INFLUENCING CHILDREN'S DEVELOPMENT

EDITORS
DENNIS BANCROFT
AND RONNIE CARR

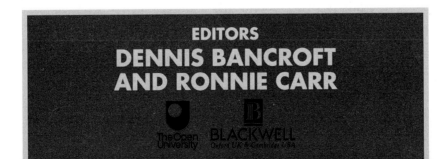

The Open University   BLACKWELL
Oxford UK & Cambridge USA

Copyright © 1995 The Open University

First published 1995 by Blackwell Publishers in association with The Open University

The Open University
Walton Hall
Milton Keynes MK7 6AA
UK

Blackwell Publishers Ltd
108 Cowley Road
Oxford OX4 1JF
UK

Blackwell Publishers Inc.
238 Main Street
Cambridge, Massachusetts 02142
USA

Cover illustration
Detail from Michael Andrews, *Melanie and Me Swimming*, 1978–79, acrylic on canvas, 72×72 ins; reproduced by kind permission of the Tate Gallery, London, copyright Michael Andrews, courtesy of the Anthony d'Offay Gallery.

A catalogue record for this book is available from the British Library.

Library of Congress Cataloguing-in-Publication data has been applied for.

ISBN 0-631-19421-5 (hbk: alk. paper) — ISBN 0-631-19422-3 (pbk: alk. paper)

Edited, designed and typeset by The Open University
Printed in the United Kingdom by The Alden Press Limited
This book is printed on acid-free paper

CONTENTS

INTRODUCTION

Dennis Bancroft and Ronnie Carr

This book is about the relationship between theory and research in developmental psychology and about the possible applications of our understanding of child development in work with children. The title of the book, *Influencing Children's Development,* suggests that psychologists can and do make a contribution to the development of children based on their psychological expertise. Of course, developmental psychology has influenced generations of teachers and clinicians, but more recently it has also been making a contribution to areas as diverse as the reliability of children's evidence as witnesses in courts of law and the implications of new technology for children's intellectual and social development.

One of us (DB) recalls always being invited to consider the 'so what?' question as an psychology undergraduate. In other words, being asked to explore the significance of the findings of psychological research both for the lives of children and for the light that such findings might shed on theoretical disputes. One purpose of this book is to address this 'so what?' question.

Another aim of the book is to encourage debate about the role of psychologists as agents of society, rather than as professionals purveying a particular body of knowledge. In some cases, cultural expectations about education and behaviour may underpin the activities of psychologists. This raises some complex issues, but it is important to be able to locate the work of psychologists within the wider community, not least because respect for the research basis of the discipline can lead to psychologists exerting a great deal of influence.

Chapter 1 sets the context for the book as a whole by looking at some of the history of the relationship between psychology and education. The chapter also considers aspects of the history of clinical psychology, and concludes by introducing some of the 'live' issues facing psychologists and the wider community. Some of these issues are revisited in other chapters of the book.

Chapter 2 takes a more detailed look at the impact of developmental psychology on teaching and learning. Chapter 3 describes the educational impact of new technology. Chapter 4 looks at how research findings from developmental psychology have affected the procedures and practices used when children must give evidence in a court of law. Recent developments in this area indicate a role for our understanding of child development in enabling children to give reliable accounts, but they also force us to recognize the wider personal and social implications of this research when people's rights and liberty are at stake.

The remaining chapters consider some aspects of the work of clinical psychologists with children. Chapters 5 and 6 can be seen as bridges between the educational and the clinical, and also serve to illustrate how arbitrary this distinction can be, for clinical conditions are likely to have educational consequences. Finally, Chapters 7 and 8 examine some of the possibilities of clinical intervention, with respect to both specific conditions and more general behavioural problems.

Underlying the chapters in this book is the large, and growing, body of knowledge generated by the research activities of developmental psychologists. Researchers investigating memory, language, social development or learning may be, in relative terms, far removed from the practicalities of delivering a psychological service to children. However, there remains a demand for the provision of developmental psychology both to professional groups, such as teachers, and directly to children. This process of delivery raises questions about the nature of psychology, the nature of children and, perhaps, the nature of psychologists themselves.

CHAPTER 1 ISSUES AND APPLICATIONS

Peter Barnes and Dennis Bancroft

CONTENTS

OBJECTIVES

When you have studied this chapter, you should be able to:

1 identify the value of psychology to teachers and discuss its place in teacher training;

2 describe the training of clinical psychologists and the range of work that they undertake;

3 distinguish between 'medical' and 'psychological' models of psychological disturbance and damage;

4 identify some important issues facing those engaged in the practical application of psychology.

1 PSYCHOLOGY AND EDUCATION

1.1 A lesson from the past

On my (PB's) bookshelf sit seven volumes of *The Teacher's Encyclopaedia*, published between 1911 and 1912. They belonged to a distant cousin of mine, a primary school teacher who entered the profession in the early 1920s, and no doubt they guided her during her training and on into her career. The title page promises coverage of the 'theory, method, practice, history and development of education at home and abroad' in the words of 'many of the most eminent educational writers, thinkers, professors and teachers of the day'. This coverage is organized in terms of subject-based contributions: Volume 1 includes chapters on 'The infant school', 'Moral instruction and training in schools', 'Dictation' and 'The teaching of drawing'.

In his introduction to the series the Editor, A. P. Laurie (Principal of Heriot-Watt College, Edinburgh), seeks to justify this form of organization as a way of handling 'such subjects as are of vital interest to the modern teacher' (p. vii), stressing the need to consider the interrelatedness of the different facets of the child's educational experience. Laurie identifies two movements as 'profoundly affecting the civilization of the day' (p. ix). One of them is of particular significance for us here.

> In the first place, there is the scientific movement which, beginning with the investigation of nature, has brought in a new ethical principle which is inspiring fresh study in all departments of knowledge, and has taught the historian, the theologian, and the philosopher that the only way to obtain knowledge which is real is to approach all these subjects from the observational and experimental point of view, in an attitude of humble inquiry, with

the determination to ask question upon question until an unassailable answer has been received. The result of this in the sphere of educational thought has been that we have been compelled to begin the study of educational problems afresh. We no longer dogmatise as to the mind of the child and its natural development; we go to the child itself, and try by careful and patient study to find out what the real nature of that development is, that we may adapt our educational methods to it and so get the best results. The outcome of this attitude of mind is the creation of the new child-psychology by which all our modern ideas of method are being controlled.

(Laurie, 1911, p. ix)

This 'movement' – the scientific study of the nature of development – is well represented in the first chapter of the first volume of the *Encyclopaedia*: an account of 'Child psychology' by John Adams, the first Professor of Education at the University of London. Adams covers a wide range of topics on which he believes psychology has something of worth to offer the teacher, including direct observation of child development, temperament, play, attention, memory, imagination, mathematics and reading. He points to the benefits for the teacher of knowing about the growing body of evidence on the subject of temperament and of taking account of the mix of temperaments within the classroom. And he refers to the recently published work of the French psychologist Alfred Binet on the development of 'mental powers', evidence of children's abilities at different ages based on systematic observation and testing, and suggests that this evidence may have implications for the ages at which emphasis is placed on subjects such as mathematics, reading and spelling.

In these and other respects Adams is keen to identify ways in which teachers can make 'practical application in [their] daily work of the psychological knowledge that has been acquired' (p. 25). In promoting this cause, however, he acknowledges a potential objection, probably one encountered over years of working with teachers: 'It is a usual complaint against psychology as an aid to the practical teacher that it is not definite enough. It is all too much in the air, too general, to be of any real service' (Adams, in Laurie, 1911, p. 30). To this charge he offers two responses:

> First, it is not desirable that the teachings of psychology should be so very definite as some teachers would like. We do not want the teacher to find in psychology a set of definite prescriptions such as one might find in a cookery book. The teacher is a worker in mind as a blacksmith is a worker in metal, and mind must be moulded by mind. It ought to be the teacher's glory that it is impossible to lay down hard-and-fast rules that apply in all cases without calling for any thought on his part. Teaching can never be carried on by machinery.

(Adams, in Laurie, 1911, p. 30)

Adams is making the point that teachers have the opportunity and the responsibility to incorporate the findings of psychological enquiry into their daily practice, but that they must be the mediators of that process, and cannot expect to be handed a set of rules that must be adhered to slavishly.

His second response is of a different kind and, as he acknowledges, somewhat inconsistent with the first: 'psychology is daily becoming more detailed and matter-of-fact. Professor Titchener [an influential contemporary psychologist] tells us that the psychology text-book of the future will be as full of formulae as the text-book of physics is today' (Adams, in Laurie, 1911, pp. 30–1).

So, on the one hand, Adams appears to be holding out to teachers the prospect of a co-operative venture in which they maintain their autonomy as practitioners, but act in a way that is informed by the knowledge of children's development generated by the enquiries of psychologists. And, on the other hand, he expects that the, as yet infant, scientific study of children's psychological development will eventually attain a degree of precision that will allow for a much more clear-cut and prescriptive set of guidelines for the teacher. In the final sentence of the chapter he offers his readers a holding position: 'there are hundreds of psychological facts that no honest teacher can afford to neglect, and there is a school attitude towards psychology that is thoroughly wholesome, and without which the teacher cannot do his best work' (Adams, in Laurie, 1911, p. 33).

We are not claiming that Adams' chapter was a significant brick in the historical edifices of either psychology or the training of teachers, despite his eminence in other regards, but it was very much in tune with the spirit of the time. Psychology was working hard to establish itself as a science, and one feature of this endeavour was a desire to establish laws about human behaviour, much as there are laws about the physical world (see Titchener's comments above). There was also the establishment of what became known as the Child Study Movement. This movement had its roots in the work of Charles Darwin and came to fruition with the encouragement of Wilhelm Preyer in Germany in the 1880s in the form of studies of children at home and at school – their drawings, play, conversation and so on. This approach was taken up by Stanley Hall at Johns Hopkins University in the USA, and as early as 1893 he organized a meeting of child psychologists at the World's Trade Fair in Chicago. Before the end of the century books were being written about the mind of the child: in England, for example, James Sully published *Studies of Childhood* in 1896.

Workers in this field were quick to recognize that what they were doing had potential relevance to education (Sully, for example, wrote *The Teacher's Handbook of Psychology* in 1886). With the passage of time two paths emerged. The first was the growth in the use of 'mental tests', beginning with the work of Francis Galton in the 1880s and reaching a significant milestone in 1905 with the first appearance of

Binet and Simon's scale of intelligence. The second path, 'experimental pedagogy', was an extension of child study beyond the investigation of child development to include topics such as methods of teaching and learning, classroom organization and problems relating to the learning of reading, writing, arithmetic and language. John Dewey, an influential educationalist, expressed support for these developments in an address to the American Psychological Association in 1899.

> While the psychological theory would guide and illuminate the practice, acting upon the theory would immediately test it and thus criticize it, bringing about its revision and growth. In the large and open sense of the words, psychology becomes a working hypothesis, instruction is the experimental test and demonstration of the hypothesis; the result is both greater practical control and continued growth in theory.
>
> (Dewey, 1900, cited in Garforth, 1966, pp. 158–9)

At the same time that enthusiasm was growing for the potential applications of this developing body of knowledge and techniques, cautions were being voiced. John Adams' moderate tone in 1911 (see page 3) is an echo of the authoritative advice of William James, one of the American founders of modern psychology. In a book entitled *Talks to Teachers on Psychology: and to students on some of life's ideals*, published in 1899, James cautioned his teacher audience as follows.

> I say moreover that you make a great, a very great mistake, if you think that psychology, being the science of the mind's laws, is something from which you can deduce definite programmes and schemes and methods of instruction for immediate schoolroom use. Psychology is a science, and teaching is an art; and sciences never generate arts directly out of themselves. An intermediary inventive mind must make the application, by using its originality.
>
> (James, 1899, pp. 7–8)

All this sets the tone for a consideration of some of the ways in which the study of psychology and the adoption of its methods of enquiry might come to have an influence on the development of children. Have the positive expectations of some of the pioneers turned out to be justified? Or have the sceptics been proved right? How can realistic, workable and effective relationships be established between the possessors and purveyors of psychological knowledge and skills and those who have a potential use for them? And to what extent and in what ways can those who are well-placed to translate that knowledge into action – those with responsibilities for children's development and welfare, such as parents, teachers, nursery nurses and social workers – acquire an understanding of psychology that is useful to them? These are questions that relate to the subjects addressed throughout this book, and in this chapter we shall seek to identify some of the issues so that you can bear them in mind as you read on.

ACTIVITY 1

Allow about 20 minutes

MAKING USE OF PSYCHOLOGICAL KNOWLEDGE

Reflect on your own experiences of psychology in relation to the development of children. For example, if you are a parent, you may have read the advice of psychologists about child rearing or about how research on children's play suggests the use of certain activities to promote cognitive development. If you are a teacher, you may have encountered psychological research on the nature of children's learning and its implications for what goes on in the classroom. You may have also had a direct working relationship with a psychologist to meet the needs of a particular child. If you are neither a parent nor a teacher, you may have observed psychologists in the media offering views on aspects of children's development about which you have opinions.

Make brief notes of the ways in which the psychological knowledge was deployed and of how 'effective' it was as you experienced or perceived it.

- If you judged it to be effective and satisfactory, to what do you attribute that?
- What form did the 'effectiveness' take? Was it that a specific problem was solved, or did you come to look at the matter under consideration in a different and more productive light?
- If you have had experiences of this sort which had negative connotations for you, how do you account for them? Were the expectations and claims unrealistic or misunderstood?
- Was the knowledge sufficient to provide useful guidance? Or was it less a question of the potential value of the knowledge than of how to make the best use of it?
- How did the direction/action advocated by the psychological guidance/advice relate to your existing view of the matter? Was it generally in accord with the way you had been thinking, or did it cause you to see things in a significantly different way?
- Did other factors outweigh the psychological aspects to such an extent that the psychological aspects became inconsequential?

If you perceive other relevant dimensions to this exercise, make a note of them too.

Any response to this activity is necessarily a personal one, so comment can only be of limited use. As you read on through this book you may encounter examples that you can relate to your own experience. In practice, when psychologists become involved in a professional capacity or as researchers the task is usually to solve a specific problem using whatever experience and skills are to hand. The skills psychologists bring to a problem are affected by their training and by their sympathy for, or adherence to, a particular theoretical position. One psychologist's approach to a set of problems may be quite different from another's, and it is often a matter of waiting for evidence to accumulate over time before deciding on the most effective way of addressing the problem (always assuming that the criteria against which 'effectiveness' is to be judged can be agreed!).

1.2 Piaget and schooling

S G

Ask many teachers for the name of a psychologist who has had a significant effect on education and Jean Piaget will be one of the first to be mentioned. In a way this is odd, in that Piaget was not, strictly speaking, a psychologist but a genetic epistemologist (someone with an interest in the biological explanation of knowledge); nor did he himself say very much about the educational implications of his work. Nevertheless, Piaget's extensive studies of children's development have been comprehensively incorporated into the fabric of developmental psychology and have stimulated a vast amount of research by those who are psychologists. In a similar fashion, the relationship between his theories and the conduct of education – particularly the education of young children – has been extensively investigated, written about and taught by many others. Indeed, it is largely through the work of those who have translated Piaget's ideas into educational contexts that his influence has spread.

In the following pages we shall identify some of these lines of influence and suggest some notes of caution about their interpretation. We shall then go on to follow up some of these issues in a rather wider context to raise questions about how the work of psychologists might affect educational practice. Some of the issues raised will also be taken up in more detail in Chapter 2.

We shall not describe Piaget's theory in any detail here, but identify two important features of it that appear to be significant for the education of children.

- In Piaget's view children are not born with knowledge that merely matures with the passage of time, nor do they acquire knowledge in a ready-made-up form from the outside world. Rather, throughout their lives, children are engaged in the *active construction of* their own development through interactions with the environment.

- The nature of children's thinking is seen as *qualitatively* different from that of adults and other children of different ages; it is not just a matter of the *amount* of knowledge of the world that they possess, but the contrasting nature of the ways in which they actually view and understand aspects of that world at different stages in their development. The idea of *stages* is an important one in Piaget's theory: children develop through three main stages (sensorimotor, concrete operations and formal operations), each involving increasing levels of organization and increasingly logical underlying structures.

ACTIVITY 2

Allow about 5 minutes

THE IMPLICATIONS OF PIAGET FOR TEACHERS

Note down, briefly, the main implications of these features of Piaget's theory for what teachers do when they teach. You do not need to think of teachers only in a formal, classroom sense; parents are teachers of their children too.

The first feature of Piaget's theory suggests that the role of the teacher is to allow children to engage with their environment in an active way and have appropriate experiences at appropriate times so as to foster their natural capacity to learn. The second feature suggests that these experiences will be educationally effective only if full account is taken of the children's level of understanding; this idea is sometimes represented in terms of the concept of *readiness*, the stage the children are at determining the sorts of educational experiences for which they are ready. Both of these implications place the child very much at the hub of the educational process and locate Piaget's theory within the *child-centred* movement in educational practice.

The Plowden Report

One measure of the power of a theory is not just the influence it has on individuals, but also how it comes to be adopted by, and subsumed within, institutionally approved policies and practices. In the case of Piagetian ideas, the Plowden Report provides an informative example. The Plowden Committee was established in the mid-1960s to look at the condition of primary education (from 5 to 11) in England and Wales and to make recommendations for changes in practices. The report, published in 1967 by the Central Advisory Council for Education, was influential in informing national education policies and actual classroom practice for many years afterwards. In particular, it resulted in a move away from 'chalk and talk' to a more child-centred approach. However, it should be noted that observational studies of young children in their classrooms have questioned the extent to which active learning takes place in practice (for example, Tizard *et al.*, 1988). And more recent government-inspired changes in education policies are rendering some of the committee's proposals increasingly marginal.

Example 1 contains some brief extracts from the Plowden Report. These extracts are indicative of some of the ways in which the Committee's thinking and recommendations were influenced by evidence from psychological research – specifically, the work of Piaget. Note the references to *developmental sequences, readiness* and *developmental age*.

Piaget was not the first person to propose child-centred education, either directly or implicitly; Rousseau advocated it in France in the eighteenth century, and schools were established in line with his principles by Froebel in Germany in 1826 and Pestalozzi in Switzerland a year later. So, while Piaget's research on children's development in one sense provided evidence for the Plowden Committee, it is important to recognize a broader context, namely a set of existing beliefs and values about the nature and needs of children. And this was potentially

> ## EXAMPLE 1
> ## EXTRACTS FROM THE PLOWDEN REPORT
>
> Knowledge of the manner in which children develop ... is of prime importance, both in avoiding educationally harmful practices and in introducing effective ones. In the last 50 years much work has been done on the physical, emotional and intellectual growth of children. There is a vast array of facts, and a number of general principles have been established ...
>
> Among the principles are present-day concepts about critical or sensitive periods, about developmental 'sequence' (that is, events which are fixed in their order but varying in the age at which the sequence begins); ... and, above all, about the complex and continuous interaction between the developing organism and its environment ...
>
> [T]he more obvious implications of it [the material presented in this chapter of the report] can be stated baldly as follows:
>
> (a) Individual differences between children of the same age are so great that any class, however homogeneous it seems, must always be treated as a body of children needing individual and different attention.
>
> (b) Until a child is ready to take a particular step forward, it is a waste of time to try to teach him to take it ...
>
> (e) Since a child grows up intellectually, emotionally and physically at different rates, his teachers need to know and take account of his 'developmental age' in all three respects. The child's physique, personality, and capacity to learn develop as a result of continuous interaction between his environmental and genetical inheritance. Unlike the genetic factors, the environmental factors are, or ought to be, largely within our control.
>
> (extracts from Central Advisory Council for Education, 1967 (The Plowden Report), paras 10, 11 and 75)

true for both those writing the report and its recipients, teachers and other education practitioners, who needed to assimilate its messages and proposals into their own views of children and their education.

The impact of theory upon practice has been presented in an interesting way by Alyson Davis, a psychologist involved in providing in-service courses for experienced teachers (Davis, 1991). When she asked teachers about the theories they had come across in their initial training and the influence these had had on their classroom practice, some reference was always made to Piaget. But these teachers were mostly unable to recall any significant detail of his theory or identify any impact of it on their own practice. Nevertheless, when they were asked to make explicit their own theories of child development, they referred to things such as the importance of active learning, qualitative differences between child and adult thinking, and the influence of environmental experience on development – all remarkably similar to Piaget's general principles. Davis explains the apparent mismatch as follows.

> Our simple answer is that these ideas have not been explicitly
> influenced by studying Piaget's ideas, and instead form part of a
> more general educational philosophy about the nature of children's
> development, stemming from early educators such as Froebel and
> Montessori who happen to share common principles with Piagetian
> ideas about development.
>
> (Davis, 1991, p. 18)

Is this inevitable? Is it good enough? If a psychological theory, supported
by evidence, can so impress the committee that wrote the Plowden Report
that they incorporate it into their recommendations for practice, should it
not be possible for psychological evidence and its implications for practice
to be presented in ways that maximize their effect?

Giving psychology away

What is it in the theories of psychology, in the ways of conceptualizing
and thinking about human beings and their development, and in the
evidence generated by psychological research, that might inform how we
lead our lives, how we bring up our children and promote their cognitive,
emotional and social development? In 1969 the American psychologist
George Miller wrote an influential paper with the title 'Psychology as a
means of promoting human welfare' (Miller, 1969). He argued that if
psychology was to have an impact on people's lives it was necessary to
'give it away', to move it out of the hands of powerful experts and into
those of ordinary people.

> ... part of the answer is that psychology must be practised by
> nonpsychologists. We are not physicians; the secrets of our trade
> need not be reserved for highly trained specialists. Psychological
> facts should be passed out freely to all who need and can use them.
> And from successful applications of psychological principles the
> public may gain a better appreciation for the power of the new
> conception of man that is emerging from our science.
>
> If we take seriously the idea of a peaceful revolution based on a
> new conception of human nature, our scientific results will have
> to be instilled in the public consciousness in a practical and usable
> form so that what we know can be applied by ordinary people.
> There simply are not enough psychologists, even including
> nonprofessionals, to meet every need for psychological services.
> The people at large will have to be their own psychologists, and
> make their own applications of the principles that we establish.
>
> Of course, everyone practises psychology, just as everyone who
> cooks is a chemist, everyone who reads a clock is an astronomer,
> everyone who drives a car is an engineer. I am not suggesting any
> radical departure when I say that nonpsychologists must practise
> psychology. I am simply proposing that we should teach them to
> practise it better, to make use self-consciously of what we believe to
> be scientifically valid principles.
>
> (Miller, 1969, pp. 1070–1)

This proposal set a demanding agenda, and it is difficult to say with any clarity what progress has been made in the direction that Miller advocated; it depends on the criteria used to judge that progress. Certainly, psychology has maintained its appeal with the public at large, as judged by the output of books, magazines, newspaper articles and television and radio programmes directed at the 'popular' market. The study of psychology as a subject in higher education is increasingly popular, with many courses heavily over-subscribed. Professional bodies, such as the British Psychological Society, have become more active in seeking to achieve an accurate and accessible reporting and dissemination of psychological 'knowledge'. How all of this knowledge and information has been received, internalized and put to some sort of use is another matter. Has human welfare been promoted as a consequence? It is difficult to know how such a question could be answered at a general level.

There are also moves which run counter to this trend. One that has a particular bearing on the discussion in this section is the marked decline in the formal status of psychology in the initial training of school teachers, a decline that began in the 1980s, and was prompted by government policies and rulings. The label 'psychology' tended to be dropped from course titles in preference for others such as 'curriculum development' and 'educational studies' (though the course contents are still concerned with psychological issues), and fewer psychologists have been appointed to the training institutions (see Tomlinson, 1992). Surely, if psychology has the potential to promote human welfare in general, it must have an even greater application to those whose professional responsibility it will be to promote and guide the intellectual, personal and social development of children. This was apparently recognized by the authors of the Plowden Report (see Example 1), and our consideration of that example led us to ask how the process might be improved. A century or so on from the events recounted earlier in this section, the debate about the relationship between psychology and education is still hotly contested. Much more is known about the nature of children's development than in the days of John Adams and William James, but the deployment of that understanding continues to be seen as problematic. We shall look at some of the dimensions of this debate, not with the intention of coming to a resolution of it, but rather to illustrate some of the arguments that are used and to consider whether they have a wider application. In doing this it may be helpful to have the following questions in mind.

(a) Have reasonable expectations been raised about the potential applications of psychological knowledge?

(b) Psychology embraces a number of theories and models, several at odds with one another. Is this a source of confusion, uncertainty and mistrust; or does it offer a 'menu' of experience and enlightenment from which people can draw selectively in accordance with their particular needs?

Is there a problem at all?

Students training to be teachers experience a variety of input which is intended to make them effective practitioners. Psychology, in various shapes and forms, has played a significant part in this experience, and until the 1980s it was usually presented as one of four 'foundation' disciplines, alongside philosophy, sociology and the history of education. There is some evidence that it was well regarded: for example, a 1980 survey of over 3,000 students on Post Graduate Certificate of Education (PGCE) courses in England and Wales found that they rated the psychology elements of the non-method (that is, school-subject-based) course the most intellectually stimulating and the most academically interesting (Bernbaum, 1985). The students also said that when they went into schools on teaching practice, the psychology courses were the most useful part of the educational theory to which they had been exposed.

This sounds encouraging and might suggest that some progress has been made. However, an alternative and less positive view of the same situation is offered by Guy Claxton, writing as a psychologist and a trainer of teachers (Claxton, 1985). He contrasts psychology with the other three 'foundation disciplines'. Philosophy, sociology and history are 'cerebral' – they ask students to *think about* the intellectual, social and historical context or content of what they are doing – whereas psychology is 'about people' and therefore might be expected to be more likely to relate to the students' personal priorities. Claxton's concern is that too often students' 'needs to be able to communicate and control, to enthuse and motivate, to create and orchestrate a harmonious and happy environment within which they and their pupils can feel that their time spent together is time *well* spent' (p. 83) are not fulfilled. Without that, intellectual facility with psychology and an ability to write good essays on the subject are not sufficient; indeed, Claxton makes the somewhat jaundiced point that such essays are the exception.

> More commonly, unfortunately, students go away having learnt the name Piaget, and that this Piaget is important, dead, and had a theory about stages. The examination papers and many of the essays that I have marked for years consistently reveal knowledge of this order. Why is it that psychology too often leaves only a faint smear on memory, a slightly bitter taste in the mouth, and as much effect on spontaneous competence as a passing face leaves in a mirror?
>
> (Claxton, 1985, p. 83)

A strong challenge! Claxton lays the responsibility for this state of affairs on the way in which psychology is taught and on a lack of understanding of the reasons for teaching it in terms of its *use* to the students once they become teachers. So, to receive a firm grounding in Piaget or learning theory, though it may be intellectually stimulating, is of limited practical benefit; it does not follow that even when something is 'properly understood' it will necessarily affect what the individual does in those areas of life to which the knowledge is potentially applicable. Claxton's concern, then, is not that psychology *as such* has a limited application for teachers, but rather that the way in which it is typically presented to them fails to deliver its potential: 'If psychology were to ransack itself for ways of helping the student teacher develop his or her competence more speedily, effectively and painlessly, it would find them. But until it does our reports must continue to read "has aptitude but lacks application", and "could do very much better"' (Claxton, 1985, p. 100).

However, isn't this to demean the theory that gives psychology its status as a science? Surely, one of the purposes of scientific enquiry is to establish theories which generate laws which in turn inform practice. Once a theory has become established, it should be possible to identify courses of action that follow from it. Isn't that what happens when theories in chemistry and physics (the so-called 'hard' sciences) are applied as technology? If so, then arguably teachers need to acquire the theory of psychology so that they can see how best to apply it. However, this underlying model has been questioned. Hastings and Schwieso (1981), for example, (cited in Schwieso *et al.*, 1992) have pointed out that in the case of the history of the 'hard' sciences and technology the relationship is *not* of this sort. Throughout the Industrial Revolution most technical advances were not the result of applying knowledge gained from scientists, but 'sprang from the work of artisans who combined practical need, commercial opportunism, tacit knowledge and forms of "suck it and see" experimental methods' (Schwieso *et al.*, 1992, p. 112). Only in the recent past have the 'hard' sciences been of direct value to technologists, and Schwieso *et al.* claim that psychology is as yet some way off from attaining that status.

> At present, understanding within psychology is not such that it normally allows very precise predictions of the consequences of certain courses of action in human situations such as the classroom. Nor can it offer confident predictions about the efficacy of any particular technique in bringing about certain desired states of affairs, say, in children's understanding; neither should psychology be expected to do such things, for the prime purpose of the discipline, as of any discipline, is to advance understanding – not practice. Basic research can yield practical benefits, but that is not its central purpose.
>
> (Schwieso *et al.*, 1992, p. 113)

This would seem to suggest that the case for psychology has been misrepresented in some respects and that some false expectations have been generated. This is not the same as saying that psychology has no contribution to make – far from it. The lessons of the Industrial Revolution offer us another perspective, a combination of practical needs and tacit knowledge – in this instance, knowledge that can be extracted from the psychological menu. This can and does take place at both a general and a more specific level. The more general level is represented in the following proposal from Margaret Sutherland: 'psychological studies can encourage in teachers the habit of regarding children … as individuals whose individual reactions can be understood in the light of general principles and whose behaviour stimulates and contributes to the greatest of all human interests, the interest in human thinking and feeling itself' (Sutherland, 1985, p. 20). Perhaps this relates to the points made earlier: namely, that being exposed to yet more psychological knowledge serves to further inform and expand existing models of children and their needs that are derived from a mix of personal experience, culturally approved ideas and the like.

More specifically, there is a move in the direction of encouraging a curiosity which draws on the thinking and the techniques of psychology and which stresses a *discipline of systematic enquiry* rather than a *body of knowledge* (Francis, 1985). This perspective sees psychology as offering a set of constructs and a set of tools with which to address questions, whether these be perennial questions, such as the nature of teaching and learning, or questions that result from changes elsewhere in society, such as the increasing impact of computer technology on people's lives or the treatment of children in the legal system (see Chapters 3 and 4).

READING

This section concludes by considering an illustration of one way in which psychology offers constructs and tools with which to tackle some practical questions.

If you were to record what goes on in the average school classroom, 'talk' in some shape or form would be an important feature; it is the medium through which much teaching and learning is conducted. Teachers typically take up about 75 per cent of the talking time, and a large proportion of this is taken up with questions to children. For example, in two studies, one of 17-year-old American high school students and the other of English pre-schoolers, the frequency of teacher questions as a proportion of all their utterances was 43 per cent and 47 per cent respectively (cited in Wood, 1988, p. 141). The questions take a variety of forms and observational research has shown that different questioning strategies elicit different sorts of answers. The reading by David Wood at the end of this chapter is a selection from research studies on the extensive literature surrounding the topic of questions and their role in teaching. As you study it, note both the detail of the studies cited and the wider implications that are suggested.

Now answer the following questions in your own words.

What are 'closed' questions, and what effect do they tend to have on children's responses?

How do questioning styles relate to educational achievement? What explanations have been offered to explain this effect?

How might a knowledge of this research inform what a teacher does in the classroom?

And finally, how has answering the above three questions (and note their characteristics) contributed to your understanding of the issues concerned? (Research on the role of questions included in printed text has suggested that well-placed, demanding questions can facilitate learning.)

ACTIVITY 3
Allow about 30 minutes

QUESTIONS ABOUT QUESTIONS

When you have an opportunity, experiment with different ways of asking similar questions of others, varying features such as:

- whether the questions are 'closed' (for example, 'What colour is it now?') or 'open-ended' (for example, 'What changes have you observed?');
- the 'waiting time' that you allow for an answer, if necessary; and
- whether you are talking to an individual or a group.

Do you detect any differences in the types of responses? Did you find it difficult to operate with an extended 'waiting time'?

This is an activity that can be done with adults or children. Afterwards, try asking the participants whether they noticed any differences between the styles of the questions.

This example illustrates two important points which relate both to the particular case of the relationship between psychology and teaching and to broader applications. The first is that the research takes place in the classroom and its findings can be clearly related to classroom practice. This is representative of an increasing trend in educational research – including that done by psychologists – namely, to base findings on what happens in real-life contexts. The teachers referred to in the Wood reading were apparently willing collaborators and may well have contributed to how the investigations were undertaken. A further implication of this is a focus on the *interaction* of teaching and learning; it doesn't just look at one or the other in isolation. The relevance and utility of the study are thus more apparent. The second feature is that much of the research is multidisciplinary. Although it isn't immediately apparent from the summaries provided, concepts and evidence deriving from developmental cognitive psychology are only a part of the story – ideas and techniques from linguistics and anthropology also play a significant role. Sometimes, in an effort to establish the contribution of psychology to a particular subject, there is a tendency to stake out and defend a particular territory and to play down the opportunity – sometimes the imperative – for a shared approach with other disciplines; this is rarely justified and usually counter-productive.

SUMMARY OF SECTION 1

- The potential for applying the scientific study of children's development to educational concerns has been recognized since the beginnings of modern psychology.

- Piaget's theory has influenced educational practice in a variety of ways. The Plowden Report provides one significant example. Teachers who claim to have been influenced by Piaget's ideas have little detailed recall of these ideas, but rather appear to have absorbed some general principles about the nature of children's development.

- The place for psychology in the initial training of school teachers has declined in recent years. Some have argued that this is because the way in which psychology was taught failed to exploit its potential.

- An alternative is to see psychology as offering a discipline of systematic enquiry rather than a body of knowledge.

- The example of styles of questioning illustrates the interactive nature of both teaching and learning as well as the location of psychology alongside other disciplines.

2 CLINICAL CHILD PSYCHOLOGY

Over the last 30 years, clinical child psychology has developed remarkably as a profession. At one time, clinical child psychologists were mainly to be found working with psychiatrists in psychiatric hospitals or units, offering primarily psychometric services such as the administration and scoring of personality and intelligence tests. There are now many more clinical child psychologists, and they work in a variety of ways in many different settings. They may still be involved in the assessment of children with difficulties, but they are also likely to be providing therapy directly, to be involved in rehabilitation or other associated services, and often to be involved in teaching and research. Table 1 should give you some idea of this variety.

This expansion and extension of clinical child psychology is due in part to changes in the organization of health services (since most, but not all, clinical psychologists are employed by health authorities), but it is also linked to the development of the profession in respect of its theoretical base and its range of available methodologies (particularly in the area of therapeutic intervention in children's lives). Advances in the understanding of child development arrived at through research, allied to a greater awareness among the public and doctors of the importance of the psychological development of children, have led to an increased demand for the services of clinical child psychologists to meet a greater variety of needs.

TABLE 1

Setting	Example
(a) *Health*	
(i) Community	
Child welfare clinics	Liaison/consultation with health visitors
Health centres	Parents groups for behavioural, sleeping, feeding problems of under-fives
GP practices	
(ii) Hospital	
Ante-natal clinics	Counselling of mothers with suspected handicapped child
	Counselling of adolescents deciding about termination of pregnancy
Intensive care neonatal units	Counselling for staff and parents
Paediatric assessment clinics	Assessment and remediation of development delays
Paediatric hospital wards	Preparation of parents/children for hospitalization
	Counselling of parents/staff dealing with terminally ill children
Casualty wards	Crisis counselling for adolescents who have taken overdoses
Psychiatric in-patient and out-patient units	Assessment and treatment with families of children showing emotional and behavioural problems
	Consultation/training of psychiatric child care staff (in psychological procedures)
(b) *Social services*	
(i) Local authority nurseries	Advice to nursery nurses concerning problems of child abuse
	Assessment of development delays
(ii) Community homes	Consultation with staff concerning management of difficult behaviour problems
	Counselling foster parents
(c) *Voluntary organisations*	Drop-in clinics for adolescents with drug taking or alcohol problems (e.g., Samaritans, Adoption Societies, Brook Advisory Centres, Grapevine, etc.)

(Source: Fielding, 1987)

The current training for clinical psychologists starts with a good pass in an undergraduate psychology degree course recognized by the British Psychological Society. This is followed by a postgraduate course (usually two or three years) at a university associated with a teaching hospital, which includes not only continued academic study but also clinical experience and small-scale personal research projects. Alternatively, the postgraduate training may involve an in-service course of three years in a hospital. The required postgraduate qualification is the BPS Diploma in Clinical Psychology, which covers adult mental health, disability and childhood problems. As well as developing professional skills, the training emphasizes the adoption of a rational, empirical approach grounded in psychological theory and scientific method. However, although the training is fairly uniform, the various theoretical perspectives in developmental psychology are reflected in a lot of variation in the basic approaches to understanding children's difficulties. As you will see in Chapter 8 of this book, psychologists involved in psychotherapeutic work adopt many different approaches and styles, ranging from a behaviourist stance based on the principles of learning theory to a psychodynamic approach making use of concepts and techniques derived from psychoanalytic theory and analytic work with adults.

As well as a great deal of diversity within the field of developmental psychology, there is also a lot of overlap between the sorts of work psychologists do with children and the work of other professionals, such as child psychiatrists (who have a medical background and training), child psychotherapists (who may have a variety of different training experiences) and specialist social workers and probation officers (who have yet other training backgrounds).

The settings in which child psychologists work, as well as their training and their theoretical leanings, will to some extent be reflected in the sorts of 'models' of children's difficulties that guide their decisions and practice. One useful distinction is that between a 'medical' model and a 'psychological' model.

2.1 The 'medical' model

Children's psychological difficulties have, until quite recently, been seen as the concern of a specialized branch of medicine, and as something to be 'treated' by professionals with a medical training. It is not surprising, then, that much of the thinking, theorizing, research and practice in this area has tended to assume a model of causation and remediation which borrows concepts and a general framework from the 'disease' model used in medicine. Clearly, there are many circumstances in which clearly identifiable disorders – such as a chromosomal difference (as in Down's syndrome) or the effects of an illness or trauma – have psychological consequences which require intervention. Where such causes are not present, or where there is more uncertainty about causation, the 'medical' model still predisposes practitioners to think of a 'condition' within the child which needs appropriate 'treatment'.

We have highlighted certain words here to draw your attention to the subtle ways in which the use of language can reflect an underlying theoretical stance.

Some of the key terms commonly used within the 'medical' model of children's difficulties include 'patient', 'disease', 'symptom', 'syndrome', 'diagnosis', 'treatment' and 'cure'. You can see how this set of labels focuses on a particular model, effectively making certain sorts of information about a child particularly relevant in deciding what might be done for them. Investigations will tend to concentrate on the child, and see the way forward as giving some form of treatment *to the child*. The model also makes other sources of information rather less relevant – for example, information about the child's parents, social circumstances and so forth.

2.2 The 'psychological' model

There has been, if not a revolution, at least a major revision in the way that psychological development has been thought about over the last few years. A growing recognition of the importance of social factors in development, particularly as far as intellectual development is concerned, has led to the new concept of social cognition being embraced by more and more psychologists. This is true of the field of clinical psychology as well as the more rarefied world of academic research and teaching, and this change can also be seen in the increasing interest in seeing children's developmental difficulties as caused and sustained by problematic social relationships. The increase in the number of practitioners involved in one form or another of family therapy testifies to this change.

In step with these changes, a new set of concepts is evolving which have a subtly different emphasis from the concepts available within the 'medical' model. Table 2 sets these new concepts alongside those already noted for the 'medical' model.

TABLE 2

Medical concept	Psychological concept
Patient	Client
Disease	Problem
Symptom	Difficulty
Syndrome	Difficulties
Diagnosis	Assessment
Treatment	Intervention
Cure	Outcome

If you compare these sets of terms you will appreciate some of the differences between the two models, and understand why it is important to attend to the words that are used to describe children and their psychological development, especially when there is cause for concern.

SUMMARY OF SECTION 2

- Clinical child psychologists have a variety of roles in their work with children, including assessment, therapy and rehabilitation. They may work in hospitals, in social services departments or in the wider community.
- The training of clinical psychologists is likely to consist of at least three years of postgraduate study. The training is usually general in nature, with specialisms such as child psychology being the focus of the latter stages of training.
- The traditional 'medical' model of children's psychological difficulties can be contrasted with the more recent 'psychological' model, which has its origins in the developmental psychological research of the second half of the twentieth century.

3 ISSUES IN APPLIED PSYCHOLOGY

3.1 Ethics and research

In recent years there has been much vigorous debate about the ethical issues that arise when animals are used in scientific research. Is it right to interfere with an animal's normal bodily functioning through surgery, medical procedures, stressful experiences and the like in the pursuit of knowledge? And if so, to what extent, under what conditions and for what purposes? Although the issues are seldom as stark when psychological research and professional practice with humans are concerned, ethical considerations still apply and must be kept under close review and treated with the utmost seriousness.

The British Psychological Society has produced a *Code of Conduct, Ethical Principles and Guidelines* (1993) which sets out standards of conduct with which psychologists are required to comply.

> The essential principle is that the investigation should be considered from the standpoint of all participants; foreseeable threats to their psychological well-being, health, values or dignity should be eliminated. Investigators should recognise that, in our multi-cultural and multi-ethnic society and where investigations involve individuals of different ages, gender and social background, the investigators may not have sufficient knowledge of the implications of any investigation for the participants.
>
> (British Psychological Society, 1993, p. 8)

The Code goes on to address the principles involved in obtaining the consent of participants in research, and it notes that children in particular, who may not be in a position to give their 'real' consent, require special safeguarding. Another central concern is the role of *deception* in research investigations, including those in which the real object of the study is not fully disclosed to the participants on the grounds that such knowledge would be likely to modify their behaviour. The problem for the psychologist is that if people understand the purpose of a study in which they are participating they may behave or speak in ways which are different from their normal behaviour. They may change their behaviour for any number of reasons: to impress, to co-operate or, indeed, to conceal and deceive.

In some research the real object of the study is not disclosed to the participants beforehand for reasons similar to those given in the preceding paragraph. One implication of this apparent need to deceive in order to investigate some aspects of human behaviour is that, once the deception becomes known, people may be annoyed in the short term and cynical about the activities and attitudes of psychologists in the longer term.

ACTIVITY 4

Allow about 20 minutes

PUBLIC PERCEPTIONS OF PSYCHOLOGISTS

Invite a few people you know to engage in a little free association. This is a technique, used by psychotherapists, which involves asking clients to respond to selected words or phrases by saying the first things that come to mind. In this case, your key word is 'psychologist' or perhaps the phrase 'I'm a psychologist'. Make a list of their replies.

Comment

Your list might include things such as 'I must be careful what I say' or 'Oh, can you read my mind?'

In any event, the responses you get may indicate something of the concerns which are felt by those who come into contact with professional psychologists. Consider the possible implications of this for psychologists attempting to establish a rapport with their clients or with participants in their research.

3.2 Terminology

The use of the term 'participants' in preceding paragraphs may have struck you as odd. During the past hundred years or so of modern psychology, people who have taken part in experimental and other investigations conducted by psychologists have usually been referred to as 'subjects' in the resulting research reports. While this term is not seen by psychologists as derogatory, it is often regarded as rather impersonal by those outside the profession. The British Psychological Society guidelines from which we have already quoted invites psychologists to use the term 'participants' instead on the grounds that 'psychologists owe a debt to those who agree to take part in their studies and that people who are willing to give up their time, even for remuneration, should be able to expect to be treated with the highest standards of consideration and respect' (British Psychological Society, 1993, p. 6).

This evolving use of terms also reflects changes in the ways in which those who participate in psychological enquiry are perceived, in some quarters at least. In an effort to be 'scientific', some traditions in psychology have tended to regard their subject matter, that is, people, as uniform objects which can be manipulated through experimental procedures and instructions into accepting and complying with the experimenter's conception of whatever it is that is being investigated. It is increasingly being acknowledged that this is not necessarily the case and that, in many situations, it is positively undesirable. The term 'participants' recognizes that those taking part in an experiment or enquiry come to it with preconceptions and frames of reference and are striving to make sense of what is happening in their own terms, and that this often needs to be taken into account in interpreting what they say and do within the context of the investigation.

Another aspect of terminology which has undergone a more widespread change in recent years is the differential reference to the sexes and the increasingly widespread adoption of non-sexist language. This has applied to the conduct and reporting of psychological research just as much as it has in other walks of life, and it is fitting that it should, since psychological investigations have made a substantial contribution to our understanding of the role of language in influencing and reinforcing sex-role stereotypes.

A third way in which the use of terminology demands attention concerns the precision with which 'technical' vocabulary is employed. This book provides examples of this very point. In Chapter 5, for example, children with a specific learning difficulty (dyslexia) are variously referred to as 'retarded readers', 'backward readers' and 'delayed readers'. Each of these terms carries with it a certain tone or loading that may not be intended by the author, and which may be quite unacceptable to the people so described and to others in the community. Terms are often adopted or adapted in order to make particular distinctions clear within the research literature, and they retain their currency for similar reasons. This may create some difficulties for authors who find themselves needing to use terms with which they themselves are uncomfortable on the grounds that they play an integral part in the literature. There are three points to bear in mind.

(a) The use of different terms to indicate the same thing or the same term to mean different things is a problem that must be resolved in order to make sensible comparisons between one study and another. The reader needs to be confident that the use of one term to describe a particular condition or group of children, say, is being used to mean the same as another term used in a similar context. Equally, it is important for the reader to be sure that when a term is employed it can be understood to mean or imply the same thing when used by different authors. In practice, these considerations are often not met, and a certain amount of confusion is the result.

(b) People are not neutral with respect to the terms applied to them. It is no part of a psychologist's work to give offence where this can be avoided.

(c) Some terms used by psychologists are more than just simple descriptions. They carry messages and meanings which are of personal significance to those being described, to their family, friends and so on. These messages also have a habit of changing in harmony with wider social and cultural trends.

3.3 Labelling

In recent years the assigning of labels such as 'dyslexic' or 'hyperactive' to children, both individually and collectively, has aroused critical comment. One reason for this is that the process of labelling can be seen as a device to avoid further thought about individuals and their particular needs by collecting them all together under a single heading. Another reason is that the label may serve to identify a gulf between the labelled child and others thought of as 'normal'. A counter view is that the process of assessment and the resulting descriptive label is a necessary part of the process of providing for a child's particular needs. We cannot pretend that all children are so similar that only one form of educational provision is adequate for all. Given considerable variety, the specific needs of children for whom a conventional education is not appropriate must also be addressed.

The problem seems to be that children who are assessed and identified as needing some particular provision may *also* suffer negative consequences. Perhaps the most damaging of these follow from the attitudes of the people who meet the labelled child. As humans we often try to reduce the complexity of our world by organizing and categorizing its contents. Once we have done this we may think of members of particular groups in stereotyped ways, often to their disadvantage. For example, people with Down's syndrome (once referred to as 'Mongolism') are a recognizable group within our community and may be thought of, collectively, as mentally 'handicapped', sociable and jolly, reticent and difficult, or whatever the stereotype happens to be. In short, people may have an understanding of what is implied by the use of a certain label to describe a certain group and then behave towards individuals in ways which are consistent with those stereotypes, even when they are quite inappropriate. The beliefs and behaviour of others can set limits upon the achievements and development of individuals. Psychologists trying to understand particular conditions or develop programmes of intervention and assistance can come to think of people as representative of a particular group, and in doing so will minimize or ignore the wide variety of talents and abilities of the members of that group. It may not be possible to eliminate this problem entirely, but it can be addressed to some extent by taking great care to use descriptive labels that have few if any negative associations. For example, nowadays children are very seldom described as 'idiots', 'Mongols' or 'educationally subnormal'. The expression in current use is 'children with special educational needs'. This is not an example of 'political correctness' but is a recognition of psychological work which has highlighted the damage done by inappropriate labelling.

3.4 Statementing

Issues of terminology and labelling apart, there are some children with special educational needs and these require identification. The 1981 Education Act attempted to shift the focus of attention towards individual children and away from the particular group to which they had been assigned. In England and Wales the Act requires local education authorities to:

- identify children with special needs
- place children in ordinary schools where possible
- make additional provision where a child's needs cannot be met by an ordinary school alone
- work closely with parents.

(Audit Commission and HMI, 1992)

While the main thrust of the Act was to integrate children with special needs into ordinary schools, it was recognized that there would be some children whose needs were such that they could not be met within a normal school alone. Education authorities are obliged to conduct an assessment of such children and, where appropriate, produce a 'statement of special educational needs'. This statement has to specify exactly what provision the child needs, and the education authority must then make this provision. At the time of the Audit Commission and HMI report, there were 168,000 pupils with a statement (2.1 per cent of the school population in England and Wales). The report identifies differences between education authorities in terms of the numbers of pupils within the authorities who are statemented. Among the reasons advanced for these discrepancies are the lack of a definition of a special educational need, and the unwillingness of some authorities to set the lower threshold too high because of the financial implications of too many children requiring additional provision. In addition, there are differences in the extent to which children who have a statement are taught in special schools. Some of these differences relate to the extent to which appropriate special provision is available within ordinary schools. (You should also note that in the Education Act (1981) Scotland, the term 'recording' is preferred to 'statementing'. The practical consequences for children remain similar.)

One crucial aspect of the statementing process is the formal assessment of a child who may have special educational needs. The assessment is a multidisciplinary exercise involving a doctor, a teacher and an educational psychologist.

3.5 Localization of the 'problem'

In some of the other chapters in this book you will find the idea that one role for psychological intervention in the development of children is to extinguish undesirable behaviours and promote desirable behaviours. In other words, when we find children whose behaviour is not what our society finds acceptable, then we have the ability and the authority to attempt to change it. It is helpful to remember that the types of behaviour which a society considers 'acceptable' are not fixed and immutable but can change. Accordingly, behaviour which our culture might find strange and even bizarre might be considered unexceptionable in some other culture. It follows from this 'cultural relativism' that the problem posed by some behaviours is one which follows from *social norms* rather than a problem located within a particular individual. Intervention with children is usually seen by psychologists as an action in the best interests of the child. An alternative perspective could see the same intervention as in the best interests of society, with the psychologist acting as an agent. All psychologists intervening on behalf of disturbed or impaired children can be faced with these competing perspectives on their activities.

3.6 Intervention

One positive consequence of investigating the psychological development of children in general, and children with disabilities in particular, is that the knowledge obtained in this way allows us to design appropriate *intervention programmes* where these are needed. Several different types of intervention have been developed over the years. Some, such as *operant conditioning*, were adopted for use with children with a wide range of developmental difficulties. Other techniques have been developed to meet particular needs, for example, *conductive education* for children with cerebral palsy. Generally speaking, the aim of intervention is to overcome or avoid the developmental difficulties posed to children by their condition.

For children with a disability there are two routes by which their development may be impaired: as a result of a *primary impairment*, such as brain damage, or as a result of a *secondary impairment* resulting from some environmental factor, such as inappropriate stimulation or lack of encouragement. When considering the effectiveness of different interventions, it is important to keep this distinction between primary and secondary impairments in mind. Ideally, intervention should be aimed at overcoming the primary impairment. For many disabilities, however, the primary impairment may be poorly understood or be inaccessible to intervention. So, in the case of conditions such as autism and Down's syndrome (see Chapter 7), intervention is usually geared to overcoming the secondary impairments.

In a world in which there are complementary and sometimes competing intervention programmes it is useful to be able to evaluate alternative approaches. In order to help both parents and professionals judge the claims made for intervention programmes designed for use for children with autism, clinical psychologists Dawn Wimpory and Veronica Cochrane (1991) produced a set of guidelines that included the following.

- *Research subjects or participating children should be clearly defined (or diagnosed)*

[Before we can judge the effectiveness of a particular therapy or intervention, we need to understand the starting point of the children who received the help. For example, in some conditions, such as autism or dyslexia, there is considerable debate about which children should be included under the descriptive term. The selection of different groups of children in different studies can make comparisons difficult.]

- *Research should compare a child's development with his/her own development before therapy began or with that of another similar child*

Children develop at different rates, and it is important when trying to establish the effectiveness of a therapy that we don't simply record the natural fast development of some children and attribute this to the therapy.

- *Research should clearly define the therapy under investigation*

The more clearly that a therapy can be defined, the firmer the research conclusion that can be drawn. If a combined therapy is employed ... [such as intervening with autistic children using Holding Therapy together with Behaviour Modification] then this 'package' needs comparison with the separate use of its component parts. Otherwise the effectiveness of one component could mask the ineffectiveness of the other ...

(Wimpory and Cochrane, 1991, p. 15)

SUMMARY OF SECTION 3

- The British Psychological Society has produced a code of conduct which sets out the ethical standards expected of psychologists. All psychological work may be judged against these standards.
- The language used by psychologists has received particular attention, including the possible negative effects of labelling people using psychological terms.
- Psychologists attempt to act in the best interests of children; however, the same act can also be perceived as being in the interests of society.
- There can be competing or complementary programmes of intervention which may be appropriate for particular children. One task for psychologists is to identify the most suitable programme.

4   CONCLUSION

One important aspect of this chapter has been to raise a number of issues to do with the relationship of the study of psychology to the practical welfare, development and education of children. These issues have ranged from questions about the ways in which the discipline has presented itself to teachers to the changing roles of clinical child psychologists and the models of children that inform their activities. Along the way we have begun to explore the significance of the use of terms to describe those who participate within psychological frames of reference, whether willingly or as a consequence of the concerns of their family, their school or wider social processes.

These are all issues that underpin many of the discussions and debates in the following chapters, and will apply in any forum in which the relationship between psychological theories and their applications is discussed.

REFERENCES

AUDIT COMMISSION and HMI (1992) *Getting In On the Act: provision for pupils with special education needs: the national picture*, London, HMSO.

BERNBAUM, G. (1985) 'Psychology in initial teacher education' in FRANCIS, H. (ed.) *Learning to Teach,* London, Falmer Press.

BRITISH PSYCHOLOGICAL SOCIETY (1993) *Code of Conduct, Ethical Principles and Guidelines*, Leicester, British Psychological Society.

CENTRAL ADVISORY COUNCIL FOR EDUCATION (1967) *Children and their Primary Schools*, London, HMSO (The Plowden Report).

CLAXTON, G. (1985) 'The psychology of teaching educational psychology' in FRANCIS, H. (ed.) *Learning to Teach,* London, Falmer Press.

DAVIS, A. (1991) 'Piaget, teachers and education: into the 1990s' in LIGHT, P., SHELDON, S. and WOODHEAD, M. (eds) *Learning to Think,* London, Routledge/The Open University.

FIELDING, D. (1987) 'Working with children and young people' in MARZILLIER, J. S. and HALL, J. (eds) *What is Clinical Psychology?*, Oxford, Oxford University Press.

FRANCIS, H. (ed.) (1985) *Learning to Teach*, London, Falmer Press.

GARFORTH, F. W. (ed.) (1966) *John Dewey: selected educational writings,* London, Heinemann.

HERBERT, M. (1991) *Clinical Child Psychology: social learning, development and behaviour*, Chichester, John Wiley and Sons.

JAMES, W. (1899) *Talks to Teachers on Psychology: and to students on some of life's ideals,* London, Longmans, Green and Co.

LAURIE, A.P. (1911) *The Teacher's Encyclopaedia*, London, Caxton Publishing Co.

MILLER, G. (1969) 'Psychology as a means of promoting human welfare', *American Psychologist,* **24**, pp. 1063–75.

SCHWIESO, J. J., HASTINGS, N. J. and STAINTHORP, R. (1992) 'Psychology in teacher education: a response to Tomlinson', *The Psychologist,* **5**, pp. 112–13.

SUTHERLAND, M. (1985) 'Psychology and the education of teachers' in FRANCIS, H. (ed.) *Learning to Teach,* London, Falmer Press.

TIZARD, B., BLATCHFORD, P., BURKE, J., FARQUHAR, C. and PLEWIS, I. (1988) *Young Children at School in the Inner City,* Hove, Lawrence Erlbaum Associates.

TOMLINSON, P. (1992) 'Psychology and education: what went wrong – or did it?', *The Psychologist,* **5**, pp. 105–9.

WIMPORY, D. and COCHRANE, V. (1991) 'Criteria for evaluative research', *Communication,* **25**, pp. 15–17.

WOOD, D. (1988) *How Children Think and Learn,* Oxford, Blackwell.

READING

Teachers' questions

David Wood

Some educationalists (e.g. Blank, Rose and Berlin, 1978) argue that teacher questions are powerful tools for encouraging pupils and students to *listen* and to *think*. To be effective, however, a teacher's questions must be of the appropriate kind and at the right 'level of demand' if pupils are to profit by them. Blank has developed an elaborate scheme for classifying questions that she offers as a way of analysing and evaluating teaching talk with pre-school and young school-children. Some questions (for example, 'What do we call this?', asked in relation to a common object) are concerned with relatively 'low level' demands and permit a very restricted range of answers, perhaps only a single word. Others, e.g. 'Why did that happen?', may call for more thought and explanation. Yet others, 'What do you think about …?' may have no obvious, correct answer but call for analytical reasoning and informed judgement.

Observations of teacher questions addressed to children of widely different ages and in a variety of disciplines have led to the conclusion that teacher questions are more often of the 'closed' type with known right answers. The responses to such questions by pupils are likely to be terse and simply correct or incorrect. When pupils answer a teacher's questions, they usually say no more and stop talking. Consequently, where such specific, closed questions are frequent, children will say little. Now, if the goal of asking questions is *only* to ascertain whether or not a child knows a particular fact or name, one can argue that such results are defensible. However, if other goals are also being sought – for example, encouraging children to reason out loud, to ask questions of their own, to state their own opinions, ideas and uncertainties, or to *narrate* – then the frequent use of specific, closed questions will not bring about the desired ends.

In one extensive study of teachers' use of questions in a number of disciplines, including natural history and physics lessons, Nuthall and Church (1973) investigated the impact of different types of questions on pupil performance. They compared lessons in which teachers used a preponderance of closed questions demanding specific factual answers with those in which they employed more open-ended questions designed to encourage reasoning, discussion and speculation. They found that the children taught through specific questions tended to do better when tested for retention of factual information. Those who were asked open-ended questions did indeed speculate, hypothesize and discuss more (though they did not learn so many specific facts per unit of teaching time). This finding may not seem surprising. It does, however, suggest that what and how children think and learn can be influenced by the way in which the teacher conducts his or her lesson!

Schools are expected to achieve a variety of different, often conflicting, goals with their children. Teachers may find some of these goals, say teaching a body of facts, to be in 'competition' with others, like fostering the development of skills in narration, self-presentation and informing others. The hope that each of these objectives can be met with the same 'register' and approach to teaching, typically the question–answer exchange in which the teacher asks almost all the questions, seems a vain one. It is not my task to try to define what the objectives of a school or teacher should be. However, the findings that have emerged from studies of classroom interaction offer teachers some practical suggestions as to how instructional means and learning outcomes might best be married. Frequent, specific questions tend to generate relatively silent children and to inhibit any discussion between them. Telling children things, giving an opinion, view, speculation or idea, stimulates more talk, questions and ideas from pupils and generates discussion between them.

If all this sounds obvious, then explain why so many studies have found that classroom talk is dominated by teacher questions.

Although Nuthall and Church found that teachers' use of specific questions led to more rapid learning of factual information by their pupils, an examination of longer-term effects of different questioning 'regimes' suggests that pupil achievement is higher when they encounter more demanding, open-ended questions (Redfield and Rousseau, 1981). Further support for this conclusion comes from a study of the questions that *parents* characteristically employ with their children. Here too, more demanding, open-ended questions from parents were found to be predictive of a number of measures of children's educational achievement (Sigel and McGillicuddy-Delisi, 1984). Sigel argues that such questions facilitate the development of educability in children because they invite them to 'distance' themselves from the immediate, short-term consequences of their experiences. In so doing, the child is enjoined to decentre, think about and reflect upon his own activities and, in consequence, becomes more analytic, less impulsive and achieves more effective control of his own learning. The notion that children 'internalize' the processes of control to which they are exposed in order to regulate their own learning and thinking emerges from a variety of research studies.

Other studies have shown that teachers can be helped to modify their own teaching styles to adopt different questioning techniques. Some of these illustrate the difficulties involved and relate back to our previous discussion of the relationship between verbal and non-verbal dimensions of communication. When teachers ask pupils questions, they tend to leave about a second of silence, on average, before they resume talking (if the children have not responded). In a study of the effects of different teacher 'wait times' on children's responses, teachers were provided with a buzzer (which only they could hear) and were asked, having posed a question, to wait until this was sounded before going on. The buzzer was controlled by an observer, who waited for three seconds after each question before activating it (again, if no response was forthcoming from the class). The increased 'wait time' allowed to children resulted in more frequent, relevant, thoughtful and 'high level' responses to the teachers' questions (Rowe, 1974; Swift and Gooding, 1983).

In face-to-face conversation … the *synchronization* of communication is finely tuned. Perhaps, when a teacher is faced with a group of pupils, the cues that enable such synchronization to emerge are destroyed or in some way inhibited, so that a teacher's timing is out of synchrony and sympathy with the pupils' responses (which are likely to vary from child to child anyway). Perhaps increasing the time allowed after a question has been asked enables most or all of the pupils to formulate their thoughts? Such results illustrate how specific features of discourse exert an important influence on the process of classroom communication. One suspects that it would prove a difficult task for teachers to sustain control over such normally spontaneous features of their classroom talk as time after questions, however.

...

> Teaching is not only a special form of conversing with others – it is an especially difficult form, if for no other reason than that the teacher must 'converse' with a large heterogeneous group of listeners. Good teaching requires one to be good at a particular kind of conversation; it is a skill not easily acquired because of the special demands it makes, and it is not a skill one can readily practise outside the classroom, since it is very rarely appropriate to any other circumstance. [Wardhough, 1985, p. 71]

The studies we have just been discussing lend considerable weight to his argument.

Classroom discourse is typically controlled by teacher questions that often demand quick, terse, factual answers and leave little time for children to respond, elaborate or reason out loud. Perhaps this explains, in part at least, why some children do not learn how to express their ideas, formulate their thoughts or say what they know. Furthermore, if the teacher asks all the questions, then he or she dictates the course of events; what will be thought about and when. We have to ask ourselves whether this provides the *pupils* with opportunities to plan, regulate, reason and explain themselves.

References

BLANK, M., ROSE, S. A. and BERLIN, L. J. (1978) *The Language of Learning: the preschool years,* New York, Grune and Stratton.

NUTHALL, G. and CHURCH, J. (1973) 'Experimental studies of teaching behavior' in CHANAN, G. (ed.) *Towards a Teaching Science*, Slough, NFER.

REDFIELD, D. L. and ROUSSEAU, E. W. (1981) 'A meta-analysis of experimental research on teacher questioning behavior', *Review of Educational Research,* **5**, pp. 237–45.

ROWE, M. B. (1974) 'Wait-times and rewards as instructional variables, their influence on language, logic and fate control. I: Wait time', *Journal of Research in Science Teaching,* **11**, pp. 81–94.

SIGEL, I. E. and MCGILLICUDDY-DELISI, I. (1984) 'Parents as teachers of their children: a distancing behavior model' in PELLEGRINI, A. D. and YAWKEY, T. D. (eds) *The Development of Oral and Written Language in Social Contexts: advances in discourse processes,* Norwood, NJ, Ablex.

SWIFT, J. N. and GOODING, C. T. (1983) 'Interaction of wait time, feedback and questioning instruction in middle school science teaching', *Journal of Research in Science Teaching,* **20,** pp. 721–30.

WARDHOUGH, R. (1985) *How Conversation Works,* Oxford, Blackwell.

Source: WOOD, D. (1988) How Children Think and Learn, *Oxford, Blackwell, pp. 142–4.*

CHAPTER 2 TEACHING AND LEARNING

Dorothy Faulkner

CONTENTS

OBJECTIVES

When you have studied this chapter, you should be able to:

1 describe the main differences between traditional and progressive models of education;

2 discuss the pros and cons of using psychological research to inform educational practice;

3 differentiate the various types of teacher–learner relationship implied by the theories of child development described in the chapter;

4 evaluate the impact of behaviourist and social constructivist views of learning on educational practice;

5 explain the importance of taking teachers' attitudes and expectations into account when evaluating children's school performance.

1 INTRODUCTION

This chapter looks at the relationship between psychological theory and research and educational practice. It will concentrate on teaching and learning, looking at both the 'cognitive' aspects of schooling (that is, the knowledge and skills children are expected to acquire), and also at more 'social' aspects (for example, what the experience of schooling means and the nature of the relationship between children and their teachers). Also, this chapter will consider the implications for education of research traditions such as behaviourism and social constructivism, and the theories of Skinner, Piaget, Bruner and Vygotsky. Before discussing these, however, it is necessary to take a brief look at some of the ways in which psychological research can inform educational policy and practice.

1.1 The great education debate

The educational system in England and Wales is currently undergoing considerable change and reform. In recent years this has been driven by the findings of a number of committees of inquiry set up by the Government and by research commissioned by the Department for Education, Her Majesty's Inspectorate, the Schools' Examinations and Assessment Council, and the like. Since the mid-1970s all aspects of education have come under scrutiny, including teaching methods and the curriculum; the types of provision made for children with special educational needs or children from minority ethnic groups; and the form of initial teacher education offered to student teachers.

In spite of all the reforms and critical appraisal, however, schools and teachers continue to be criticized from all sides for apparently failing to provide the kind of education and training that young people need to be

'This term's topic is on educational reform ... I'd like it in by tomorrow morning.'

successful in today's society. The nature of effective teaching – and whether children should be taught using so-called 'traditional' methods, or whether the 'progressive' child-centred methods advocated by the Plowden Committee in 1967 are more effective – has been a continual source of controversy in educational circles particularly with relation to primary schooling. (A comparison of the main features of these two methods is given in Table 1.) In 1976, Prime Minister James Callaghan initiated what came to be known as the 'great education debate'. In an influential speech delivered at Ruskin College, Oxford, he declared himself to be uneasy about the effectiveness of informal child-centred methods of teaching, particularly when practised by inexperienced teachers.

This speech generated a considerable amount of interest and research into the effectiveness of teaching methods in schools, such as Leicester University's *Observational Research and Classroom Learning Evaluation* (ORACLE) project (Galton, Simon and Croll, 1980) and the study by members of the Thomas Coram Research Institute, *Young Children at School in the Inner City* (Tizard *et al.*, 1988). Generally speaking, these studies showed that a multitude of factors influence how well children are or are not taught. These factors interact in complex ways and cannot be understood by simply examining the question of whether schools use traditional or progressive teaching methods. These studies have failed to convince the 'traditionalist' camp, however, and in the 1990s the great debate continues.

TABLE 1 A comparison of traditional and progressive teaching methods as applied to primary school education

Features	Traditional	Progressive
Underlying rationale	Education involves the transmission of knowledge from adult expert to child novice through direct instruction; accurate retention of content knowledge is emphasized	Education involves the construction of knowledge by children through processes of discovery learning; process – learning how to learn – is emphasized
Classroom organization	Whole-class teaching; classes organized according to age and ability; children may be streamed according to ability	Mixed ability classes; children within any one class taught in small groups; groups organized according to ability, friendship, or age
Curriculum organization	Individual subjects are taught separately by specialist teachers	Subjects are taught by the same teacher through topics or themes which cover many different areas of the curriculum simultaneously.

Emotive newspaper headlines about education are commonplace. Depending on which newspaper one reads, these articles either defend attempts to reform the educational system in the face of a perceived rising tide of illiteracy, truancy and falling standards, or they vilify what is seen to be a misguided attempt on the part of the Government to 'return to basics'.

Over the years psychologists have built up a considerable body of knowledge in areas such as language development, the acquisition of reading skills, the development of children's understanding of scientific and mathematical concepts, and so on. Yet, as has been dramatically demonstrated by the vigorous and long-standing debate on the teaching of reading, this knowledge does not seem to be helping teachers and education specialists to resolve their differences. One might want to ask why it is the case that psychological research apparently plays a relatively minor role in informing educational policy and practice.

1.2 Educational policy and research

The opinions of educational policy makers concerning the usefulness or otherwise of psychological research clearly affects the extent to which psychologists can make a contribution to educational practice. For example, both the Plowden Report (Central Advisory Council for Education, 1967) and the Bullock Committee's Report, *A Language for Life* (DES, 1975), which investigated the teaching of English language and literacy, clearly recommended not only that the study of child development should be a necessary component of all teacher education courses, but also that there should be a reciprocal relationship between academic research and educational practice. The Plowden Committee described the relationship of research to practice as follows:

> The willingness of teachers to experiment, to innovate and to change has been one of the mainsprings of progress in the primary schools. This source of improvements will continue so long as we have forward and inventive teachers. At the same time, in spite of the slender resources devoted to it, educational research has contributed much to progress since the turn of the century. ...

> Because education is an applied discipline, the relation between research and practice is and should be reciprocal. From studies of what individual teachers are doing, useful pointers can be obtained to fruitful directions for experiment and research: research in education or in such ancillary sciences as child development, social psychology, or learning theory will throw up ideas with which the innovating teacher can experiment. In this very important sense, *research and practice are parts of a whole, and neither can flourish without the other.*

> (Central Advisory Council for Education, 1967, paras 1151, 1152, p. 423; my italics)

The Bullock Committee, however, was more critical of the potential of research:

> Generally speaking, there exists something of an uneasy relationship between research and teaching. The findings of research studies are not always pertinent to the problems of teachers or of much practical value in the classroom. On the other hand, some have had considerable relevance and a great deal to offer schools and yet have not been taken up. It is sometimes said of teachers that they ignore research findings and of researchers that they fail to respond to the day-to-day problems of the classroom. There is clearly a pressing need for better communication and a closer understanding ...
>
> (DES, 1975, p. 552)

Whereas the Plowden Report recommended that teachers should 'experiment' with new ideas generated by research, the Bullock Report went further. In order to bridge the 'confidence gap' between teachers and researchers, it recommended that teachers should conduct their own research:

> In our view, teachers should be involved not only in experimenting with the outcomes of research but also in identifying the problems, setting up hypotheses, and carrying out the collection and assessment of data. ... This kind of participation can help teachers to a better understanding of the discipline, methods, and limitations of research, and can ensure that the outcomes are put to practical use.
>
> (DES, 1975, p. 553)

The 'teacher-as-researcher' movement is now very strong in both England and Wales, and also in Scotland. The Scottish Council for Research in Education actively supports teacher research by awarding prizes and grants to teachers who wish to carry out research in their own schools and classrooms, and co-ordinates an information exchange network for teachers and educational researchers. The Classroom Action Research Network performs a similar function for teachers in England and Wales, and many of the Open University's education courses provide training for teachers wishing to engage in research. Nowadays there are many instances of fruitful and productive collaboration between teachers, schools and university research units, as the example given in Research Summary 1 shows.

Maths work in a primary classroom.

> ### RESEARCH SUMMARY 1
> ### LANGUAGE COUNTS IN THE TEACHING OF MATHEMATICS
>
> Susan Wright, a primary school teacher, carried out an in-depth case study of six 6- to 7-year-old children's understanding of mathematical terms and concepts. She wanted to find out why some children appeared to experience difficulty in coping with the specialized language used in maths lessons. She decided to focus on children's understanding and use of language in three areas: Time, Length and Weight. She collected data on the six children over a six month period using systematic observation, tape-recordings of children's language during maths lessons, and recordings of her own question-and-answer sessions with the children.
>
> She found that the children experienced more difficulty with the abstract concept of Time than they did with Length and Weight. They also found it difficult to make simple predictions based on their own experience. From the audiotapes, Wright found that she asked many more questions of the children than they asked of her; 'The topics of Time and Length contained only thirty-four children's questions as opposed to about five hundred of mine'. Approximately 50 per cent of her questions asked for factual knowledge answers. Less than 10 per cent required the children to make predictions and reason.
>
> She concluded that: 'There should be greater use of reasoning questions by the teacher and more opportunity for children to hypothesize about their work; children's active use of mathematical vocabulary should be encouraged together with an awareness of the need to extend the personal vocabulary of some children ...'
>
> (Wright, 1990, p. 150)

As you can see from Research Summary 1, Susan Wright's findings are similar to those discussed by David Wood in Reading A of Chapter 1. This example also shows how the relationship between research and practice can follow the reciprocal models advocated by the Plowden and Bullock Reports and more recently by Rudduck (1991). It would be fair to say, however, that the relationship between research and teaching is more often an 'uneasy' one. As knowledge of learning and development clearly is relevant to teaching, perhaps psychologists need to ask themselves why this should be so.

1.3 Psychologists and teachers

One reason why teachers do not find it easy to see how research on children's development is relevant to classroom practice is that much of the research is designed to shed light on theoretical issues rather than applied issues. For example, many psychologists who carry out research on children's reading are more interested in describing the development of psychological processes, such as word recognition and phonological decoding, than they are in questions concerning how to teach reading (Oakhill, 1995, discusses this issue in more detail).

Secondly, even when psychologists carry out their research in classrooms, as opposed to the laboratory, the relationship between researchers and teachers is frequently unequal. Researchers may be reluctant to communicate the true nature and purpose of their investigations to the teachers for fear of biasing their results. Also, they may be unwilling to accept that teachers have useful insights into children's learning as these may not be based on systematic observation. The 'expert theoretician' finds it difficult to enter into meaningful dialogue with the 'expert practitioner' and vice versa, and, as with all clashes between experts, this can produce a climate of mutual distrust and lack of communication. If teachers and psychologists are to enter into meaningful dialogue, the research model adopted must be one which recognizes that the skills of each, though different, are complementary.

The next section looks at how different theoretical traditions in psychology describe the relationship between learning and development, and the implications of this for models of the teacher–learner relationship.

SUMMARY OF SECTION 1

- There has been considerable debate over the past 30 years about whether children should be taught using traditional or progressive methods of education.
- Psychological research does not appear at first sight to have had a direct impact on this debate, although it is clear that it does have a significant role to play in helping teachers understand child development.
- Both the Plowden Report and the Bullock Report have argued that the relationship between psychological research and educational practice should be reciprocal in nature.
- Although the relationship between psychologists and teachers has not always been equitable in the past, nowadays teachers are actively encouraged to participate in the research process.

2 THE RELATIONSHIP BETWEEN LEARNING AND DEVELOPMENT

In many ways the debate introduced at the beginning of Section 1 concerning the advantages and disadvantages of traditional and progressive education is a false one. Research studies which have examined why some schools are more effective than others have shown that most schools adopt a mixture of both traditional and progressive methods (e.g. Galton, Simon and Croll, 1980). Periodically, however, books, Government reports, and policy documents are released which attempt to evaluate the current state of education. In the 1980s and 1990s these have been increasingly critical of child-centred methods, and by implication, theories of child development. For example, in 1992 Professors Robin Alexander, Jim Rose and Chris Woodhead produced an influential discussion paper on the quality of teaching in primary schools. This stated:

> To teach well, teachers must take account of how children learn. We do not, however, believe that it is possible to construct a model of primary education from evidence about children's development alone: the nature of the curriculum followed by the pupil and the range of teaching strategies employed by the teacher are also of critical importance. Teaching is not applied child development. It is a weakness of the child-centred tradition in primary education and teacher training that it has sometimes tended to treat it as such and, consequently, to neglect the study of classroom practice.
>
> (Alexander, Rose and Woodhead, 1992, p. 14)

What have developmental psychologists to say by way of defence? For those of us who are interested in the practical applications of our discipline, it is quite clear that there is currently a conceptual muddle concerning: firstly, the nature and purposes of education; secondly, the relationship between learning and development; and, finally, the relationship between teaching and learning.

A traditional science lesson in a secondary school.

2.1 The behaviourist model

According to devotees of the traditional 'transmission' model of education, the purpose of education is to impart to children a range of knowledge and skills through the medium of direct instruction. According to this model children are seen as empty or partially filled vessels into which knowledge and skills are to be poured. They are passive recipients of knowledge delivered by their teachers, and learning consists of successful retention of facts and information. According to Vygotsky (1978), the theoretical position underlying this model is that there is no distinction between learning and development; learning *is* development. This is the position most commonly associated with behaviourist models of learning.

2.2 The Piagetian tradition

As you saw in Chapter 1, the 'progressive' child-centred tradition sees education as providing children with the means to develop their own knowledge and skills, at their own pace, according to their individual aptitudes. This tradition recognizes that children take an active part in their own development and that, provided they have access to a rich and stimulating environment, they will construct their own knowledge and understandings. According to Vygotsky, this tradition is based on the assumption that development is *independent* of learning:

> [Learning] merely utilizes the achievements of development rather than providing an impetus for modifying its course.
>
> [...]
>
> Because this approach is based on the premise that learning trails behind development, that development always outruns learning, it precludes the notion that learning may play a role in the course of the development.
>
> (Vygotsky, 1978, pp. 79–80)

This tradition implies that children do not have to be directly taught in order to learn. The function of teachers is to facilitate and to organize the learning environment in such a way that it allows children to develop concepts and skills by themselves. This tradition is the one derived from Piagetian theory.

Children working independently on a range of tasks in a primary school classroom.

2.3 Bruner's viewpoint

The third theoretical position is that learning and development are mutually dependent and interactive:

> Schematically, the relationship between the two processes could be depicted by two concentric circles, the smaller symbolizing the learning process and the larger the developmental process evoked by learning.
>
> (Vygotsky, 1978, p. 83)

This position is the one originally advocated by Bruner who claimed that:

> [The] intellectual development of the child is no clockwork sequence of events; it also responds to influences from the environment, notably the school environment. Thus instruction in scientific ideas, even at the elementary [primary school] level, need not follow slavishly the natural course of cognitive development in the child. It can also lead intellectual development by providing challenging but usable opportunities for the child to forge ahead in his development. Experience has shown that it is worth the effort to provide the growing child with problems that tempt him into [the] next stages of development.
>
> (Bruner, 1974, p. 417)

You can see from this quotation that not only does Bruner see a role for teaching and instruction, he also claims that given the right kind of instruction, learning can *lead to* development.

2.4 Vygotsky's model

As is pointed out in Das Gupta and Richardson (1995), Vygotsky (1978) took this argument one stage further when he claimed that we must pay attention to two distinctly different developmental levels: the child's 'actual developmental level' (concepts, skills and ideas that have already been mastered), and the child's 'potential developmental level' (concepts, skills and ideas which the child has not fully grasped, but which he or she can cope with, given help and guidance by a more experienced child or adult).

Although he maintained that learning should not be equated with development, Vygotsky claimed that 'properly organized learning' within a child's zone of proximal (or potential) development 'sets in motion a variety of developmental processes that would be impossible apart from learning' (Vygotsky, 1978, p. 90). Contrary to the positions discussed earlier, then, Vygotsky implies that both *teaching* and *learning* have a definite role to play in leading the child from one level of development to the next. According to this fourth model, instruction (or teaching) assumes as much importance as learning in development. Children's learning needs to be organized and structured by teachers in such a way as to allow them to derive maximum benefit from the learning experience.

Fortunately for developmental psychologists, this position also appears to have informed recent educational thinking. Although Alexander, Rose and Woodhead (1992) criticized the child-centred tradition in their report on primary school teaching, they also acknowledged that:

> Recent research into children's learning does, however, emphasise young children's immense cognitive and linguistic competence. In the 60s and 70s, Piagetian theories about developmental ages and stages led to chronologically fixed notions of 'readiness', thus depressing expectations and discouraging teacher intervention. More recent studies demonstrate what children, given effective teaching, can achieve ... They show that learning is essentially a social and interactive process. They place proper emphasis on the teacher as teacher rather than 'facilitator'. Such insights are, in our view, critical to the raising of standards in primary classrooms.
>
> (Alexander, Rose and Woodhead, 1992, p. 14)

These brief descriptions of various educational traditions and the possible different relationships between learning and development are necessarily somewhat oversimplified. For our purposes, however, it is important to realize that not only do the educational traditions differ about the *purposes* of education, they also differ in terms of how they regard the *relationship between teacher and learner*. Similarly, psychological models of learning and development can also be distinguished according to how they describe the dynamics of the teacher–learner relationship. As you will see later in the chapter, elements of all four models currently exist alongside each other in schools, and changes to educational practice do not mean that one model is simply replaced by another, lock, stock and barrel.

SUMMARY OF SECTION 2

- As most schools employ elements of both traditional and progressive teaching methods, the debate concerning their relative advantages and disadvantages is misleading.
- Several different models of the relationship between learning and development are possible, depending on which psychological tradition one is working within.
- According to the behaviourist tradition there is no difference between learning and development; they are one and the same.
- The Piagetian tradition maintains that development and learning are independent, and that teaching and instruction cannot directly influence development.
- According to Bruner, learning and development are mutually interdependent. Teaching has a vital role to play in bringing about development.
- Vygotsky maintains that development occurs when teaching and learning are located within the child's zone of proximal development.

3 IDEAS ABOUT THE NATURE AND PURPOSES OF EDUCATION

As we saw in Section 2, as well as thinking about the relationship between learning and development, and that between teaching and learning, it is also necessary to think about the nature and purposes of education. Any one society's ideas about education, and how best to prepare its young members for adulthood within that society, will be heavily influenced by historical and cultural factors. Developmental psychologists are beginning to pay much closer attention to the influence of culture on children's development, and also to its effects on educational systems.

One way of thinking about the influence of culture on schooling and educational practice is to imagine what would happen if you were asked to design an educational system from scratch. The result would be likely to reflect the cultural values, conventions, knowledge systems and preferred behaviours of the society you belonged to. Also, the educational priorities driving the new system would indicate your views on what well-educated people ought to be like, and how young children should be educated in order to achieve this.

ACTIVITY 1

Allow about 30 minutes

EDUCATION AND CULTURE

Given generous funds and a free rein, briefly imagine how you would redesign an educational system with which you are familiar. Focus on the types of knowledge and skills that you would consider necessary for someone to come out of your system as a well-educated person. Do not spend too long on this (about ten minutes). You might like to make a note of your ideas so that you can think about them later.

Now read the following extract from Howard Gardner's *The Unschooled Mind* (1993), which describes three different kinds of educational system. Identify the teacher–learner relationships implied by each system.

> In any society, knowledge will be encoded in a variety of forms. There will be many skilled performances, much factual information, and numerous, sometimes competing concepts and theories about the world. ... In a Confucian society, for example, you would make sure that youngsters were instructed in how to render calligraphic characters, how to play a musical instrument, how to pour tea, how to draw a bow, and how to dress like a member of the gentry or a warrior. The well-educated person in such a society can carry out exquisitely a whole set of performances ....
>
> You might decide on further reflection, that a host of highly proficient performances is less desirable than the possession of considerable bodies of information. ... You would then make

sure that starting very young, youngsters committed to memory as much information as possible. They would learn the words and rules of many languages, both living and dead; gain familiarity with numerous stories, works of music, and works of art; master the various arithmetical tables, geometric proofs, and scientific laws that have been established; commit to memory lists of facts and figures about past and contemporary societies, practices, and achievements. By adulthood, a graduate of such a program would resemble a well-stocked vessel, capable of exhibiting the knowledge that we associate with a successful quiz show contestant or a winner in a game of Trivial Pursuit.

A third tack would be to minimize skilled performances of valued cultural practices and/or the mastery of prized facts, striving instead for the attainment of a rich understanding of the concepts and principles underlying bodies of knowledge. ... [The] person who understands deeply has the capacity to explore the world in a number of ways, using complementary methods. She arrives at concepts and principles in part on the basis of her own explorations and reflections, but she must ultimately reconcile these with the concepts and principles that have evolved in various disciplines. The test of understanding involves neither repetition of information learned nor performances of practices mastered. Rather it involves the appropriate application of concepts and principles to questions or problems that are newly posed. ... [The] 'compleat understander' can think appropriately about phenomena of consequence in her society, particularly ones that she has not previously encountered.

(Gardner, 1993, pp. 116–17)

Do Gardner's hypothetical educational systems bear any resemblance to the one you thought up? Before you read on, spend five to ten minutes thinking about the sort of teacher–learner relationship implied by each of Gardner's three examples. What sort of teacher–learner relationship is implied by your own ideal educational system?

Comment

Obviously, in the above extract, Gardner was caricaturing three fairly distinct types of educational systems and sets of cultural values. Nevertheless, at least two of the descriptions, the last two, must strike common chords in those who have experience of British and American education. I hope that carrying out this activity has helped you appreciate the relationship between society, culture and education.

If learning is viewed as the acquisition of skilled performances, as in the Confucian society described by Gardner, then this implies that in schools the teacher–learner relationship should be that of master and apprentice. Here the master teaches by example, and the novice learns by imitation. By contrast, if knowledge acquisition is a society's or culture's goal, then teaching will consist of delivering information to pupils in an easily digestible way, and in order to learn children will need to find or be given strategies, such as rote repetition, to help them commit the material to memory. Here the acquisition of knowledge is 'reproductive' and involves simple repetition and retention of what has been taught (Nunes, 1995, offers an extended discussion of this type of knowledge acquisition). This system has much in common with the 'traditional' system of education outlined at the beginning of this chapter.

If, on the other hand, education is seen to involve 'the attainment of a rich understanding of ... concepts and principles' (Gardner, 1993, p. 117) and the wherewithal to apply this understanding to new phenomena, then clearly the learner is expected to take a much more active role in the construction of his or her own understanding. Here, the acquisition of knowledge can be described as 'generative', as it encourages children to generate new facts and principles on the basis of those they have already discovered. This system seems to embody many of the principles of 'progressive' education derived from the application of Piagetian theory to educational practice. As you saw in Section 2, however, Piaget did not accord much importance to direct instruction.

Gardner's third idealized educational system implies that instruction has a very definite role to play in learning, when he says that the learner 'must ultimately reconcile' the results of his or her own 'explorations and reflections' with 'the concepts and principles which have evolved in various disciplines' (Gardner, 1993, p. 117). When it comes to learning about formal disciplines such as science and mathematics, children cannot discover new ways of thinking, and make

Young children working with their teacher.

conceptual changes to their established ways of thinking, completely independently; they need to be explicitly instructed in the formal language, concepts and discourses of these disciplines. They also need to be exposed to other people's ideas through intellectual conflict and discussion (see Das Gupta and Richardson, 1995, for a more extended treatment of this argument). This perspective is derived from the work of Vygotsky and Bruner. As you saw in Section 2, their positions allow teachers a much more interactive role in the teacher–learner relationship whereby they work within the child's zone of proximal development and guide them towards an understanding of socially constructed systems of knowledge.

Barbara Rogoff (1991) has extended the ideas of Vygotsky and Bruner by proposing that the roles of children and adults in teaching and learning situations should ideally be complementary. Children's learning, or their cognitive growth and development, should rely as much on their own efforts as on those of the teacher: 'They do not simply receive the guidance of adults, they seek, structure, and even demand the assistance of those around them in learning how to solve problems of all kinds' (Rogoff, 1991, p. 68). Rogoff describes this kind of relationship as 'guided participation'. This formulation seems to be the one best fitted to promoting the kind of learning and development outlined by Gardner in his third idealized educational system.

In this section of the chapter, we have looked at the influence of culture on education, and at idealized forms of the teacher–learner relationship in fairly abstract terms. The next sections will consider how the various theories translate into practice, and will examine the influences they have had on current educational thinking.

SUMMARY OF SECTION 3

- This section introduced the idea that not all cultures have the same views about the nature and purposes of education. If we accept that learning and development are mutually dependent, then this has implications for the study of children's development, as other societies and cultures will adopt different methods of providing for learning and education.

- Three idealized educational systems were compared. Each of these systems has a different view of the nature of knowledge and how children might be expected to acquire an understanding of the knowledge, skills and values of their particular culture.

- It was argued that when a genuine understanding of knowledge systems and formal disciplines is an educational and cultural goal, then a 'guided participation' model of the teacher–learner relationship is the one to aim for.

4 PSYCHOLOGICAL THEORIES IN PRACTICE

In the previous section we looked at cultural influences on the teacher–learner relationship. This section will examine the implications of various psychological theories of learning and development concerning the nature of this relationship. First we shall look at the teacher–learner relationship from the point of view of behaviourist theories of learning before moving on to look at the theories of Piaget, Bruner and Vygotsky.

4.1 The behaviourist tradition

Programmed instruction

Early behaviourists such as Pavlov (1849–1936) and Watson (1878–1958) were committed to the view that learning could be regarded as a biologically universal phenomenon. This view implied that once the laws of behaviour could be defined, these would apply to all species – including human beings. This conviction justified the study of learning through experimental research on laboratory animals such as the rat. Watson and Pavlov explained learning in terms of *classical conditioning*. According to this theory, learning is said to take place when an animal has been conditioned through reinforcement to produce a particular response to an artificial, experimentally controlled stimulus.

Edward Thorndike (1874–1949) also adhered to the principle of biological continuity, but he explained learning in terms of *operant* or *instrumental conditioning* (see Das Gupta, 1994, for a discussion). According to this theory, learning takes place when animals form new stimulus–response associations in naturally occurring situations when one out of a range of possible responses has a particularly favourable effect or outcome for the animal. Thorndike formulated the 'law of effect' to explain this phenomenon:

> Of several responses made to the same situation, those which are accompanied or closely followed by satisfaction to the animal will, other things being equal, be more firmly connected with the situation, so that, when it recurs, they will be more likely to recur; those which are accompanied or closely followed by discomfort to the animal will, other things being equal, have their connections with that situation weakened, so that, when it recurs, they will be less likely to occur.
>
> (Thorndike, 1911, p. 244; quoted in Roth, 1990, p. 265)

Unlike classical conditioning, Thorndike's law of effect had the potential to explain how learning takes place in natural contexts. Later behaviourists such as Skinner (b. 1904) applied the principles of operant conditioning to explain learning in humans. Skinner was particularly interested in how the theory might be applied in education. His writings on education have been particularly influential in the United States, and

Reading A describes how he came to formulate a method of teaching known as 'programmed instruction' based on the principles of operant conditioning.

'I opted out of the rat-race and decided on a career in education'.

READING

Reading A, 'Educational applications of operant conditioning principles', comes from a textbook for teachers published in the USA in 1993 where the behaviourist approach to teaching is widely used in everyday classroom contexts. It describes Skinner's dissatisfaction with the conventional teaching techniques operating in the United States in the 1940s and 1950s, and explains why he devised a set of instructional principles which could be used to design teaching programmes for use in schools.

ACTIVITY 2
Allow about 20 minutes

SKINNER'S THEORY, TEACHING MACHINES, AND PROGRAMMED INSTRUCTION

Use Reading A to help you answer the following questions:

1   Why does Skinner have such a low opinion of traditional North American educational practices? Thinking back to your own schooling, do his criticisms strike any chord?

2   What is the key idea behind Skinner's approach to teaching?

3   What, according to Skinner, are the advantages to the learner of teaching materials based on the principles of programmed instruction?

4   How would you describe the teacher–learner relationship and the roles of teacher and learner implied by this theory?

5   Can you see any problems with this theory?

Comment

You can see from Reading A that Skinner's theory implies that it is possible for teachers to shape children's learning behaviour in much the same way that experimenters can shape the behaviour of animals in a laboratory. The role of the teacher, therefore, is that of a programmer, and he or she must be able to design, or work with, carefully structured teaching programmes, where the aims, objectives and goals are clearly specified. The learner's role is essentially passive. He or she simply has to work through the programmed sequences at a comfortable pace, until all the material has been mastered.

According to Gammage (1982) the advantages and disadvantages of programmed instruction are as follows:

Advantages

- Well-designed programmes give immediate feedback to children and their mistakes are corrected immediately.
- Computerized instruction programmes can be closely matched to a child's age and level of ability, and he or she can work through them at his or her own pace.
- Well-designed programmes can cater for differences in individual children's learning styles by providing different routes through the programme.

Disadvantages

- Poorly designed instruction packages are repetitive and boring and do nothing to motivate children to learn.
- Programmed learning can rarely cope with more creative and open-ended styles of learning.
- Children's learning benefits from exchanging ideas with teachers and peers, even where these ideas are wrong. Programmed instruction cannot provide this kind of social interaction.

Nowadays, programmed instruction is not much used in British schools, although it did have a place in language laboratories in the 1970s. Skinner's teaching machines have been superseded by more sophisticated, interactive computer programs which give children and teachers much more control over the learning process. The latest developments in computerized instruction are discussed in the following chapter by Karen Littleton, who gives a more detailed critique of behaviourist-inspired methods of instruction.

Behaviour management techniques

Although behaviourist learning techniques are not generally used in Britain for the teaching of academic subjects, they continue to be used in many other countries, including the United States. In British schools, structured learning programmes are more usually employed as a method for teaching children with special educational needs.

Behaviourist learning principles are frequently used in Britain, however, in the area of classroom management. In previous decades the prevailing educational philosophy with regard to classroom management was that bad behaviour should be punished. Skinner pointed out, however, that children often behave badly because they are trying to gain attention, and that attention, even in the form of punishment, can therefore be reinforcing to the child. He maintained that a more sensible approach to behaviour problems was to use operant conditioning techniques, and a system of rewards or reinforcers to reshape children's behaviour gradually in the desired direction.

Behavioural approaches to classroom management draw on the principles of behaviourism, but emphasize the fact that the successful design of intervention programmes requires careful measurement of the occurrence of the problem behaviour before, during and after the intervention (Presland, 1993) and the identification of what triggers the undesirable behaviour in the first place. One way of doing this is to carry out an 'ABC' analysis. 'ABC' stands for 'antecedent', 'behaviour' and 'consequent'. First the teacher observes the troublesome child or group to identify what triggers the undesirable behaviour (the antecedent); he or she then notes what form this takes (the behaviour); and, finally, observations are made so as to determine what is reinforcing or maintaining the behaviour (the consequent).

Frank Merrett and Dorothy Blundell (1986) have described how the behavioural approach was applied to help 13-year-old Timothy increase his concentration and the time he spent attending to his work. Timothy was in the remedial class of a large secondary school in the West Midlands. He found language work particularly difficult, and had a reading age of 6.9 years. His teacher, Dorothy Blundell, observed that when he was asked to work alone Timothy became anxious, and instead of doing his work he would try to entertain the other children. For half an hour a day for two weeks she measured the amount of time Timothy actually sat and got on with his work by noting down whatever he was doing every time she heard a tape recorded signal. These observations showed that Timothy only spent about 30 per cent of his time 'on-task'. A ten week intervention programme was designed to help Timothy (see Example 1, overleaf). By the end of the programme, his behaviour had improved and he was spending 60 per cent of his time on his school-work. Timothy's on-task behaviour continued to improve after the intervention programme had come to an end.

It is important to note in this example that Timothy's behaviour did not improve simply because of the official reinforcing activity, i.e. being given time to colour in. All sorts of 'unofficial' social reinforcements – such as praise from his teacher, and the interest of other children in what he was doing – were also important. The behavioural approach, as it is now advocated, acknowledges the importance of establishing good social relationships between children and their teachers. By contrast, Skinner's original formulation does not take into account the social and cultural dynamics of the teaching and learning situation.

EXAMPLE 1
TIMOTHY: A BEHAVIOURAL APPROACH INTERVENTION

Timothy was very fond of using a 'Doodle Art' sketch pad to colour in a cartoon picture and this was made contingent upon on-task behaviour … The boy was accordingly given the opportunity to tally his on-task behaviour using the same definition, observation schedule and signal as his teacher. He knew that the teacher would be recording at the same time and understood that only those tally marks for on-task behaviour which were agreed between them would count. Ten such agreed tally marks could be exchanged for two minutes of the reinforcing activity, i.e. colouring in the 'Doodle Art' picture.

[…]

Improvement in agreement rates in tallying, achievement of minutes of earned time and completion of the colouring task all gave opportunities for the teacher to deliver social reinforcement in the form of praise, approval and other encouragement. This was added to by the interest and co-operation of the rest of the class and other members of staff and culminated when the picture was completed and displayed in the school corridor for everyone to see. It was later taken home so that the parents could register approval and praise. Thus, one of the chief effects of the intervention was that Timothy began to receive positive reinforcement for well-defined acceptable behaviours instead of for 'clowning' and other avoidance strategies. This could be looked upon as the first stage on the way to his becoming subject to the natural, intermittent schedules of reinforcement which keep most of us in line with the expectations of our group.

(Merrett and Blundell, 1986, pp. 152–3)

4.2 The social constructivist tradition

Sections 2 and 3 described various positions regarding (a) the relationship between learning and development, and (b) different types of teacher–learner relationship implied by these positions and by different cultural models of the educational process. It was pointed out that in contrast to the behaviourist and early Piagetian models, which emphasize the individual nature of children's development, social constructivist theories, such as those of Bruner, Vygotsky and Rogoff, view learning and development as being embedded in social relationships. In terms of school practice, the introduction of these later theories has resulted in there being a much greater emphasis on the role of social processes in cognitive development. In particular this has meant that more consideration is given to fostering children's communication skills and promoting effective group work.

The Piagetian constructivist philosophy of 'learning by discovery' has not been entirely abandoned, however, nor has Piaget's notion that children progress through well-defined developmental stages. In some formulations of his theory Piaget did acknowledge that social relationships had an important part to play in children's development, particularly in the domains of moral reasoning and scientific thinking (e.g. Piaget, 1932). Later research by psychologists such as Willem Doise and Anne-Nelly Perret-Clermont, working with Piaget in Geneva, led to the view that children needed to be exposed to socio-cognitive conflict in order to progress from one stage of development to the next (e.g. Doise, 1990; Perret-Clermont, 1980). According to this view children will make most progress in their understanding when their own ideas and explanations are challenged, or set against those of another child. Even though both children's initial ideas may be wrong, in working together to resolve the discrepancies, they may come up with an alternative, more cognitively sophisticated explanation. Karen Littleton reviews the evidence for and against this research in the following chapter.

Like Vygotsky, then, in later formulations of his theory Piaget also described how development could occur through social interactions between children. The work on socio-cognitive conflict as a mechanism for development has led to a great deal of interest and research on the potential of 'peer tutoring', where children teach each other, as an educational technique. The key principles underlying peer tutoring will be discussed later. Section 4.3 describes a topic-based approach to teaching primary school children which has been very popular in recent years. This approach relies in part on Piaget's original 'discovery learning' model, but it has been extended to incorporate aspects of Bruner's and Vygotsky's social constructivist stance. It places a great deal of emphasis, therefore, on joint discovery and children learning through talk and teacher-guided discussion.

4.3 Teaching and learning in early childhood

READING

In Reading B, 'Toy project', Rachel Pinder describes some topic work based around the theme of 'toys' which was carried out with a class of 6 and 7 year olds. The reading is taken from her book *Why don't teachers teach like they used to?*, in which she discusses the influence of various philosophical and psychological traditions on primary school practice in the late 1980s and early 1990s. Like others, she sees the 'traditionalist versus progressive' debate in education as being a red herring, and she sets out to show how elements of both traditions have been incorporated into good primary practice.

In the section from which this reading is taken Pinder discusses the concept of 'the integrated day' where different groups of children work on a range of different tasks all related to a particular cross-curricular theme, or topic. Work on the topic can extend over several weeks, with children rotating round the tasks so that they cover the whole curriculum. A particular feature of this approach is that at times the class come together for whole-class teaching, sometimes they work independently, and at other times they work in pairs or small groups.

Before you turn to this Reading, look at the flow diagram for the toy project shown in Figure 1. Note how all the curriculum areas are covered, and also how some activities have been especially designed to encourage co-operation between children.

As you work through this Reading, make a note of the various intellectual, social, and linguistic skills that the children are developing by working in this way.

FIGURE 1   The toy project – based on teacher's flow diagram for term's work (Pinder, 1987, pp. 132–3).

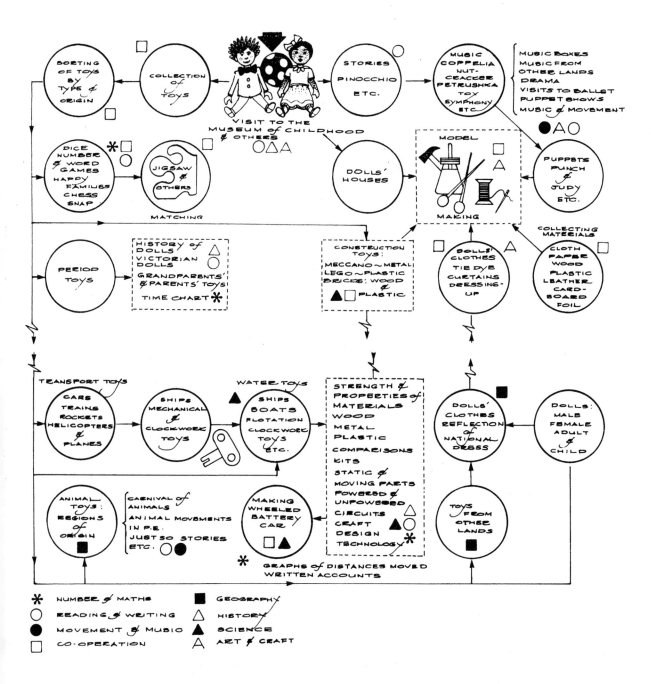

ACTIVITY 3

Allow about 45 minutes

MATCHING PRACTICE TO THEORY

Using the notes you made in connection with Reading B, see if you can identify some of the elements of the developmental theories discussed in this chapter which match up with the various skills the children were acquiring through their work on the toy project. This activity is designed to help you understand how the educational implications of psychological theories and research work in practice.

Comments on this activity are given in the text.

In terms of intellectual skills, the 6- and 7-year-old children described by Pinder were being exposed to the ideas of category formation and classification through the various sorting operations they carried out on the toys. They were also introduced to Piagetian notions of class inclusion (which toys could be categorized under more than one category label), and they were learning about the physical properties of objects through operations such as weighing and measuring.

Socially, the children were gaining practical experience of group collaboration which involved them in negotiation and decision making. For example they had to decide amongst themselves how to sort the toys, on rules for games, and rules for sharing out and caring for the toys. In this kind of situation one can also see how children cope with socio-cognitive conflict of the type described by Piaget and by Doise (1990). For example, there was a conflict when the children had to sort the toys according to function and found that some toys fitted more than one category.

As you can see, however, there was more Vygotskian-type collaboration taking place than there was socio-cognitive conflict. According to Piagetian theory, these 6 to 7 year olds are at the preoperational/concrete operational transition stage. Had they been working alone, it is unlikely that they would have discovered such diverse and sophisticated ways of sorting and categorizing the toys. Through discussion with each other and their teacher, they were able to achieve a better understanding of these activities than they would have been able to do working alone. This is a good example of what Vygotsky means when he talks about development occurring in and around the zone of proximal development. You can also see how, in Bruner's terms, the teacher carefully scaffolds the children's work through her skilful use of questions and activities.

Finally, when we consider the types of language skills the children were developing, you can see that not only were they learning new concepts and vocabulary, they were also developing conversational and discussion skills as well. Speaking and listening skills were encouraged through story work, and when the children were invited to discuss their experiences of listening to music and visiting the ballet. They also discussed what they thought they had learned from the project. In terms of the more formal, literary aspects of the language curriculum such as reading and writing, again we can see the influence of Vygotsky and Bruner, both of whom maintain that children should be taught to read and write through a functional approach to literacy. In discussing how children should be taught how to read and write Vygotsky made the following claim:

> ... writing should be meaningful for children, ... an intrinsic need should be aroused in them, and ... writing should be incorporated into a task that is necessary and relevant for life. Only then can we be certain that it will develop not as a matter of hand and finger habits but as a really new and complex form of speech.

(Vygotsky, 1978, p. 118)

The writing and reading tasks built into the toy project clearly reflect this thinking. For example, right at the beginning of the project the children had to write a letter home to explain why they needed to bring their toys into school; reading was carried out in the context of doing research on toys and toy making; the children wrote and presented their own puppet plays; and had to design their own posters, all activities which were highly meaningful and relevant in the context of the project. In Bruner's terms, these children were learning to use the 'cultural tool', written language, in ways that made sense to them (Bruner, 1974, p. 528).

As you can see from the example, the teacher's role has moved a long way away from that of someone who merely facilitates children's development through the provision of an appropriately organized environment. Similarly, although the children are actively learning through structured play, they are no longer engaged in the individual discovery learning described by Piaget. Although they are being encouraged to develop a sense of autonomy and control over their own learning, in that their teacher does not directly supply them with answers to the problems they are working on, they are also actively collaborating with their peers in order to discover ways of categorizing objects, finding solutions to problems and devising their own rules for games and so on.

So far in this section we have looked at how developmental theories have affected educational practice in the early years of primary schooling over the past 30 years or so. What about older children in the later stages of primary schooling and in secondary schools? Has practice here been similarly influenced?

4.4 Teaching and learning in middle to late childhood

As children grow older the curriculum becomes progressively more subject-based, although cross-curricular work is encouraged, especially in the case of language work and mathematics. Studies by Gammage (1987) and by Edwards and Westgate (1987) have shown that in both primary and secondary schools the pressures of working towards examinations and covering the syllabus mean that whole-class teaching is common, and that children are taught using fairly traditional methods. This and other research (e.g. Bennett and Dunne, 1989) has also shown that although children may be seated in groups, they tend to work individually: genuine collaborative group work is the exception rather than the norm. Nevertheless, there have been significant movements towards making the middle and secondary years of schooling more 'child-centred', as Example 2 illustrates. There has also been a drive to encourage genuine collaborative learning through peer tutoring, and to develop the kinds of functional language skills discussed earlier.

EXAMPLE 2
HOLT HALL, 1940: A RESIDENTIAL 'LIVING HISTORY' PROJECT

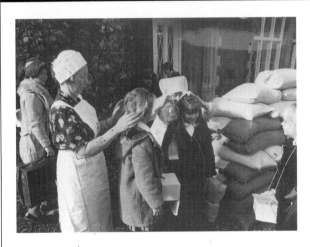

In 1990 a group of Norwich teachers designed an ambitious 'living history' experience for children aged 7 to 13. Holt Hall, a residential field study centre in Norfolk, was transformed for two weeks into a Second World War evacuee reception centre (in 1940, children living in cities in England were evacuated to the country to escape from German bombing raids). The aim of the project was to investigate the effectiveness of using role-play and drama and the use of 'empathy' to encourage children to appreciate historical causes and their consequences.

Alan Childs and Mike Pond describe the experience as follows:

'So we came to 5 November 1990 not quite knowing what would happen to the children or to us during the experience. The first party of evacuees "from Gravesend" arrived by 1940s charabanc at the remote station outside the village of Weybourne. The bus drove away having unloaded everything, but the journey by rail was not to be. Waiting in the carriages the children were informed by the station master that the line had been damaged in the previous night's air raid and the coach with its "irate" driver was summoned back. On the way to Holt Hall the bus encountered a military road block on the edge of the heath and, dishevelled and tired, the evacuees at last drew up in front of the house ...

'Little about the house was of 1990. The transformation had been carried out carefully. In the corner of the entrance hall was a period radio from which the 9 o'clock news would later be broadcast. Games, comics and newspapers of 1940 were around for children to use. Their meals and sweet rationing were authentic — as were the coins they handled.

'For the next 2½ days the children went through a series of both mundane and exciting events, all fully researched and set in the autumn of 1940. Their teachers were of course with them, equally baffled by some of the happenings but ready to deal with the "3 Rs" or put them through their paces with "PT" [Physical Training] ...

'From the writing of the children, from the interest of the media ... from the enthusiastic feedback of the sixty or so adults who created the authenticity by brilliant role-play, we were able to build up an extensive evaluation of the experience from the educational standpoint and were much encouraged by what we saw and heard.'
(Childs and Pond, 1992, pp. 18–19)

This 'living history' project shows how educational environments can be created where teachers and learners participate jointly in the learning experience. Clearly, this kind of project is exceptional (and expensive). Howard Gardner, whose ideas were discussed in Section 3, sees projects like this as the way forward, however, as they allow the creation of environments where children can be 'educated for understanding', and where 'the "compleat understander" can think appropriately about phenomena of consequence in her society, particularly ones that she has not previously encountered' (Gardner, 1993, p. 117).

In the United States Gardner has been particularly active in promoting the idea of children's museums and discovery centres to complement formal schooling. Linked in with this is the idea that the teacher–learner relationship should operate on a master–apprenticeship model, with children learning through 'guided participation'. Discussing the idea of children's museums he states that:

> As part of this educational scene, adults are present who actually practise the disciplines or crafts represented by the various exhibitions. …
>
> During the course of their schooling, youngsters enter into separate apprenticeships with a number of these adults. Each apprenticeship group consists of students of differing ages and various degrees of expertise in the domain or discipline. … The student's apprenticeships deliberately encompass a range of pursuits, including artistic activities, activities requiring exercise and dexterity, and activities of a more scholarly bent. In the aggregate, these activities incorporate the basic literacies required in the culture – reading and writing in the dominant language or languages, mathematical and computational operations, and skill in the notations drawn on in the various vocational or avocational pursuits.
>
> (Gardner, 1993, pp. 200–1)

Gardner is highly critical of the 'disembedded' nature of much of school learning. He proposes that children's development is best served when learning is embedded in real-life practical contexts. Only in this way can children appreciate the functional nature of the skills and concepts they are being asked to acquire. If all this seems very futuristic, you might like to think of opportunities available in your immediate locality which can and do provide this type of educational experience. It need not be a museum or discovery centre, it could be any kind of place of work. Also, if you have teenage children you will be familiar with the practice of 'work placement' where young people spend differing amounts of time out of school gaining an apprenticeship-type of experience in the kind of work they might want to take up when they leave school.

As yet little psychological research has been carried out which evaluates the developmental gains of this kind of educational innovation, although in the United States psychologists such as Barbara Rogoff are

Peer tutoring in the early
years.

actively investigating the apprenticeship model of teaching and learning. Much more effort has been expended on investigating the potential of peer tutoring and collaborative group work. Some of this research is discussed in the next chapter by Karen Littleton in relation to children working with computers, so only a brief discussion will be given here.

In the strict sense, peer tutoring involves pairing an older child (the tutor) with a younger child (the tutee) so that the younger child can learn from the more experienced older child. This type of pairing has been frequently used in the teaching of reading. In a detailed review of the various studies which have been carried out in the area, Keith Topping (1992) reported that while many studies showed significant learning gains on the part of both the tutor and the tutee, other studies showed no effects.

As you will recall from the discussion in Section 2, Vygotsky originally proposed that learning in the zone of proximal development could best be achieved when the child was guided by a more knowledgeable adult or older peer. Recently, this notion has been challenged as many studies have shown that 'reciprocal peer tutoring' has considerable potential for helping children's learning. In reciprocal peer tutoring there is no marked difference in the age or ability between children in a pair or group, and each child takes turns at acting as tutor or tutee. Reviewing the evidence concerning how well this technique works, Topping states that: 'The effectiveness of reciprocal peer tutoring would appear to highlight the importance of task-focused structured interaction in co-operative learning pairs or groups' (Topping, 1992, p. 155). In other words, for reciprocal peer tutoring to work, children need to be given specific preparation and guidance from their teacher – both about the learning task, and also about how to work together effectively when the teacher is no longer present. It is not sufficient simply to pair children up and then leave them to get on with the task of teaching each other.

Frank Hardman and Sue Beverton have shown that 'discussion strategies need to be explicitly taught through analysis and reflection, with pupils becoming aware of the roles that they can play in discussion, the suitability of those roles in different situations and so on' (Hardman and Beverton, 1993, p. 147). Example 3 (overleaf) gives their description of how they attempted to teach these skills to a mixed-ability class of 14 year olds during their English lessons. They argue that children need to develop *metacognitive knowledge* concerning their own abilities in situations where they have to enter into meaningful discussion. Hardman and Beverton have coined the term 'metadiscoursal awareness' to describe the kind of knowledge one needs to develop in order to participate effectively in group discussions.

EXAMPLE 3
DEVELOPING METADISCOURSAL SKILLS

The teacher had been working with the class for two terms to raise their awareness and understanding of the strategies and roles they would employ in the management of group work. This included, for example, knowledge of how to question or challenge, of how to listen and take a positive interest in the progress of their group and of turn-taking, yielding a turn and holding the floor. It also involved developing an awareness of how discourse markers (such as 'well', 'then', 'I think') can be helpful in managing talk, and discussing the effects of changes in tone and emphasis, and of para-linguistic features (such as establishing eye contact, sitting in friendly formation), on conversation. His teaching strategies included videoing, analysing and providing feedback on group discussions, role-play and simulation that drew on chat show and news interview techniques, and modelling a range of roles while interacting with groups. In analysing such work with the class, the teacher aimed to explicate the 'rules', strategies and routines of collaborative talk in order to develop the pupils' metadiscoursal awareness.

(Hardman and Beverton, 1993, p. 147)

A similar training programme has been developed by A. Palinscar and Ann Brown (1986) to help older children develop their reading comprehension skills. As older children's learning relies heavily on the ability to comprehend and analyse information from written texts, this type of programme is extremely important. In Palinscar's and Brown's programme the teacher initially works with a small group of pupils as they analyse a text. The teacher models processes such as predicting, questioning, generating ideas from the text, summarizing and clarifying for the pupils, who then practise these processes by taking turns to act as group leader. The group leader begins the discussion by posing a question about the text's context. The leader also summarizes the resulting discussion for the rest of the group at the end of the session. The technique involves pupils in taking shared responsibility for understanding the text, and for providing each other with feedback and support. It also relies upon pupils internalizing, and making their own, the discussion techniques modelled for them by their teacher. Palinscar and Brown describe their programme as 'reciprocal teaching', and claim that it can yield impressive gains in the development of children's comprehension and reasoning skills.

ACTIVITY 4
Allow about 20 minutes

A COMPARISON OF PRIMARY AND SECONDARY SCHOOL PRACTICE

Using the notes you made for Activity 3, use the following table to summarize the similarities and differences, in the way developmental theories have been applied to primary and secondary school practice, that have emerged from the above discussion.

	Similarities	Differences
Primary school		
Secondary school		

How do current teaching methods as described in the chapter relate to the ways in which you were taught at school?

Comment

Clearly there are similarities in the way developmental theories can be applied to primary and secondary school practice. The benefits of active discovery learning techniques apply at all ages although in secondary school these are more likely to be associated with particular subject areas than with cross-curricular topics. Similarly, given appropriate training and support, most children can be encouraged to learn from each other in pairs or small groups. Also, teachers can model the development of effective discourse skills at all ages, although you may have noted that whereas the aim of teachers in secondary schools is eventually to hand over control of a discussion to their pupils, this is less likely to be the aim of primary school teachers. Younger children will continue to need a large measure of teacher input in order to sustain meaningful talk about the topic in hand. It is also doubtful that very young children could be trained to develop the kind of abstract metadiscoursal awareness discussed by Hardman and Beverton.

Secondary school students discussing a text.

None of the teaching and learning methods discussed in this section could be described as formal. The teacher–pupil relationships described are supportive rather than didactic in nature. Nevertheless, these apparently more relaxed and informal methods of teaching require a lot of detailed planning on the part of teachers if they are to work successfully. The 'toy project' flow chart (Figure 1) shows just how much careful thought goes into designing learning activities which are engaging, and relevant to young children but which also cover the academic curriculum. Similarly, the 'living history' project also shows just how much planning some teachers are prepared to undertake in the design of new types of learning environment. Finally, when it comes to children learning through group discussion, teachers have a very active role to play in scaffolding the discussion process by modelling appropriate discourse skills for their pupils.

SUMMARY OF SECTION 4

- This section described Skinner's behaviourist model of learning and its educational applications.
- This model was criticized for failing to take into account the dynamic social exchange of ideas between children and their teachers which is an important component of the learning experience.
- Current topic-based methods of teaching young children were described, and it was shown that although these retain the spirit of the 'child-centred' philosophy outlined in the Plowden Report, they have also incorporated many features of the social constructivist tradition.
- There is now a greater emphasis on talk and collaborative group work, and on developing children's language and literacy in functional contexts.
- The potential of using carefully designed out-of-school learning environments for increasing children's understanding of particular knowledge areas was discussed. Projects like the 'living history' one show how the master–apprenticeship model of teaching and learning can work in practice.
- Finally, the chapter discussed peer tutoring and the use of structured group work with older children. These techniques are most effective when children receive instruction in managing group discussions and in analytical techniques.

---

5 PUPIL–TEACHER RELATIONSHIPS AND TEACHER EXPECTATIONS

When reading the previous section, you might be tempted to think that establishing good teacher–pupil relationships is relatively unproblematic. Provided the teacher has taken care to structure the learning environment and scaffold children's learning in appropriate ways, then in theory all should go well, classrooms should be full of well-motivated children eager to engage in the learning process. Yet, as Timothy's case in the section on behaviour management illustrates, not all children find school learning easy. There are a variety of reasons why this may be the case. One of these is that regardless of the style of relationship teachers adopt, the quality of that relationship is not necessarily experienced in the same way by all children. No matter how determined teachers might be to treat all children equally, their personal attitudes and expectations can profoundly affect the way they interact with different children. Similarly children have expectations about school which influence how they behave towards their teachers.

5.1 Relationships and attitudes to learning

In a study comparing children's attitudes to home and school, Jacqueline Goodnow and Ailsa Burns found that children of all ages have three main expectations of school:

> First, there is the expectation that you are going to learn, and that the teacher will make it possible: 'They give you education', to use a first-grader's comment. It is also hoped that the teacher will be human and friendly. He or she, in the words of a sixth-grader, 'should be a person, not a policeman'. Then, there is the expectation that you will be an accepted member of the class, and be respected at least as much as anyone else. Classrooms are large groups, and the problems of rivalry are even more complex than they are in families. A child generally wants to be noticed by the teacher and at the same time be an accepted member of [their] peer group, not a 'teacher's pet'. He or she usually hopes for at least 'equal' treatment.
>
> (Goodnow and Burns, 1985/91, p. 202)

Young people are also aware of their teachers' expectations concerning themselves and other pupils in their class, as the following quotation from a study by David White and Peter Brockington illustrates:

> Teachers didn't get me involved. People expected me to be like my brothers who'd been there before me. The first comment I got was, 'Oh, no, not another Bird.' It made me feel really out of it and because that's what they'd expected, that's what I was like. I gave up too easily at school. Teachers ought to try and find out where kids get their anti-school attitudes from.
>
> (21 year old quoted in White and Brockington, 1983, p. 56)

Using structured interviews, White and Brockington asked young people aged 16–23 years to reflect on aspects of their schooling. Theirs is just one of many ethnographic studies conducted over the past 10 to 15 years which have looked at young people's experience of schooling. Without fail, all of these studies have shown that the experience of schooling leaves 'marks on the memory' which can profoundly affect the ways we feel about ourselves in later life.

 Social psychologists such as Harter (1986) have shown that children's sense of self-worth is affected in important ways by how well their personal ambitions match the realization of those ambitions. For example, children who want to perform well at school, and who do perform well, will feel more positive about themselves than children

'It's a figurative interpretation of the emotional interaction of a pupil–teacher relationship'.

who want to do well, but who are having difficulties with their work. Harter also found that other people's opinions and reactions are also important in determining the ways in which we feel about ourselves. In the school context, this means that when children have a positive and supportive relationship with their teacher they are also likely to feel positive about their own competence as learners, unlike the young person quoted above, who 'felt really out of it' from his first day at school, because his teacher was not really reacting to him as an individual.

Previously it was pointed out that these early experiences stay with us as adults, and that they can affect both the way in which we relate to other people, and how we feel about ourselves as learners. It has also been recognized that teachers' own childhood experiences as pupils colour the ways they themselves develop as teachers.

> Teachers are the product not merely of their training but of their unique intellectual attributes, their personality, attitudes and cumulative experiences. Their own experiences as children (or parents) may profoundly influence their approach to the children they teach.
>
> (Alexander, 1984, p. 3)

For this reason student teachers are encouraged to reflect on their own early experiences and examine the assumptions and ideas about children which they hold and which might affect the relationships they later make with their pupils. The intention behind this sort of exercise is to make teachers aware of their unconscious attitudes, and of the effects these can have on children. Activity 5 gives you a chance to try this type of exercise for yourself.

ACTIVITY 5

Allow about 30 minutes

TEACHING AND LEARNING – PERSONAL EXPERIENCE

The questions are taken from White's and Brockington's study mentioned earlier. It is designed to encourage you to reflect on your own experiences as a pupil, and to explore some of the childhood influences which have affected the way in which you now think about yourself as a learner.

First, spend about 10 minutes thinking back to your own days at *secondary* school. Can you remember your favourite teacher? Why was he or she special? What influence did he or she have on you: (a) as a learner, and (b) personally?

Now answer the following questions.

1   Did you look forward to going to secondary school?
2   How did it compare to primary school?
3   Can you describe the school?
4   What did you enjoy about (a) subjects, (b) teachers?
5   What didn't you enjoy about (a) subjects (b) teachers?
6   Why did you enjoy or not enjoy these?
7   Did you get into any trouble?
8   How did you get on with the teacher?
9   What makes a good teacher, do you think?
10 Can you remember situations where you thought teachers were treating kids unfairly? or vice versa?
11 Was there a noticeable sex bias in the teaching or in subject choice?
12 How do you think school has helped you in terms of what you are doing now?

(Adapted from White and Brockington, 1983, pp. 157–8)

Having answered these questions, try to draw up a list of features of, and characteristics that you feel make a contribution towards, what was for you an effective teaching style. Can you identify elements of your schooling which may have made you feel confident or unconfident about your own learning abilities?

Comment

As everyone who attempts this activity will have very personalized recollections of their own school days it is only possible to comment in a very general way. What I hope has come out for you is that the way we are taught and the personalities and styles of our teachers can have very powerful effects in shaping our attitudes towards ourselves as learners and our perceptions about which school subjects we are good at and want to work at, and which we are 'hopeless' at and abandon. Exercises such as this can reveal the source of some of our often hidden assumptions about and attitudes towards teaching and learning. As was pointed out earlier, today's teachers are just as likely as other people to have been influenced by their experiences as pupils.

Teachers' childhood experiences of schooling are not the only factors which affect how they develop their own personal teaching styles and ways of relating to children. Social and cultural attitudes and values can also affect the expectations they hold about certain 'categories' of children. For example, many societies have particular attitudes about differences in boys' and girls' academic abilities. These attitudes colour expectations about how well boys and girls will perform in school, and can affect the type of encouragement and opportunities provided for them (e.g. Croll and Moses, 1990). This in turn can have significant effects on pupils' measurable academic achievements and later success or failure in the educational system.

5.2 Teachers' expectations and children's performance

A famous study by two American psychologists, Robert Rosenthal and Lenore Jacobson (1968), provided evidence in support of the argument that individual levels of achievement are partly a function of the assumptions teachers make about children's learning potential (see Research Summary 2). Rosenthal and Jacobson showed that often these assumptions were not based on any real assessment of a child's potential, instead they were related to how children had been previously labelled by other teachers.

Since Rosenthal and Jacobson carried out this research, there have been many studies of the effects of teachers' expectations on children's learning and development, and, as is common with psychological research, later findings do not present such a clear-cut picture. In their discussion of this research, Biehler and Snowman (1993) point out that subsequent studies found that teachers' expectations only had an effect during the early years of schooling, and that even here the effects on children's achievements were not nearly as great as those claimed by

---

RESEARCH SUMMARY 2
THE PYGMALION EFFECT

Rosenthal and Jacobson (1968) gave an intelligence test to all 6 to 12 year olds in a school in San Francisco to provide a base-line measure against which later gains in intelligence could be compared. Children were then *randomly* assigned to either an experimental or to a control group. Their teachers were told that children in the experimental group were 'high achievers' likely to make significant intellectual gains over the school year. In reality, there was no difference at all in the test scores of these children and the children in the control group. When the two groups were re-tested after a year, however, children who had been labelled as high achievers showed significant gains in IQ scores compared with those in the control group. Rosenthal and Jacobson claimed that the reason for these gains was that teachers' expectations subtly altered the ways in which they taught the two groups, and also that the children themselves responded either positively or negatively to their teachers' expectations.

Rosenthal and Jacobson. Other studies showed that while teachers certainly did have expectations based on what they perceived children's potential to be, these were more likely to maintain children's existing tendencies than to change them radically. Summarizing the research evidence, Biehler and Snowman state that the following factors have been shown to be important in creating high or low teacher expectations:

> Attractive children are often perceived by teachers to be brighter, more capable, and more social than [other] children.
>
> Teachers tend to approve of girls' behavior more frequently than they approve of boys' behavior.
>
> Female teachers tend to perceive the behavior of girls as closer to the behavior of 'ideal students' than do male teachers.
>
> Middle-class pupils are expected ... to receive higher grades than lower-class students.
>
> Teachers are more influenced by negative information about pupils (for example, low test scores) than they are by neutral or positive information.
>
> Teachers appear to spend more time and to interact more frequently with high achievers than with low achievers.
>
> High-achieving pupils receive more praise than low-achieving ones.
>
> (Biehler and Snowman, 1993, pp. 570–1)

Although Rosenthal and Jacobson's original methodology and findings have been severely criticized, nevertheless their research did initiate an important and continuing debate in both psychology and education about the effects of expectations on children's performance and self-esteem. This and other more recent research has highlighted the fact that children try to live up to their teacher's expectations. Where these expectations are too low, or are unrealistic, then the whole quality of the teaching–learning experience is adversely affected – usually to the detriment of the child, and his or her educational achievement.

SUMMARY OF SECTION 5

- This section has looked at some of the social factors which influence the quality of the teacher–learner relationship.
- Both children and teachers have expectations about each other. Children's perceptions of these expectations can affect the ways in which they think of themselves as learners. These perceptions can have lasting effects on children's self-esteem and developing sense of themselves as learners.
- Teachers' own experiences of schooling can shape their own teaching styles and the way they relate to the children they teach.
- Teacher expectations can have profound effects on children's educational success.

CONCLUSION

This chapter has described how two important psychological traditions, behaviourism and social constructivism, have influenced and continue to influence educational practice in Britain and the United States. It was pointed out initially, however, that although there may be general agreement amongst psychologists and educators that research on children's learning and development should play an important role in informing educational practice, and vice versa, this opinion has not always found favour with politicians and policy makers.

From the discussion of these and the other issues raised in this chapter I hope that three main points have emerged. Firstly, in our society it is not possible to evaluate the influence of psychological theory on educational practice without taking historical, cultural and political factors into account. Secondly, it is possible to take a number of different positions on the relationship between learning and development, and also on the nature and purpose of education. These positions are associated with different models of the teacher–learner relationship, and with alternative methods of instruction. Finally, as was pointed out in Sections 4 and 5, learning and development are embedded in social relationships, and it is not sufficient to look at the effects of schooling on children simply in terms of their intellectual development. It is also necessary to take into account the social relationships between teachers and children, and between children and their peers, in order to understand fully the processes of teaching and learning.

FURTHER READING

DARLING, J. (1994) *Child-centred Education and its Critics*, London, Paul Chapman Publishing Co.

GARDNER, H. (1993) *The Unschooled Mind: how children think and how schools should teach*, London, Fontana Press.

PINDER, R. (1987) *Why don't teachers teach like they used to?*, London, Hilary Shipman.

ROGERS, C. and KUTNICK, P. (1990) *The Social Psychology of the Primary School*, London, Routledge.

REFERENCES

ALEXANDER, R. (1984) *Primary Teaching*, London, Cassell.

ALEXANDER, R., ROSE, J. and WOODHEAD, C. (1992) *Curriculum Organisation and Classroom Practice in Primary Schools: a discussion paper*, London, DES.

BANCROFT, D. (1995) 'Categorization, concepts and reasoning' in LEE, V. and DAS GUPTA, P. (eds), *Children's Cognitive and Language Development*, Oxford, Blackwell/The Open University (Book 3 of ED209).

BENNETT, N. and DUNNE, E. (1989) *Managing Classroom Groups*, Hemel Hempstead, Simon and Schuster.

BIEHLER, R. F. and SNOWMAN, J. (1993) *Psychology Applied to Teaching*, seventh edition, Boston (Mass.), Houghton Mifflin.

BRUNER, J. (1974) *Beyond the Information Given: studies in the psychology of knowing*, ANGLIN, J. M. (ed.), London, George Allen and Unwin.

CENTRAL ADVISORY COUNCIL FOR EDUCATION (1967) *Children and their Primary Schools*, London, HMSO (The Plowden Report).

CHILDS, A. and POND, M. (1992) 'Holt Hall, 1940: a residential "living history" project', *Teaching History*, July, pp. 17–19.

CROLL, P. and MOSES, D. (1990) 'Sex roles in the primary classroom' in ROGERS, C. and KUTNICK, P. (eds), *The Social Psychology of the Primary School*, London, Routledge.

DAS GUPTA, P. (1994) 'Images of childhood and theories of development' in OATES, J. (ed.), *The Foundations of Child Development*, Oxford, Blackwell/The Open University (Book 1 of ED209).

DAS GUPTA, P. and RICHARDSON, K. (1995) 'Theories of cognitive development' *in* LEE, V. and DAS GUPTA, P. (eds), *Children's Cognitive and Language Development*, Oxford, Blackwell/The Open University (Book 3 of ED209).

DEPARTMENT OF EDUCATION AND SCIENCE (DES) (1975) *A Language for Life*, London, HMSO (The Bullock Report).

DOISE, W. (1990) 'The development of individual competencies through social interaction' in FOOT, H., MORGAN, M. and SHUTE, R. (eds), *Children Helping Children*, Chichester, Wiley.

EDWARDS, D. and WESTGATE, D. P. (1987) *Investigating Classroom Talk*, Lewes, Falmer Press.

GALTON, M., SIMON, B. and CROLL, P. (1980) *Inside the Primary Classroom*, London, Routledge and Kegan Paul.

GAMMAGE, P. (1982) *Children and Schooling: issues in childhood socialization*, London, George Allen and Unwin.

GAMMAGE, P. (1987) 'Chinese whispers', *Oxford Review of Education*, **13**, pp. 95–109.

GARDNER, H. (1993) *The Unschooled Mind: how children think and how schools should teach*, London, Fontana Press.

GOODNOW, J. and BURNS, A. (1985/91) 'Teachers: a child's eye view' in WOODHEAD, M., LIGHT, P. and CARR, R. (eds) (1991) *Growing up in a Changing Society: a reader*, London, Routledge/The Open University.

HARDMAN, F. and BEVERTON, S. (1993) 'Co-operative group work and the development of metadiscoursal skills', *Support for Learning*, **8**, pp. 146–50.

HARTER, S. (1986) 'Processes underlying the construction, maintenance, and enhancement of the self concept in children' *in* SULS, J. and GREENWALD, A. G. (eds), *Psychological Perspectives on the Self*, vol. 3, Hillsdale (N.J.), Lawrence Erlbaum Associates.

MERRETT, F. and BLUNDELL, D. (1986) 'Self-recording as a means of improving classroom behaviour in the secondary school' in WHELDALL, K. MERRETT, F. and GLYNN, T. (eds), *Behaviour Analysis in Educational Psychology*, London, Croom Helm.

NUNES, T. (1995) 'Mathematical and scientific thinking' in LEE, V. and DAS GUPTA, P. (eds), *Children's Cognitive and Language Development*, Oxford, Blackwell/The Open University (Book 3 of ED209).

OAKHILL, J. (1995) 'Development in reading' in LEE, V. and DAS GUPTA, P. (eds), *Children's Cognitive and Language Development*, Oxford, Blackwell/The Open University (Book 3 of ED209).

PALINSCAR, A. S. and BROWN, A. L. (1986) 'Interactive teaching to promote independent learning from text', *The Reading Teacher*, **39**, pp. 771–7.

PERRET-CLERMONT, A. N. (1980) *Social Interaction and Cognitive Development in Children*, New York, Academic Press

PIAGET, J. (1932) *The Moral Judgement of the Child*, London, Kegan Paul.

PINDER, R. (1987) *Why don't teachers teach like they used to?*, London, Hilary Shipman.

PRESLAND, J. (1993) 'Behavioural approaches' in CHARLTON, T. and DAVID, K. (eds), *Managing Misbehaviour in Schools*, London, Routledge.

ROGOFF, B. (1991) 'The joint socialization of development by young children and adults' in LIGHT, P., SHELDON, S. and WOODHEAD, M. (eds), *Learning to Think*, London, Routledge/The Open University.

ROSENTHAL, R. and JACOBSON, L. (1968) *Pygmalion in the Classroom*, New York, Holt, Rinehart and Winston.

ROTH, I. (ed.) (1990) *Introduction to Psychology*, vol. 1, Hove, Erlbaum/The Open University.

RUDDUCK, J. (1991) 'The language of consciousness and the landscape of action: tensions in teacher education', *Journal of the British Educational Research Association*, **17**, pp. 319–32.

THORNDIKE, E. L. (1911) *Animal Intelligence*, New York, Macmillan.

TIZARD, B., BLATCHFORD, D., BURKE, J., FARQUHAR, C. and PLEWIS, I. (1988) *Young Children at School in the Inner City*, London, Erlbaum.

TOPPING, K. (1992) 'Co-operative learning and peer tutoring: an overview', *The Psychologist*, **5**, pp. 151–7.

VYGOTSKY, L. S. (1978) *Mind in Society: the development of higher psychological processes*, COLE, M., JOHN-STEINER, V., SCRIBNER, S. and SOUBERMAN, E. (eds), Cambridge (Mass.), Harvard University Press.

WHITE, R. and BROCKINGTON, D. (1983) *Tales out of School: consumers' views of British education*, London, Routledge and Kegan Paul.

WRIGHT, S. (1990) 'Language counts in the teaching of mathematics' in WEBB, R. (ed.), *Practitioner Research in the Primary School*, Basingstoke, Falmer Press.

READINGS

Reading A   Educational applications of operant conditioning principles

R. F. Biehler and J. Snowman

By arranging conditions and supplying reinforcement according to the principles [of operant conditioning], Skinner succeeded in shaping the behavior of rats and pigeons in quite amazing ways, as pigeons playing ping-pong and the xylophone attest. Because he was so successful in getting animals to learn new forms of behavior, he concluded that similar techniques could be used to shape human behavior ...

His daughter was a student in public school. When he asked her what the class had done each day and examined the books and assignments she brought home, Skinner became increasingly appalled about the kind of education his child was receiving. He concluded that traditional teaching techniques were terribly confused and inefficient and also primarily negative, in the sense that most children study to avoid negative consequences. It appeared to Skinner, for example, that his daughter studied most diligently to avoid being embarrassed or punished or to avoid a low grade. When he analyzed teacher–pupil behavior with reference to principles of operant conditioning, he was especially bothered by the fact that there was almost always a substantial interval between the point at which pupils answered questions and the point at which they received feedback as to whether their responses were correct or incorrect. Skinner realized that it was physically impossible for a teacher responsible for a class of thirty to respond to more than a few students at a time, but he was still bothered by the situation. Finally, he noticed that lessons and workbooks were often poorly organized and did not seem to lead students to any specific goal. Skinner became convinced that if the principles of operant conditioning were systematically applied to education, all these limitations could be either reduced or eliminated.

In the intervening forty-five years, little has changed, according to Skinner. In an article written in 1984 titled 'The Shame of American Education,' Skinner makes the following assertion:

> I claimed that the school system of any large American city could be so redesigned, at little or no additional cost, that students would come to school and apply themselves to their work with a minimum of punitive coercion and, with very rare exceptions, learn to read with reasonable ease, express themselves well in speech and writing, and solve a fair range of mathematical problems. (p. 954)

Skinner's claim is based on four prescriptions related to operant conditioning: (1) Be clear about what is to be taught; (2) teach first things first; (3) allow students to learn at their own rate; and (4) program the subject matter. The primary means by which this group of goals would be accomplished are programmed instruction and teaching machines (that is computer-assisted instruction) ...

Programmed instruction

The key idea behind Skinner's approach to teaching is that learning should be *shaped*. Programs of stimuli and consequences should be designed to lead students step by step to a predetermined end result. In the mid-1950s Skinner turned this shaping approach into an innovation called programmed instruction.

Programmed instruction can be described as specially designed written material that presents small amounts of written information to the student in a predetermined sequence, provides prompts to draw out the desired written response, calls for the response to be repeated in several ways in order to produce mastery, immediately reinforces correct responses, and allows the student to work through the program at his or her own pace.

According to Skinner (1968, 1986) when programmed materials are well designed and appropriately used, they produce the following effects:

1. Reinforcement for the right answer is immediate.
2. The teacher can monitor each student's progress more closely.
3. Each student learns at his or her own rate, completing as many problems as possible within the allotted time.
4. Motivation stays high because of the high success level designed into the program.
5. Students can easily stop and begin at almost any point.
6. Learning a complex repertoire of knowledge proceeds efficiently.

When programmed materials were first made commercially available during the mid-1950s, they were designed to be presented to students in one of two ways: in book form or incorporated into mechanical teaching machines. The earliest teaching machine were simple mechanical devices. A program was inserted into the machine and the first statement or question was 'framed' in a viewing window. (That is why the individual steps of a program are called **frames**.) The student printed an answer on a designated line then moved a knob that pulled a transparent cover over what had been written (to prevent erasing a wrong answer). At the same time, information appeared in the opening, revealing whether or not the response was correct. After checking the correctness of the response, the student turned another knob, which presented the next frame, and so on.

Developing a program

The first step in developing a program is to define precisely what is to be learned (the terminal behavior). Then, facts, concepts, and principles must be arranged in a sequence designed to lead the student to the desired end result. This requires first making the steps (the knowledge needed to go from frame to frame) small enough so that reinforcement occurs with optimal frequency, then putting them in the proper order and arranging them so that students will be adequately prepared for each frame, or numbered problem, when they reach it.

[…]

In composing a program, the writer strives to progressively reduce the degree of *prompt*, or the number of *cues* necessary to elicit the correct answer. In the language of programming, the prompt is *vanished*. But in reducing cues, it is important to remember Skinner's experiments with pigeons and not go too far too fast.

References

SKINNER, B. F. (1968) *The technology of teaching*, New York, Appleton-Century-Crofts.

SKINNER, B. F. (1984) 'The shame of American education', *American Psychologist*, **39**(9), pp. 947–54.

SKINNER, B. F. (1986) 'Programmed instruction revisited', *Phi Delta Kappan*, **68**(2), pp. 103–10.

Source: BIEHLER, R. F. and SNOWMAN, J. (1993) Psychology Applied to Teaching, seventh edition, Boston (Mass.), Houghton Mifflin, pp. 334–7.

Reading B   Toy project

Rachel Pinder

The idea of a project on toys was discussed with a class of six- and seven-year-olds who responded with enthusiasm and promised to bring in toys of all descriptions. After discussion about the feasibility of this, it was agreed that their parents might feel concern at this prospect, and they decided that a letter home explaining the purpose of the toy collection would be a good idea. The children wrote the letters, with their teacher's help, and the teacher countersigned each one.

The next morning several toys were brought in, and a larger number of parents than usual came to ask the teacher about the project. Interest was keen, and the toy collection grew quickly. There was discussion about how the toys were to be sorted and displayed. Someone suggested 'girls'' and 'boys'' toys, but after consideration the class came to the conclusion that most toys were enjoyed by both sexes; boys in the class played with the dolls in the house corner and the girls were keen on woodwork and construction sets. The next suggestion was 'soft' and 'hard', and this was felt to be more useful. The teacher then asked which materials would be considered hard, which led the children to think about the different materials used. Eventually they decided to sort them by the chief material used in their composition. This led to five main groups: wooden toys, metal toys, plastic toys, soft toys, and paper toys (which included kites). Games, it was agreed, would have to be a separate category. Playing with the toys was also discussed, and, although everyone would want to try out the various toys, it was generally felt that the permission of the owner should be sought and given. A code of conduct for the treatment of toys was worked out, and two of the children volunteered to write it out for display. One clause which everyone was definite about was that any trespass on the code would result in immediate loss of the privilege of playing with the toys.

The next task was the recording of ownership and provenance: Derek's electronic game had been a birthday present only two weeks earlier, while the rocking horse which Mandy's father had brought had been used by him when he was a child and was at least 30 years old. Four children were given the job of recording ownership and collecting as many details about each toy as was available. Another five children sorted the toys out into their appropriate sets, while five more arranged each set in its agreed display area, which meant quite a lot of classroom rearrangement, involving consultation with the teacher. Four more children were engaged in sorting out board games into number games, word games, and others, which included chess and draughts. Another group had been asked by the teacher to think of other ways of dividing the toys into sets, while the two remaining children had been sent to the school library, with the class helper, to find books about toys of different kinds and about toy-making, list their titles and display them. This involved them in making attractive posters which would draw the attention of the class to the book collection.

By late afternoon, most of the tasks had been satisfactorily completed and the children were able to sort themselves into groups and choose one toy or game to play with, the choices being made in a disciplined way, on the whole, with the teacher as final arbiter.

As, over the weeks, the numbers of toys increased, new categories were defined, so that sorting could be by age – those toys older than the class (some even older than the teacher!) and new toys. Sorting by function was tried and found to be a useful method: water toys, toys for babies, toys for sleeping with, toys for building things, toys which moved, toys to move with (e.g. hoops, skipping ropes, balls, bicycles) and musical toys, were the main categories decided on. Dolls proved difficult because although the collection included male, female and baby dolls, some moved, some made sounds, some were designed for babies, and so on. It was agreed that dolls would form a special set which would be divided into sub-groups. Transport toys posed a similar problem; some moved, some did not. Graphs were made showing the number of toys which fell into the different categories, and the different ways in which toys could be sorted.

During this time the teacher read a variety of stories about toys – *Pinocchio* proved a favourite – and the children grew interested in the idea of making puppets. *The Toy Symphony* was used as a basis for their music and movement, and later, when they were spending some time looking at animal toys, *The Carnival of the Animals* was used in a similar way. The work on animal toys led to comparisons with real animals and a world map was used to plot the countries of origin of the various animals.

A visit was arranged to a nearby toy museum, where the children were particularly interested in the old dolls and dolls' houses, puppets and puppet theatres, and lead soldiers. On their return they opted to make puppets and a puppet theatre. It was decided to make stick and glove puppets, because string puppets were likely to be too difficult. This part of the project took up the rest of the half-term. The music to *The Nutcracker* and *Coppelia* stimulated the children's interest in ballet and a visit to either a puppet theatre or a ballet performance was discussed by the class for the following half-term. A majority preferred the ballet visit because, they said, they were making their own puppets and would be performing their own plays, and while two or three of the girls attended ballet classes, most of the children had never seen a live ballet performance.

At the half-term holiday, since the classroom had become *very* overcrowded, most of the toys were sent home with thanks, except for the dolls, puppets and games, because these were the areas which were going to be further investigated in the following half-term.

Source: PINDER, R. (1987) Why don't teachers teach like they used to?, London, Hilary Shipman, pp. 129–34.

CHAPTER 3 CHILDREN AND COMPUTERS

Karen Littleton

CONTENTS

1 INTRODUCTION

If you were to make a list of the activities that occupy children today and compare it with a list of those that you and your generation engaged in when children, you would doubtless find both similarities and differences. Some experiences remain constant across time and place: children have been kicking footballs around or playing with dolls for centuries. Others are 'crazes' with particular moments of popularity: hula-hoops, Rubik's cubes, teenage mutant hero turtles and the like. However, there is a further category, that of innovations which take hold in society at a particular time and have an impact on children's worlds with effects that are both long-lasting and pervasive. One relatively recent example is television: almost all children in the UK have access to television and studies have shown that the average child up to the age of 15 years watches around 23 hours per week (Gunter *et al.*, 1991). There has been much speculation and research over the past 30 or so years on its supposed effects on children's development, both the educational benefits and possible imitation of violence or absorption of 'undesirable' attitudes. In the early stages, there were worries about effects on children's health, together with feelings that the hours spent watching TV were taking up time that could be spent more profitably on other pursuits – particularly ones that involved more social interaction.

A second significant innovation, which began in the late 1970s, has been the availability of computer technology. Computers are constantly becoming cheaper and more accessible and offer an ever-widening range of experiences, from arcade-type games, through complex numerical calculations to educational packages of various sorts. These experiences are available to children both in schools and at home: one survey of secondary-aged children in the UK in the mid-1980s found that about 45 per cent had access to a computer at home and that 80 per cent of those said that they made some use of it (Shotton, 1989). As you read this, such figures are almost certainly obsolete; as the technology becomes cheaper and more powerful in the range of things it can do, access and usage rates will undoubtedly rise.

ACTIVITY 1

Allow about 10 minutes

CHILDREN AND COMPUTERS – WHAT ARE THE ISSUES?

Like television, computers have stimulated questions that relate to their effect on children's psychological development. From your own experience, your observations of those around you or just plain speculation, note down some of the issues raised by children's engagement with computer technology.

Comment

Some questions are broadly positive in tone, others more negative. Of the positive sort are questions like:

- Can computers help children to learn more quickly and more effectively?
- Can computers enable children to think in different ways?
- Can computers make children more confident in their ability to control and manage parts of their world?
- Is working with computers more motivating than other learning media?

Of the negative sort are:

- Is working with computers a socially isolating experience? Can it affect the ability to interact with other human beings?
- Does reliance on computers as a teaching medium remove important features of the teaching–learning relationship?
- Can children become addicted to or dependent on computers to an undesirable degree?
- Do some computer games encourage violent and antisocial behaviour?

As with television, research has responded to these questions by focusing on the potential of and anxieties about computers. This chapter will look at some of this research, in particular on how computer technology has been adopted within educational settings and on its potential benefits. You will see that it is possible to identify relationships between different psychological theories and the ways in which computers are used.

I've already stressed the need for caution with figures of home-computer availability and use because of the speed with which these become out of date. The same can be said for figures on the spread of computers in schools. Nevertheless, it's possible to detect some informative patterns. At the beginning of the 1980s, very few primary schools in England were using computers: one survey (Jones, 1980) claimed that as few as 30 fell into this category. Since then, expansion has been rapid. A series of surveys by the Government Statistical Service (Department for Education, 1995) found that the percentage of children in English primary schools with 'hands-on' experience of microcomputers rose during the ten years from 1984 to 1994 from 70 per cent to 99 per cent.

In 1994, the estimated number of micros in the primary sector was 185,000, over five times more than in 1984, and the ratio of pupils to micros fell over the same period from 107:1 to 18:1. In secondary schools, the surveys found that the percentage of pupils with 'hands-on' experience rose from 73 per cent in 1984 to 94 per cent in 1994; the number of micros in schools had, as in the primary sector, increased more than five-fold; and the ratio of micros to students had decreased steadily from 60:1 in 1984 to 10:1 in 1994.

For those children who get to use computers in school, what sorts of experiences do they have, what is the computer used to do, and what impact does the experience have on the developing child? So far I have talked as if 'the computer' provides some sort of uniform and common experience, but that is far from being the case. Important differences can be seen in both the *hardware* – the features which give the computer its power – and the *software* – the programs or instructions which enable the machine to be used in particular ways. Advances in computer technology have meant that machines have become more powerful in that they have a greater capacity, can respond faster and can offer features such as coloured screens. At the same time the programs – the software – have taken advantage of hardware developments to provide experiences which are more user-friendly, more visually appealing and more responsive.

It is important to look beyond the surface attractiveness of the program to what it is attempting to achieve and the principles and aims that lie at the heart of it, and particularly, in our case, to the sort of intellectual experience it is providing for the child. It may help to think of this in terms of a continuum of open-endedness. At one end of the continuum – the 'closed' end – are those programs designed to execute a single task. If we want to use the computer to provide 6 year olds with some exercises in simple computation, it is relatively easy to find a program to present them with addition and subtraction sums of varying levels of difficulty. The program would tell the child when a correct answer has been entered and provide praise or some other reward, identify an incorrect response and provide the correct one, determine the level of difficulty of the problems presented in the light of performance thus far, log the child's progress, etc. Programs of this sort are usually labelled *drill-and-practice* for obvious reasons; they provide automated practice and testing and as such can substitute for this part of the teacher's role in the child's educational experience.

By contrast, at the 'open' end of the continuum are programs which allow many different things to be achieved by the user. I am writing this chapter using a word-processing package on a computer. I'm able to change what I want to say, move sections of text around, experiment with different layouts, and so on. The program isn't an end in itself but rather a 'tool' with which to achieve my aim of writing an interesting and informative chapter. A few years ago I would have used a pen to achieve a similar end but I now believe that it's more efficient to use this technology. Just as this is an option for me, so it is increasingly becoming part of the experience of children in school. There are other ways, too, in which the computer can be used in this open-ended way as a tool to achieve a variety of goals. The example of programming will be considered later in this chapter.

Some implications for education are neatly summarized in the following quotation:

> The computer is not a passive addition to the classroom; it is not a neutral black box. It is versatile, and because of its ability to support many educational philosophies it forces us to reflect actively upon which form of education we want for our children. After all, we have never asked whether or not a blackboard or a book will replace the teacher, but we do ask that question about computers. At intellectual, social, economic and pragmatic levels, computers are a challenge to current educational practice.
>
> (Underwood and Underwood, 1990, p. 4)

This leads us to look in more detail at some of these uses of computers, the philosophy and psychology that underlie them and the evidence about their impact on children and their learning. We will start at the 'closed' end of the continuum.

2 NEW TECHNOLOGY, NEW TEACHING?

2.1 The computer as teaching assistant

The underlying principles of drill-and-practice programs have already been described. These place them broadly within behaviourist theory and they are in many respects the successors to Skinner's teaching machines. As with those machines, the rationale is that children learn most effectively by repeating tasks which are tailored to their own particular level of competence. Children can work at their own pace through the tasks, which can be broken down into a sequence of steps with rewards for the successful completion of each one, so that each child is enabled to work up to the required level of performance.

Here, then, the computer is seen to offer *individualization* of the teaching–learning process. It serves as a patient teaching assistant, working with one child on routine tasks and continually giving direct and immediate feedback designed to shape subsequent performance and ensure a steady build-up of understanding. While all children encounter essentially the same teaching sequence, each individual is free to progress through the sequence of tasks at their own pace and to repeat or practise each sub-component, especially those which prove particularly problematic or difficult. Programs of this sort tend to concentrate on low-level cognitive skills such as basic mathematics, word recognition and spelling. How effective are they when judged in their own terms?

The substantial body of research evaluating this particular genre of software leads to the conclusion that its impact on children's learning is modest (Kullik *et al.*, 1985) with some significant exceptions (Hughes, 1990, p. 125). But there is still a case to be made for these sorts of programs in their place. The lower-order skills on which they tend to concentrate are important ones:

> If we must concentrate on the spellings of words and on the formation of letters with a pencil, then we will have less time available to think about the meanings of the sentences being composed. As we automatize the lower-order skills, then so our minds become free to plan, guide and review. The tedious activities then take care of themselves, but only when they have been practised and over-practised. Drill-and-practice serves the purpose of releasing our minds.
>
> (Underwood and Underwood, 1990, pp. 22–3)

So, while worthy and valuable in its place, drill-and-practice appears to take little advantage of the potential of computers, certainly when it comes to providing tools for creative thinking. For that we must move to the other end of the continuum and consider the impact of computer programming on children's thinking.

2.2 Logo and the development of thinking skills

Perhaps the boldest claims for the potential of computers to influence development have concerned the computer-specific activity of programming. Since the late 1960s, many have claimed that the

experience of programming itself helps to develop thinking skills. The most influential advocate of this notion is Seymour Papert, who helped design Logo, a programming language with many powerful features. In one of these features – turtle graphics – children are able to write programs to control a 'turtle', a small wheeled robot which moves around on the floor or on a table. Built into the turtle is a pen which can be lowered so that it leaves a trace on paper as the device moves; in this way the turtle can draw patterns and pictures as directed by the program. Alternatively, the turtle can be simulated on a computer screen where its movements appear as patterns traced on the screen.

A floor turtle.

EXAMPLE 1
LOGO PROGRAMMING

This example is designed to give you an appreciation of some of the features of Turtle Graphics.

1 You can select commands to make the turtle *move forward* a set distance leaving a trace:

PENDOWN (lowers the pen on to the page)

FORWARD 70 (makes the turtle move forward the specified distance)

PEN UP (lifts the pen clear of the page)

The resulting trace would look like this:

2 The turtle can also be made to turn right or left a specified number of degrees:

PENDOWN
FORWARD 70
RIGHT 90 (makes the turtle turn 90 degrees to the right)
FORWARD 70
PEN UP

The resulting trace would look like this:

3 You can repeat commands:

PENDOWN
FORWARD 70 RIGHT 90
FORWARD 70 RIGHT 90
FORWARD 70 RIGHT 90
FORWARD 70
PEN UP

The resulting trace would look like this:

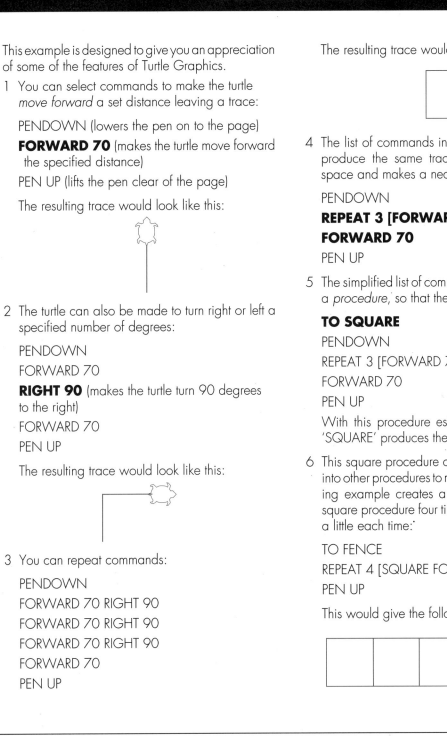

4 The list of commands in (3) can be simplified to produce the same trace. This saves computer space and makes a neater program:

PENDOWN
REPEAT 3 [FORWARD 70 RIGHT 90]
FORWARD 70
PEN UP

5 The simplified list of commands can be defined as a *procedure*, so that the computer is told:

TO SQUARE
PENDOWN
REPEAT 3 [FORWARD 70 RIGHT 90]
FORWARD 70
PEN UP

With this procedure established, merely typing 'SQUARE' produces the same trace as in (3).

6 This square procedure can then be incorporated into other procedures to make patterns. The following example creates a fence by repeating the square procedure four times and moving forward a little each time:

TO FENCE
REPEAT 4 [SQUARE FORWARD 35 RIGHT 90]
PEN UP

This would give the following trace:

ACTIVITY 2

Allow about 10 minutes

A FLOWER PROGRAM

Read through Example 1. How would you create a 'flower' like the one shown below?

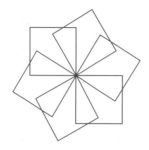

My answer is at the end of this chapter.

Papert's claims

Papert set out his vision of the educational use of microcomputers in an influential book, *Mindstorms*, published in 1980. In it he made many assertions about the way Logo could benefit children's thinking. As Example 1 illustrates, turtle graphics provide children with a way of exploring mathematical shapes and ideas. For Papert, encouraging exploration within this environment offers them a key to understanding ideas in arithmetic, algebra and geometry. The turtle serves as an 'object to think with', something that leads children from their own personal experience and knowledge to an appreciation of more formal, abstract mathematics. These experiences help to make the task of learning mathematics more relevant by creating a meaningful context in which they can experiment with mathematical concepts. Papert thought of this in terms of providing children with a living language with which to talk mathematics to the computer. So, just as one good way of learning a language such as French is to live in France, one aim of Logo is to provide an environment, which Papert called 'Mathland', where speaking the language of mathematics becomes second nature (Papert, 1980, p. 6).

Papert's claims for Logo are not restricted to the realms of learning mathematics, however. Rather, he sees learning to communicate with the computer as having the potential to change the way in which learning takes place. The act of programming helps to develop skills such as that of breaking down problems into manageable units, and these skills can then be applied to other situations. Papert refers to these generalizable problem-solving skills as 'powerful ideas'.

Your own experience of completing Activity 2 may have illustrated how, in order to construct a program to create a flower, plans have to be thought out and then specified in a concrete form. The thinking that lies behind this becomes visible and open to scrutiny and, in this respect, Papert points to the opportunity that programming provides for children to reflect on their own thinking. This, in turn, he argues, results in them being able to exercise greater control over their own mental processes.

> Even the simplest Turtle work can open new opportunities for sharpening one's thinking about thinking. Programming the Turtle starts by making one reflect on how one does oneself what one would like the Turtle to do. Thus teaching the Turtle to act or to 'think' can lead one to reflect on one's own actions and thinking. And as children move on, they program the computer to make more complex decisions and find themselves engaged in reflecting on more complex aspects of their own thinking.
>
> (Papert, 1980, p. 28)

The Piagetian influence

Underlying Papert's philosophy is the theory of Jean Piaget and its distinction between 'concrete' and 'formal' thinking: Papert regards the computer experience as a way of making concrete and personal the abstract and formal:

> ... it is not just another powerful educational tool. It is unique in providing us with the means for addressing what Piaget and many others see as the obstacle which is overcome in the passage from child to adult thinking. I believe that it can allow us to shift the boundary separating concrete and formal.
>
> (Papert, 1980, p. 21)

In Papert's view, the role of the adult or teacher is largely restricted to helping to create a supportive environment in which children are free to explore and discover. In certain circumstances, interventions on the part of the teacher may be of some value but the emphasis is on the individual constructive activity of the child and on Logo as a kind of 'enabling device'. Adults support children 'as they build their own intellectual structures with materials drawn from the surrounding culture. In this model, educational intervention means changing the culture, planting new constructive elements in it and eliminating noxious ones' (Papert, 1980, p. 32). Papert sees the individual benefiting from developing, testing and removing errors from computer programs, and showing this in heightened intellectual reflectiveness. So, although the experience of children programming turtles is usually a social one involving other learners, Papert's focus, inspired by Piaget, is on the creative engagement of the individual with the computer and leaves little room for any analysis of the interpersonal dimensions of the learning process.

Evaluating the claims

What evidence is there to suggest that there are cognitive benefits associated with the activity of computer programming? Papert's claims for the power of Logo as a resource for the development of abstract thought and high-level thinking skills have been the subject of intensive and continuing research (for reviews see Simon, 1987; Johanson, 1988). Martin Hughes (1990, p. 132) has identified key themes and provided some tentative conclusions emerging from this research literature.

Enhanced problem-solving?

First, Hughes notes that the experience of programming in Logo does not in itself result in enhanced problem-solving capabilities. While some research has demonstrated that computer programming can result in significant improvements in performance on certain problem-solving tests, many other studies have revealed only modest effects, or indeed, none at all. Papert, however, is unconcerned by such findings, since he believes that something as unique as the Logo experience cannot be evaluated adequately by the standard experimental design typically employed by researchers in this area. This usually involves the measurement of children's problem-solving capabilities at the start of the study (the pre-test) and then again after exposure to Logo (the post-test). Their performance is compared with that of a control group of children who did not have experience of Logo or who were engaged in some other activity. However, Papert contends that it is unsatisfactory to regard Logo in this way as isolated technical knowledge, just another 'treatment' which either does or does not have an effect. Rather, Logo can only realize its potential when it is integrated into a 'culture'.

In much of the evaluative research, the nature of children's encounters with Logo falls well short of Papert's vision. To experience Logo as he intended, they would need to do a lot of programming. Given that they didn't, it is perhaps not surprising that where cognitive benefits were observed, they were rarely impressive. However, before agreeing that children should spend more time working with Logo, we should consider what that implies. More time with Logo means less of the school day for other topics. If the price for developing critical thinking skills in this way is complete immersion in Logo, it may be too high a price to pay. But before dismissing the potential of the computer to influence cognitive development, we should consider Hughes's second tentative conclusion.

Where gains are observed

Research indicates that gains are more likely to be observed when encounters with Logo are carefully structured by the teacher. For example, Clements (1986) compared the progress of three groups of 6 to 8 year olds. One group was given a 22-week introduction to Logo, the second experienced a schedule of computer-aided instruction of similar length, and the third (the control group) participated in their normal scheduled lessons. The children in the Logo group encountered a highly structured sequence of activities, with the teacher (who was present throughout) introducing them to increasingly difficult and complex concepts and ideas. Those concepts of central importance were explicitly taught and the teacher emphasized the need for pre-planning and the careful contemplation of the effects of programs. Subsequently, tests of higher order thinking revealed that the children in the Logo group demonstrated significant improvements relative to those in the other two groups. Findings such as these raise the possibility that the negative results of other studies may tell us more about the 'discovery method' of learning so strongly advocated by Papert than about the effectiveness of Logo itself as a means of fostering intellectual development.

Working together

Hughes describes the third provisional conclusion emerging from his review of the Logo research as being 'somewhat unexpected'. Although most evaluations of the impact of Logo have focused on *individual* cognitive skills, one clear finding was that the experience of working on the computer had a more profound effect on children's *social interaction* (see Clements and Nastasi, 1988). This is supported by the anecdotal evidence of teachers using Logo in their classrooms and the results of case studies undertaken by Hoyles and Sutherland (1986, 1989) who claim that children's social interactive learning can benefit substantially from the experience of Logo programming. The contrast between this *social* dimension to learning and the image of computer use as an essentially *solitary* activity is a striking one and it has provoked a good deal of informative research, as we shall see in the next section.

SUMMARY OF SECTION 2

- 'Drill-and-practice' programs provide individualized teaching, usually of basic skills.
- Evaluations of 'drill-and-practice' software indicate only modest benefits for children's learning.
- Seymour Papert claims that Logo and turtle graphics help children to understand aspects of mathematics and to develop 'powerful ideas'.
- Drawing on Piaget's theory, Papert sees the experience of Logo programming as a way of helping children make the transition from concrete to formal ways of thinking.
- Papert sees the the teacher's role as largely restricted to the creation of a supportive environment in which children are free to explore and discover.
- Research suggests that programming in Logo does not in itself result in enhanced problem-solving capabilities, but cognitive gains are more likely to be observed when the experience is carefully structured by the teacher.
- Working with Logo opens up possibilities for social interaction.

3 COMPUTER USE BY GROUPS

Until fairly recently, both popular and theoretical accounts of computer use have neglected what really happens in many schools. At primary level in particular, computers are scarce (Jackson *et al.*, 1986). So, for what appear to be pragmatic reasons, children are often to be found working at the computer in either pairs or small groups and without the direct involvement of a teacher. But economy is not the only reason for this pattern of computer use. Many teachers believe that the introduction of computers into schools has provided children with an excellent environment in which they can learn to work together in groups. This view is supported by evidence from observational studies (e.g. Bennett, 1987; Galton, 1989) which show that computer work represents one of the few classroom-based activities where children genuinely collaborate rather than merely work alongside one another. They talk about the task in hand and are more likely to ask each other (rather than the teacher) when they need help. One study (detailed in Sheingold *et al.*, 1984) compared sessions in which children were learning to program in Logo with ones where they were working without computers. There was much more interaction between children in the Logo sessions, ranging from sustained systematic collaboration and explicit requests for help through to almost casual 'stopping by' or 'dropping in' at the computer.

The pattern of interaction around the computer depends, not surprisingly, on the type of software being used. For example, Crook (1987) reported that children solving mazes with a piece of computer-aided-learning (CAL) software typically adopted a turn-taking style of interaction. This contrasted with their response to software involving completing a series where they interacted in many different ways as they discussed various solutions.

Computer use by a group.

ACTIVITY 3
Allow about 5 minutes

ASSESSING THE EFFECTS OF COLLABORATIVE WORKING

If computers have this sort of impact on the ways in which children work, does this in turn affect their learning? Before addressing this question we need to consider how such effects might be assessed. Note down any suggestions you may have. What evidence would you look for to see whether interaction around the computer did affect children's learning?

Comment

One point you might have raised is whether we should be concerned with the achievements of the *group operating as a group* or focus instead on the *individual* learning outcomes of the group members. The former isn't usual in education, but objectively there is no compelling reason for the focus being solely on what the ex-group members subsequently achieve as individuals. After all, outside the classroom much problem-solving is typically undertaken in groups. Whether emphasis is placed on the group or on the individual will depend to some extent on the personal values of the researchers and the cultural context within which the investigations are conducted. It is, perhaps, a reflection of the strong individualistic ethos in our own society that many researchers have been concerned mainly or exclusively with individual learning outcomes (Light, 1993). Thus a question that researchers have been addressing of late is whether children who work together at the computer in small groups subsequently demonstrate better individual learning outcomes than those who work alone.

3.1 Do children learn better when working together?

A study by Zemira Mevarech and colleagues (1991) can shed light on this issue. Mevarech charted the progress over a four month period of five classes of 12 year olds using arithmetic drill-and-practice software. A third of them worked alone on the computer, while the remainder worked together in pairs of similar ability in mathematics. These pairs were actively encouraged to share the keyboard, help each other and discuss and agree solutions to the problems. Would the children who worked in pairs on the arithmetic problems learn more than those working alone? The answer to this question was determined by giving them an individual 'post-test' comprising all the types of problems that they had been working on. This was done at the end of the four months and again two months later. The results were unequivocal: on both sets of tests those children who had worked in pairs made significantly greater achievement gains than those who had worked individually.

This comparison of children working alone and in pairs at the computer has been explored with other sorts of tasks, too. For example, Blaye *et al.* (1991) asked 11-year-old children to work on a complex route-planning task (known as 'King and Crown' – see Research Summary 2 in Section 5) on three successive occasions. The task was presented as an adventure game in which the children were required to find a way of transporting an object from one place to another, overcoming certain restrictions and avoiding obstacles along the way. They had three separate attempts at the task. On the first two, they either worked on their own or paired with a child of the same sex. In the third 'post-test' session all the children tackled the task on their own. On this final occasion the task was varied so that they had to apply the experience gained in the previous sessions to a slightly different representation of the problem. To succeed, they had to get the object to the appointed place within the time allowed.

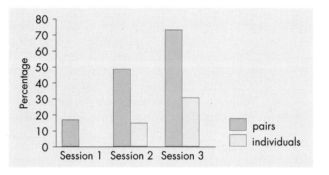

FIGURE 1
Percentages of pairs as against individuals who solved the task (Blaye *et al.*, 1991, p. 477).

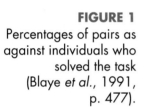

ACTIVITY 4

Allow about 5 minutes

ASSESSING COLLABORATIVE VERSUS INDIVIDUAL MODES

Some results from this study are presented in Figure 1. The solid bars indicate the percentage of *pairs* succeeding, while the shaded bars represent the percentage of *individuals* solving the task. In the final session where all the children worked individually the distinction is between those who had previously worked in pairs and those who had worked individually throughout.

What conclusion might be drawn from this evidence?

Comment

Very few children in either condition managed to complete the task in the first session. On the second session, however, about 50 per cent of the pairs of children successfully completed the task while fewer than 20 per cent of those working individually succeeded. In the final individual ('post-test') session, over 70 per cent of the children who had previously worked in pairs succeeded in solving the variant of the task while only about 30 per cent of those who had previously worked individually managed to do so.

These studies indicate that children who have had the experience of working in a pair are better at solving similar problems when they subsequently work alone. This is not always the case, however.

Simply getting children to work together on a computer-based task is not an educational panacea: other research shows that pairs or groups of children working together do not always out-perform individuals, and even when they do, this advantage does not necessarily carry over to individual post-tests (see Light and Blaye, 1990). It is interesting to note, however, that in none of the research do individuals fare significantly better than children in pairs or groups.

One way of trying to explain these inconsistencies is to look at the interaction patterns of the learners and how these are affected by features of the computer tasks. Particular features of the computer software, for example, can be critical in determining whether what is known as 'peer facilitation' of learning occurs. An illustration of this is provided by Light *et al.* (1987) who conducted a series of studies using a computerized version of the Towers of Hanoi problem (see Figure 2). Children were required to move a series of differently sized rings from one peg to another in as few moves as possible. The rules dictate that only one ring may be moved at a time and a larger ring may not be placed on top of a smaller one. With three rings the best solution is seven moves.

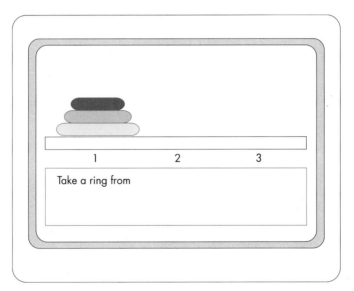

FIGURE 2
The computer-screen presentation of the Towers of Hanoi task (Light *et al.*, 1987).

ACTIVITY 5

Allow about 5 minutes

THE TOWERS OF HANOI

Try the Towers of Hanoi task for yourself. Mark out three positions (to represent the three pegs) on a piece of paper. Next make a tower of three different sized coins at position 1 with the largest at the base, followed by the next largest and then the smallest on the top of the pile. Now see if you can move all the coins to position 3 in just seven moves and following the rules given above.

(The solution is provided at the end of this chapter.)

In the Light *et al.* studies, 8 year olds were randomly assigned to work on the task either in same-sex pairs or individually. A week later each child was individually tested on a slight variant of the task. The first study found that the children who had worked in pairs did not do significantly better than those who had worked on their own. This was somewhat unexpected as previous work using a non-computerized form of the problem had demonstrated clear evidence that working in pairs had helped learning (Light and Glachan, 1985). However, closer scrutiny of what went on in the pairs revealed that many of the children had either adopted a non-interactive turn-taking pattern of working on the computer or else had developed a way of working in which one dominant member assumed sole responsibility for handling the task. In the non-computerized form of the task, both children were actively involved in making each move as the rings had a handle on either side and moving them had to be a joint effort. There was no equivalent feature in the computerized form of the task.

In a subsequent study, Light and colleagues adapted the computer program so that *both* children had to type a pre-determined command (the so-called 'dual-key constraint', i.e. the equivalent of having the two handles) in order to make each move. Under these conditions, how did the performance of children who worked alone compare with those who worked in pairs with the dual-key constraint and those who worked in pairs without such constraint? There was no difference in the performance of children in the individual and no-constraint groups, but significantly more children in the dual-key group solved the problem in the optimal number of moves. This suggests that, for peers to facilitate learning, children have to engage actively both with the computer and with one another.

Further evidence of this is provided by Blaye (1988) who worked with 5 to 6 year olds on a computer-based task where they had to complete a matrix filling task. She found that the experience of working in a pair did sometimes result in enhanced individual progress, particularly when the pair was working under conditions in which one child used a light pen to indicate the chosen move while their partner used the keyboard to affirm that choice. Once again, then, there are indications that the computer of itself doesn't guarantee peer facilitation of learning. Rather, working conditions must be such that they foster both the children's engagement with the task and their engagement with one another. So, having seen that under 'supportive' conditions, peers can facilitate individual learning, let us turn to consider the possible psychological mechanisms underpinning such learning.

3.2 Explaining peer-facilitation effects

The evidence from the research described above indicates that the computer affects children's thinking and learning in a much less direct way than Papert thought. The focus here is not on the potential of the computer to foster the development of 'powerful ideas'. Rather, the computer is seen as providing an effective environment for supporting productive interactions *between* children.

ACTIVITY 6

Allow about 10 minutes

POSSIBLE EXPLANATIONS

How would you explain the peer-facilitation effects you have just been reading about? List your explanations and keep them in mind as you read through the remainder of this section.

Affect and motivation

We can think in a number of different ways about the effects of having a partner. It may be that the presence of a partner has significant affective and/or motivational effects which themselves have consequences for performance both as a pair and subsequently when acting as an individual. For example, it might make a task less threatening or more fun for those involved. Alternatively, working with a partner on the computer might lead to increased self-confidence. While such explanations are undoubtedly plausible, researchers have had very little to say about children's affective experiences of computer-based learning situations. The clear focus has been on cognitive accounts of peer facilitation of learning. Some of these accounts are considered below.

Talking about problems

How useful is it to talk about a problem to someone else? Does it help to clarify one's thoughts and so result in more effective learning? Some evidence on this comes from a study in which 9 to 11 year olds worked on a specially designed computer-based problem-solving task, a spaceship simulation game in which they had to find out three things needed to achieve a particular target, such as the number of passengers on board (Fletcher, 1985). The children worked on the task either individually or in groups of three. Some of the individual children worked silently while others were asked to talk aloud about each decision taken and to explain why that decision was made; the experimenter was present but did not interact with them. The children who worked in groups of three were asked to talk among themselves and to agree on each of the decisions. Analysis of the results revealed that on three of the four performance targets, both the groups and the talking individuals took fewer steps to reach the specified targets than the individuals working silently. Fletcher concluded that overt verbalization may have some part to play in peer-facilitation of performance. This is not to say that all the benefits of peer interaction arise as a direct consequence of verbalizing, rather that in some circumstances it may be an important factor.

While Fletcher looked at the role of talk as such, others have chosen to look at the *quality* of the interaction and to examine the relationship between this and learning outcome. Webb *et al.* (1986), for example, observed pairs of 11 to 15 year olds following a course in BASIC programming and measured their spontaneous verbal and interactive behaviours. On completion of the course, the children were each given a test designed to assess their individual programming competence. Did the quality of the paired discussion predict subsequent individual programming ability? Analysis of the data showed that giving and receiving explanations, receiving responses to questions and talking aloud when using the keyboard were all associated with individual programming competence.

Conflict and disagreement

However, the sorts of measures of interaction used by Webb were rather limited. They did not ask, for example, whether disagreement and argument can help learning. Your answer to Activity 6 may have indicated that this might be important. Attempts to resolve such disagreements may well cause people to consider the other's point of view. Perhaps, by seeing an alternative way of tackling the problem – even if that supposed solution is itself wrong – each individual makes cognitive gains that can subsequently be demonstrated when they are solving problems on their own account.

This way of thinking about the role of social interaction in cognitive development has been pursued by Willem Doise, Gabriel Mugny and Anne-Nelly Perret-Clermont (e.g. Doise and Mugny, 1984; Perret-Clermont, 1980). They drew their inspiration from some of Piaget's early work in which he showed awareness of social influences on cognitive development. Piaget's key concept of egocentrism identified the principal barrier to the pre-school child's progress as being an inability to decentre, to take account of other people's points of view. He portrayed children of this age as being unable to appreciate that the first thing that strikes them about a problem might not be the only way the problem can be thought about; they cannot reflect on alternatives or understand how different factors might interact with one another. At this stage in his own thinking Piaget saw particular sorts of social experiences as combining to overcome this egocentrism. The child's social relations with adults did not have this effect because of the differences in power and status; children could not balance their own views against those of adults. By contrast, the more equal relationships between children did allow them to consider different and conflicting views ('centrations') and balance them against their own. By doing so, they might integrate these partial views into a new and more complete perspective, and this could be viewed as progress along the road towards higher level – 'operational' – thinking.

Doise and Mugny (1984) investigated these ideas using one of Piaget's classic conservation tasks, the transfer of liquid from one container to another container of a different shape. Typically, children below the age of about seven will say that the amount of liquid has changed; either that there is more in the second container because it is wider, or that there is less because the level of liquid is lower than in the first container. According to Piaget, the children are centering their attention on just one of the relevant aspects of the problem and failing to notice equally important ones. Doise and Mugny noted that if children at this stage worked on the conservation problem in pairs or small groups and found that there were differences in the solutions proposed, their attempts to resolve these differing points of view would more often than not result in decentring, with all children going on to give higher-level, conserving solutions. And this happened even when the solutions being proposed were incorrect. They argued that these experiences of socio-cognitive conflict play a significant role in children's cognitive development.

This notion of socio-cognitive conflict has stimulated inquiry into the nature and significance of the activity that may go on when children are working in pairs or small groups around a computer (see Research Summary 1).

RESEARCH SUMMARY 1
MASTERMIND

One study observed 8 year olds playing a computerized version of the code-breaking board game, 'Mastermind' (Light and Glachan, 1985). The game involves trying to establish the correct sequence of four concealed coloured pegs in as few moves as possible. The player sets out an array of four pegs and is told whether any of the chosen colours correspond to the concealed set and whether any one or more of the pegs is of the right colour and in the right place. The player then sets out another array in an effort to establish which pegs are generating this positive feedback. Skilled players use a variety of strategies in drawing on the feedback to inform their next move. In this study, though, the children played the game in pairs with each child being expected to propose and justify a particular move. In some instances the alternative proposals led to conflict as to which was the better suggestion; in others the discussion was judged to be supportive. All the children then played the game again on an individual basis. If socio-cognitive conflict works in the way claimed, then those children who had been in pairs where there had been argument should have performed better than those from the harmonious pairs when working on their own, and that was what in fact happened.

S G Support for the idea of socio-cognitive conflict also comes from Christine Howe and colleagues. They looked at children's predictions about objects dropped from planes (Howe *et al.*, 1991). Children – and indeed adults – offer a variety of judgements about when to release an object from a plane travelling at a given speed in order to land on a particular target and about the course likely to be followed by that object. Howe put 12- and 14-year-old children into pairs on the basis of their initial individual predictions (the pre-test). Some pairs were of children whose individual predictions were similar, the others were different. These pairs then tackled further trajectory problems together before individually completing a further series (the post-test). As with the 'Mastermind' study, it was the children who had been in the pairs characterized by *differences* in predictions who made the greatest improvement between the pre-test and post-test.

Co-construction of knowledge

We have seen that work on the role of conflict has its roots in Piagetian thinking, but some of the more recent research into the impact of peer interaction on learning draws on a theory of Vygotsky's, that knowledge is co-operatively produced and shared (see Chapter 2). This notion of the 'co-construction of knowledge' is usually applied to interactions between adults and children – so-called *asymmetrical interactions* – because the partners are unequal in status. More recently, however, researchers looking at children and computers have begun to apply the concept to *symmetrical interactions* between children. For example, Sylvia Barbieri and Paul Light investigated some of the interactions of pairs of children working together on a computer-based problem-solving task (The King and Crown game described in Research Summary 2) (Barbieri and Light, 1992). Among the sorts of interactions that they noted were whether they talked about their plans for solving the problem and whether they negotiated with each other what the next move should be; both of these might be seen as constructing knowledge together. A week after they had worked on the problem in pairs, the same children were given a similar problem to do on their own. The key question for the researchers was whether there was a relationship between how the children had interacted in pairs and how they performed, both in the pairs and subsequently as individuals. The evidence was that the sorts of interactions thought to be co-constructions of knowledge did predict how successful the children would be, both as pairs and in their individual performance.

The Vygotskian view of learning within adult–child relationships sees the adult as 'scaffolding' the child's learning, helping the child to understand the sort of problem it is (so-called *metacognitive awareness*) and facilitating planning. It may well be that notions of this sort also apply to the co-construction of knowledge in symmetrical interactions of the sort typically found when children work around the computer. Most of the relevant research to date has focused on *pairs* of children and it remains to be seen what happens in larger groups. In focusing primarliy on comparisons of group versus individual performance we have neglected a number of potentially important factors such as the size of the group and the ability of the individual group members. Nevertheless, there are grounds for thinking that social processes in computer-based learning are a good deal more significant than, say, Papert's emphasis on the individual activity of the child would have us believe.

Much of the work described above has looked at children and computers with the implication that computers are, in some way, a necessary part of the process. But are they really essential for such apparently productive interaction? After all, the benefits of group work were being advocated long before the computer revolution, for example in the Plowden Report of the late 1960s (Central Advisory Council for Education, 1967).

ACTIVITY 7	WHY USE COMPUTERS TO SUPPORT GROUP WORK?
Allow about 5 minutes	Note down the particular benefits of using computers to support interaction between learners.

Although numerous official education reports have emphasized the potential educational value of discussion and interaction between children, in practice many schools have found this difficult to achieve (Galton, 1989). In the busy classroom environment some teachers may be unable to provide the structuring and monitoring of small group activity that they would wish. Given suitable software, then, the computer may be able to offer something that other teaching and learning situations sometimes cannot, namely an effective environment for supporting and sustaining well-structured learning interaction between children. The introduction of computer technology into the classroom may ultimately enable teachers to achieve the effective management of less 'teacher-centred' learning environments and thereby alter the entire pattern of relationships currently associated with classroom learning. This picture of the potential of the computer to transform dramatically both the nature and organization of the learning environment is discussed in the next section.

SUMMARY OF SECTION 3

- Working in pairs or groups can have a substantial positive effect on children's learning.

- However, pairs or groups of children working together at the computer do not always out-perform individuals, and even when they do, the advantage does not necessarily carry over to individual post-test assessments.

- The features of the computer itself cannot guarantee peer facilitation of learning. Working conditions must be such that they foster both the children's engagement with the task and their engagement with one another.

- Explanations of peer-facilitation effects suggest that the computer has an effect on children's thinking and learning which is much more indirect than that advocated by Papert.

- The computer can provide an effective environment for supporting productive interactions *between* children, and research is attempting to pinpoint the particular features of interaction which lead to enhanced performance and learning.

- There are several different explanations for peer facilitation of learning. Particular emphasis has been placed on the role of socio-cognitive conflict.

- Work on the role of conflict has its roots in Piagetian thinking. More recent research on the impact of peer interaction is being conducted in a Vygotskian framework.

- The use of computers to support group work in schools may help to ameliorate some of the organizational problems associated with group-based methods of teaching.

4 THE COMPUTER AS 'MEDIUM'

How might the computer transform educational institutions? Cole and Griffin contrasted two metaphors for computer–student interaction:

> The first [metaphor] assumes that the computer is an agent, operating as a 'partner in dialogue'. This view implies that the student–computer system can be viewed as an analogue to the student–teacher system with the computer replacing the teacher. Within the framework provided by this perspective, it is important to look at the computer's potential for providing structured hints, well-timed feedback, and a wealth of factual knowledge. It is this metaphor that underlies the bulk of research on computers and education at the present time …
>
> A second metaphor … is of the computer as a 'medium', not replacing people, but re-organizing interactions among people, creating new environments in which children can be educated and grow by discovering and gaining access to the world around them. This metaphor emphasizes the potential of computers for re-organizing instruction within the classroom and for making possible the extension of education beyond the classroom.
>
> (Cole and Griffin, 1987, pp. 45–6)

The first metaphor presents an image of the computer which is somewhat akin to that we saw in the first part of Section 2. The metaphor of computer as 'medium', however, regards the computer as a *socio-cognitive tool* which shapes interaction in specific ways, ways that then emerge in distinctive forms of cognition. In other words, the extent to which computers become part of everyday life serves to transform the ways in which activities are organized, and in doing so may affect such things as how we reason, remember and solve problems.

When this idea of the computer as a socio-cognitive tool is applied to the classroom it raises a different set of questions from those we have been considering so far, not least concerning the relationships between learner, teacher and computer. Neil Mercer has identified some of the implications:

> The quality of understanding that learners acquire through the use of information technology in the classroom is not, and never will be, determined by the quality of the 'interface' between the learner and the technology. Quality of understanding, the nature of educational knowledge, is determined by a much more complex contextual system which is inseparable from how education is defined in our culture … this culturally based contextual system is continually created and re-created in the classroom through interactions between teachers and learners.
>
> (Mercer, 1993, p. 37)

READING

Neil Mercer and colleagues have begun to explore these relationships and some of their thoughts can be found in the reading at the end of this chapter, which you should now read. Note especially the comments about the responsibility of teachers and make a list of the ways in which the teacher plays an influential role.

4.1 When the child is the expert

One notable feature of many classrooms at the moment is that, where computers are concerned, many children know more than their teachers.

ACTIVITY 8

Allow about 5 minutes

CHILD 'EXPERTS' AND 'NOVICE' TEACHERS

Read the following news item from the *Guardian*.

> **Pupils lead way on computers**
> The maddening child who knows far better than its parents how computers work is also helping explain information technology to teachers and fellow pupils, according to education inspectors.
>
> A report by Her Majesty's Inspectors finds schools are recognizing such a 'pupil expert' can be a great asset.
>
> School visits since 1988 have found schools using increasingly complex equipment. 'Pupils turn to information technology without reticence or trepidation, unlike many of their elders.'
>
> (*Guardian*, 24 December 1992)

What do you consider to be the implications of such a classroom dynamic? Do you think the teacher's authority could be undermined?

One investigation of 'expert' children and 'novice' teachers (Shrock and Stepp, 1991) looked at the social interaction surrounding a computer in an American elementary school (equivalent to first or primary) classroom. The teacher was relatively inexperienced in computer use and so designated a child 'expert' as the resource person for students learning to use the computer. The observed negative effects on the role definition of 'teacher' and the frequency of interactions not conducive to learning led the researchers to warn of the potential danger of child experts becoming 'gatekeepers' of knowledge and competing authority figures in the classroom. Whether or not this is a real danger, it draws attention to the significance of the relationship between pupil and teacher and the need for a clearer understanding of how that is affected, in this instance, by the increasing deployment of computers in classrooms.

4.2 Defeating time and space

As well as reorganizing interactions between people, computer technology has the potential to create *new educational environments*. For example, the opportunities offered by computer-mediated communication, through networks, mean that joint activity can be supported which may be separated in time and space.

Such technology also allows for the possibility of the extension of education beyond the classroom. Charles Crook, who has taken a particular interest in these developments, has summarized its potential:

> This form of communication opens up exchanges between children who are growing up and learning in, perhaps, very different cultural contexts ... It can also create real audiences for their work and a real possibility of intellectual co-ordination with peers in pursuit of joint projects.
>
> (Crook, 1992, p. 221)

But although computers may have the potential to reorganize learning interactions in a variety of significant ways, everyday experience suggests that social institutions have a remarkable capacity for neutralizing the effects of new developments, technological or otherwise. Classrooms may prove to be too well 'buffered' to be much affected by computers, and indeed may assimilate computers entirely into their existing way of doing things. Only time will tell whether computer technology will radically alter the ways in which children's thinking is developed and extended.

SUMMARY OF SECTION 4

- The computer can be seen as a 'medium', not replacing people but re-organizing interactions among them, creating new environments in which children can be educated and grow by discovering and gaining access to the world around them.
- Computers may have the potential to transform uniquely the way in which human cognitive activity is organized. To date there has been very little research designed to address this issue.
- There is a pressing need for studies which consider (a) the special relevance of computers for re-ordering the contexts of education by re-organizing interactions among people and (b) the potential of the computer to create new educational environments.

5 GENDER DIFFERENCES

Skill with computer technology can endow high status in today's society. Given this, could educational computer technologies worsen present social inequalities?

ACTIVITY 9

Allow about 5 minutes

IDENTIFYING DISADVANTAGE

Make a list of the inequalities which might be amplified by the growing presence of computers in schools and note the ways in which the effects are likely to be felt.

Comment

An American study from the Laboratory of Comparative Human Cognition (LCHC) may be used to set the tone for a response to this activity. It concluded that 'the manner in which computers are being employed in America's classrooms has caused the level and involvement with technology for women and minorities to decrease relative to Anglo/male norms' (LCHC, 1989, p. 74). The LCHC researchers cited a national survey in America which revealed that:

1   more computers are being placed in the hands of middle- and upper-class children than poor;

2   when computers are placed in schools for poor children they are used for rote drill and practice instead of the cognitive enrichment that they provide for middle- and upper-class students;

3   female students have less involvement than male students with computers in schools, irrespective of class or ethnicity.

(LCHC, 1989, p. 74)

To what extent do these observations apply to the UK? There are certainly grounds for seeing an association between experience of computers and economic and social advantage. Common sense suggests that not only are children from better-off backgrounds more likely to have more experience of computers at home but also the financial support that such families are able to offer their children's schools is likely to ensure that they are better equipped and more able to offer a richer educational experience to their pupils. Whether or not there is a qualitative difference in the experience within and between schools (point 2 above) is a different matter and some have provided evidence of children from all social and economic backgrounds working on a wide variety of computer tasks.

On the third point, that of an imbalance of involvement related to gender, there is more widespread agreement. Celia Hoyles has summarized the state of affairs in the UK as follows:

> While girls and boys might show a similar appreciation of the significance computers might have for their personal futures, boys tend to be more positively disposed than girls towards computers, are more likely than girls to take optional computer courses in school, to report more frequent home use of computers and tend to dominate the limited computer resources that are available in school.
>
> (Hoyles, 1988, p. 1)

Before moving on to consider these differences in more detail, it is worth noting that one form of potential disadvantage not mentioned by LCHC is that related to physical and mental disability. In the UK, at least, there are many examples of the use of computers in schools to extend the potential of children with disabilities or learning difficulties, both in the areas of basic skills and in extending them beyond their apparent limitations.

Over the last few years, many educationists have commented that the increasing deployment of computer technology in schools could potentially place girls at a disadvantage to boys (e.g. DES, 1989; Hoyles, 1988). Such comments are made in light of the growing body of research summarized in the quotation from Hoyles above. Girls typically are much less enthusiastic about computer use than boys (e.g. Martin, 1991; Todman and Dick, 1993) and both boys and girls tend to see use of the computer as an activity more 'appropriate' for boys than for girls (Hoyles, 1988). And, even where girls and boys express equally positive attitudes, it is clear that both believe that boys like and use computers more than girls do (Hughes *et al.*, 1987). The following extracts from a class discussion with 5 year olds illustrate just how early these gender biases in attitudes show up:

TEACHER: Do you think that computers are more useful for girls or for boys?

MALCOLM: Boys!

TEACHER: Why do you think that is?

MALCOLM: Because boys can do more complicated things than girls.

TEACHER: Why can boys do more complicated things than girls?

MALCOLM: They know better things.

TEACHER: What makes you think that?

MALCOLM: My Daddy told me.

...

TEACHER: What do you think, Ellen?

ELLEN: Girls!

TEACHER: Why do you think that is?

ELLEN: Girls play nicer games than boys.

TEACHER: Really?

ELLEN: Yes. My Daddy told me.

...

TEACHER: Martin, you have a computer at home, don't you? Who
            uses it?

MARTIN: Daddy.

TEACHER: Does Mummy use it at all?

MARTIN: Sometimes.

TEACHER: Does she? What does she use it for?

MARTIN: Not much. She really does the housework because
            Daddy's too lazy.

(Straker, 1989, pp. 231–3)

Straker also notes that, in primary schools, computers are used more by
boys and male teachers than by girls and female teachers. And this
imbalance persists into the secondary school. For example, Culley found
that:

> In most schools fewer girls than boys participate in optional
> computing activities such as computer clubs, where girls were less
> than 10 per cent of regular attenders. Computer rooms in most
> schools were regarded as male territory and girls report being made
> to feel very uncomfortable by the attitudes and behaviour of the
> boys. Several schools have recognized this problem and responded
> by establishing certain times as 'girls-only'. Such schemes were only
> partly successful, however. The tendency was for the open sessions
> to become the *boys'* sessions and thus reduce even further the
> access of girls to computers. In one school the 'open' sessions' were
> overseen by a male computer teacher, while the girls-only sessions
> were staffed by a female teacher who had no computing expertise.

(Culley, 1988, p. 4)

Observations in the classroom also showed that girls tended to get less
time than boys on the computers and to receive less attention and
assistance from the teachers, much of whose time was taken up by the
boys' demands.

By contrast, when observations were made in girls-only schools, the girls
were more positive about computers (Culley, 1988). This might suggest
that segregating boys and girls for this part of their experience in mixed
gender schools would allow girls to be less inhibited and thus to learn
more. However, the evidence from research provides mixed messages on
this matter: some shows that girls are particularly disadvantaged by
working with boys (e.g. Underwood *et al.*, 1990) but others suggest that
this is by no means always the case (e.g. Hughes *et al.*, 1988; Littleton *et
al.*, 1992).

Girls' low level of participation in computer-related activities is also
reflected in the relative number of girls and boys being entered for public
examinations in computer studies and computer science (Hughes, 1990).
And the gap appears to be getting wider as the proportion of girls
studying computer science grows smaller (Buckley and Smith, 1991).

5.1 Explaining the differences

ACTIVITY 10

Allow about 10 minutes

POSSIBLE EXPLANATIONS

Can you think of possible explanations for gender differences in computer use of the sort just described? Compare your explanations with those offered by researchers in the following section.

A variety of explanations has been proposed to account for the differences. One is that they are inextricably interwoven with the issue of individual versus collaborative modes of working. Hoyles and colleagues, for example, argue that when computers are used individually or perhaps even competitively, girls tend to find the experience alienating. This contrasts sharply with what happens when the computer is associated with a collaborative mode of working, when girls are typically just as enthusiastic as boys in their response to computer technology (Hoyles *et al.*, 1991).

Alternatively, Sherry Turkle has suggested that there may be differences in the *cognitive styles* of boys and girls which affect the ways in which they relate to computers (Turkle, 1984). She sees the prevailing computer culture as one in which the methods of working require formal analytical skills which she claims are indicative of masculine styles. If this argument is accepted, it is necessary for girls to be helped to reject such conventions and negotiate with computers in ways with which they are better suited.

Although the evidence on gender differences in attitudes towards computer-related activities, levels of participation with computers and styles of computer use tends to be consistent, it appears that girls perform just as well as boys when they engage with computer-based learning tasks and programming activities (Underwood and Underwood, 1990).

An idea of some of the complexities of the issue of gender differences may be gained from Research Summary 2, an account of a research project I have been involved in (Littleton *et al.*, 1992).

RESEARCH SUMMARY 2
PIRATES AND PICNICS

King and crown

A sample of 11 to 12 year olds, with equal numbers of boys and girls, was asked to play a problem-solving adventure game presented on a computer. To succeed in the game, which was known as 'King and Crown', they had to find the king's crown and transport it back to a specified town for the feast that was to take place there. The children had to give the computer instructions to move three characters (a driver, a pilot and a captain) by means of different forms of transport (car, plane and ship) along defined routes, avoiding somepirates in the process. In order to complete the game successfully, the player had to search for relevant information and devise a way of reaching and retrieving the crown which took account of how the characters were allowed to move about and avoided the hazards presented by the pirates.

Honeybears

As part of the same study, a comparable group of children played another computer game which was essentially the same task but with different characters and storyline. This version drew on ideas from the children's song, *The Teddy Bears' Picnic*, and a television advertisement involving a 'honey monster'. The problem to be solved is identical to that in the 'king and crown' game, only here it is to retrieve some honey for a picnic and the characters are three bears – Ponybear, Airbear, and Waterbear – who travel by pony, balloon and boat, avoiding the honey monsters as they go.

The solution strategy is identical in the two tasks. The differences lie in the designation of the characters and the context and storyline of the plot.

In both conditions of the experiment the boys and girls worked individually at the computer and were told that they had a maximum of 30 minutes to try to solve the problem. They were given points depending on how close they got to the solution in that time. The results are shown in Figure 3.

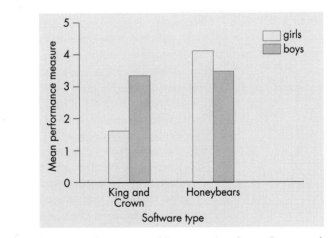

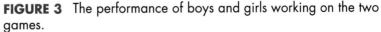

FIGURE 3 The performance of boys and girls working on the two games.

ACTIVITY 11

Allow about 5 minutes

INTERPRETING DATA ON GENDER DIFFERENCES

What can be concluded from the data presented in Figure 3? The vertical axis is the scale of performance on the task: the higher the score, the further towards the correct solution. The bars show the boys' and girls' average scores on the two versions of the game.

How would you explain these results?

Comment

Clearly the boys' performance was little affected by the version of the game they were using; it averaged approximately 3.5 on both. The girls' performance, however, was substantially affected by the version they used, it being far better for honeybears.

Some clues to why these differences may have occurred come from our observations of the children as they played the games (Littleton *et al.*, submitted). It seemed that boys found both versions equally appealing while girls appeared to find the king and crown game less motivating and enjoyable than honeybears. Many of the girls seemed to identify with the characters of the bears and after playing the game talked spontaneously about which bear was their favourite. More than one talked about taking particular bears on their journey to get the honey because 'they wouldn't want to get left behind'. This kind of identification with the characters was not apparent when they played the king and crown game, nor was it exhibited by the boys on either version. This suggests that what might be thought to be surface features of games or tasks can have a differential effect on those engaging in them. In themselves, these kinds of identification and projection do not help to solve the task – indeed, they could potentially hinder the solution – but it would appear that, given an initial motivation to engage with the task, the girls were every bit as capable of handling the interface with the computer and thinking their way through the problem as the boys.

Whatever the precise explanation for these findings, the evidence suggests the need for caution in thinking that gender differences in computer use are in some way inevitable and immutable. The metaphors and imagery used in the presentation of the task can have an influence out of all proportion to their significance for the designer of the software. This is a case where context exerts a critical influence on cognitive performance and can affect not just the absolute difficulty of a task but also its relative difficulty for different groups of children. Technologies arise in the context of existing social relations and may carry the potential for the further development and transformation of those relations. The comparison of boys' and girls' performance on these two computer games is but one example of the subtlety of how these effects may occur. Translating the message into the context of children working with computers in the classroom underlines the challenge facing those who are committed to providing equal opportunities for all children.

SUMMARY OF SECTION 5

- There are grounds for concern about the potential of educational computer technologies to amplify pre-existing patterns of social inequality.
- There are concerns that the increasing deployment of computer technology in schools could potentially place girls at a disadvantage relative to boys.
- Girls tend to have a less favourable attitude to computer use than boys, and use computers much less.
- While there are gender-related differences in terms of children's style of computer use, level of participation in and attitudes towards computer-related activities, such differences are not generally associated with performance on computer tasks.
- Gender differences in performance are far from immutable. The metaphors and images used in the presentation of the task can be critical in determining girls' success on computer-based tasks.
- Technologies arise in the context of existing social relations but may carry the potential for their further development and transformation. The introduction of computers into the classroom should, therefore, go hand-in-hand with a commitment to equal opportunities for all children.

6 CONCLUDING COMMENTS

In the space of less than two decades the nature of computers and their impact on our lives have changed in dramatic ways. In this chapter we have seen how changes in the technology have interacted with ideas about its potential for influencing children's development. The coverage has, of necessity, been selective but it reflects some of the past and present concerns of practitioners and researchers. As the power and potential of the technology continues to change, new opportunities will arise and, doubtless, new dilemmas for teachers, software designers, psychologists and others. Crystal-ball gazing is a hazardous occupation so I will refrain from it here. One important message of the chapter, however, concerns the shift in the focus of interest from examining the relationship between the individual learner and the machine towards investigating some of the ways in which computer technology can encourage and support collaborative learning opportunities and can provide the means for new forms of discovery and understanding. It will be interesting to observe how these are realized and how they impact upon wider social concerns such as equal opportunities. This chapter should have provided you with a platform from which to make such observations.

FURTHER READING

CROOK, C. (1992) 'Cultural artefacts in social development: the case of computers' in MCGURK, H. (ed.) *Childhood Social Development: contemporary perspectives*, Hove, Erlbaum.

HUGHES, M. (1990) 'Children's computation' in GRIEVE, R. and HUGHES, M. (eds) *Understanding Children*, Oxford, Blackwell.

LIGHT, P. and BLAYE, A. (1990) 'Computer-based learning: the social dimensions', in FOOT, H., MORGAN, M. and SHUTE, R. (eds) *Children Helping Children*, Chichester, Wiley.

PAPERT, S. (1980) *Mindstorms: children, computers and powerful ideas*, Brighton, Harvester Press.

SCRIMSHAW, P. (ed.) (1993) *Language, Classrooms and Computers*, London, Routledge.

UNDERWOOD, J. (ed.) (1994) *Computer-based learning: potential into practice*, London, David Fulton Publishers.

UNDERWOOD, J. and UNDERWOOD, G. (1990) *Computers and Learning: helping children acquire thinking skills*, Oxford, Blackwell.

REFERENCES

BARBIERI, M. S. and LIGHT, P. (1992) 'Interaction, gender and performance on a computer-based problem solving task', *Learning and Instruction*, **2**, pp. 199–213.

BENNETT, N. (1987) 'Co-operative learning: children do it in small groups – or do they?', *Educational and Child Psychology*, **4**, pp. 7–18.

BLAYE, A. (1988) 'Confrontation socio-cognitive et résolution de problème', unpublished doctoral thesis, University of Provence.

BLAYE, A., LIGHT, P., JOINER, R. and SHELDON, S. (1991) 'Collaboration as a facilitator of planning and problem-solving on a computer based task', *British Journal of Developmental Psychology*, **9**, pp. 471–83.

BUCKLEY, P. and SMITH, B. (1991) 'Opting out of technology: a study of girls' GCSE choices' in LOVEGROVE, G. and SEGAL, B. (eds) *Women into Computing: selected papers 1988–1990*, Heidelberg, Springer-Verlag.

CENTRAL ADVISORY COUNCIL FOR EDUCATION (ENGLAND) (1967) *Children and their Primary Schools*, London, HMSO (the Plowden Report).

CLEMENTS, D. H. (1986) 'Effects of Logo and CAI environments on cognition and creativity', *Journal of Educational Psychology*, **78**, pp. 309–18.

CLEMENTS, D. H. and NASTASI, B. K. (1988) 'Social and cognitive interactions in educational computer environments', *American Research Journal*, **25**, pp. 87–106.

COLE, M. and GRIFFIN, P. (1987) *Contextual Factors in Education: improving science and mathematics education for minorities and women*, Madison, Wisconsin Center for Education Research.

CROOK, C. (1987) 'Computers in the classroom: defining a social context' in RUTKOWSKA, J. C. and CROOK, C. (eds) *Computers, Cognition and Development*, London, Wiley.

CROOK, C. (1991) 'Computers in the zone of proximal development: implications for evaluation', *Computers in Education*, **17**(1), pp. 81–91.

CROOK, C. (1992) 'Cultural artefacts in social development: the case of computers' in McGURK, H. (ed.), *Childhood Social Development: contemporary perspectives*, Hove, Erlbaum.

CULLEY, L. (1988) 'Girls, boys and computers', *Educational Studies*, **14**, pp. 3–8.

DEPARTMENT FOR EDUCATION (DFE) (1995) *Survey of Information Technology in Schools*, Statistical Bulletin 3/95.

DEPARTMENT OF EDUCATION AND SCIENCE (DES) (1989) *Information Technology from 5 to 16*, London, HMSO.

DOISE, W. and MUGNY, G. (1984) *The Social Development of the Intellect*, Oxford, Pergamon.

FLETCHER, B. (1985) 'Group and individual learning of junior school children on a micro-computer-based task', *Educational Review*, **37**, pp. 251–61.

GALTON, M. (1989) *Teaching in the Primary School*, London, David Fulton Publishers.

GUNTER, B., McALEER, J. and CLIFFORD, B. (1991) *Children's Views about Television*, Aldershot, Avebury.

HOWE, C., TOLMIE, A. and ANDERSON, A. (1991) 'Information technology and group work in physics', *Journal of Computer Assisted Learning*, **7**, pp. 133–43.

HOYLES, C. (ed.) (1988) *Girls and Computers*, London, University of London, Institute of Education (Bedford Way Papers No. 34).

HOYLES, C. and SUTHERLAND, R. (1986) 'Using Logo in the mathematics classroom', *Computers in Education*, **10**, pp. 61–72.

HOYLES, C. and SUTHERLAND, R. (1989) *Logo Mathematics in the Classroom*, London, Routledge.

HOYLES, C., SUTHERLAND, R. and HEALY, L. (1991) 'Children talking in computer environments: new insights on the role of discussion in mathematics learning' in DURKIN, K. and SHIRE, B. (eds) *Language in Mathematical Education: research and practice*, Milton Keynes, Open University Press.

HUGHES, M. (1990) 'Children's computation' in GRIEVE, R. and HUGHES, M. (eds) *Understanding Children*, Oxford, Blackwell.

HUGHES, M., BRACKENRIDGE, A., BIBBY, A. and GREENHOUGH, P. (1988) 'Girls, boys and turtles' in HOYLES, C. (ed.) *Girls and Computers*, London, University of London, Institute of Education (Bedford Way Papers No. 34).

HUGHES, M., BRACKENRIDGE, A. and MACLEOD, H. (1987) 'Children's ideas about computers' in RUTKOWSKA, J. and CROOK, C. (eds) *Computers, Cognition and Development*, London, Wiley.

JONES, R. (1980) *Microcomputers: their use in primary schools*, London, Council for Educational Technology.

JOHANSON, R. P. (1988) 'Computers, cognition and curriculum: retrospect and prospect', *Journal of Educational Computing Research*, **4**, pp. 1–30.

KULLIK, J., KULLIK, C. and BANGERT-DROWNS, R. (1985) 'Effectiveness of computer-based education in elementary schools', *Computers in Human Behaviour*, **1**, pp. 59–74.

LABORATORY OF COMPARATIVE HUMAN COGNITION (LCHC) (1989) 'Kids and computers: a positive vision of the future', *Harvard Educational Review*, **59**(1), pp. 73–86.

LIGHT, P. (1993) 'Collaborative learning with computers' in SCRIMSHAW, P. (ed.) *Language, Classrooms and Computers*, London, Routledge.

LIGHT, P. and BLAYE, A. (1990) 'Computer-based learning: the social dimensions' in FOOT, H., MORGAN, M. and SHUTE, R. (eds) *Children Helping Children*, Chichester, Wiley.

LIGHT, P., FOOT, T., COLBOURN, C. and MCCLELLAND, I. (1987) 'Collaborative interactions at the microcomputer keyboard', *Educational Psychology*, **7**, pp. 13–21.

LIGHT, P. and GLACHAN, M. (1985) 'Facilitation of problem solving through peer interaction', *Educational Psychology*, **5**, pp. 217–25.

LIGHT, P., LITTLETON, K., MESSER, D. and JOINER, R. (in press) 'Social and communicative processes in computer-based problem solving', *European Journal of Psychology of Education*.

LITTLETON, K., LIGHT, P., JOINER, R., MESSER, D. and BARNES, P. (1992) 'Pairing and gender effects on children's computer-based learning', *European Journal of Psychology of Education*, **7**, pp. 309–23.

LITTLETON, K., LIGHT, P., JOINER, R., MESSER, D. and BARNES, P. (unpublished) 'Pirates and picnics: gender and software interactions in children's computer-based problem-solving'.

MARTIN, R. (1991) 'School children's attitudes towards computers as a function of gender, course subjects and availability of home computers', *Journal of Computer Assisted Learning*, **7**, pp. 187–94.

MERCER, N. (1993) 'Computer-based activities in classroom contexts' in SCRIMSHAW, P. (ed.) *Language, Classrooms and Computers*, London, Routledge.

MEVARECH, Z., SILBER, O. and FINE, D. (1991) 'Learning with computers in small groups: cognitive and affective outcomes', *Journal of Educational Computing Research*, **7**(2), pp. 233–43.

PAPERT, S. (1980) *Mindstorms: children, computers and powerful ideas*, Brighton, Harvester Press.

PERRET-CLERMONT, A.-N. (1980) *Social Interaction and Cognitive Development in Children*, London, Academic Press.

SHEINGOLD, K., HAWKINS, J. and CHAR, C. (1984) *I'm the Thinkist, you're the Typist: the interaction of technology and the social life of classrooms*, New York, Bank Street College of Education (Technical Report 27).

SHOTTON, M. (1989) *Computer Addiction?: a study of computer dependency*, London, Taylor and Francis.

SHROCK, S. and STEPP, S. (1991) 'The role of the child micro-computer expert in an elementary classroom: a theme emerging from a naturalistic study', *Journal of Research on Computing in Education*, **23**(4), pp. 545–59.

SIMON, T. (1987) 'Claims for Logo: what should we believe and why?' in RUTKOWSKA, J. C. and CROOK, C. (eds) *Computers, Cognition and Development*, Chichester, Wiley.

STRAKER, A. (1989) *Children Using Computers*, Oxford, Blackwell.

TODMAN, J. and DICK, G. (1993) 'Primary children and teachers' attitudes to computers', *Computers in Education*, **20**(2), pp. 199–203.

TURKLE, S. (1984) *The Second Self: computers and the human spirit*, London, Granada.

UNDERWOOD, G., McCAFFREY, M. and UNDERWOOD, J. (1990) 'Gender differences in a co-operative computer-based language task', *Educational Research*, **32**, pp. 16–21.

UNDERWOOD, J. and UNDERWOOD, G. (1990) *Computers and Learning: helping children acquire thinking skills*, Oxford, Blackwell.

WEBB, N., ENDER, P. and LEWIS, S. (1986) 'Problem-solving strategies and group processes in small groups learning computer programming', *American Educational Research Journal*, **23**, pp. 243–61.

ANSWERS TO ACTIVITIES

ACTIVITY 2

TO FLOWER
REPEAT 6 [SQUARE RIGHT 60]

ACTIVITY 5

The optimal solution to the Towers of Hanoi task is:

1   Small coin to peg 3
2   Medium coin to peg 2
3   Small coin to peg 2
4   Large coin to peg 3
5   Small coin to peg 1
6   Medium coin to peg 3
7   Small coin to peg 3

READING

The nature of computer-based activity in the classroom

Neil Mercer and Eunice Fisher

A common view, held by teachers, software designers and many education technology researchers, is that the nature of any computer-based learning activity is almost entirely defined by the software. Teachers typically attribute the future or success of any activity to 'good' or 'poor' programs. Although software is of course a defining influence on activities (to greater or lesser extents for different kinds of programs: compare, say, some adventure games with word-processing packages), our observations show that in practice the procedures and outcomes of any computer-based activity will emerge through the talk and joint activity of teacher and pupils. That is, the same software used by different combinations of teachers and pupils on different occasions will generate distinctive activities. These distinctive activities will operate to different time scales, generate different problems for pupils and teachers and will almost certainly have different learning outcomes. Apart from the software itself, the main defining influence on the structure and outcomes of a computer-based activity will be that of the teacher, through any initial 'setting up' of the activity, through the nature of the interventions he or she makes during the activity, and through the ways (before and after the time spent at the screen) that pupils are enabled to relate the activity to other educational experience. As Crook (1991) suggests, there is a need for the computer to:

> ... become a topic of classroom discourse such that the experience can be interpreted and blended into the shared understanding of the participants. This is a more demanding and perhaps more intrusive role for the teacher than has otherwise been identified.

(p. 87)

We should not decry or attempt to diminish the powerful influence of the teacher on computer-based activities, for the teacher's responsibility is to ensure that children's computer-based experience contributes to their education. That responsibility cannot be delegated to even the most sophisticated software or to the children themselves. If we can describe and evaluate the ways that teachers attempt to 'scaffold' children's learning with computers, we might then be able to help teachers to perform that role more effectively and also contribute to the design of more classroom friendly software

Reference

CROOK, C. (1991) 'Computers in the zone of proximal development: implications for evaluation', Computers in Education, **17**(1), pp. 81–91.

*SOURCE: MERCER, N. and FISHER, E. (1992) 'How do teachers help children to learn? An analysis of teachers' interventions in computer-based activities', Learning and Instruction, **2**, pp. 339–55.*

CHAPTER 4 CHILDREN AS WITNESSES

Ray Bull and Peter Barnes

CONTENTS

OBJECTIVES

When you have studied this chapter, you should be able to:

1 give an account of the ways that psychologists and lawyers have collaborated to further the interests of children involved as witnesses in court;

2 identify ways in which research on children's development has informed policy and practice relating to child witnesses;

3 describe the features of different ways of interviewing child witnesses and evaluate their strengths and weaknesses;

4 identify the rationale behind other ways in which children are helped to give accurate testimony;

5 give an account of the factors that appear to influence adults' judgements of the accuracy and admissibility of children's testimony.

1 INTRODUCTION

In their everyday lives children talk about the things that happen around them all the time. They tell us what their teacher said and did at school, about the fight in the playground, the goings on in the latest episode of a TV serial. We may sometimes suspect that their recall is partial or even that at times they may over-dramatize. But, for the most part we tend to take children's ability to observe and report on events for granted and to expect them to give accurate accounts. And we acknowledge that adults are probably just as likely to remember selectively and to elaborate.

However, such apparent faith in children's relative reliability and honesty is rather more variable when viewed in the context of the legal system. Can the evidence that children give in court be trusted? How old do they need to be before the court can be satisfied that they are competent to tell the truth? These are questions with a long and often complex history (see Spencer and Flin, 1990). For a long time the courts declared that a child could give evidence so long as the judge was satisfied that he or she understood the importance of telling the truth. The 1933 Children and Young Persons Act permitted children to give unsworn evidence in criminal cases and there were examples of children as young as 2 years old doing so. However, in 1958 the climate changed following a case in which a 5-year-old girl, called as a witness against her father, who was charged with incest, could not be persuaded to say anything once in the witness box. This provoked a judicial ruling to the effect that no child should be considered competent to give even unsworn evidence before the age of 6, and the more cautious practice grew up that they should not be called until they reached the age of 8. However, that position is now changing as a result of increasing public and professional concern about the sexual abuse of children. In cases of sexual assault there is often no conclusive forensic evidence and where the child victim is the only witness to the assault, a prosecution is not possible unless the child's evidence can be heard.

This chapter aims to show how psychological research, particularly that conducted in the late 1980s and early 1990s, has contributed to a more positive assessment of children's competence to provide a valid account of what they have witnessed.

But first there are two important distinctions to make clear. The first is that between *civil* and *criminal* proceedings. In civil proceedings (which include divorce and child protection) the standard of proof for evidence is based on a *balance of probabilities*; the court needs only to be convinced, say, that a child has *probably* been abused rather than that she has not. In criminal proceedings (trials for offences such as murder, rape, sexual assault), by contrast, it is necessary to prove this *beyond reasonable doubt*. In such cases the status of children's evidence is particularly critical because imprisonment may well be the result of criminal proceedings, but not of civil proceedings. The significance of the distinction is perhaps best illustrated by cases where a parent is acquitted of abusing a child following a criminal prosecution but then a civil court subsequently removes the child from home following a judge's finding that the parent was responsible (Spencer and Flin, 1990).

Having established the distinction, it is perhaps surprising to discover that little is known officially about the numbers of child witnesses who appear in legal proceedings nor, indeed, in what types of cases they are involved. One study conducted in Glasgow over a nine month period in the late 1980s found that 1000 children between the ages of 5 and 15 were summonsed to testify as witnesses in criminal trials (Flin and Bull, 1990). Table 1 indicates the sorts of offences that were involved and their occurrence relative to each other.

TABLE 1 Nature of trials to which children were called to give evidence and the frequency of each as a percentage of the total.

Assaults	32
Breaches of the peace	16
Theft	15
Lewd and libidinous behaviour, incest/sodomy	6
Murder/attempted murder	4
Road traffic accidents	2
Other	25

Source: Flin and Bull, 1990

Note, however, that the evidence in Table 1 comes from Scotland; it does not follow that a similar pattern would be found in England and Wales, a point that introduces the second important distinction. In the UK there are three separate legal systems, for England and Wales, for Northern Ireland and for Scotland. The first two are broadly similar, but the Scottish legal system is quite different. In Scottish law, for example, a conviction cannot be made on uncorroborated evidence (i.e. evidence from a single source, for example, on one person's word alone) – and this applies to adults as well as to children. For this reason the prosecution in a case frequently needs to use every piece of evidence that they have access to and this means that children are likely to be called more often than south of the border. Here we will mainly be concerned with the law as it applies in England and Wales; this is partly for simplicity, but also because, at the time of writing, Scottish law is undergoing extensive changes in the areas that we will be discussing. The main message of this chapter, though, is less to do with any particular code of legal practice than with how the evidence from psychological research has come together with the concerns of the legal profession to establish new practices and procedures.

In doing this, three main questions are addressed:

(a) Are children capable of giving accurate and truthful evidence? How do we know when they have acquired the capacity to do so?

(b) How can children be enabled to give evidence in ways which meet the demands on the legal system to dispense justice? How can and should the law be changed to allow this?

(c) How can children be protected from the possible stressful aspects of giving evidence?

We will be looking at these issues from the perspective of psychology but it is important at the same time to recognize that there are other considerations besides the needs and entitlement of children, in particular the principles of justice. And here another major difference between the civil and criminal law comes to the fore. In civil proceedings concerning children's welfare, the law is guided by the principle that the child's welfare must be the paramount consideration. In a criminal prosecution of an offence against a child, however, the child witness's welfare may not necessarily be the primary consideration. The law must maintain the accused's right to a fair trial and avoid cases of wrongful conviction.

2 THE COMPETENCE OF CHILD WITNESSES

ACTIVITY 1

Allow about 15 minutes

GROUNDS FOR SUSPICION?

Imagine that you are a member of a jury hearing a case where an 8-year-old child is called to give evidence about a sexual assault.

Make a list of your thoughts about how you would respond to what the child has to say. What sorts of concerns would you have? On what are they based?

Are the grounds for these concerns amenable to empirical investigation? What sort of research evidence would you want to be able to draw on to help you decide whether or not the child was a competent witness?

Finally, make brief notes on some of the reasons why people may question whether children's ability to give evidence is significantly different from that of adults.

Comment

Some of the questions and concerns that you have raised may be reflected in the following extract from a book about evidence written by an English lawyer:

> First, a child's powers of observation and memory are less reliable than an adult's. Secondly, children are prone to live in a make-believe world, so that they magnify incidents which happen to them or invent them completely. Thirdly, they are also very egocentric, so that details seemingly unrelated to their own world are quickly forgotten by them. Fourthly, because of their immaturity they are very suggestible and can easily be influenced by adults and other children. One lying child may influence others to lie; anxious parents may take a child through a story again and again so that it becomes drilled in untruths. Most dangerously, a policeman taking a statement from a child may without ill will use leading questions so that the child tends to confuse what actually happened with the answer suggested implicitly by the question. A fifth danger is that children often have little notion of the duty to speak the truth, and they may fail to realise how important their evidence is in a case and how important it is for it to be accurate. Finally, children sometimes behave in a way evil beyond their years. They may consent to sexual offences against themselves and then deny consent. They may completely invent sexual offences. Some children know the adult world regards such matters in a serious and peculiar way, and they enjoy investigating this mystery or revenging themselves by making false accusations.
>
> (Heydon, 1984, p. 84)

Some of these claims relate to children's perceptual and cognitive competence, others to their moral maturity and yet others to their susceptibility to pressure and influence from adults. Heydon states his case with a certain authority, but are his assertions about children's behaviour in these circumstances themselves based on 'admissible evidence'? All of these questions are the proper subject matter of developmental psychology, so it is reasonable to expect that psychology will itself have 'evidence' to offer on the validity of the charges being levelled against children as witnesses. How well that evidence stands up to critical scrutiny and how those concerned, particularly members of the legal profession, might be better informed as to its strengths and weaknesses form one important strand of this chapter.

In the mid-1980s considerable publicity was given in the media to cases concerning the sexual abuse of young children. At that time, under the law of England and Wales, children below the age of 6 were never allowed to give evidence. Children over 6 were rejected as witnesses unless they 'were of sufficient intelligence to justify the reception of their evidence' (Home Office, 1933, pp. 5–38). Furthermore, unless their evidence was given on oath (which it usually was not) it could not result in a conviction unless there was corroboration. The media publicity accompanying such cases, together with pressure from children's charities and child development researchers led the Home Office (Hedderman, 1987) to publish a review of research, most of it psychological in origin, relating to:

- children's ability to remember events reliably;
- their suggestibility in the face of questioning;
- their ability to distinguish fact from fantasy;
- their propensity to lie.

A consequence of this review was the Criminal Justice Act 1988 which removed the corroboration requirement so that, in this regard, young children (even when giving evidence unsworn) were to be treated in the same way as adults. Given that adults themselves by no means always remember reliably, can be suggestible in the face of questioning, sometimes have difficulty determining between fact and fiction, and sometimes tell lies, this was a sensible development. Nevertheless, continuing legal suspicion meant that children (at that time) of less than 6 years of age were still prevented by case law from giving evidence in criminal trials in England and Wales. (They had for many years been allowed to do so in Scotland, because of the corroboration requirement.) However, in 1990 this restriction changed when the Court of Appeal (for England and Wales) ruled that children of *any* age could give evidence provided the judge assessed them and thought them sufficiently intelligent and able to understand the duty of speaking the truth.

Why, then, in the period between 1958 and 1990 were young children prevented from testifying in criminal trials? This was partly due to lawyers' general suspicions about their evidence, but Hedderman (1987) also pointed to the influence of Freud's view that the reports of many of his female patients that they had been sexually abused as children were in practice mere childhood fantasies. The impact of these ideas was that, when children claimed to have been victims of or witnesses to abuse, adults tended not to believe them. This, in turn, fuelled suspicions that *any* child witness's evidence – not just regarding sexual abuse – was questionable. Nowadays, such children's accounts are more likely to be believed, in part owing to the publication of extensive surveys which have suggested that child sexual abuse is much more common than was previously thought (Glaser and Frosh, 1988; Spencer and Flin, 1990). In addition, when it comes to looking at the extent to which children fantasize, what little research there is indicates that even young children have the capacity to discriminate fact from fantasy.

Heydon's perceptions of the reliability of children's powers to observe and remember (see Comment following Activity 1) are at odds with our own assertions at the start of this chapter. Who is right? This is a question that is amenable to experimental investigation, and since the late 1980s there have been many such studies reported (e.g. Goodman and Bottoms, 1993). One of these is described in Research Summary 1, which you should read now.

RESEARCH SUMMARY 1
HOW ACCURATELY DO CHILDREN AND ADULTS RECALL A DRAMATIC EVENT?

Rhona Flin and colleagues compared the accuracy of recall of an event by two groups of children, one aged 5 to 6 years and the other 9 to 10, and by a group of university undergraduates. They all watched a talk by a nurse about foot hygiene, illustrated with slides. The children were told that the talk was about how to look after their feet and that they should listen carefully to what the nurse said. The adults were told that they were being asked to listen to the presentation as part of a study evaluating the perceived utility of such talks for children.

In fact the whole procedure was staged, and the nurse and her two assistants (who were professional actresses) followed a prepared script. So each of the three groups witnessed as near identical an event as possible. As the nurse was being introduced, the two assistants set up a projector and loaded slides into the carousel. Just before the talk was due to start the assistants made as if to leave and in the process one of them tripped over the projector cable, causing the carousel to crash to the ground, scattering the slides. The assistants then began to argue, progressively more angrily, about the accident until, after about 30 seconds, the nurse said she could manage without the slides and asked them to leave. However, the assistants continued with their argument so that the nurse had to adopt a sterner tone to ask them to go. One left in a huff; the other apologized and offered to pick up the slides. The nurse declined the offer, the second assistant left the room and the five-minute talk began.

After the talk the children returned to their classrooms and the students continued with their normal lecture, having first completed a brief questionnaire rating the talk for its appropriateness to different age groups of children.

On the following day both children and adults were interviewed and asked to recall as much as they could about the incident. Standard questions were asked about such things as the sequence and content of the events, the content of the nurse's talk, and the clothing worn by those involved. Analysis of what they provided showed that the amount of information correctly recalled was not related to the respondents' age. Out of a possible maximum score of 26 on the interviewer's questions, the 6 year olds averaged 17, the 9 year olds 19 and the adults 18.

However, when they were interviewed again five months later (a delay period typically experienced by children called to court to give evidence about a crime they had earlier witnessed), the 9 year olds and the adults remembered as much as they had after one day, but the 5 year olds recalled about 40 per cent less. It is worth noting that, at all ages, very little of what was reported was actually incorrect.

Source: Flin et al., 1992.

Research of this sort has consistently found that even young children (e.g. from 4 years old) usually provide accurate accounts, though they are sometimes less full in their details than those of older children and adults. Both adults and children are affected by the way they are interviewed. When the procedures used are misleading, biased or suggestive, this often leads to deficits in recall accuracy.

ACTIVITY 2

Allow about 10 minutes

QUESTIONING THE RESEARCH EVIDENCE

Research of the sort described in Research Summary 1 is, of necessity, based on *simulations*.

How far do you think the findings are likely to hold true with respect to actual court proceedings? Suggest some of the differences that may affect a child's ability to give evidence.

Comment

The interviews Flin and her colleagues conducted with the children were unlikely to be particularly distressing. Neither was the incident itself. The children were not directly involved in the incident, nor was the subject matter 'taboo'.

By contrast, giving evidence in court is profoundly stressful, even for most adults, and it normally involves cross-examination which is often deliberately hostile. The child in court may have to testify in front of the accused person. And, in such circumstances, the child will probably understand that the consequences of what they say may be far-reaching; it could result in someone they know being sent to prison.

You may have thought of other differences. The important point to bear in mind is that caution needs to be exercised when considering the implications of research based on simulations for the real-life experience of children.

SUMMARY OF SECTION 2

- Some of the grounds on which children's testimony might be called into question have been identified.
- Research has had an impact on changing legal practices concerning how children are regarded as witnesses.
- A study by Flin *et al.* indicates that children are as good as adults at recalling the details of an incident when questioned about it the day afterwards, but that younger children (aged 5) recall significantly less after an interval of five months.
- Research based on simulations may be of limited relevance to the experience of children in actual court cases.

3 RESPONSES TO A STRESSFUL EXPERIENCE

The ability to provide accurate testimony is just one factor to be considered where decisions are being taken about children acting as witnesses. Is it in young children's interests that they should be allowed or required to testify in court, especially in criminal trials in which they will be cross-examined? For example, if giving evidence in court is very stressful for abused children, especially young ones, is this in itself likely to result in further distress for the child? There can be a moral dilemma here between upholding the interests of the child and upholding the interests of justice.

READING

Despite widespread concern about child witnesses being exposed to the demands of a criminal trial, there has been only one empirical study in Britain of children's behaviour in the witness box. This research was conducted by Rhona Flin, Ray Bull, Julian Boon and Anne Knox and an account of it is provided as a Reading at the end of this chapter. You should read this now.

As you read it, note how the research was conducted and the aspects of the children's behaviour and demeanour that were measured. Are there any clear differences which relate to age? Flin *et al.* conclude that 'children's experiences while giving evidence in court are dependent on a host of internal and external factors'; make a list of the ones referred to in the Reading. Note the problems inherent in replicating these in a simulation.

The findings of the limited amount of research on this topic are that while some children are stressed by the experience of giving evidence, others are not. Many professionals – social workers, police officers, lawyers – remain of the view that it is generally much more stressful for child witnesses to give their accounts than it is for most adults (Spencer and Flin, 1990). One factor likely to be of significance here is the *reason* for seeking a child's account. If the child was the victim or witness to a crime, the crime itself may well have negative psychological effects on the child. Researchers are faced with the difficult problem of disentangling these often powerful effects from those associated with giving evidence. Nevertheless, legislators in many countries have decided to try to modify aspects of trial procedure which, opinion has it, may well be stressful for child witnesses.

Potential sources of stress include coming face-to-face with the alleged perpetrator and being in a strange environment with unusual procedures and rules and a lot of unfamiliar people. What can be done to reduce such stress without compromising

FIGURE 1 ... some children are stressed by the experience of giving evidence, others are not. (*And When Did You Last See Your Father?*, by William Frederick Yeames)

the rights of the accused person? In 1989 the Court of Appeal ruled that the growing practice in trials of using screens to prevent child witnesses being intimidated by their surroundings was not unfair or prejudicial to the accused, and legislation has allowed children to give evidence via live video-links and through video-recorded interviews.

3.1 Live video-links

The 1988 Criminal Justice Act allowed child witnesses in criminal trials in England and Wales to testify from another room in the court building linked to the trial court by closed circuit television. (Similar legislation was introduced in Scotland in 1990.) Those in the court can see the child, and the child can see the person questioning her/him, but not the defendant. Graham Davies, a psychologist, conducted with colleagues a two-year evaluation for the Home Office of the usefulness of this new 'live-link'. From surveys of court personnel they concluded that the 'live-link has been demonstrated to have positive and facilitating effects on the courtroom testimony of children and to have widespread acceptance among the various professional groups involved in the processes of justice' (Davies and Noon, 1991, p. 138).

However, the live-link should not be seen as a panacea for all the problems facing child witnesses. In 1990 the first trial in a pilot scheme which enabled children to give evidence via closed-circuit television collapsed when the 13-year-old alleged victim remained silent in front of the camera, and the judge directed the jury to acquit the defendant (*The Times*, 31 January, 1990, p. 17). Such problems were not readily resolved as the following newspaper report illustrates:

Detective calls for child interview evidence on video

Abuse case dropped after girl falters

A couple accused of subjecting their two daughters to sexual abuse and cruelty were cleared yesterday after the elder child was unable to continue giving evidence.

Judge Gerald Butler QC ordered the jury at Southwark crown court, south London to return verdicts of not guilty to cruelty, indecent assault and gross indecency charges against the 43-year-old father. He also ordered that the 40-year-old mother, who was charged with cruelty against her daughters then aged nine and 12, be similarly cleared.

After the case Detective Constable Charles Timms, who investigated the allegations, called for legislation to allow video recordings of children's first interviews at police stations to be used as evidence.

Peter Clarke, prosecuting, said the police investigation began after teachers at the elder girl's school noticed she was pulling her hair out. 'She pulled almost all of her hair out of her body even her pubic hair.' He said the girl, now aged 13, would screech, and shout words like 'bosoms', and touch female staff on their breasts and buttocks.

He said she was subjected to 'unspeakable' abuse. She had made a statement to police alleging in detail how her father repeatedly abused her and forced her to watch him in 'bizarre' sex acts with his wife.

During the 38 minutes she gave evidence on Wednesday, the girl was in a room linked to the court by closed circuit television.

She said she had not wanted her father to live at their home in Mitcham, south London. When Mr Clarke asked why she replied: 'Because of those naughty things ... I didn't like him doing those sorts of things. I didn't like him pulling his trousers down.' When he asked her to describe the 'things' she said: 'I am too shy.'

Mr Clarke said the mother was charged with cruelty because she allegedly failed in her duty to protect the children.

He told the court yesterday that the situation had been carefully considered overnight: 'Although the Crown has seriously considered calling the younger girl, I take the view that it would not be in her or the public's interest to pursue this trial.' He offered no further evidence on the charges.

Det Con Timms said afterwards that letting children give evidence through closed circuit television was not enough. 'Too many cases of this kind are halted because children cannot bring themselves to tell the full story'. It had to be made easier for them to give evidence. The elder girl was still receiving psychiatric counselling. Both children were in care but their parents were entitled to apply for their return.

(*Guardian*, 22 June 1990, p. 4)

3.2 Video-recorded interviews

Pressure for the use of video recordings of children's testimony in court had begun to build up during the 1980s and in 1988 the Home Office responded by setting up a committee chaired by Judge Pigot. (This inquiry considered England and Wales; the issue was also examined by the Scottish Law Commission.) The committee's report, which took particular note of child development research, recommended the introduction of such video recordings as a way of reducing stress for child witnesses and also preserving the children's contemporaneous accounts (thus avoiding the sort of problem identified in Research Summary 1). In addition, the report suggested the provision of a code of practice for interviewing, something which became especially important once the interviewers' behaviour was available for scrutiny via the video recording.

Several of the Pigot Committee's recommendations were incorporated into the 1991 Criminal Justice Act which permitted (from October 1992) video-recorded interviews with child witnesses to be used as their evidence-in-chief in criminal trials. ('Evidence-in-chief' is explained in the Reading). Since child witnesses more often appear for the prosecution than for the defence, these interviews are usually concerned with allegations against a defendant. The Act expects the judge to order that the child not be examined-in-chief on any matter which, in the opinion of the court, has been dealt with in the video-recorded interview. In this way the recording can take the place of the child's evidence-in-chief if the interview is deemed acceptable to the court. Cross-examination (and any re-examination) still, however, has to be conducted live, usually using a video-link. The 1991 Act also contains a provision designed to abolish the *competency requirement*: the requirement that a child be able to understand the duty to tell the truth before the court will listen to his or her evidence. However, this provision is obscurely drafted, and it remains to be seen whether the courts will interpret it as having this effect.

One reason why some of the provisions of the Criminal Justice Act were introduced was that the government was trying to make the criminal justice process more considerate towards the needs of child witnesses. If a criminal court deems admissible all or part of a video recording made by the joint police/social work child protection team, this replaces live examination of a child's evidence-in-chief by a lawyer. However, the Act allows the court to reject part or all of a video recording if, for example, it considers that questioning has been improperly done with respect to rules of evidence. Thus, the skills of the interviewer must be of a good standard. Similarly, in civil courts the way in which the interview is conducted is very relevant. This is why the Pigot Committee's report suggested that the Home Office produce a code of practice on interviewing.

SUMMARY OF SECTION 3

- We have identified findings from research which has illustrated some of the stresses on children giving evidence in court and how these are responded to; there is no clear relationship between age and performance.
- Changes in the law have allowed for children to give evidence via live video-links and video-recorded interviews in an effort to reduce stress caused to them.
- Research has concluded that live video-links have positive and facilitating effects in the way intended.
- The increased use of video-recorded interviews has focused attention on the importance of interviewing techniques for use with children.

4 THE ACT OF INTERVIEWING CHILDREN

In 1991 there was wide concern over the circumstances in which some young children living in Orkney were removed from their homes and families by social workers acting on suspicion that they were being ritually sexually abused. In October 1992 Lord Clyde presented to the Secretary of State for Scotland the report of his inquiry into the affair (Clyde, 1992). The report described the interviewing skills of those who spoke to the alleged child victims as inadequate and deficient. A newspaper report of the time quoted a Scottish Office spokesman as saying that it was widely accepted that this was a difficult area: 'What we don't know about interviewing children would fill books.' (*Independent*, 28 October 1992).

In 1991 the Home Office asked the first author of this chapter, together with Di Birch, a lawyer from the University of Nottingham, to produce a draft code of practice for video-recorded interviews. They also set up a policy steering group consisting of senior representatives from a number of relevant bodies of lawyers, police officers, social workers, children's charities, psychiatrists and psychologists to help produce the code. The involvement of people from different disciplines and backgrounds showed a recognition of the importance of finding a way forward which took account, amongst other things, of both evidential and child development knowledge. The finalized version of the code was published in August 1992 as a *Memorandum of Good Practice on Video Recorded Interviews with Child Witnesses for Criminal Proceedings* (Home Office, 1992).

The *Memorandum of Good Practice* covers a wide range of issues, including advice on the legal conditions that may need to be satisfied before a video recording will be accepted in court and guidance on the legal rules to be observed in producing a recording of evidence which is acceptable. It gives guidance on what to do prior to an interview, including when and where to conduct the video-recording, and what equipment to use. An essential component gives advice on conducting the interviews so that children can give as full an account as possible without undue influence taking place (see Bull, 1992).

ACTIVITY 3

Allow about 10 minutes

FEATURES OF A GOOD INTERVIEW

Imagine the case of a girl aged 11 who has been sexually assaulted by a man while walking home from school alone. What would be the characteristics of a 'good' interview with the girl? What should be avoided? What considerations do you think that a professional interviewer should bear in mind? Think in terms of the structure of the interview and the nature of the questions asked.

Compare your notes with what follows.

The aim of an interview with a child witness is to obtain as full and reliable an account as possible. Past criticisms have focused on some of the questioning techniques employed, in particular that interviewers have biased the child's account by the use of suggestive, leading, or pressurizing questions. What 'good practice' has developed as a response, and to what extent is it based on research?

4.1 The *Memorandum of Good Practice*

In 1988 David Jones, a British child psychiatrist experienced at interviewing children who may have been abused, recommended dividing interviews with them into four phases (Jones and McQuiston, 1988):

(a) rapport;

(b) free narrative;

(c) questioning; and

(d) closure.

These four phases, which are supported by child development research, form the basis of the procedures recommended in the *Memorandum of Good Practice*. Some of the features of these phases are outlined and illustrated in the following paragraphs. It needs to be understood, however, that interviewing is a highly skilled business requiring considerable training if it is to be carried out properly. This brief account in no way equips the reader to be an interviewer.

Rapport

The essential first phase in any interview – with children or adults – is the establishment of a rapport between interviewer and interviewee. The aim of this is to help the child to relax and feel comfortable talking to an adult who, in all probability, is unfamiliar to them. As with similar forms of initial social interaction this typically takes the form of chatting about a TV programme or a hobby or it might involve play with toys or drawing. As well as helping to initiate the interaction it also provides the interviewer with a picture of the child's communicative and social development which may help to inform how the interview itself is conducted.

Free narrative

Research such as that described in Research Summary 1 has found that, when asked simply to describe what happened in their own words, children usually produce reliable accounts. So, the recommendation is that this phase of the interview should allow children to do just that. Research has also found that younger children sometimes report less than older ones and in their case some encouragement may be necessary from the interviewer, typically in the form of prompts that do not lead the child's narrative in any particular direction.

Research can inform practice in a number of respects, even in an area which appears superficially straightforward, such as enabling a child to give an account, in their own words, of something that has happened to them. Recall the research described in Chapter 1 which showed that, in the school classroom, teachers obtained fuller replies from pupils if they were able to wait longer than three seconds before intervening to speak once pupils appeared to stop speaking. Such findings are likely to apply outside the classroom, too.

Research into young children's understanding of the world can also be put to effective use. McGurk and Glachan (1988) found that children under 6 years old are reluctant to believe that they know anything useful that adults do not already know. They may not appreciate that the interview is a situation in which some of the usual rules of conversation with adults are reversed or altered; the adults *don't* already know the answers. Also, young children often assume that because one adult (i.e. the perpetrator) knows what has happened to them, other adults may somehow be privy to that knowledge (Toglia *et al.*, 1992).

Questioning

Valuable though the free narrative account may be, there is invariably a need for the interviewer to ask further questions. There are different forms of questions, and how and when these are deployed may contribute both to the fullness and to the accuracy of the account given, and perhaps, in due course, to its reception and credibility in court.

(a) *Open-ended questions* invite the child to provide further information but in a way that does not lead or seem to apply pressure. This may well take the form of the sorts of prompts that have already been described as a feature of the free narrative phase, inviting the child to say more about a particular episode (e.g. 'Could you tell me more about the man you saw by the railway bridge?'). Research has helped to inform good practice: 'why' questions are best avoided as they may be interpreted by children as attributing blame or guilt; repeating a question soon after it has been answered may be interpreted as a criticism of the original response and consequently met by a different answer in the belief that the first one was incorrect (Poole and White, 1991); and open-ended questions need to be phrased in a way which implies that an inability to remember or not to know the answer is acceptable, since most children are socialized at home and school into thinking that 'don't know' answers are frowned upon by adults (Moston, 1990).

(b) *Specific yet non-leading questions*: the free narrative account typically produces information which is potentially relevant to the matter in hand but lacks the desired level of precision. Children do not always understand what is relevant in a situation, and this sort of questioning can guide them into focusing their accounts better. The characteristics of this sort of question (e.g. 'What colour was the man's jacket?') are that they give no hint that there is a particular answer that the interviewer wants. Even apparently simple questions that invite one of two possible responses or ask for a 'yes' or a 'no' answer are problematic: children (and, indeed, adults) are more likely to choose the second of two alternatives or to give the positive answer 'yes' (Choi, 1991).

(c) *Closed questions*: specific yet non-leading questions may not be sufficient in themselves and there may be situations in which the interviewer needs to offer a limited number of alternative responses to the child (e.g. 'Was the man's jacket green, or red, or blue?') Some of the problems this may present have already been described.

(d) *Leading questions* such as 'Was the man's jacket green?' imply the answer. As such they are more likely to produce responses which are attributable to the type of questioning than to reliable remembering. Questions of this sort are not usually permitted as part of a child's live evidence-in-chief in a criminal trial and in court counsel can object to such questions before a witness giving evidence-in-chief responds to them. It may be possible in an interview, however, to revert to one of the non-leading styles (i.e. (a) to (c), above) once some potentially relevant information has apparently been generated by a leading question.

In practice, it may not be humanly possible for interviewers to avoid altogether the sorts of leading and closed questions which are common in everyday adult conversation but which run the risk of biasing replies. There is some evidence, however, that warning children in advance that some questions may be 'tricky' helps to reduce the unwanted effects of leading questions (Warren *et al.*, 1991).

Closure

The fourth and final phase of the interview procedures recommended by the *Memorandum of Good Practice* is important in two ways. First, it allows the interviewer to check the things that the child has said, which may subsequently be important when offered as evidence in court, using the child's own language and not a summary provided by the interviewer in adult language. Secondly, it provides a necessary opportunity to try to ensure that the child has not been distressed by the experience of the interview and is left in a positive frame of mind and not feeling, for example, that they have failed because they have been unable to remember something. In these respects this phase is a complement of the establishment of rapport with which the interview needs to begin.

The *Memorandum of Good Practice* which informed these interview procedures was closely based on a combination of child development research and professional legal opinion. However, the approach advocated may not be possible in every instance. Where children are very reticent, very young or have special or particular needs, or where decisions about child protection need to be made, supplementary or alternative measures need to be considered. These, too, have been developed on the strength of research evidence.

4.2 The cognitive interview

The nature of memory – and more particularly how information is *retrieved* from memory – is of obvious significance to those with an interest in witness testimony. The *cognitive interview* (CI) is a procedure which has recently been developed by psychologists on the strength of research as a way of aiding witnesses' retrieval of information (see Fisher and Geiselman, 1992; Memon and Köhnken, 1992). It was originally developed for use with adult witnesses and it employs four cognitive techniques.

How well something is remembered can be influenced by the compatibility between the *encoding* context and the *retrieval* context. Typically, an experience is encoded into memory within a context. This might include the features of the room in which it occurred – the position of the furniture, the colour of the curtains, the picture on the wall – or the people who were present. This information is encoded, either intentionally or incidentally, along with the critical event which later needs to be retrieved from memory. The first technique in the cognitive interview seeks to enhance the recall of these critical events by mentally reinstating the context in which they occurred. While there is considerable debate about the potency of such effects, proponents of the cognitive interview claim that it is a crucial part of their procedure that does assist witnesses to recall more information.

The second technique involves instructing witnesses to recall information from a variety of perspectives (e.g. another person's) once they appear to have remembered all they can from their own perspective. In a study by

Anderson and Pichert (1978) participants read a story about a house that contained information of interest both to a home buyer and to a burglar. After that they were asked to recall the story from the perspective of either a home buyer or a burglar. When they were subsequently asked to recall the story a second time, from the other perspective, it was found that they remembered significantly more correct information than those asked to recall again from the same perspective.

The third technique has the interviewees recalling the events in a different order so that, for example, having done their best to recall from the beginning through to the end in the usual fashion, they are encouraged to do so in *reverse* order by asking 'What happened just before ... ?' The psychological theory behind this technique relates to the notion of scripts. McCartney and Nelson (1981) have described a script as a mental representation of the sequence of actions called for in a familiar situation. For example, a typical script for having a meal at a restaurant might include (i) arrive at restaurant, (ii) wait to be seated, (iii) take off coat, (iv) give coat to waitress, (v) look at menu, (vi) order drink, (vii) order food, (viii) drink and eat, (ix) have coffee, (x) ask for bill, (xi) pay bill, (xii) get coat, (xiii) leave restaurant. Memon and Bull (1991) contended that the retrieval of information from memory is influenced by people's prior knowledge and their scripts. So, when witnesses are trying to remember what has happened they tend to use their scripts to recall aspects of the event in the order in which they believe such an event would *usually* take place. Asking witnesses, once they have done this, now to recall in a *different* order may well produce further information which is script-inconsistent, unusual, and atypical, yet valid.

The fourth CI technique asks witnesses to report everything they can, however inconsequential it may seem to them. This is another device for encouraging recall of things that are script-inconsistent.

Adult witnesses to both mock and real crimes who have been interviewed using these techniques recall significantly more information than witnesses who are simply asked to do their best or who are interviewed by police officers using their own interview methods. Fisher and Geiselman (1992) have further developed the procedures by adding techniques which include asking open rather than closed questions, not interrupting (both familiar from the *Memorandum* procedures), asking the witness to concentrate, and letting the witness have more control over the interview.

Rather less attention has been paid to the usefulness of the cognitive interview with children and such findings as there are have been very mixed. McCauley and Fisher (1992) found that interviews with children employing the CI approach led to more recall. However, as they mixed other interviewing strategies with the CI techniques it wasn't possible to determine whether it was the CI retrieval techniques as such that produced the effect. Saywitz et al. (1992) reported some success in using cognitive interviews with 8 to 12 year olds, but they noted that elements of the technique, such as asking the child to recall from another person's perspective, were problematic, especially with the younger children. Köhnken *et al.* (1992) found that the CI enabled 9 and 10 year olds to recall more but it also produced more confabulations.

Bull's (1995) review of these and other studies concluded that CI can be accommodated to a child-centred approach because it encourages listening to, rather than quizzing, the child and it therefore sat well with the latest government reports and recommendations. But at the same time the procedures are in need of some modification for use with children, especially younger ones. In work with Amina Memon the first author of this chapter found that children aged from 5 to 9 years required some further explanation and prompting when the CI techniques of 'change perspective', 'change order', and 'reinstate context' were being employed (Bull, 1995). At this age children may not have reached a sufficient level of cognitive development to respond readily to such techniques. As expected, the 9 year olds correctly recalled more information than the 5 year olds, but no significant differences were found between children interviewed using the cognitive interview techniques and those merely instructed to 'try harder'. In addition, the youngest children made more errors with the 'change order' instruction. As we've just seen, the thinking behind the use of the changed order instruction with adults is that it forces them not to rely on their scripts, so increasing the likelihood of recall of unusual, script-inconsistent, information. The age at which children develop scripts is much debated (Bull, 1995) and until further research has clarified this matter, the usefulness to young child witnesses of the CI change order instruction (and, indeed, the other CI instructions) is unknown.

4.3 Improving with practice

For most children the sorts of interview procedures described in this chapter would be an unfamiliar experience. Does this novelty have an adverse effect on the efficiency of their recall? Would their performance be improved by some sort of practice? John Yuille, a Canadian researcher, has recommended that children should experience two practice recall attempts about topics totally unrelated to the reason why they are being interviewed before being asked to provide information relating to the incident in question (Yuille *et al.*, 1993). And there is evidence that providing practice recall sessions of this sort when using the cognitive interview can considerably improve the amount that children recount (Saywitz *et al.*, 1992).

4.4 The use of 'props'

It seems well established that younger children tend to provide less complete accounts than do older children, though *what* they say is no less accurate. Is this because the younger children have less available in their memories on which to draw, or is that material there, but for some reason less available through the technique of free recall? Questioning is not a satisfactory alternative if this leads them to give erroneous information in an effort to satisfy what they think the questioner wants to hear, and this seems to be the tendency with younger children. A less direct option is to use 'props' such as toys, models or puppets to aid recall. These props might help to recreate the room in which the incident supposedly happened, and to identify, for example, who sleeps where.

DeLoache (1990) reported that even children as young as 3 years had sufficient cognitive development to use models and toys to represent real events. This evidence needs to be interpreted with caution since the tasks she used were far less complex than those that typically occur in investigative interviews. Nevertheless, work by Pipe *et al.* (1993) does suggest that props may be useful in such interviews and the approach received support in the *Memorandum of Good Practice*. But there are contrary voices. One objection (Raskin and Esplin, 1991) is that props, just like questions, may be suggestive or distracting and, furthermore, that they lack a scientific basis. This is similar to the sorts of criticisms levelled at the use of children's drawings as an indication of emotional state.

There has been some systematic research on the use of props, but not a lot. A review of the available evidence by Pipe *et al.* (1993) found that props usually led to increased recall, but that on some occasions this increased recall contained more errors. This increase in errors seemed to depend on the way the props were introduced to the children, on how representative they were of the real-life equivalent, and on the nature of the associated questioning. If critical problems like this are to be avoided it is very important that interviewers be trained in the effective use of props and be knowledgeable about relevant child development. But in order for such training to be effective it is first necessary to understand better the processes by which props may facilitate remembering.

4.5 Children with communication difficulties

One group of children for whom props might prove particularly useful is those who find oral communication difficult. There is some evidence that such children are particularly prone to acquiescing to spoken questions – tending to answer 'yes' to 'yes/no' type questions – and to give answers that are inappropriately influenced by question structure and wording (Sigelman *et al.*, 1981). The same researchers found that 'either/or' questions produced better remembering than did 'yes/no' questions, particularly if they were presented pictorially rather than verbally. And Helen Dent (1986) found that general rather than specific questions produced better recall and had less of a biasing/suggestive effect when used with child witnesses with learning disabilities. Generally, though, more research is needed to provide informed guidance on the most effective techniques that will help children with communication difficulties give valid accounts of what has happened to them.

SUMMARY OF SECTION 4

- This section has been concerned with how interviews may be used to enable children to provide accurate accounts that are suitable for use in court. The *Memorandum of Good Practice* has sought to make recommendations about practice based on a growing body of research.

- One account sees interviews as incorporating four phases, each with its own function. Some of the links to research evidence have been described.

- The 'cognitive interview' is another development which draws on research into human memory in an effort to facilitate fuller and more accurate recall; however, its use with children is less well established than with adults.

- Aids to recall such as practice sessions and props can help to generate better accounts, though they need to be employed with caution.

- Research has also suggested ways in which children with communication difficulties can be enabled to give valid accounts.

5   CHILDREN IN COURT

5.1 Who is telling the truth?

ACTIVITY 4

Allow about 5 minutes

POWERS OF DETECTION

Do you consider yourself a good judge of whether or not people are telling the truth? Is it easier to tell in the case of a child than an adult? What do you base your judgement on?

Comment

You may have singled out certain non-verbal behaviour – avoiding eye contact, blushing, perspiring, trembling voice – as sure-fire indicators of dishonesty. However, although we may like to believe that we are quick to detect when someone is lying to us, psychological research (e.g. summarized by Köhnken, 1990) suggests that we are very often mistaken. One reason for this unrealistic self-assessment is simple:

> When we are asked to estimate our ability to detect deceptions, we remember only the gross and awkward lies which were easily detected. Most of the skilful, clever, successful lies, on the other hand, are never noticed. In fact, this is the very reason why they were successful. Hence, they will not influence our judgement of our own detection accuracy.

(Köhnken, 1990, p. 40)

Although the sorts of non-verbal behaviours just described, particularly those involving the face and eyes, are thought to be indicators of deception, they are also easily controlled by most determined liars. Children learn that parents interpret lack of eye contact as an indicator that they may be lying and so realize that in order to lie effectively they should look at the other person when doing so. We might expect to find that children are less accomplished at this than adults who have had rather more experience and who may also have greater insight into how non-verbal behaviour is interpreted. The limited research on this question supports such a notion. Feldman and Philippot (1991), for example, found that adults were more accurate at detecting whether children were lying than they were for other adults. However, some young children were judged to be lying when they were telling the truth, and vice versa.

If non-verbal behaviour is not necessarily a good guide to whether people's stories are a true account of events they have actually experienced, what other more effective ways are there? For example, in Germany, in 1954, the Supreme Court decided that in every criminal case where a child was alleged to have been sexually abused, and the main evidence regarding this allegation came from the child, the court should appoint an expert psychologist to interview the child. This was done to try to ensure that valid accounts from children would be heard by the courts and not dismissed as fantasy stories. One of the main ways in which such experts have tried to decide whether or not the account is of a genuinely experienced event is to scrutinize the written transcript of their interview with the child to see if certain criteria thought to be indicative of genuinely experienced events were present. *Statement criteria analysis*, as this procedure is known, draws on 19 separate aspects of a statement; these are listed in Table 2.

TABLE 2   Content criteria of statement analysis

General characteristics	10 Accurately reported details misunderstood
1 Logical structure	11 Related external associations
2 Unstructured production	12 Accounts of subjective mental states
3 Quantity of details	13 Attribution of perpetrator's mental state
Specific contents	*Motivation-related contents*
4 Contextual embedding	14 Spontaneous corrections
5 Descriptions of interactions	15 Admitting lack of memory
6 Reproduction of conversation	16 Raising doubts about one's own testimony
7 Unexpected complications during the incident	17 Self-deprecation
	18 Pardoning the perpetrator
Peculiarities of content	
8 Unusual details	*Offence-specific elements*
9 Superfluous details	19 Details characteristic of the offence.

Source: Köhnken, 1990.

Many of these criteria relate to children's cognitive development. For example, criterion 2, 'unstructured production', looks to see if the child's account is disorganized, with fragments of the event scattered throughout the statement in a rather jumbled way. If so, this is taken as an indicator of credibility. By contrast, fabricated testimonies and fantasies are usually structured, with the events recounted in a generally chronological manner and with causal connections made between them. Criterion 10, 'accurately reported details misunderstood', also rests on the developmental assumption that children (especially younger ones) may recount aspects of sexual behaviour in a factually accurate way but with obvious misunderstanding of their meaning.

These criteria were formulated on the basis of German psychologists' clinical experience (rather than via experimental research) dating back to the 1930s. And although statement criteria analysis was employed by psychologists in both Germany and Sweden for decades, it was not until the late 1980s that methodologically rigorous experimental research was conducted to determine whether the criteria do, in practice, discriminate successfully between accounts of actually experienced events and fictional ones. For example, in one study reported by Steller and Boychuk (1992) children of 7 and 11 years were asked to tell two stories, one about an event they had experienced and one a fictitious account of an event they had not experienced. This was done in the context of a storytelling competition. Typed transcripts of these stories/accounts were then examined by researchers trained in the use of statement criteria analysis, and they had to decide which were accounts of events that had been genuinely and directly experienced by the children, and which were not. This study found many of the 19 criteria in Table 2 to be present significantly more often in the accounts of genuinely experienced events.

Other similar studies have found support for the notion that the criteria are sometimes useful in assisting to determine whether a child witness's account is of a genuinely experienced event. However, the uncertainties that remain mean that there is plenty of scope for disputes in court over the interpretation of such evidence, with 'experts' making contradictory claims. More work is now needed to ascertain the theoretical bases of the various criteria to determine *why* they should discriminate. Even so, this approach holds promise, especially because of the limitations of the alternative: trying to tell if children are giving valid accounts merely by observing their behaviour.

5.2 Adults' expectation of child witnesses

This chapter began by raising the doubts of lawyers and the public alike concerning children's competence as witnesses; recall Heydon's list of their apparent shortcomings in Section 2. The nature of this mistrust has been investigated in a variety of ways. The age of the witness has an effect in some ways, but not others. For example, Goodman *et al.*(1987) asked young adults, simulating a jury, to read a summary of a trial; the testimony remained the same but participants were told different ages (6, 10 and 30) for the key witness. The 6-year-old witnesses were rated as less credible than the 10 year olds, who were rated as less credible than the 30 year olds. However, witness age had no effect on ratings of guilt or innocence. Leippe and Romanczyk (1987) similarly asked young adults to read a transcript of a case in which a grocer was killed during a robbery from his shop. As in the previous study, the age of the eyewitness testifying was variously described as being 6, 10 or 30 years. In addition, the other evidence was varied to create a strong, ambiguous or weak case against the defendant. When this evidence was strong and the eyewitness an adult all of the participants returned a guilty verdict, whereas only 58 per cent did so under the same conditions when the witness was a child. When the other evidence was weak or ambiguous no significant effects of witness age were found.

Research Summary 2 outlines findings from two studies which have attempted to identify further which features of witnesses and their performances have an influence on mock jurors.

RESEARCH SUMMARY 2
WHAT INFLUENCES ADULTS' PERCEPTIONS OF CHILDREN'S CREDIBILITY AS WITNESSES?

David Ross and colleagues, using a survey, established that adults expected less of child witnesses (as compared with adults) where accuracy and suggestibility were concerned, and would give less weight generally to children's testimony. By contrast, they made no distinction between children and adults on the matter of honesty.

Ross et al. explored these differences further by asking adults to watch one of two video recordings of a simulated court trial. In one version the testimony was given by an 8 year old, and in the other by a young adult. The observers rated the testimony of the child as more accurate, truthful, forceful, confident, consistent and trustworthy than the identical testimony given by the adult. However, age was not found to be a factor in judgements about guilt.

How might this apparent contradiction be explained? Were there, perhaps, some uncontrolled differences, besides age, between the actors providing the evidence? Ross et al. repeated the study, replacing the video recordings with identical written transcripts so that all that varied was the witness's given age. Once again, the child witness condition produced more positive ratings (but no effect on guilt).

In a similar vein, Nigro et al. (1989) found the testimony from an 8 year old to be rated as more credible than the same testimony attributed to a 25 year old. In addition they found that if the witness's testimony was presented in a 'powerful' rather than 'powerless' speech manner (i.e. one which included hesitations, 'uhs' and 'ums') the child's testimony led to more guilty decisions.

(Ross et al., 1990; Nigro et al., 1989)

ACTIVITY 5

Allow about 5 minutes

WHY THE DIFFERENCE BETWEEN CHILDREN AND ADULTS?

Consider the differences between children and adults that are described in Research Summary 2 and suggest reasons why they might have occurred.

Comment

One possible explanation of these findings is that adults have an expectation that children's testimony will be poor (as shown in the survey results from Ross *et al.*) and are then favourably impressed when their actual performance is confident, consistent and forceful. However, Ross is appropriately cautious about this interpretation since the conditions of this experiment may unwittingly have produced an impressive child witness but only an average adult one. This consideration was taken into account in a further study which is described in Research Summary 3.

RESEARCH SUMMARY 3
CONFIDENCE AND CREDIBILITY

David Luus and Gary Wells (1992) asked children (aged 8 and 12) and adults to watch a video recording of a simulated crime – an abduction. Next day they were asked to describe it in their own words. These descriptions were video-recorded. Adults watched the videoed descriptions and rated the witnesses for credibility and confidence. No significant differences were found in these ratings between the three age groups. Those witnesses rated as confident were also rated as credible. This suggests that child witnesses who give their testimony with confidence may well be judged as credible. Luus and Wells made the point that 'people might imagine children to be incapable of delivering accurate, convincing testimony, but these preconceived negative views seem quickly to be discarded upon actually observing a child testify' (p. 85).

How big a part does this surprising apparent contradiction of low initial expectations actually play? Luus and Wells asked other adult participants to read transcripts of what the 8-year-old children and the adults had said as witnesses. Some participants were led to believe that the transcripts from the children were actually those of adults and vice versa. Their credibility ratings were unrelated both to the true age of the witnesses whose transcripts were used and to the age as given to the participants. So, it would appear that they were not giving the younger children higher credibility scores by virtue of their age but rather it was the *confidence* with which witnesses presented their testimony that had a stronger effect on observers.

(Luus and Wells, 1992)

Research of this kind has obvious implications for legal practices though it is open to the criticism that it takes the form of simulations rather than being based on real-life experience. Do people behave in the same way when they have the real responsibility of being on a jury? That remains an open question.

5.3 Preparing children to give evidence

At various points during this chapter we have seen how particular events or trends in crime statistics appear to have been significant in prompting changes in legal practice so far as the treatment and status of child witness testimony is concerned. A further example of this comes from Canada where, in the mid-1980s, a Royal Commission Inquiry reported into the incidence of child sexual abuse, child pornography and juvenile prostitution. They noted over 10,000 documented cases of child sexual abuse and expressed concern about the ability of the criminal justice system to cope with the problem. Among the Commission's proposals was the suggestion that there be fundamental changes to the law to allow children to be able to speak directly for themselves at legal proceedings.

In 1987 the Canadian government passed Bill C-15 bringing in new legislation in this area. Some of its provisions were designed to enable very young children to testify in court, to reduce the need for corroboration and to enable the use of video and of screens between the child and the defendant in court. A research project was commissioned with the aim of designing procedures to help children prepare for giving evidence in court. One problem identified by previous research was that many children had a very poor understanding of what actually went on in court, so one aim was to overcome this ignorance. Second, children were seen to need help with dealing with the stress and anxiety understandably related to testifying; existing knowledge of anxiety reduction techniques offered a way of responding to this. And third, the sort of research evidence described in the previous section illustrated the need for children to be properly prepared for being interviewed and for giving their evidence competently in court.

An important part of the research project was to evaluate the impact of these procedures (Dezwirek-Sas, 1992). When child witnesses who had experienced them were compared on a number of psychological and other measures with those who had not, it was found that prosecutors rated more positively the real-life court room testimony of the children who experienced the new procedures. In addition, these children had better adjustment on some of the measures of fear and better knowledge of court than did the control group.

Although there has been a fair amount of research into effective ways of preparing children for medical procedures, there is correspondingly little directed at how to assist children to recall events effectively in court. One such study (Saywitz *et al.*, 1990) drew on research into how children encode memories and then retrieve them, in order to train 7 to 11 year olds to recall more of a staged live event. The training included getting the children to use external visual cues such as drawings representing 'who was there', 'what happened', 'where did it happen' and also encouraging them to report in appropriate detail on categories of information that would be useful in a criminal investigation (i.e. the setting, participants, conversations, affective state, actions and consequences). The children trained in this way were compared with a group which received instructions to be as complete as possible but received no training, and a control group which received neither instructions nor training. The trained group correctly recalled significantly more information than did the other two (which did not differ from each other). However, the trained children also produced significantly more *incorrect* recall. When this recall was analysed separately for use with and without the visual cues, it was found that the trained group's higher incorrect recall was occasioned solely by the use of the visual cues. This study illustrates how preparing children to give evidence may well be worthwhile but at the same time demonstrates how further research is needed into the ways in which accurate information is best elicited.

SUMMARY OF SECTION 5

- An important aspect of assessing children's testimony is knowing whether they are telling the truth. This is not as easy to do as may appear at first sight. Statement criteria analysis offers one way forward, though it is by no means foolproof.

- A subtle influence on how adults regard children's testimony is the interplay between expectations of how children will perform and the way that they do actually give evidence. Research suggests that the confidence with which children give evidence has a significant effect on their perceived credibility.

- Canadian research has indicated ways in which children can be prepared and trained to give their evidence more competently in court.

6 A WAY FORWARD

This chapter has illustrated how, up until the 1980s, many lawyers were very sceptical about young children testifying in court. However, a surge of activity in child development research in that decade demonstrated that young – even very young – children were able to give valid accounts, especially if they were interviewed in particular ways. The 1980s also saw the start of a good working relationship between lawyers and psychologists, members of professions who hitherto had only rarely met or shared their needs and knowledge. One example of this was the attendance of the entire Pigot Committee (see Section 4) at a conference where psychologists were presenting the results of relevant research, a conference which was opened by the Lord Chancellor. A further example was the collaboration between John Spencer (a legal scholar) and Rhona Flin (a psychologist) which led to the publication of *The Evidence of Children* in 1990. Not only did lawyers and government become more receptive to the results of child development research, but some of those conducting such research designed their studies so that their outcomes would be of directly perceived relevance to lawyers. In Britain, government brought in legislation that not only recognized that young children could be competent witnesses but also went some way toward meeting the needs of children in legal cases.

Although important progress has been made, there remain many outstanding challenges. For example, providing an account of a witnessed crime remains stressful for some witnesses (whether they be children or adults). One way of reducing this stress, and at the same time obtaining an uncontaminated account from witnesses, is to interview them appropriately in a way that is based on knowledge of child development gained by careful research studies. But more research is necessary on the practice of interviewing child witnesses, particularly the very young and those with particular problems such as communication difficulties.

Although official views have now accommodated the idea that young children are able effectively to bear witness in court, the general public – the potential members of juries – appear to be less sure about this. They have rather low expectations of children's capabilities, though they can be very impressed by a competent and confident child. One dilemma facing those conducting research on how best to prepare children to act as witnesses concerns ways of assisting the child to give a valid account but not in a way that appears too adult or too confident (even coached), which may result in jurors not believing the child if they expect children to be incompetent. And this has implications for interviewing procedures. Shuy (1986) suggested that jurors may be more impressed by a free narrative account from a child than by the more controlled, brief answer, fragmented testimony which often follows from certain styles of questioning.

ACTIVITY 6

Allow about 10 minutes

REAPPRAISING THE EVIDENCE

In Activity 1 you were invited to note your own thoughts about the trustworthiness of children's evidence in court. How have your views been affected by what you have read in this chapter? How convincing do you find the evidence offered? What types of future research would you identify as having potential value in progressing our understanding of the important issues in this area?

FURTHER READING

DENT, H. and FLIN, R. (1992) *Children as Witnesses,* Chichester, Wiley.

GOODMAN, G. and BOTTOMS, B. (eds) (1993) *Child Victims, Child Witnesses: understanding and improving testimony*, New York, Guilford.

OPEN UNIVERSITY (1993) *Investigative Interviewing with Children* (K501), Milton Keynes, Open University.

SPENCER, J. and FLIN, R. (1990) *The Evidence of Children: the law and the psychology,* London, Blackstone.

WALKER PERRY, N. and WRIGHTSMAN, L. (1991) *The Child Witness: legal issues and dilemmas*, Newbury Park (Calif.), Sage.

REFERENCES

ANDERSON, R. and PICHERT, J. (1978) 'Recall of previously unrecallable information following a shift in perspective', *Journal of Verbal Learning and Verbal Behaviour,* **17**, pp. 1–12.

BULL, R. (1992) 'Obtaining evidence expertly: the reliability of interviews with child witnesses', *Expert Evidence,* **1**, pp. 5–12.

BULL, R. (1995) 'Innovative techniques for the questioning of child witnesses especially those who are young and those with learning disability' in ZARAGOZA, M., GRAHAM, J., HALL, G., HIRSCHMAN, R. and BEN-PORATH, Y. (eds), *Memory and Testimony in the Child Witness,* Newbury Park (Calif.), Sage.

CHOI, S. (1991) 'Children's answers to yes-no questions: a developmental study in English, French, and Korean', *Developmental Psychology,* **27**, pp. 407–20.

CLYDE, J. (1992) *The Report of the Inquiry into the Removal of Children from Orkney in February, 1991*, Edinburgh, HMSO.

DAVIES, G. and NOON, E. (1991) *An Evaluation of the Live Link for Child Witnesses,* London, Home Office.

DeLOACHE, J. (1990) 'Young children's understanding of models' in FIVUSH, R. and HUDSON, J. (eds) *Knowing and Remembering in Young Children,* New York, Cambridge University Press.

DENT, H. (1986) 'An experimental study of the effectiveness of different techniques of questioning mentally handicapped child witnesses', *British Journal of Clinical Psychology,* **25**, pp. 12–17.

DEZWIREK-SAS, L. (1992) 'Empowering child witnesses for sexual abuse prosecution' in DENT, H. and FLIN, R. (eds) *Children as Witnesses*, Chichester, Wiley.

FELDMAN, R. and PHILIPPOT, P. (1991) 'Children's deception skills and social competence' in ROTENBERG, K. (ed.) *Children's Interpersonal Trust*, New York, Springer-Verlag.

FISHER, R. and GEISELMAN, R. (1992) *Memory-enhancing Techniques for Investigative Interviewing: the cognitive interview*, Springfield (Ill.), Thomas.

FLIN, R., BOON, J., KNOX, A. and BULL, R. (1992) 'The effect of a five-month delay on children's and adults' eyewitness memory', *British Journal of Psychology*, **83**, pp. 323–36.

FLIN, R. and BULL, R. (1990) 'Child witnesses in Scottish criminal proceedings' in SPENCER, J., NICHOLSON, G., FLIN, R. and BULL, R. (eds) *Children's Evidence in Legal Proceedings*, Cambridge, Faculty of Law.

FLIN, R., BULL, R., BOON, J. and KNOX, A. (1993) 'Child witnesses in Scottish criminal trials', *International Review of Victimology*, **2**, pp. 319–39.

GLASER, D. and FROSH, S. (1988) *Sexual Abuse*, Basingstoke, Macmillan.

GOODMAN, G. and BOTTOMS, B. (eds) (1993) *Child Victims, Child Witnesses: understanding and improving testimony*, New York, Guilford.

GOODMAN, G., GOLDING, J., HEGELSON, V., HAITH, M. and MICHELLI, J. (1987) 'When a child takes the stand: jurors' perceptions of children's eyewitness testimony', *Law and Human Behavior*, **11**, pp. 27–40.

HEDDERMAN, C. (1987) *Children's Evidence: the need for corroboration*, Research and Planning Unit, Paper 41, London, Home Office.

HEYDON, J. (1984; 2nd edn) *Evidence: cases and materials*, London, Butterworth.

HOME OFFICE (1933) *Children and Young Persons Act, 1933*, London, HMSO.

HOME OFFICE (1992) *Memorandum of Good Practice on Video Recorded Interviews with Child Witnesses for Criminal Proceedings*, London, HMSO.

JONES, D. and McQUISTON, M. G. (1988) *Interviewing the Sexually Abused Child*, London, Gaskell.

KÖHNKEN, G. (1990) 'The evaluation of statement credibility: social judgement and expert diagnostic approaches' in SPENCER, J., NICHOLSON, R., FLIN, R. and BULL, R. (eds) *Children's Evidence in Legal Proceedings: an international perspective*, Cambridge, Faculty of Law.

KÖHNKEN, G., FINGER, M., NITSCHKE, N., HÖFER, E. and ASCHERMANN, E. (1992) 'Does a cognitive interview interfere with a subsequent criteria-based content analysis of a statement?', paper presented at the meeting of the American Psychology–Law Society, San Diego.

LEIPPE, M. and ROMANCZYK, A. (1987) 'Children on the witness stand: a communication/persuasion analysis of jurors' reactions to child witnesses' in CECI, S., TOGLIA, M. and ROSS, D. (eds) *Children's Eyewitness Memory*, New York, Springer-Verlag.

LUUS, D. and WELLS, G. (1992) 'The perceived credibility of child eyewitnesses' in DENT, H. and FLIN, R. (eds) *Children as Witnesses*, Chichester, Wiley.

MCCARTNEY, K. and NELSON, K. (1981) 'Children's use of scripts in story recall', *Discourse Processes*, **4**, pp. 59–70.

MCCAULEY, M. and FISHER, R. (1992) 'Improving children's recall of action with the cognitive interview', paper presented at the meeting of the American Psychology–Law Society, San Diego.

MCGURK, H. and GLACHAN, M. (1988) 'Children's conversation with adults', *Children and Society*, **2**, pp. 20–34.

MEMON, A. and BULL, R. (1991) 'The cognitive interview: its origins, empirical support, evaluation and practical implications', *Journal of Community and Applied Social Psychology*, **1**, pp. 291–307.

MEMON, A. and KÖHNKEN, G. (1992) 'Helping witnesses to remember more: the cognitive interview', *Expert Evidence,* **1**, pp. 39–48.

MOSTON, S. (1990) 'How children interpret and respond to questions: situational sources of suggestibility in eyewitness interviews', *Social Behaviour*, **5**, pp. 155–67.

NIGRO, G., BUCKLEY, M., HILL, D. and NELSON, J. (1989) 'When juries "hear" children testify: the effects of eyewitness age and speech style on jurors' perceptions of testimony' in CECI, S., ROSS, D. and TOGLIA, M. (eds) *Perspectives on Children's Testimony*, New York, Springer-Verlag.

PIPE, M.-E., GEE, S. and WILSON, J. (1993) 'Cues, props and context: do they facilitate children's event reports?' in GOODMAN, G. and BOTTOMS, B. (eds) *Child Victims, Child Witnesses: understanding and improving testimony,* New York, Guilford.

POOLE, D. and WHITE, L. (1991) 'Effects of question repetition on the eyewitness testimony of children and adults', *Developmental Psychology*, **6**, pp. 975–86.

RASKIN, D. and ESPLIN, P. (1991) 'Statement validity assessment: interview procedures and context analysis of children's statements of sexual abuse', *Behavioural Assessment*, **13**, pp. 265–91.

ROSS, D., DUNNING, D., TOGLIA, M. and CECI, S. (1990) 'The child in the eyes of the jury: assessing mock jurors' perceptions of the child witness', *Law and Human Behavior*, **14**, pp. 5–23.

SAYWITZ, K., GEISELMAN, R. and BORNSTEIN, G. (1992) 'Effects of cognitive interviewing and practice on children's recall performance', *Journal of Applied Psychology*, **77**, pp. 744–56.

SAYWITZ, K., SNYDER, L. and LAMPHEAR, V. (1990) 'Preparing child witnesses: the efficiency of memory training strategy', paper presented at the Annual Convention of the American Psychological Association, Boston.

SHUY, R. (1986) 'Language and the law', *Annual Review of Applied Linguistics*, **7**, pp. 50–63.

SIGELMAN, C., BUDD, E., SPANHEL, C. and SCHOENROCK, C. (1981) 'Asking questions of retarded persons: a comparison of yes-no and either-or formats', *Applied Research in Mental Retardation*, **5**, pp. 347–57.

SPENCER, J. R. and FLIN, R. (1990) *The Evidence of Children: the law and the psychology*, London, Blackstone.

STELLER, M. and BOYCHUK, T. (1992) 'Children as witnesses in sexual abuse cases: investigative interview and assessment techniques' in DENT, H. and FLIN, R. (eds) *Children as Witnesses*, Chichester, Wiley.

TOGLIA, M., ROSS, D. and CECI, S. (1992) 'The suggestibility of children's memory: a social-psychological and cognitive interpretation' in HOWE, M., BRAINERD, C. and REYNA, C. (eds) *The Development of Long-term Retention*, New York, Springer-Verlag.

WARREN, A., HULSE-TROTTER, K. and TUBBS, E. C. (1991) 'Inducing resistance to suggestibility in children', *Law and Human Behavior*, **15**, pp. 273–85.

WHITE, S. (1990) 'The investigatory interview with suspected victims of child sexual abuse' in LA GRECA, A. (ed.) *Through the Eyes of the Child*, Boston, Allyn and Bacon.

YUILLE, J. (1988) 'The systematic assessment of children's testimony', *Canadian Psychology*, **29**, pp. 247–62.

YUILLE, J., HUNTER, R., JOFFE, R. and ZAPARNIUK, J. (1993) 'Interviewing children in sexual abuse cases' in GOODMAN, G. and BOTTOMS, B. (eds) *Child Victims, Child Witnesses: understanding and improving testimony*, New York, Guilford.

READING

Children giving evidence in criminal trials

R. Flin, R. Bull, J. Boon and A. Knox

Research method

The Flin *et al.* study was based in Glasgow. The research team received notification from the Procurators Fiscal (public prosecutors) of all children under 16 years of age called to give evidence as prosecution witnesses in the criminal courts. An attempt was made to observe as many of these children as possible within a period of 12 months. It should be emphasized that the majority of witnesses cited to give evidence do not actually find themselves in the witness box or even in court; accused persons frequently change their 'not guilty' pleas to 'guilty' in the run up to the trial, not all witnesses cited are required to give evidence, and not all trials listed will run on the first date scheduled. Over the 15-month study period (1988–9), 366 children were 'tracked' up to their attendance at court and 89 of these were observed to give evidence in 40 trials. In view of the large number of cases and the location of courts in different parts of the city it was necessary to adopt a prioritizing policy as to which cases the two research staff should attend in the event of more than one trial going ahead on a given day. The priorities in such instances were to attend the most serious cases and those trials which involved the youngest children.

With the permission of the presiding judge, the researcher sat in a discreet position as near to the child as possible to permit unobtrusive observation and the recording of data. Data were entered on a schedule which consisted of three subsections designed to record a comprehensive picture of the court, the people present, the case, the examinations and the demeanour of the child witness.

The first six children observed giving evidence were rated by both of the research staff and the inter-rater agreement was found to be 95%. However, good inter-rater reliability does not of itself mean that the rating scales are valid or accurate. These are obviously subjective impressions of the child's behaviour and responses and therefore the ratings can only be regarded as indicative of emotional state or linguistic competence.

Examinations-in-chief, cross-examinations and re-examinations

The children were questioned (i.e. examined) firstly by the prosecution and then, usually, by the defence lawyer(s). There were wide variations in terms of the number of examinations given, their duration, and the number of adjournments. Following the initial examination-in-chief (see explanation below) by the prosecution lawyer, 65 of the 89 children were cross-examined by one or more defence lawyers. A further examination was then required by the prosecution lawyer for 20 of the children who had been cross-examined. The average duration of the examination-in-chief was 16 minutes but this disguises large variations: they ranged from three to 92 minutes. The average duration of the subsequent cross-examination was 20 minutes but again there were wide variations around the mean figure (1–59 minutes). For those children who were re-examined by the prosecution the average duration was 4.5 minutes (range: 1–18 minutes).

The number of examinations which the court required of the child witnesses became less predictable where there were multiple accused. Although 52 (58%) of the children appeared in cases which were brought against a sole accused, 26 (29%) gave evidence in cases where there were five or more accused. The effect of having multiple accused could be dramatic, since each defence lawyer has the right to cross-examine the witness – a right which would almost certainly be exercised if the witness gave incriminating evidence regarding their client during the examination-in-chief. This meant, for example, that in one case involving eight accused, a child was examined no less than ten times: once with the examination-in-chief, eight cross-examinations by different lawyers, and a final re-examination by the prosecution!

Demeanour of child witnesses

When a child is a witness for the prosecution the aims of the three stages of legal examination are as follows. The initial examination-in-chief is an interview conducted by the prosecution lawyer in which questions are asked which are designed to elicit from the child the basic facts he or she knows relating to the alleged crime. This may then be followed by a cross-examination in which the defence lawyer attempts to cast doubt on the testimony previously given. In doing so it is usually necessary to ask questions which directly challenge the child such as, 'Are you sure that you saw X?', 'I put it to you that what you saw was in fact Y'. However, these sorts of questions are not solely the preserve of the defence. If, during the cross-examination, the child retracts something which was said during the examination-in-chief, the prosecution may wish to exercise its right to conduct a re-examination. If this happens, the prosecution may well need to put questions of an equally challenging nature to those put previously by the defence. It is not, therefore, simply the defence lawyers who may apply pressure to the child, but both sides, depending on the circumstances of the case and what has been said in the preceding examinations.

In the examination-in-chief and cross-examinations approximately 50% of the children were rated as being either unhappy or very unhappy, with 40% of those who were re-examined by the prosecution appearing unhappy. Similarly, half the children were rated as being tense or very tense during their examination.

The majority of children gave their evidence without becoming so obviously upset that they were reduced to tears. In the examinations-in-chief there were only five children who cried. In the 65 cross-examinations, five children were seen crying, while only one of the 18 children re-examined by the prosecution was moved to tears. Perhaps surprisingly, it was not usually the youngest children who cried but the older ones. To the extent that it is possible to generalize on the basis of these small numbers, there were three common strands. First, all those who cried were giving evidence in Sheriff or High Court cases; secondly, the evidence they gave was in relation to serious charges (i.e. murder, incest or assault to severe injury); and thirdly, it was at the point that they were questioned about the critical part of the incident that they broke down. However, while children may not in general become tearful in the courtroom, a much higher percentage appeared to be unhappy and tense while giving their evidence.

Ratings were also made as to the degree of self-confidence the children showed while delivering their evidence. These were made on the basis of the child's demeanour while giving evidence and not the degree of confidence a child expressed in his or her statements to the court. For example, some children were observed who seemed very shy and timid in the delivery of their testimony but who were clear and firm as to the sequence and nature of events which they were asked to describe. Conversely, some children showed highly confident and unabashed irritation at being pressed for details which they had already indicated they could not remember clearly. The children varied considerably in the degree of self-confidence which they showed. The ratings indicate that in the initial examination-in-chief and the cross-examination, 46% of the sample were able to cope at least to a reasonable extent, with a further 40% showing some degree of confidence. The remaining 14% of children were rated as lacking self-confidence.

Fluency of children's evidence and linguistic difficulties

While observing the children giving evidence, the researcher made ratings of their verbal performance and the appropriateness of the questioning technique used. There were six scales which recorded fluency, amount of detail, appropriateness of the vocabulary used by the lawyer, age-appropriateness of the grammar used by the lawyer, confidence in their statements and the number of 'don't know' or mute responses. The majority of children were relatively fluent and able to provide at least some detail.

Difficulties could emerge as a consequence of questions being put by the examining lawyer which were age-inappropriate either in terms of vocabulary or grammar. Although the majority of children (85%) were asked age-appropriate questions in terms of grammar, 12% of examinations-in-chief, and 40% of cross-examinations contained some vocabulary that the child appeared not to understand. The problem of incomprehension included instances where children were wrong-footed by questions containing double negatives, language which was unfamiliar, or grammatical constructions which were too difficult. Sometimes children answered with what they thought the lawyer wanted to know rather than asking for the question to be explained.

Where problems in understanding did occur they were by no means concentrated upon the younger children. One probable reason for this was that with very young witnesses the lawyers appeared to be conscious of the need to keep questions as simple as they could. Several instances were observed where there was a sense of frustration for all concerned at the failure to achieve an understanding of even questions relating to simple matters. The following examples of lawyers' questions to young children which were heard in court help to illustrate this:

'Did you form an impression about the piece of wood?'

'Did he then take offence?'

'May I take you back to the evidence you gave earlier?'

'What was the nature of the street lighting?'

'What is your position regarding …?'

Comparison of the effects of prosecution and defence questioning

The data showed that the children were no more likely to be rated as being unhappy, tense, faltering or lacking in self-confidence when answering the prosecution's questions than when answering the questions of the defence. Many defence lawyers would not be surprised that the children appeared to react in the same way to them as to the prosecution lawyers. They argue that it would not be in their interests to be seen putting children under pressure in the witness box since it might well lose them, and therefore their client, the sympathy of the court. This point, coupled with that made above concerning the need for prosecution lawyers sometimes to apply pressure, might account for the comparability in the ratings during the prosecution and defence examinations.

In terms of the language used, again little difference was found between the prosecution and the defence lawyers. No significant difference was found in the age appropriateness of the vocabulary used in questioning. However, significant differences were found with respect to the age appropriateness of the grammatical structures. These indicated that, on average, the prosecution lawyers were more successful in putting questions during the examination-in-chief at levels which the children could understand than were the defence lawyers during their cross-examinations.

Overview and conclusions

Misunderstandings on the part of both the lawyers and the children were observed regarding children's linguistic ability to cope with the questions which were put to them. These findings do not provide support for the view that the defence cross-examination is necessarily the most difficult part of the trial. While differences did emerge between defence and prosecution styles and the children's responses to them, they appeared to be a function of the style of examination being conducted rather than a simple distinction between defence and prosecution *per se*. Children's experiences while giving evidence in court are dependent on a host of internal and external factors.

One of the principal concerns about children as witnesses is that they are disadvantaged compared with adults in terms of their relative ability to understand the court proceedings, to give coherent evidence, and to cope with this experience. While the findings of this study indicate that the majority of children were able to give their evidence reasonably well in terms of providing at least some detail relatively fluently, a large percentage of children did appear tense and unhappy while doing so.

Source: adapted from Flin et al., 1993.

CHAPTER 5 LANGUAGE IMPAIRMENT AND DYSLEXIA

Dennis Bancroft

CONTENTS

1 INTRODUCTION

After this short introduction, this chapter consists of two separate, though related, sections. The first (Section 2) discusses the possibility that children who experience difficulty or delay in language development are vulnerable when they begin to learn to read, write and spell. Jane Oakhill has explored the view that there is a continuity between language development and literacy (Oakhill, 1995). This part of the chapter is intended to extend that discussion. Section 3, the largest part of the chapter, explores some of the psychological research which bears on the issue of developmental dyslexia. I argue that psychologists have a role to play in establishing the existence or otherwise of dyslexia, in making clear the development of literacy skill in children who have difficulties and, finally, in identifying appropriate remediation.

1.1 Terminology

Psychological investigations of children who have some difficulty with aspects of literacy often differ in the terms and expressions they use. Terms like 'retarded reader' are no longer acceptable to the wider community and have been replaced by descriptions which are less perjorative. In addition, psychologists who feel that they have novel material to convey may coin a new term or give a new meaning to an expression. In short, one problem facing a reader in this area is that of the varied and sometimes inconsistent use of terms. Another related problem is that some terms do not have general acceptance either in psychology or indeed elsewhere. The term 'dyslexia' is one of these. In my descriptions of research studies, I have retained the terms used by the original authors. Where a dispute exists, I try to identify it and outline some of the alternative positions.

2 LANGUAGE IMPAIRMENT

2.1 Literacy: a definition

Alison Garton and Chris Pratt (1989) offer a much broader definition of 'literacy' than is usual. They argue that the concept of literacy should embrace spoken language in addition to notions of reading and writing. Literacy is defined by them as 'the mastery of spoken language *and* reading and writing' (their emphasis) (Garton and Pratt, 1989, p. 1). The point that these authors develop is that there is a continuity between the spoken and written forms of the language in terms of development in addition to the commonplace idea that someone who is literate is also likely to be verbally fluent. In the introduction to their book, Garton and Pratt use two arguments to support this wider definition of literacy. The first is that written language is a 'second-order acquisition', dependent upon ('parasitic upon' is the expression they use) spoken language. The second is the claim that the process of learning each of these forms of language is similar in one important respect: in each case, the learner requires assistance from an interested and supportive adult.

This second argument is strongly implied in much of the literature concerning language development (see, for example, Bancroft, 1995), but is difficult to test experimentally. It was reported in antiquity that the following 'experiment' was conducted to investigate the natural course of development without adult intervention. Infants removed from their parents at birth were placed in the care of a mute person living in a remote spot. The idea was that, without the contaminating influence of a particular community's language habits, the language that the infants developed would determine which language was the natural language of humans. Post-experimental reporting was vague at the time and so much detail is lost. Supporters of the social constructivist view of language development will be relieved to know that the infants were described as developing no language at all.

The relationship between *normal* language development and reading skills is explored in detail by Jane Oakhill (1995). In the section that follows I look at some findings which have pointed to the relation between *impaired* language development and subsequent difficulties with reading. The ability to read is a crucial asset in our community and the basis of much formal education. A little later on I will describe research work which considered the development of groups of children. Before that, here are two 'case studies' of individual children. These descriptions are of real children although the names have been changed.

2.2 Case study: Graham

Graham is 10 years old and is in his last year at primary school. He has always enjoyed going to school and particularly likes football and maths (in that order). He has recently become unhappy and withdrawn at home and at school. He told his mother that he couldn't read and that he was scared of transferring to secondary school. His teachers share his concern and say that his reading is at 'the six year level'. He has received a lot of extra help from the 'special needs' teacher in his school. In fact, he has been withdrawn from his class for extra reading several times a week for the last three years.

Graham has felt increasingly resentful at missing other lessons and embarrassed that the other children knew that he needed extra help. This feeling has turned into anger towards the teachers and himself as he has realized that he is making no progress. Graham also has great difficulty in constructing words and sentences. He has plenty of ideas about what he wants to write but spends long periods waiting in the queue for the teacher to write the next word in his personal 'spelling dictionary'.

A language specialist visited Graham at school and assessed his language. The assessment took place over several visits and was conducted in a variety of contexts. Graham's speech is described as indistinct and hard to understand. The school records show that Graham had been referred for speech therapy when he was four years old. Graham had attended sporadically for 18 months and then stopped going altogether. The records also showed that Graham had had 'glue ear' (i.e. his hearing was impaired) as a small child and continued to suffer from catarrh. After his language assessment, Graham was seen, once again, by a speech therapist who discovered that he found it difficult to distinguish between some English sounds. For example, Graham found it difficult to distinguish between the vowel sounds themselves and between some sound groups like 'str' and 'dr'. (This means that a word like 'drain' could be 'strain' or 'drone' as far as Graham was concerned.)

Graham was apparently unable to 'hear' the sounds as different. His teachers had concentrated on helping Graham match letter sounds to printed letters and he had made a little progress but because of his difficulty in distinguishing sounds he was unable to work at the level the teachers intended.

The problem was identified for Graham and related to his earlier difficulties with hearing and speech. Graham, reassured that he was not 'stupid', was able to accept the regular input from the various specialists. With this attention and increasing confidence he began to enjoy reading and made progress. After a year Graham has much improved although he still reads slowly and sounds out words when writing.

ACTIVITY 1

Allow about 15 minutes

UNDERSTANDING GRAHAM

List some of the effects that Graham's dulled hearing might have on his language and the language of people around him.

(a)

(b)

(c)

(d)

Comment

You might have pointed to the connection between the disturbance to Graham's hearing and his ability to distinguish between some of the subtle (but crucial) sound distinctions of English. Most people use language skill as an indicator of ability and pitch their input accordingly. You might therefore have suggested that Graham would be spoken to in a simpler way. This exposure to a simplified linguistic environment could reduce Graham's chances of learning or practising more sophisticated usage (see Chapter 6).

2.3 Case study: Catherine

Catherine is aged 7 and attends a unit for children described as having speech and language difficulties. The unit is attached to her school. Catherine started at her local primary school at the age of 5 but her teacher and, later, an educational psychologist observed that she had difficulty understanding what was said to her. She was unable to sit and listen to a story and constantly interrupted when other people were talking or reading aloud.

Catherine was happy to talk to the other children in her class but her stories and anecdotes were disconnected and she seemed to lose her way in the telling. When she was told to sit down, or when other children lost interest in what she was saying, she became truculent. At first it was thought that Catherine's difficulties were caused by a 'behaviour problem'. Her parents contested this view, saying that they thought that Catherine had difficulty in understanding and in expressing herself.

A language specialist confirmed this opinion and noted that while Catherine could understand individual words and phrases, she could not understand when they were part of a connected narrative or part of a complex instruction. Catherine experienced particular difficulty with connectives (such as 'and', 'so' and 'because') and with temporal adverbs (such as 'before' and 'after'). These words, together with grammatical order, indicate the relationships between events and persons.

ACTIVITY 2

Allow about 20 minutes

UNDERSTANDING CATHERINE

The purpose of this exercise is to try to allow you to observe something of Catherine's world for yourself. First, cut a short article out of a newspaper. Ink out all the instances of the following words: 'and', 'so', 'then', 'now', 'if', 'because', 'before', 'after', 'while', 'during', 'still', 'but'.

Once you have done this, get someone else to read the passage and tell you what it means. They should experience considerable difficulty, although their implicit knowledge of grammar will be a help.

2.4 Research investigations

Several research strategies are available to investigate the relationship between language and literacy. One is to begin with a sample of children who are experiencing difficulty with reading and/or spelling and to check their history to see if they had delayed or unusual language development. Some of the earliest investigations in the field were of this kind. One finding was that children with reading difficulties were often reported as being 'late talkers'. This finding suggests a link between language development and reading difficulties but lacks specificity and is problematic since records of children's language development vary in quality and accuracy. There could be a range of factors contributing to reading difficulty, of which delayed language skill was only one. Retrospective studies of this kind do not easily allow researchers to isolate the influence of the various possible factors.

A second strategy is to follow the development of children who are identified as being late or aberrant talkers. Once the children are identified, they are revisited at points during their development when further measures are made. The study by Bishop and Adams (1990), described below, is of this kind.

A third option is to investigate the language skills of children who have been identified as having difficulty with reading. There are two problems with this approach. First, children with reading problems may have had some difficulty with language which is no longer apparent, and second, it is often difficult to distinguish between consequence and cause (for example an apparent lack of verbal fluency may be a consequence of limited success in reading rather than the cause of that limited success). This last issue is a problem which has dogged the efforts of researchers, particularly with respect to investigation of dyslexia. It will be treated more fully later on in the chapter.

A study of language impairment and reading disorder

Dorothy Bishop and colleagues conducted a series of investigations, beginning in the early 1980s, of the relationship between language impairment and reading disorder. The same group of children was used throughout. In this longitudinal approach, measures of the children's performance are made at each stage, so that relationships between early development and later difficulties can be identified. Bishop and Edmundson (1987) had around 90 children referred to them by speech therapists and paediatricians. The children were all about 4 years old. They were referred because they had some impairment of language development which could not be attributed to low intelligence, hearing loss or physical defect. Some of the group of referred children were considered to have delayed non-verbal as well as delayed verbal development. The 19 children who were so identified were described in the study as the 'general delay group'. This left a remainder of about 70 children who were described as having a specific language impairment (SLI). That is to say, the difficulties experienced by these children could not be attributed to any other factor since those children where this might have been the case were omitted from the sample.

The SLI children were given a range of tests at the ages of 4.5 and 5.5. By the time the children in the sample had reached the age of 5.5, some of them no longer showed any evidence of impaired language. On this basis, Bishop assigned the SLI children to one of two groups which they called the 'good outcome at 5' group and the 'poor outcome at 5' group.

> In classifying children into these subgroups, we do not wish to imply that there are sharp divisions between those with good and poor outcomes ... However, the distinction can be of use ... where one wishes to ask such questions as whether language-delayed children who appear to have recovered by 5.5 years will go on to have literacy problems.
>
> (Bishop and Adams, 1990, p. 1028)

Most of the children seen in this study were revisited when they had reached 8.5 years and given a battery of tests designed to investigate their current language and literacy skills. The range of tests given to the children at each stage was quite comprehensive and covered such matters as receptive vocabulary, grammatical understanding, comprehension, knowledge of sounds, mean length of utterance (MLU), reading and spelling. In addition to the children who had been referred, the experimenters also saw a control group of 30 children who were matched to the referred children in terms of age. There were equivalent proportions of girls and boys in the referred and control groups.

Accuracy and comprehension in reading

The data from the different parts of the study were investigated using a range of statistical techniques which identify relationships between the various measures. One outcome was that the results at age 8.5 indicate that the children who had been referred (the whole group is known as the language-delayed group) were reading as *accurately* as the children in the control group but were worse than these children in terms of *comprehension*. Further investigation allowed Bishop and Adams to conclude 'the poor reading comprehension scores obtained by the language-delayed group can be explained in terms of their generally poor language understanding' (Bishop and Adams, 1990, p. 1034).

Within the 'language-delayed group' are three sub-groups, those with a 'general delay', those who had improved by the age of 5 (the good outcome group) and those who had not improved by the age of 5 (the poor outcome group). After the researchers had established that the language-delayed children were reading as accurately as the controls, they investigated the data further to see if the children in the 'good outcome' group, in particular, were reading *using the same strategies* as the control group. The researchers wondered whether the 'good outcome at 5' children who had a history of language impairment might have a problem in learning the sounds of words. If this was so, they might be less able to use this knowledge of sounds to work out the overall sound of words and would be obliged to learn words as wholes.

In order to investigate this possibility, the researchers asked the children to read and spell non-words (words like 'siv' and 'drange'). Since none of the children would have come across these words before, Bishop

TABLE 1   The mean phoneme errors out of 25 in reading and spelling non-words.

| | Control | Language-delayed group | | |
		Good outcome at age 5	Poor outcome at age 5	General delay
	N = 30	N = 29	N = 37	N = 16
Non-word reading	7.7	5.3	12.3	16.1
Non-word spelling	5.7	3.4	8.1	16.3

N = number of children in each group.
Source: Bishop and Adams, 1990, p. 1034.

and Adams reasoned that children who were able to use knowledge of sounds would be better at reading and spelling them than the children who could not.

As you can see from Table 1, the children in the second column (good outcome at age 5) made rather fewer errors than the control group of normally developing children. Statistically, the difference between these two groups is small and could have easily occurred by chance. Both the other groups of children made many more phoneme (sound) errors which suggests that these were the children who were forced to use the strategy of 'recognition' which is not effective with new (or non-) words.

To summarize:

• Children referred for impaired language development are not all the same. Some appear to be more generally delayed while some appear delayed in language alone. Of the latter, some then catch up by 5 while others do not.

• By the time the referred children are 8 they read as accurately as normally developing children but with less comprehension.

• Finally, the referred children who appear to catch up (the 'good outcome' group) can use sound-based strategies for reading and spelling in a similar manner to children in the control group.

Predicting problems

Bishop and Adams raise and discuss many other issues in their paper. The one most pertinent to this chapter is that of prediction. Which of the many tests and measurements they made at the beginning of the study would predict later difficulty with reading and spelling? There are several possibilities. First, that

> children with phonological disorders [problems with the sounds of words] will be at particular risk for reading and spelling difficulties, and their problems will be characterized by lack of awareness of letter–sound correspondences, i.e. they should have particular difficulty with non-words.
>
> (Bishop and Adams, 1990, p. 1039)

Another possibility is that children who have difficulty with the rules of language structure (syntax) and/or the meaning of words and expressions (semantics) will have difficulty with reading and spelling. Each of these possibilities can be investigated using the data collected by Bishop and colleagues.

Does early phonological disorder mean later reading problems?
The way the researchers chose to investigate this possibility was to
identify those children who, at the beginning of the study, had *only*
phonological disorders. They found 12 such children. The extent of the
disorder ranged from mild to severe. Bishop reports that this group of
children were able readers and spellers by the time they reached 8 years
of age, and in fact were reading and spelling as well as the children in
the control group.

Returning to the whole group of children when they were 5 years old,
Bishop and Adams also looked at those children who had shown a range
of problems when first seen and who had improved, leaving only some
residual phonological difficulty. This group of children was investigated
also. As before it was found that when these children had reached 8
years of age they were, in general, reading and spelling as well as the
children in the control group.

Although children who had early problems with the sounds of language
caught up well, a further analysis revealed they *were* able to use one
particular phonological measure, that of children's ability to produce the
range of sounds in the language, to predict a child's reading accuracy at
the age of eight. The authors concluded:

> Expressive phonology [ability to make language sounds] did not
> begin to show substantial correlations with literacy test scores
> until 5.5 years of age, when the child was first learning to read.
> Phonological competence in 4–5 year olds ... did account for a
> significant proportion of variance in reading accuracy once the
> effects of general language competence had been allowed.

> (Bishop and Adams, 1990, p. 1043)

What do these rather complex results seem to be saying? First, children
who had early difficulties with *distinguishing* language sounds
nonetheless develop literacy skills which are the equal of the control
group children. However, performance on a test in which children had to
produce a range of sounds was related to later reading accuracy. It is
clear that further research is needed to clear up this apparent
contradiction. A detailed scrutiny of data like these can take our
understanding further forward but, as in this case, it can also suggest
new and possibly fruitful lines of enquiry to follow up.

Syntactic skills and literacy problems
The children in Bishop's study were given many different tests of
language development and ability. Using statistical techniques, the
researchers investigated the results from these tests to see if there were
relationships between the language test given at the age of 4 and the
literacy measures given at the age of 8. 'The strongest and most
consistent 4.5 year old predictor of subsequent reading ability is MLU'
(Bishop and Adams, 1990, p. 1041).

'MLU' is short for 'mean length of utterance' which was calculated for
children at ages 4 and 5 by counting the number of morphemes (the
meaning-bearing parts of words) produced in response to two particular

tests of vocabulary. MLU is usually obtained by counting the number of words spoken and dividing this by the number of times the child spoke. In order to get a high MLU, one needs to produce long grammatical strings of words within each utterance. The lowest MLU one could get would be an MLU of 1, which would be the MLU of a child who always gave one-word answers. (The nature and value of the MLU measure is discussed by Bancroft, 1995.) It seems therefore that the *amount* of connected speech produced by pre-literate children is related to subsequent performance in reading and writing.

Bishop and Adams conclude that:

> Contrary to what we expected, children who grow out of their early language difficulties (our group with good outcome at 5 years) were not at risk for literacy problems. Children who still have evident language impairment at the age of 5.5 years are likely to have reading and spelling difficulties, but these will not be isolated problems, but will occur in the context of persisting deficits in comprehension and expression of spoken language.
>
> (Bishop and Adams, 1990, p. 1046)

In the remainder of the chapter we will turn our attention to a different although perhaps related area of literacy difficulties, developmental dyslexia. In this area also, psychologists have been busy trying to understand the nature of a problem which confronts some children and to suggest suitable tactics for remediation. It may be the case that overlap between language impairment and developmental dyslexia will depend on the definition of developmental dyslexia that is used. As Bishop and Adams point out, if dyslexia is defined as a problem with literacy alone in the presence of otherwise normal abilities, and if 'normal abilities' include both *verbal* and *non-verbal* ability, then some children with literacy problems will not be described as dyslexic because they have language impairment, i.e. lower than normal verbal ability. If verbal ability is excluded and the criterion is a literacy problem associated with normal non-verbal ability, then there will be some overlap between language impairment and dyslexia. Verbal and non-verbal ability is usually assessed by measuring a child's performance on an intelligence test (see Example 1).

READING

The reading by Jane Oakhill at the end of this chapter describes something of the importance of literacy and its contribution to a person's development. At this point in the chapter you have been introduced to the relationship between language development and the development of literacy. Parents and educators are usually very concerned when confronted by a child who is having difficulty in becoming literate. Before going on to the next section, read what Jane Oakhill says as it will give you a psychological basis from which to appreciate this concern.

EXAMPLE 1
VERBAL AND NON-VERBAL INTELLIGENCE

Tests of intelligence can consist of a range of different 'sub-tests' measuring things like vocabulary and pattern matching. These sub-tests can be grouped into those which investigate verbal ability and those which investigate those aspects of intelligence not involving language. By this means it is possible to measure something of the intellectual ability of a person who has little or no language skill. If, as in this case, 'language' is under investigation, it is useful to have a means of investigating ability which is independent of language.

By way of example, verbal measures include tests of comprehension and vocabulary while non-verbal measures might involve matching patterns or completing puzzles.

SUMMARY OF SECTION 2

- The concept of 'literacy' can embrace skill with spoken language as well as the more widely understood skills of reading and writing. In other words, there may be a continuity between the spoken form of the language and other forms.

- Research strategies investigating links between early and later language skills have been of various kinds. Among the most effective have been longitudinal studies which follow children through the process of becoming literate.

- In order to establish a continuity between language development and later difficulties with literacy, I have described in some detail one particular study which is representative of several others and which has proposed some conclusions, two of which are particularly important.

- The first is that children with some forms of early language impairment are likely to experience continuing difficulties in comprehending spoken language as well as some related problems with reading and spelling.

- The second is the observation that children who recover from impairment make progress which is every bit as good as that of the children in the control group.

- The contribution of these psychologists to the development of children with language impairment is twofold: first, they have pointed to particular areas of language which predict later development; and secondly, they have found that recovery (and perhaps remediation?) can lead to apparently normal development.

3 'DYSLEXIA': A SUITABLE CASE FOR TREATMENT?

3.1 Introduction

"IT WAS SUPPOSED TO BE CALLED 'A NO SMILA' — BUT LEONARDO WAS DYSLEXIC."

In this part of the chapter I will consider some aspects of the issue of 'dyslexia' (more specifically *developmental dyslexia* to distinguish our topic from the problems that can result from neurological damage). It is important to be aware, at the outset, that not everyone would agree that there is a definable group of children, different from all others, that can be described as 'dyslexic'. There are two broad positions. The first is that there is such a group whose development of the literacy skills of reading and spelling is different in *kind* from other children. The other view accepts the idea that there are children for whom the development of these skills is a particular problem, but sees these children as developing in a similar way to others, differing only in the *extent* of their difficulty. Research evidence in this area offers some support for each position without ruling out either. However, one positive consequence of interest in this area has been the development of techniques which may assist most children learning to be literate, whether or not they can be described as 'dyslexic'.

The dispute between these two positions is no mere academic pastime as the educational experience (and success) of some children depends upon which view is taken. Since the 1981 Education Act, local education authorities are obliged to meet any special educational needs that are identified. If there is a group of children with an identifiable educational need, then resources must be found to meet that need. In times of scarce resources, local authorities can be reluctant to accept that the condition of 'dyslexia' exists. If they take this position, then they also take the view that they do not need to provide additional resources. Alternatively, some parents, educators and psychologists *do* consider that dyslexia is a specific learning difficulty which constitutes a need to be met under the provisions of the 1981 Act.

Research directed at resolving this issue is a clear point of contact between psychology and the concerns of people in the wider community. It can take the matter further in two ways. First, by recognizing that there are a number of children with no known explanation for their difficulty in developing literacy skills, psychologists have been involved in clarifying the reading and spelling strategies used by poor readers and those used by normal readers. Secondly, psychologists have been concerned to develop and evaluate appropriate remedial techniques. This latter development clearly depends upon the successful identification of the particular problems that children can experience.

ACTIVITY 3

Allow about 20 minutes

TERMINOLOGY

At the beginning of the chapter, I drew your attention to the range of descriptions applied to those children who are experiencing difficulty with literacy. Using the chart below, make a note of as many of these as you can find together with your assessment of them as positive, negative or neutral terms.

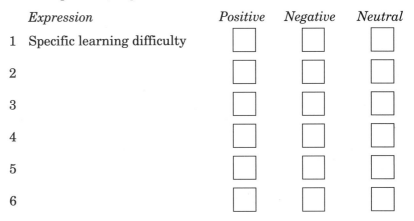

	Expression	Positive	Negative	Neutral
1	Specific learning difficulty	☐	☐	☐
2		☐	☐	☐
3		☐	☐	☐
4		☐	☐	☐
5		☐	☐	☐
6		☐	☐	☐

Comment

There are at least two forces at work behind the introduction of new terms. One of these is the concern that children should not be identified in negative terms where this can be avoided. Secondly, it is sometimes the case that psychologists employ a new term to more accurately capture what they see as the particular characteristics of the children in their study. In both cases, without general agreement, the results can be confusing.

3.2 Some definitions

As was hinted in the final paragraph of the preceding part of the chapter, which children become identified and described as 'dyslexic' can depend on the definition that is used. Some writers insist that the condition is specific and no children whose reading difficulties may result from some other factor should be included. They suggest that children may fail to read and spell for a variety of reasons, many of which are external to the child. The first definition below is of this form. It comes from the World Federation of Neurology report of 1968.

Definition 1

[Dyslexia is] a disorder manifested by difficulty in learning to read despite conventional instruction, adequate intelligence and socio-economic opportunity. It is dependent upon fundamental cognitive difficulties which are frequently of constitutional origin.

(quoted in Snowling, 1987, p. 2)

As Margaret Snowling (1987) observes, there are considerable problems with this definition, not least because many of its terms lack definition. For example, how much intelligence is 'adequate' and what is 'conventional instruction'? It is assumed in this definition that its subject children are a definable group distinguishable from other children. As we have seen, not everyone accepts this view. One other point to note about this definition is that it is medical in origin and dates from the time when reading difficulties were thought to be a medical problem.

Definition 2
Developmental Dyslexia [is] a learning disability which initially shows itself by difficulty in learning to read, and later by erratic spelling and by lack of facility in manipulating written as opposed to spoken words. The condition is cognitive in essence, and usually genetically determined. It is not due to intellectual inadequacy or to lack of socio-cultural opportunity, or to emotional factors, or to any known structural brain defect. It probably represents a specific maturation defect which tends to lessen as the child grows older, and is capable of considerable improvement, especially when appropriate remedial help is offered at the earliest opportunity.

(Critchley and Critchley, 1978, p. 149)

ACTIVITY 4

Allow about 10 minutes

COMPARING DEFINITIONS

(a) You now have two definitions, both deriving from a medical viewpoint. Compare the two and list the similarities and differences that have surfaced in the ten years between them.

(b) Do the differences represent an advance? If so, in what way(s)?

Comment

You might have noted that both definitions make a point of saying what the dyslexic child is *not*. That is, he/she is not the victim of poor teaching or lack of opportunity and so forth. Differences include greater detail in the second definition and an indication that improvement is possible, especially if remedial help is forthcoming. Perhaps you have been able to identify other differences.

One important idea which follows from these definitions is that in order to identify a child as dyslexic one needs to establish that there is no other possible cause for the child's difficulties. This includes establishing that the child's intellectual ability is at least average to eliminate the possibility that the child's problems are a consequence of a lack of general ability. The psychological assessment of children thought to be dyslexic often follows this line. The child's ability is established by a formal intellectual test and then the child's literacy skills are assessed. A pronounced mismatch between the two is taken as evidence of a *specific* problem. Critchley (1970) lists some common features of 'dyslexic' reading and spelling which include:

(a) reversals and rotations of letters;

(b) omissions of syllables;

(c) difficulty in keeping place when reading;

(d) the inability to pronounce unfamiliar words.

Such checklists have been much used and are, indeed, useful for focusing attention upon a child's reading and spelling performance. However, there are three problems with such lists. The first is that many of the 'signs' are produced by children whose development is normal so it becomes difficult to know how frequent a sign needs to be to indicate the existence of a problem. Secondly, it may be the case that some signs are of greater significance and diagnostic value than others. No information is given concerning this possibility. Finally, it is not clear how many of these 'signs' need to be present for a diagnosis to be made.

To summarize where we have got to so far:

- The wider community is not neutral with respect to research into dyslexia, and so great care and objectivity is needed if the psychological contribution is to be recognized as of value.

- There have been attempts to define a condition of 'dyslexia'. Not infrequently these take the form of definitions by exclusion, i.e. saying what the condition is *not* rather than what it is.

- Although definitions and checklists seem to be plausible and helpful, they turn out to be somewhat problematic.

3.3 The task of readers

Before we go on to look at research into reading, you may find it helpful to explore something of the nature of the task facing children learning to read English. We will consider research into the process of reading development. With this background, we will move on to explore the nature of difficulties experienced by backward readers. It will be possible to identify some of the means of assisting reading development. I will end this section by discussing some of the wider issues concerning the nature of reading difficulty and the contribution made by psychological research.

Historical origins of English spelling

Much psychological research has been directed at trying to understand the problems some children have in learning to read. It is possible that one problem can be located in the nature of the *task* confronting children, i.e. in the language itself. It seems possible that the earliest form of writing where symbols were used to represent words was derived from pictures or (more abstractly) pictograms. Some modern languages still have this character. For example, written Chinese is composed of stylized forms of an earlier picture writing. Such a language is described as 'logographic'. A more flexible development of writing occurred when symbols were used to represent the *sounds* used in language. The important points to note here are that written languages are derived from spoken languages and that most modern written languages use symbols to represent the sounds of a language rather than concepts.

Horse   Forest

Cart   Growing field

FIGURE 1
Some Chinese words.

Although it is generally true that the sounds of individual letters are closely related to the sounds of words, in some languages this relationship is closer than in others. Andrew Ellis (1984) uses the term 'transparent' to describe those languages in which the sound of a word is conveyed unambiguously by the letters which make it up. An example of a 'transparent' language is Italian and an example of a partially transparent language is English. Pleas for transparency in the spelling of English words have not always met with approval. For example, the eighteenth-century writer Jonathan Swift took the opposite view:

> Another cause, which hath maimed our language, is a foolish opinion that we ought to *spell* exactly as we speak.
>
> (Swift, quoted in the definition of 'spell' in Johnson's *Dictionary*, 1773)

There are some words in written English which are transparent: their pronunciation closely follows an assembly of the sounds of their component letters, for example 'cat' and 'jump'. There are also many English words whose letters do not easily relate to the sound of the word as a whole, for example 'women' and 'yacht'. Andrew Ellis reports that this was not always so and that in earlier times 'words were spelled as they were pronounced ... [so] ... spellings varied from place to place as their dialect pronunciations varied' (Ellis, 1984, p. 5).

Transparent spellings of the previous examples are 'wimin' and 'yot'. Two main factors have probably contributed to our present spellings. The first is the introduction of printing, which, among other things, had the effect of standardizing spelling. The second is the influence of spelling reformers who altered transparent English spellings like 'sythe' to the less clear 'scythe' in order to stress the supposed classical (and therefore high status) origins of the word. The process of fixing the spellings of English words was largely completed by dictionary writers in the eighteenth century. Until this time a spelling was 'right' if its pronunciation sounded right. The quotations from Dr Johnson's famous *Dictionary* found in this section are in memory of his contribution to the difficulties faced by present generations of English-speaking school children.

Although the rest of the chapter is concerned with the difficulties that some children have in learning to read and spell, we should remember that the language which they are learning appears, at times, to be contrived to make life difficult for them. In other words, the problem does not lie solely with them or with their teaching.

3.4 Reading difficulty and research

We have arrived at a point where we have some idea of the task facing children when they begin to learn to read English. In addition, psychologists have elucidated something of the usual course of development. For example, one prominent model of the development of reading (Frith, 1985) describes a progression from the recognition of particular words as complete entities (logographic stage), through the ability to analyse words in terms of their component sounds (alphabetic stage) and finally to rapid recognition (the orthographic strategy used by mature readers; see Oakhill, 1995, for an extended discussion). There are some children for whom the task of learning to read presents enormous difficulties. One early explorer in the field was a Glaswegian eye surgeon, James Hinshelwood, who noted cases of what he termed 'word blindness' (Hinshelwood, 1917). Hinshelwood considered the condition to be congenital, to occur in otherwise normal children and to resist ordinary methods of teaching. Although Hinshelwood's work has long been superseded, the expression 'word blindness' still has some currency. This is unfortunate since as well as being literally untrue (the children are not in any sense 'blind'), it implies a perceptual deficit which has misled some subsequent workers. Hinshelwood, however, is due some credit for drawing attention to the problem.

In the United States, Samuel Orton noted that one of the most striking features of poor readers was that they seemed unable to preserve the order of letters in words they were asked to read and spell (Orton, 1937). Orton also suggested that there was a genetic involvement and that among children with this difficulty there was some evidence of mixed laterality (e.g., being right-handed and left-footed). It is to Orton that we owe the imposing term 'strephosymbolia' (literally 'twisted symbols') as a description of the condition. Orton also described some difficulties with the ordering of the components of a word, for example 'enemy' might be read as 'emeny'. Other striking observations concerned what he termed 'reversals'. These could be of two forms. The first was the tendency to reverse the order of letters in a word, e.g., 'was' being read as 'saw'. The second kind of reversal involved the substitution of one letter for a similar letter having a different orientation, for example reading 'b' as 'd'. One final point to note about these pioneers is that they were both medical men. Part of their legacy has been the idea that failure to read is a medical condition (see the discussion of medical and psychological models in Chapter 1).

As we noted above, this is not the only view that can be taken. One operational definition found in the research literature takes a 'backward reader' to be a child of average or above average ability, whose reading and/or spelling performance is two years less than that reasonably expected given the child's intellectual ability as indicated by a standard test. In order to 'unpack' this operational definition, one should note that no cause is presumed. Children are given standard measures of literacy and ability. All other things being equal, one would expect that children of average intellectual ability would be reading/spelling also at the average level, i.e. a level consistent with their overall ability.

The research conducted by Rutter and Yule (1975) on the Isle of Wight is often cited as the basis for this expectation. This study, which was on a very large scale, showed something of the expected relationship between literacy skills and measures of general ability although the correlation found was not very strong. One problem with the operational definition above is that children of low ability are excluded, presumably on the grounds that any reading or spelling difficulties that they have

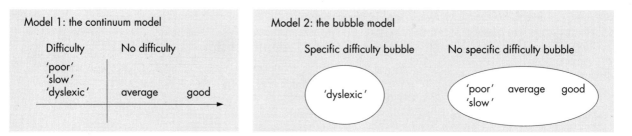

FIGURE 2
Two models of reading ability.

could be attributed to their level of ability rather than a particular difficulty with reading. While the exclusion of these children may have a sound methodological basis, there could be a practical disadvantage for these children if they are thought not likely to benefit from remedial intervention.

Another problem relates to the debate I referred to at the beginning of this section between those who think that what is called dyslexia is a characteristic of a specific group of children, and those who think that children described as dyslexic are not an identifiable group but are at one end of the continuum of all persons learning to read. The problem is that the operational definition asserts what the research seeks to establish, hardly an open-minded approach.

In summary,

- Part of the process of learning to read involves learning the relationship between letter and letter groups and words.
- Learning to read can be problematic because in some languages the relationship between the sound of some words and the sounds of their components is not transparent.
- While most children master this problem, there are some children for whom it remains difficult.
- Early medical interest in the problem focused attention on the perceptual and cognitive difficulties experienced by an apparently definable group of children.

In other words, we have identified a problem and have some ideas about its cause. We should now look at the outcomes of research investigations to see if the problem remains as originally specified and if the proposed causes have some substance. We will also be interested to resolve which of the alternatives, continuum or syndrome, is supported by the evidence.

Dyslexia as a problem of visual memory

Definitions of dyslexia found in the literature seek to describe the whole condition of a person. The research I am about to describe has a much narrower focus as it deals with specific aspects of difficulty. For example, as I noted above, some of the earliest suggestions made to account for otherwise able children's difficulty in learning to read involved the idea that they might have some specific perceptual problem. Perhaps, it was thought, children with reading difficulties might have a poor visual memory and, as a result, be unable to recognize parts of words and common groups of letters.

ACTIVITY 5

Allow about 30 minutes

DESIGN A STUDY

(a) Sketch out a research study to investigate the possibility that poor readers have worse visual memory than other children. Your study will need some groups of children to compare with each other and a suitable task for them to do.

(b) What groups of children will you choose? What task seems appropriate?

Comment

An obvious research technique much employed in this area is to compare the performance of poor readers with a similar group of normal readers. 'Similar' in this case usually means similar in terms of mental age or chronological age. The groups of children might be presented with brief exposures of groups of letters or words. The dependent variable or outcome would be how accurate the various groups were in recognizing the target words.

Suppose your study finds a difference in performance between the two groups. Would this not point to a problem in the processing of visual material as the cause of the reading difference? Unfortunately, as many writers have pointed out, your data indicates a difference but gives no indication as to its cause. The problem is that we know that a person's performance on tasks of this kind is not static throughout life and one can improve through experience. The kind of experience that might help to improve one's ability to recognize and recall letter groups might well be the experience that comes from reading itself. If this is so, reading could be the *cause* of improved performance rather than poor reading being the *consequence* of a perceptual problem.

In order to avoid this problem you might have chosen to compare groups of poor and normal readers matched on the basis of their reading age (thus removing the possible advantage of experience from the normal

---

RESEARCH SUMMARY 1
CAUSE OR EFFECT?

A study of the kind described above was done in 1973 by Frank Vellutino and colleagues. He matched children of the same age and compared the performance of normal and dyslexic readers on a task which asked them to copy from memory words of about four letters which the children had been shown briefly. As one might expect, the dyslexic group were worse on this task than the normal readers. So far we don't know if this outcome is a cause or a consequence of the reading difficulty. In a separate part of the study Vellutino repeated the task, only this time using words written in Hebrew rather than in English. None of the children was familiar with this sort of writing. The dyslexics were just as good as the normal readers on this task. This finding supports the view that the difference in performance found in the first part of the study was a consequence of reading experience rather than a cause of reading failure.

readers). Any difference found between the groups now could not be as a result of the greater reading experience of the normal readers. This somewhat complex reasoning appears to have defeated any number of psychologists and as a result many of the studies purporting to identify the deficits of children with specific reading difficulty do no such thing.

ACTIVITY 6
Allow at least 40 minutes

A MEMORY TEST

(a) Make a set of ten cards (postcard-sized). Print a different group of four letters of English (e.g. 'chdl' or 'setz') on each of five cards (be sure not to use proper words). On the other five cards, print a group of four Greek symbols, e.g., 'δαφτ'. Here are some for you to choose from:

$$\delta \, \epsilon \, \iota \, \sigma \, \beta \, \alpha \, \nu \, \chi \, \rho \, o \, \phi \, \tau$$

(b) The next step is to find a subject. Show your subject each card *very briefly* (one or two seconds). After they have seen each, give them time to write down the letters they had been shown before showing the next. Keep your cards and the subject's notes in the same order (it may help if you have unobtrusively numbered your cards).

(c) Average the number of correctly copied letters for, first, the English and, second, the Greek versions. Any difference you find is likely to be as a result of your subject's greater familiarity with the English alphabet.

Presumably your subject's memory will have the same capacity in each case although familiarity with English might help them *use it* more efficiently. By the by, why is it a good idea to make sure that your subject is not a mathematician?

Dyslexia as a problem of memory

Remaining with the issue of memory, there has been considerable interest in the possibility that children with reading difficulty have poor memories in general. This would become apparent not only in reading where one needs to remember words and letters, but also in other aspects of life such as remembering shopping lists or the order of the months of the year. This possibility has been investigated by several groups of researchers. For example, Holmes and McKeever (1979) presented two groups of 13 year olds with the task of recalling faces and words. The group of poor readers was worse than the normal readers when the task involved recalling words. As before, because this research used an age match we are not able to decide whether this outcome is the cause or consequence of poor reading. In the other part of the study, comparing recall of faces, the two groups were equally proficient. Although, with this design, evidence which indicates differences between normal and poor readers is ambiguous, evidence which shows no difference can be accepted. The reason is that where some skill, like face recognition, is equally present in both groups, it can have no direct effect on any other difference, such as reading ability.

To summarize,

- Much of the research into reading difficulty uses designs that do not allow us to resolve the issue of cause.
- Suggestions that reading difficulty is experienced by children who have some visual or memory deficit do not seem to be supported by the evidence.
- Poor readers experience difficulty with tasks involving words and letters, although it is not clear if this difficulty is the cause or consequence of the reading difficulty.

Longitudinal studies of reading development

We have criticized the tactic of comparing groups of children matched by age or intelligence. There are several other possibilities. One is to match children on the basis of their reading age, thus equalizing reading experience. Another tactic is to conduct a longitudinal study which would follow the development of a number of children over several years. Using this technique, one might be able to detect differences between the children before they begin to read and relate these differences to subsequent reading development. In Dorothy Bishop's longitudinal study, children were referred to the study because they showed some signs of language impairment. Alternatively, another research strategy would be to select a sample who were representative of all children. Only some of these would experience difficulty as they began to learn to read.

Peter Bryant and Lynette Bradley (1985) have conducted such a longitudinal study. The study involved nearly 400 children who were first seen around the age of 4 years. This group of children were studied over the following four or five years. At the beginning of the study, none of the children could read. When it finished, the children were around 9 years of age and most were well on with learning to read. The children's memory for words was investigated at the beginning of the study. Some children were better than others on this test.

Later on in the study, the children were given other tests, this time tests of reading and spelling. If poor memory led to or caused reading difficulties, then those children who were poor at the memory task when they were 4 would be the children who were experiencing difficulties with reading and spelling at the age of 6 or 7. No such relationship was found. At the end of the study, Bryant and Bradley gave the children a different test of memory. If reading experience contributed to the development of memory skills, then one would expect that the children who were reading best at 6 or 7 would be those children who performed best on the memory test at the age of 9. This *was* the outcome found.

Before we accept this result uncritically, one should be aware of the possibility that memory strategies used at the beginning of the study might have been different from those in use at the end. As John McShane observed ' ... it is possible that reading difficulties occur among children who have difficulty with the new strategy, which affects both memory and reading performance' (McShane, 1991, p. 302).

With this reservation in mind, we seem to be in a position to accept that at least some aspects of memory are developed through the exercise of reading. In virtually eliminating 'memory deficit' as a cause of reading and spelling difficulty we have clarified the position by removing one source of explanations.

Awareness of sounds

Peter Bryant and Lynette Bradley pointed out in their 1985 book (which discusses reading problems) that having a language composed of a relatively small number of sounds greatly simplifies what has to be learned. The many thousands of distinct words in English are built from collections of this small number of sounds. These sounds are related to letters and to groups of letters. An awareness of sounds and their relation to written language would seem to be a great advantage to the child learning to read and spell. A difficulty in this area would imply a considerable disadvantage. There is also, as we have noted, the separate problem that many words in English have sounds that do not relate in an obvious way to the sounds of the letters in the words. The suggestion is that, although an awareness of sounds is no guarantee that written words can be recognized, the skill is a considerable assistance. It is of most help in the early stages of learning to read.

Several studies have shown that awareness of sounds in words is achieved late in childhood. For example Bruce (1964) set children aged between 5 and 9 years the task of saying what particular words would sound like with one of the letters missing (e.g. late without the 'l'). He found that it was only after the age of 8 years that children could solve this task reliably. The conclusion reached from this and other studies was that an awareness of sounds is one of the gains which comes from learning to read.

The perception of rhyme is one particular form of an awareness of sounds and similarity. On the basis of the work of Bruce and others, one might argue that the ability to perceive rhyme would depend on the experience of sounds which comes when learning to read. If this were true, then people who were illiterate would be unable to perceive rhyme. Bryant and Bradley scorn this conclusion and observe that most of Chaucer's audience were illiterate and yet were able to appreciate the power of his rhyming. On a somewhat less literary plane, we know that children experience and enjoy rhyming in the form of games and nursery rhymes well before learning to read. The Russian educationist Kornei Chukovsky went so far as to claim:

> [Rhyme-making from the second year of life on] helps [the child] to orient himself to his language and to enrich his speech. Under the influence of beautiful word sequences, shaped by a pliable musical rhythm and richly melodic rhymes, the child playfully, without the least effort, strengthens his vocabulary and his sense of the structure of his native language.

(Chukovsky, 1971, p. 87)

In an early investigation of the possibility that the ability to detect rhymes might contribute to the later process of learning to read, Bryant and Bradley (1978) compared the performance of a large group of what they termed 'backward readers' with a group of younger children of a similar reading age. The children were presented with groups of four spoken words. Three of each group shared some common sound, either the first sound (a test of alliteration) or some other part of the words (a test of rhyming). The group of backward readers, although older than those children reading normally for their age, found the tasks more difficult. Bryant and Bradley concluded that backward readers were relatively insensitive to sound. Because reading levels were the same for each group, it seems unlikely that this insensitivity was the result of the reading problem and may indeed have been part of the cause of it. This possibility led Bryant and Bradley to propose that some test of sensitivity to rhyme taken *before children began to read* might predict how well they were able to cope with the task of learning to read.

This line of reasoning led the two psychologists to embark upon what is perhaps their most significant contribution to research in this area. The significance lies in the possibility that at least one source of reading problem might be identified and, more importantly, in the possibility that some appropriate early intervention might be identified.

A longitudinal study of rhyme and reading

This longitudinal study involved around 400 children and its outcomes were described in the early to mid-1980s. The children were selected because they showed no signs of reading at the time the study began. Each child was investigated using three sorts of measure. One of these took the form of the alliteration and rhyming test described above. The other measures were measures of memory and verbal intelligence.

After about four years, when the 400 children were now about 8 or 9 years of age, they were re-tested. By this time the children were all reading, but some were reading much better than others. The psychologists compared the performance of the children on the earlier tests (of sensitivity to rhyme and alliteration) with their later reading performance. The results seem to be quite clear. The children who were having difficulty with the earlier task were also those who were having difficulty in learning to read. Bryant and Bradley also report that there was no relationship between poor performance on the rhyming test and later performance in other areas like mathematics, strongly suggesting a specific relationship between rhyme and reading.

3.5 Remediation and intervention

> By pasting on the vowels and consonants on the sides of four dice, he has made this a play for his children, whereby his eldest son in coats, has played himself into *spelling*.
>
> (John Locke, quoted in Johnson's *Dictionary* in the definition of 'spell', 1773)

Here John Locke is recording his interest in the possibility that one can teach spelling by means which engage a child's own interests, in this case in playing with dice. It seems that the verbal games which form a part of many children's play may have a similar useful role. By identifying the relationship between early experience of sound games like rhyming and later ability to deal with the task of learning to read, Bryant and Bradley feel able to claim that backward readers are not a special group but are part of the continuum of all readers. More importantly, their work identifies an area where intervention might be able to address the difficulty experienced by some children in recognizing sounds.

Research in America suggests that practice with sounds at an early age can contribute to subsequent reading development. David Goldstein (1976) compared the performance of two groups of 'bright' 4 year olds when he taught one group about letter sounds and the other letter names and the order of letters. He used the same materials with both groups, each for a similar amount of time. Once the thirteen-week period of training was over, Goldstein tested the children and found that the letter–sound group performed much better on a reading test than the other group.

Bryant and Bradley, as part of their large study, took four groups of 6 year olds and gave each lengthy periods of training. The training differed for each group. Two groups were given training which involved rhyme and alliteration. Children who were given this kind of training were up to 14 months in advance of the other groups of children in reading and spelling at the end of the study. More recent work which indicates the value of being sensitive to sound similarities comes from Usha Goswami (1986) who showed that children by the age of 6 are able to use sound patterns in words that they know to derive a spelling for similar sounding words that they haven't tried to write before. This is a form of *reasoning by analogy* which may be unavailable to 'backward readers' who are less able to recognize similarities between words on the basis of their sounds.

Giving children help to develop sound discrimination skills before and during the early years of the development of reading is intended to promote a skill of doubtful value (Snowling, 1987). Margaret Snowling also points to an alternative strategy of intervention which might make the skill of sound discrimination less important in the reading process. This alternative is to introduce children to larger units of reading than letter–sound or letter-group–sound correspondences. She argues that if children can be brought to process larger groups of letters, then the ability to decompose words into letter–sound correspondence is not needed as much.

A third intervention strategy has been developed from some early suggestions by Samuel Orton (1937) together with his collaborators Gillingham and Stillman (1956). This technique is described as a 'structured multisensory method'. When a child is introduced to some new spelling pattern, they see it, say it, read it and feel it (in the form of wooden letters). It has turned out to be very effective in addressing the reading difficulties experienced by some children and it has some experimental support. Charles Hulme (1981) has demonstrated in several experiments that poor readers are better able to remember strings of letters if they are able to trace them. The beneficial effect was present for all readers but greatest for the poor readers. The idea is to encourage children to use all their senses in concert and by this means to circumvent any particular sensory weakness whether it be the cause or consequence of the reading difficulty.

SUMMARY OF SECTION 3

- There are two main positions on the question of the existence of developmental dyslexia. One of these sees dyslexia as an identifiable condition which some children who have difficulty with reading and spelling have. The other position maintains that children 'with dyslexia' are not different but are at one end of a continuum of all children learning to read and spell. This distinction is important in a practical sense since whichever view is taken has implications for the legal obligations of local authorities to provide support.

- Several attempts have been made to define dyslexia. Some definitions specify what dyslexia is not rather than what it is. Psychologists avoid the difficulties of definition by relying on 'operational definitions' or working hypotheses.

- Much research interest has focused on investigating the skills of children becoming literate and on areas of difficulty that they may have. A more neglected problem resides in the language itself, which, in the case of English, seems to have been contrived to pose problems to learners.

- Using a longitudinal study, Bryant and Bradley have suggested that rhyming skills and rhyming games contribute to an awareness of sound similarities and differences, which contributes to the later development of reading and writing.

- One outcome of this research is the suggestion that practising and developing rhyming and other sound-based skills is a potentially fruitful technique.

4 CONCLUSIONS

Reading problems are a source of considerable anxiety to children, teachers and parents. There is, consequently, a great deal of emotional investment in the issues of 'cause' and 'remediation'. To some extent Section 3 has sought to avoid some of the more heated discussion by concentrating on three particular issues.

(a)   Is there an identifiable group of children who are dyslexic, or are children with reading difficulties part of the continuum of all readers?

It must be admitted that this issue is unresolved. Bryant and Bradley have suggested that their evidence supports the 'continuum' view. Others advance data to support the 'identifiable group' view. The debate is clouded by the supposition by some (often teachers) that if 'dyslexics' turn out to be an identifiable group, they will be given resources at the expense of other children not so 'fortunately' labelled. Others (often parents) suppose that if children with reading difficulties are not an identifiable group then they will not receive the attention and resources to address their specific problems.

(b)   What are the particular characteristics of the children who experience difficulty in learning to read?

Here psychology has given us some helpful pointers. After several false starts and dubious methodology, research findings have identified some of the areas in which children with specific reading difficulties perform as well as other children and some of the areas where there are clear differences. There are several areas of fruitful investigation in addition to those briefly described here, particularly those explored by the psychophysiologists.

(c)   What are the possibilities for remediation?

Intervention and remediation are best informed by adequate conceptual and research work. Once again, psychology has helped in several ways.

First, in identifying the strengths of children with specific reading difficulties which constitute the basis for development; secondly, in exposing the doubtful value of much of the early research findings; and thirdly, in identifying differences between these children and other readers. As we have seen, there are several possible lines of teaching intervention which may be tried.

This chapter has introduced two areas of psychological interest in developing literacy. First, the possible relation between early language impairment and reading difficulty and, second, the nature and remediation of developmental dyslexia. To return to our starting point, it may turn out, as Garton and Pratt have suggested, that these two topics are not distinctly different but closely interrelated. Current research is, in part, directed at exploring this possibility.

REFERENCES

BANCROFT, D. (1995) 'Language development' in LEE, V. and DAS GUPTA, P. (eds) *Children's Cognitive and Language Development*, Oxford, Blackwell/The Open University (Book 3 of ED209).

BISHOP, D. V. M. and ADAMS, C. (1990) 'A prospective study of the relationship between specific language impairment, phonological disorders and reading retardation', *Journal of Child Psychology and Psychiatry*, **31**(7), pp. 1027–50.

BISHOP, D. V. M. and EDMUNDSON, A. (1987) 'Language-impaired 4-year-olds: distinguishing transient from persistent impairment', *Journal of Speech and Hearing Disorders*, **52**, pp. 156–73.

BRUCE, D. J. (1964) 'The analysis of word sounds', *British Journal of Educational Psychology,* **34**, pp. 158–70.

BRYANT, P. E. and BRADLEY, L. (1978) 'Differences in auditory organisation as a possible cause of reading backwardness', *Nature*, **271**, pp. 746–7.

BRYANT, P. E. and BRADLEY, L. (1985) *Children's Reading Problems,* Oxford, Blackwell.

CHUKOVSKY, K. (1971) *From Two to Five,* Berkeley (Calif.), University of California Press.

CRITCHLEY, M. (1970) *The Dyslexic Child,* London, Heinemann Medical Books.

CRITCHLEY, M. and CRITCHLEY, E. A. (1978) *Dyslexia Defined,* London, Acford.

ELLIS, A. W. (1984) *Reading, Writing and Dyslexia: a cognitive analysis*, London, Laurence Erlbaum Associates.

FRITH, U. (1985) 'Beneath the surface of developmental dyslexia' in PATTERSON, K. E., MARSHALL, J. C. and COLTHEART, M. (eds) *Surface Dyslexia: neuropsychological and cognitive studies of phonological reading*, Hillsdale (N. J.), Laurence Erlbaum Associates.

GARTON, A. and PRATT, C. (1989) *Learning to be Literate*, Oxford, Blackwell.

GILLINGHAM, A. M. and STILLMAN, B. U. (1956) *Remedial Training for Children with Specific Disability in Reading, Spelling and Penmanship*, New York, Sackett and Wilhelms.

GOLDSTEIN, D. M. (1976) 'Cognitive-linguistic functioning: learning to read in pre-schoolers', *Journal of Educational Psychology*, **68**, pp. 680–8.

GOSWAMI, U. (1986) 'Children's use of analogy in learning to read: a developmental study', *Journal of Experimental Child Psychology*, **42**, pp. 73–83.

HINSHELWOOD, J. (1917) *Congenital Word Blindness*, London, H. K. Lewis.

HOLMES, D. R., and MCKEEVER, W. F. (1979) 'Material specific serial memory deficit in adolescent dyslexics', *Cortex*, **15**, pp. 51–62.

HULME, C. (1981) *Reading Retardation and Multi-sensory Teaching*, London, Routledge and Kegan Paul.

JOHNSON, S. (1773; 4th edn) *A Dictionary of the English Language in which the Words are deduced from their Originals and Illustrated in their Different Significations by Examples from the best Writers*, London, W. Strahan.

MCSHANE, J. (1991) *Cognitive Development*, Oxford, Blackwell.

OAKHILL, J. (1995) 'Development in reading' in LEE, V. J. and DAS GUPTA, P. (eds) *Children's Cognitive and Language Development*, Oxford, Blackwell/The Open University (Book 3 of ED 209).

ORTON, S. T. (1937) *Reading, Writing and Speech Problems in Children*, New York, Norton.

RUTTER, M. and YULE, W. (1975) 'The concept of specific reading retardation', *Journal of Child Psychology and Psychiatry*, **16**, pp. 181–97.

SNOWLING, M. (1987) *Dyslexia*, Oxford, Blackwell.

VELLUTINO, F. R., PRUZEK, R. M., STEGER, J. A. and MESHOULAM, U. (1973) 'Immediate visual recall in poor and normal readers as a function of orthographics-linguistic familiarity', *Cortex*, **9**, pp. 370–86.

READING

The consequences of being literate

Jane Oakhill

In this article, I shall consider the value of literacy skills within our society, and will assess some of the evidence that literacy affects cognitive development and thinking. Many scholars, from a range of disciplines, consider the introduction of writing systems into social life to be a watershed in human history. There is often seen to be a 'great divide' between those who 'have' literacy, and those who do not. The precise terms differ, but literacy is variously viewed as separating history from prehistory; primitive societies from civilized societies; modern societies from traditional societies. On this view, literacy is generally seen as 'a good thing' and 'more advanced'. Such judgements are based on the profound social changes that often accompany the introduction and adoption of writing systems, though this view has been challenged recently, most notably by Brian Street (see, for example, Street, 1984), whose views will be discussed later. There is general agreement that written records provided the crucial technology for the rise of the arts and sciences over the last two-and-a-half thousand years. Literacy was also instrumental in the development of commercial and administrative networks (though some see literacy as merely an enabling factor and not a primary causal factor in such developments). Few doubt that the printing press and the book provided the technological basis for the rise of industrial society.

In modern societies, we expect people to be literate. Everyday activities, such as filling in forms, reading road signs, recipes, instructions and newspapers all assume a reasonable level of literacy. The stigma attached to illiteracy in our society is far greater than that attached to innumeracy. Our main interest here is in the *psychological* consequences of literacy. Literacy skills could have their effects on cognition by altering the ways in which people get information, how they store information, and how they retrieve it. Literate people will also have access to a potentially much broader range of ideas – they can assimilate knowledge and information from written text. In this way, literacy skills can be seen as serving a number of intellectual and cognitive functions. Literacy also opens the world of literature. But does the acquisition of reading and writing have any important effects on the structure and functions of the mind? Some make the more radical claim that the mastery of written language affects not only the *content* of thought, but also the *processes* of thinking: how we classify, reason and remember.

Let us consider some of the arguments for this claim. Goody and Watt (1968) noted that alphabetic literacy in post-Homeric Greece came at the same time as new academic disciplines – history and logic. They argue that literacy was the precondition and precursor for these disciplines, and posited a change in thought processes as the mediating link. Goody and Watt stress the implications of the permanency of writing (because it is represented in visual symbols). New intellectual operations, which would not be possible with transient oral utterances, could be performed on this 'frozen' language. Readers could, for example, compare sets of statements to look for inconsistencies. They also claim that alphabetic literacy led to new ways of classifying knowledge, and fostered the development of logic. Although there is a generally accepted idea that the possession of written language promotes abstract thinking, analytical reasoning, new ways of categorizing, such claims are rarely supported by any evidence that people in literate societies do, in fact, process information about the world any differently from those without literacy.

Indeed, Street (1984) challenges Goody's views, claiming that he overstates the significance that can be attributed to literacy *per se*, rather than the social order in which it is found. An additional, largely untested, assumption is that changed modes of thinking come about *because of* linguistic changes and these *lead to* the cultural changes. The challenge to psychologists has been to try to demonstrate that such hypothetical links between literacy and the nature of thought exist. Several have attempted to do so, and we will consider some of their efforts here. The Russian psychologist, Luria (see Luria, 1976) studied the ways in which literacy and schooling affect intellectual functions. In the 1930s he led an expedition to a region in central Asia where rapid changes made possible a comparative study. Luria compared three groups from similar village backgrounds who were being exposed to differing levels of education. The groups were: non-literate farmers, those doing short literacy courses, and participants in short teacher-training programmes. Luria used a variety of experimental tasks (to assess perception, word association, concepts, classification and reasoning) and found differences between the groups. Those without literacy or schooling tended to perform the tasks in what he classed as a concrete, context-bound way, and were guided by perceptual and functional attributes of objects. By contrast, the most highly-schooled group could be characterized as taking a more abstract approach, and seemed to be responsive to the conceptual and logical relations among things. The minimal literacy group fell in between. However, Luria's groups differed in other respects: their age, for instance, and their experience of other activities such as collective management and planning of agricultural operations. This possible link between literacy level and other major changes in life experience is a major problem in such research.

More recent work on this topic has been carried out by Greenfield (for example, Greenfield, 1972). She studied cultural influences on concept formation among Wolof children in Senegal, West Africa. In many tasks, she found differences in performance between the children attending school, and matched, unschooled children. For example, in one task which required the children to put together familiar objects or pictures which were 'most alike', schooled and unschooled children differed systematically in some of the ways they grouped objects together, and how they responded to questions about their groupings. For instance, the children were asked about the reasons for their groupings. Like schooled American and European children, the schooled Wolof children were readily able to answer the question 'Why do you *say* (or *think*) these are alike?' The unschooled Wolof children did not seem to understand the question, but could answer readily if they were asked, 'Why *are* these alike?' Greenfield argued that this evidence suggests that the unschooled Wolof lacked self-consciousness – i.e. they did not differentiate between their own thoughts about something and the object itself. She argued that the concept of a personal point of view appeared to be absent: when asked about *their* view, they were unable to answer the question. Greenfield links the use of verbal forms such as 'I think' to cognitive flexibility. The unschooled Wolof children grouped objects and pictures according to only one attribute, even though there were several different bases for classification (colour, form, function, for instance). The Wolof school children, by contrast, like Western school children, were more flexible in assessing an object from different points of view. Greenfield interpreted these findings as arising because of the schooled children's capacity for context-independent, abstract thought, and linked this type of thinking with literacy. Her argument was that differences between the schooled and unschooled groups derive from fundamental differences between written and oral language. Those who have only an oral language, which relies on context to communicate meaning, take for granted a common point of view. Greenfield's views have not gone unchallenged. Street (1984) argues that it is ethnocentric to dismiss illiterate people as lacking in important cognitive skills, and that the inferences Greenfield makes from her data are exaggerated. It may be simply that the conventions that unschooled Wolof children use to talk about their thinking were different from those of the researcher herself. Street suggests that the differences between schooled and unschooled Wolof children can perhaps more appropriately be described as differences in conventional uses of explicitness than as differences in 'abstraction'. He suggests that the schooled Wolof children may have learned the convention of adopting a 'detached' role, but that the ability to adopt such conventions will not tell us anything about the child's facility with abstraction, nor their logical performance. He concludes:

> The unschooled, oral Wolof do not, then, lack the abilities of abstraction, symbolization and formal logic that schooled, literate children are claimed to have. The differences between the groups cannot be couched in such grandiose terms. There is not a 'great divide' between them as Greenfield would have us believe.
>
> (p. 38)

Olson has focused on comparisons of pre-literate pre-school children and older children of various ages to test his hypothesis that literacy permits the development of a unique form of logical competence (Olson, 1977; Olson and Torrance, 1983). His hypothesis is that an important conceptual transformation occurs during the early school years, which depends on children's developing ability to attend to the *structure* of language, as distinct from the *meanings* it conveys. Written text, he suggests, is largely responsible for permitting people to differentiate the form of the language from its content – what is *said* from what is *meant*. Thus, literacy is seen as allowing people to master the logical functions of language, and to separate them from its interpersonal functions. For example, adults can appreciate the 'say/mean' distinction. Most adults appreciate the ambiguity in questions such as 'Can you say that chickens have fur'? They might reply, 'Well, you can *say* it, but it wouldn't be true'. Children do not seem to see the ambiguity (Olson and Torrance, 1983). In one study, 5-year-old children were read a story concerning a dispute between two children about the distribution of some popcorn (Olson and Hildyard, 1981). One of the children complained, 'You have more than me!' When asked what this story character had *said*, more than half of the 5 year olds claimed he had said, 'Give me some!', which is of course not exactly what he said, but a likely interpretation of the utterance's intended *meaning*. By contrast, most of the 7 year olds could report precisely what was said, but, when asked, indicated that they knew what was meant as well. Evidence that pre-school children lack the ability to distinguish between 'say' and 'mean', while older children and adults have this ability, has been claimed by Olson as support for the idea that literacy has its effect on cognition by encouraging children to treat language as an object of thought (in other words, by aiding their *metalinguistic* development).

However, Olson and Torrance acknowledge that the ability to distinguish between what is said and what is meant could derive, not from learning to read and write, but from any one of a number of other sources: from classroom talk, from conversations with literate adults, from pre-school literacy-related activities, for instance. This point highlights a problem with all the experimental projects outlined above: they fail to support the *specific* claims made for literacy's effects. The main difficulty is that all of the comparisons are between schooled and unschooled children, and unwarranted generalizations are often made about the effects of literacy. The changes observed cannot be attributed to literacy *per se* because schooling and literacy are confounded in these studies, and whether literacy has a causal function in cognitive development remains unproven. Over a wide range of cultures and experimental tasks, schooled children consistently outperform unschooled children on cognitive tasks indicative of intellectual functioning. However, it is possible to disentangle hypotheses about the effects of mastering written language from general effects of schooling by looking at cultures in which schooling and literacy can be separated.

Such an instance is Scribner and Cole's (1981) study of the Vai people of Liberia. They have a writing system *of their own invention*, a syllable-based script which they use in commercial and personal affairs. Since this script is not taught in school, but at home, Scribner and Cole were able to separate the effects of schooling from those of literacy since they could find some people who had learned to read and write, but who were unschooled. They compared Vai, Arabic or Qur'anic literacy and English (school) literacy, all of which were found amongst the Vai. They found that some cognitive skills were enhanced by practice in specific scripts. For example, knowledge of Vai, but not of Arabic, facilitated explicit verbalization skills, as measured by ability to explain the rules of a board game to another person. Knowledge of Arabic script enhanced some types of memory task. However, by far the majority of the skills they assessed were related to schooling rather than literacy. The children who had been to school were, for example, able to give more adequate explanations of their logical inferences in reasoning tasks, of their classification strategies, and of their knowledge about language than were those who were literate in the Vai script, but who had never been to school. On such tasks, those who were literate in Vai but who had not been to school performed similarly to unschooled subjects who were not literate. Scribner and Cole's conclusion was that specific uses of literacy have specific implications: 'particular practices promote particular skills'. Schooling enhanced performance on most of the tasks they used, but there were some instances where non-school literacy improved performance even when schooling did not. Scribner and Cole conclude that knowledge of reading and writing without schooling does not have the same intellectual consequences as literacy with schooling. Another major problem in enterprises that attempt to ascertain the effects of literacy on thought is that literacy has a variety of uses in different societies. These differences make it impossible, therefore, to state in any general way the cognitive consequences of literacy (Olson and Torrance, 1983).

To conclude this article, we should note that there is less equivocation over the effects of literacy on children's thinking about, and conceptions of, language structure. Children's language awareness, their ability to use terms such as 'letter', 'word' and 'sentence', and understanding of the way in which spoken language is comprised of small sounds (phonemes) seem to grow with reading ability, rather than preceding it. Although literacy is regarded as very important in our society, there is no good evidence that literate people think in qualitatively different ways from illiterate ones. The only differences found when literacy and schooling are deconfounded are very subtle ones.

Summary

Evidence for the claim that literacy *per se* induces people to think in qualitatively different ways is hard to find. In studies where the effects of literacy and schooling have been deconfounded, it is schooling that has the more dramatic and general effects on thinking.

There is clearer evidence that literacy helps children to think about language and reading-related concepts, and to appreciate the phonemic structure of the language.

References

GOODY, J. and WATT, I. (1968) 'The consequences of literacy' in GOODY, J. (ed.) *Literacy in Traditional Societies*, New York, Cambridge University Press.

GREENFIELD, P. (1972) 'Oral or written language: The consequences for cognitive development in Africa, US and England', *Language and Speech*, **15**, pp. 169–78.

LURIA, A. R. (1976) *Cognitive Development: its cultural and social foundations*, Cambridge (Mass.), Harvard University Press.

OLSON, D. R. (1977) 'From utterance to text: The bias of language in speech and writing', *Harvard Educational Review*, **47**, pp. 257–81.

OLSON, D. R. and HILDYARD, A. (1981) 'Assent and compliance in children's language' in DICKSON, W. P. (ed.) *Children's Oral Communication Skills*, New York, Academic Press.

OLSON, D. R. and TORRANCE, N. G. (1983) 'Literacy and cognitive development: A conceptual transformation in the early school years' in MEADOWS, S. (ed.) *Developing Thinking*. London, Methuen.

SCRIBNER, S. and COLE, M. (1981) *The Psychology of Literacy*, Cambridge, Cambridge University Press.

STREET, B. V. (1984) *Literacy in Theory and Practice*, Cambridge, Cambridge University Press.

SOURCE: specially written for this book by Jane Oakhill.

Susan Gregory

CONTENTS

OBJECTIVES

When you have studied this chapter, you should be able to:

1 recognize the distinction between being born deaf and becoming deaf later in life, and describe some of the consequences of pre-lingual profound deafness for development;

2 understand how psychological knowledge has informed practice in the following areas:
   (a) early interaction and language development;
   (b) the development of literacy skills;
   (c) the development of identity and self-esteem in deaf children;

3 appreciate the ways in which the study of deafness can inform our understanding of psychological processes;

4 critically discuss the linguistic status of British Sign Language and reflect on the possibilities of its use with pre-lingually deaf children;

5 understand the deficiency model of deafness and contrast this with other perspectives.

1 INTRODUCTION

For most of us, our understanding of deafness comes from knowing someone who has become deaf or is going deaf. To lose one's hearing is a characteristic of the ageing process. For example, 34 per cent of people over 60 and 74 per cent of people over 70 experience some degree of hearing loss. For those becoming deaf it can be a frustrating and isolating experience as familiar sounds become less and less distinct and conversations, particularly in a group, are more difficult to follow. Family and colleagues too, experiencing the effects of deafness at second hand, are likely to feel irritated and become impatient as they are asked to repeat what they say, or comments and questions are simply not heard.

There are fewer of us, however, who will have met or even know of a person who was born deaf. This is not surprising, since there are around 10 million people in the UK with some hearing loss, while only around 55,000 of them were born with a significant hearing loss. The latter group, however, may experience their hearing loss in a very different way and for them it is not a loss, but a state of being deaf. This group is the focus of attention in this chapter.

ACTIVITY 1
Allow about 10 minutes

BORN DEAF AND BECOMING DEAF: DIFFERENCES AND SIMILARITIES

What do you think are the main differences and similarities between people who are born deaf and people who become deaf? Try to write down at least three of each. Some suggestions are provided at the end of this chapter.

Differences   **Similarities**

Our focus for this chapter is on those who are born deaf and we examine the consequences of this for development. Deafness has always been both intriguing and challenging to psychologists. It is intriguing because deaf people constitute a unique group who, because they cannot hear, are likely to experience and understand the world in a different way. In addition, many born-deaf people communicate using sign language, a language unlike others and inaccessible to most hearing people. At the same time deaf people present a challenge to psychologists and educationists since, despite the fact that their intellectual potential is the same as that of hearing people, they consistently underachieve at school. The attainments of deaf children in the UK, as in other countries throughout the western world, are depressing and disappointing, with the majority of deaf children leaving school with poor educational achievements and literacy skills and low self-esteem.

This chapter will look at both sides of the equation: how psychological knowledge influences practices with deaf children and how the study of deaf people itself informs psychology. Towards the end we shall examine whether the implicit view of deafness in much psychological writing inadvertently contributes to the low achievements of deaf pupils through its emphasis on a deficiency view of deafness, and whether a more positive view can be developed.

2 ISABEL AND PHILIP

ACTIVITY 2

Allow about 40 minutes

ISABEL AND PHILIP

As an introduction to this topic you should read through the following two case histories. Both of them are true, although names have been changed to protect confidentiality. They concern two deaf people born into hearing families. Each is based on three interviews: two of them were with the parents, one when their son or daughter was 2–3 years old and a further one when they were 19–21 years old, and a third was carried out with the young deaf people themselves at this later age.

As you read through, identify those issues that are of concern to the parents. You should also specify those that could be the subject for psychological investigation.

2.1 Isabel

> I have always felt, and I still feel, that they are grovelling in the
> dark as far as the education of deaf children is concerned. No one
> really knows, it is all experimental. 'We will do this now for a bit,
> see how that works, if it does not work we will try something else.'
> I have always felt that and I still feel it.

The quote above is taken from an interview with the mother of Isabel.
At that time, Isabel was 21 years old. She was born deaf and is fluent in
English and sign language. She has a good job, though not one that fully
recognizes her abilities, and has a lively social life with both deaf and
hearing friends. In spoken conversation she is dependent on lip-reading
and her speech would not be easy for everyone to understand.

Although her parents suspected from an early age that Isabel was deaf,
diagnosis did not take place until she was 2 years old. Although this was
stressful at the time, her mother suggests it may have had a positive
side to it.

INTERVIEWER: How do you feel about early diagnosis?

MOTHER: Oh yes I do [agree with it]. But there again, sometimes I
wonder if I would have treated Isabel as normally as I did
in those first two years if I had known she was profoundly
deaf. If a professional person had said to me then, 'Yes,
Isabel is profoundly deaf' at 14 days old, would I have
treated her in the way I did, because I treated Isabel as a
normal child. I did not want to know she was deaf. I
mean, I knew she was. I had my suspicions there at the
back of my mind, but I really did not want to believe that.
So I treated her as a normal child.

For a short time following diagnosis the family had a visiting peripatetic
teacher of the deaf, whose help they valued. She emphasized treating
Isabel as normally as possible, but also using every possible opportunity
to speak to her, to expose her to as much spoken language as possible.
She was given hearing aids at the age of three, but her parents never
really felt she benefited from them and she herself did not like to wear
them. As a child she only wore them at school and as an adult she has
discarded them.

At the age of 3 years she went to the local school for the deaf and by the
age of the first interview with her parents, when she was nearly 4 years
old, she could say 'hello', 'no' and 'flower'. Her parents found they had to
use some gestures to communicate with her, although they had been
advised not to as it was said that this could inhibit the development of
her language, and they felt somewhat guilty about using them.

Neither Isabel nor her family was happy with this local school, although
Isabel enjoyed the contact with other deaf children. It was here that she
saw sign language being used for the first time, although its use at
school was discouraged. Interestingly Isabel comments on the fact that
she never met deaf adults at school or outside.

ISABEL: When I was very young, 4 or 5, I thought my hearing would improve. I didn't realize I would stay deaf … When we were at school we all talked. We thought our mothers talked fast and we would be able to do that one day. By 7 or 8 I realized I would be deaf permanently.

Her parents' dissatisfaction with the school arose from the low expectations it had of the pupils. The only other possibility was a boarding school over 100 miles away and Isabel's parents were understandably reluctant to send her away when she was of primary age. However, when she was 11 years old they decided it would be better for her to go although they were still not happy about it. The school was strongly oral in its approach in that it emphasized listening and lip-reading skills and any form of signing was outlawed.

ISABEL: If I signed at … school, they smacked my hand, they threatened I would have to leave the school. This wasn't right because signing helped me.

At the time she went, her parents endorsed the oral policy of the school, although now it is an area of doubt for them. This was a recurring theme through the later interview and her mother said:

MOTHER: The reason I sent her to … school, the main reason was, because they taught in an oral way. It was pure oralism. And I, in those days, was totally against British Sign Language. But now I don't feel that any more. I feel that total communication should be used in all schools for the deaf and I strongly believe that now.

But later in the same interview, she explains things slightly differently:

MOTHER: I was absolutely terrified that if she learnt sign language right from the word go, as a very young child, that that would be her only form of communication. You see with her being profoundly deaf I felt if she once gets into this sign language, into the swing of it, it would be her only form of communication. Now, horrible as this sounds, she is in the minority and she has to go out into a hearing world and everybody is not going to learn sign language for Isabel, you see. So I felt she must learn to communicate with hearing people on their level.

While Isabel did well at school, her family do not feel she reached her full potential. In particular, they feel she never really developed her reading ability above a basic minimum. Writing also did not come easily to Isabel.

The family feel she is fortunate to have obtained work; however, in response to a question about whether Isabel is happy in her work her mother says, 'No, she thinks it is totally boring.'

2.2 Philip

You should now compare the experience of Philip and his family with that of Isabel, focusing on the issues that are of concern to parents.

PHILIP: I was not happy at school. I did not understand. It was a waste of time. I want to forget about school … It was left up to me to make it out. They were teaching and I was not understanding.

Philip feels he got little out of school, as the quote above indicates, and that his life began when he started at college. He has recently successfully completed his time there during which he studied drama. He greatly enjoyed his course, which was designed for both deaf and hearing students working together. Sign language interpreters were provided some of the time, though Philip had difficulty at first as, when he arrived there, he had no knowledge of signing. However, he gradually became competent and was able to participate more and more fully. The vast majority of students at the college itself were hearing. He had the offer of a job in the theatre in London but he would not earn enough to cover his living expenses. He has appeared in a production in a London theatre, and on television, mostly in programmes for deaf children. He now has a job in printing which he enjoys although he would prefer to be an actor. His speech is difficult to understand for people who do not know him, but he is fluent in sign language which is now his preferred means of communication.

When he was young he felt bad about being deaf. He says, 'When I was young, that was a bad time, I remember the pain … I asked my teacher, "Is it possible to become hearing?" My friends were all the same, we talked about it, we wanted to become hearing.'

Now he is 19 years old, he does not want to change into a hearing person, and he says, 'I realize I am deaf and it does not bother me.'

His parents suspected he was deaf very early on; they took him to the doctor when he was 3 months old but were told, wrongly, that it was not possible to diagnose deafness so early, and the diagnosis was not confirmed until he was 11 months. He was given a hearing aid at this age which he gradually came to wear, although he did not like it at first. He now wears it all the time and finds it very valuable.

His parents followed the advice they were given to talk to Philip and not to use gestures.

MOTHER: It was just talking and talking.

FATHER: It wasn't sign was it?

MOTHER: No. No sign. Just talk and talk.

INTERVIEWER: Was that the right advice?

FATHER: No, no we didn't know. We hadn't got the experience … we should have had both [speech and sign].

At the first parental interview when Philip was 2 years old he had no language. He often had temper tantrums where he would throw himself on the floor and kick in the air. His parents felt this was due to his lack of communication.

He was educated in schools with partially hearing units although the small number of deaf children in the school meant he was often the only deaf child in a particular class. He never saw sign language at school, although in his teens he became aware of it outside school. He asked his teacher about it.

PHILIP: I was told to ignore sign language. The teacher did not want to know that sign language existed. I asked them why they were not involved in sign language but they were not interested. I was always arguing the point. They did not know about it because they were hearing, but I think it was part of their job to know!

He was frustrated most of the time at school, and as the quotation that heads this section indicates, he found it difficult to follow what was going on.

PHILIP: The teachers thought I could understand but I could not.

He believes in integrated education and is opposed to any separation between deaf and hearing people. He was asked how he thought deaf chidren should be educated.

PHILIP: It is a hard question but interesting. Deaf school is good but we need a higher level of education. There needs to be more interest in integrating schools properly, in learning from one another. There should not be a lecture style of teaching. There should not be one deaf pupil in a class of hearing pupils but four or five in each class. I know the feeling of being on my own, my tension and frustration. If you are with other deaf people there is a natural bond.

The main issue for his parents was his low level of attainment. They explained that when he was young they did not think much about educational concerns as they were relieved that something was happening in terms of school placement. Their main concern at this stage was that Philip had to leave home so early to go to school and was taken there by taxi. For his mother this meant that, as she could not take him to school and meet him, the informal contacts with the school and other mothers were lacking. It was therefore more difficult to find out what was happening at school and this was compounded by the fact that Philip's language was limited at this time and he could not talk to her about it. It was at the junior and particularly the secondary stage that they began to get worried about his progress.

FATHER: And from that stage on, I don't think we, as parents, paid enough attention. That's how I felt. I felt guilty that I didn't pay enough attention to what was going on. But Philip as we said could pick up a book and not be able to understand it but could write a computer program. So he is obviously quite bright in certain areas and we think he is quite bright, don't we?

Philip sat six GCSEs. He obtained a Grade 1 and a Grade 3, and failed all the others. His father described their disappointment with the results.

FATHER: And when we see his examination results come out like this we are pleased that he's passed something. I'm very pleased but I am disappointed because I know potentially there was an awful lot more. And if we hadn't been conned by the teachers saying everything is fine, everything is OK. For me it was when I sat down with Philip, when he was going through his mock papers, and realized he hadn't been taught it.

The extent of his low attainments only first became clear with the first report they received on Philip, when he was just over 16 years old, which was produced at the interview.

PARENTS: This was his first report. And his reading age at that time was 9.8 and his vocabulary age was 7 ... His written language it says, 'Philip's written language is poor.'

On leaving school he was still not able to read well enough to read a newspaper. However, the thing that upset Philip's parents the most was that his attainments at school, which seemed poor to them, were actually viewed as acceptable by those responsible for his education.

FATHER: That's the level they expect, you see ... 'Well,' they have said to me, 'he has reached an above average say for a deaf person.' But to me that's not good enough. I mean he's a clever young man. So we shouldn't say 'Well it's good because it's average with the deaf.' We should try and improve it so other good lads can rise to the top.

Comment

You will have probably identified a number of concerns for the parents which could include:

(a) the problem of diagnosing deafness early and reactions to diagnosis;

(b) issues around the development of early language;

(c) decisions about the choice of school;

(d) the generally low attainments at school including, in particular, poor literacy skills;

(e) the use of sign language with deaf children;

(f) the development of a deaf identity;

(g) career choice and the problem of underemployment.

You may also have suggested worries about the future, family, social life and work.

In identifying those areas amenable to psychological investigation, you may have asked:

(a) What strategies are most effective for parents to employ with their young deaf children?

(b) What would be the consequence of using sign language in the education of deaf children?

(c) Why are the academic attainments of deaf children so low?

In carrying out the activity, you may have started to experience some frustration, either because the information did not seem to be sufficient or because you need to know more about aspects of deafness.

Three particular areas seem to need clarification:

(a) How deaf are these young people and what difference does the degree of deafness make?

(b) What is the effect of hearing aids?

(c) What is sign language and what is its relevance to deaf children and adults?

The following two sections provide information on these issues.

SUMMARY OF SECTION 2

- In Section 2, through studying the case histories of Isabel and Philip you have identified a number of issues which are likely to concern hearing parents of deaf sons and daughters. You also should have reached conclusions as to which of these issues are amenable to psychological investigation.

3 HEARING LOSS AND HEARING AIDS

3.1 Degree of deafness

Very few children or adults are totally deaf and hear nothing at all. Hearing loss can range from minor losses to very severe losses. Hearing loss is usually measured in decibels (dB). For example, a 20 dB loss, in very general terms, means a person cannot hear sounds which have a loudness of 20 dB or less.

To give some general guidance, these are the intensities in decibels of some common sounds.

TABLE 1 Decibel level of different sound sources.

Intensity in decibels	Sound source
20	watch ticking
30	whispered conversation
60	spoken conversation
80	shouting
90	pneumatic drill
120	jet aircraft

Thus, in general, a child with a 30 dB loss, without hearing aids, would not hear a whisper, and all other sounds would be less distinct, while a child with an 80 dB loss would not hear speech. This is an oversimplification as this loss refers to average hearing loss. Hearing loss can be measured at different sound frequencies; the consonants, particularly 's', are high frequency and the vowels are low frequency sounds. Hearing loss is calculated by averaging five frequencies – those that cover the speech range – for the better ear. Thus, two people described as having a 70 dB loss may be affected very differently depending on its differential effect over the speech frequencies.

In educational terms, children with an average loss of 71–95 dB are usually described as severely deaf, while children with a loss greater than 95 dB are described as profoundly deaf (British Association of Teachers of the Deaf, 1981). However, while recognizing that degree of hearing loss is important, the categories must be treated with some caution. While most educationists would agree that, at a basic level, they provide information about a child, they should be considered alongside other factors. As already mentioned, different patterns of loss may be categorized in the same way but will have different consequences. Moreover, individuals vary in their attitude to hearing aids and the extent to which they are able to benefit from them.

3.2 Hearing aids

A recent research project with young deaf people who had received them found that two-thirds (39/58) found hearing aids useful but one-third (19/58) did not (Gregory, Bishop and Sheldon, in preparation). Hearing aids can only amplify those speech frequencies where there is already some hearing. Whereas normal hearing is selective, hearing aids amplify everything including background noises. This can be compared to a recording by a tape-recorder which in a noisy room will pick up unwanted sounds. Radio aids are better and are often used in school but to be used to maximum effect they require the speaker to wear a microphone and thus are only suitable for some situations.

3.3 Isabel and Philip

Audiograms (the chart which shows the extent of loss over the different frequencies) were not available for Isabel and Philip, as is often the case for deaf adults. Much emphasis is placed on audiograms within the education system, yet after leaving school little notice is taken of them. Both reported themselves to be profoundly deaf. This too is usual, for if deaf adults are asked for an assessment of their own hearing, the distinction they are likely to make is between not hearing anything useful which will be labelled 'profoundly deaf', or having useful hearing which they would label 'partially hearing' or 'hard of hearing'. A functional assessment was carried out for Isabel and Philip in which profound deafness was defined as 'little or no response to sound, no response to the human voice' and severe deafness as 'some response to human voice but only in situations when the individual is attending'. It correlates approximately with loss assessed by audiograms.

Isabel was classified as severely deaf. Without her aid she could only hear very loud sounds such as disco music or other loud noises. With her aid she could hear sounds such as the telephone ringing or a shout although she would not be able to identify what was said. Although she can hear more with her aids, this has never benefited her enough to make her want to wear them and as an adult she has rejected them entirely. Philip was described as profoundly deaf. He could hear nothing without his aids. With his aids he was aware of various sounds although he did not feel it was really hearing. He was aware of a dog barking, a telephone ringing and an aeroplane flying overhead. He chose to wear his aids all the time.

SUMMARY OF SECTION 3

* Section 3 has described how hearing loss can differ in degree. The effect of hearing aids has also been considered. It suggested that hearing aids are more useful to some deaf people than to others and some deaf people reject them entirely.

4 BRITISH SIGN LANGUAGE

Throughout the histories of Isabel and Philip you will notice references to sign language. Neither was introduced to sign language prior to school, and both were educated through an oral approach to education, which concentrates on listening, speaking and lip-reading and avoids the use of signs. However, both, as adults, see a role for sign language in the education of deaf children. But what is sign language?

British Sign Language (BSL) is a visual gestural language. It is produced in space by movements of the hands, although the body and the face are also significant. Its lexical unit (words are the lexical unit of speech) is the sign. There is not a one-to-one match between signs and words; for example, there is a single sign for the three words 'he helped me' but the word 'hammock' would require a sequence of signs.

Signs are combined in certain systematic ways to convey meaning. The order of signs in a sign sentence will not necessarily be the same as the order of words in an English sentence with equivalent meaning. It is not possible to use BSL and English simultaneously. Thus, there is not a direct match between BSL and English just as there is not a direct match between Punjabi or Portuguese and English. Not as immediately obvious is the fact that sign languages differ from each other. BSL and ASL (American Sign Language) differ despite the fact that the UK and USA share a common spoken language.

For as long as there have been records of deaf people it seems that some form of sign language has been used. It is mentioned in the works of Saint Augustine (AD 354–430), *De Quantitate Animae Liber Unus*, Chapter 18). The first documenation of sign language is found in the books of Bulwer: *Chirologia: or the natural language of the hand* (1644) and *Philocophus: or the deaf and dumb man's friend* (1648). Yet signing has only been recognized as a full language in the last 30 years. The term ASL was first used in 1960 and BSL in 1975 (see Brennan, 1976). In 1988 the European Parliament called on member states to grant official recognition for their own sign languages, but at the time of writing this has not yet been granted in the UK.

For many years, much of the discussion of British Sign Language has been concerned with whether it can be afforded full linguistic status.

ACTIVITY 3

Allow about 10 minutes

WHAT IS LANGUAGE?

You should spend a few minutes thinking about what features are necessary for something to be ascribed the status of a language. It is a question that has challenged philosophers and you should not try to arrive at a definition but describe three or four elements you would expect to see. You might find it useful in thinking about what is, or is not, a language to consider specific examples such as music, talking parrots, dogs obeying owners' commands, computer 'language', etc.

Comment

You should compare your features with those that are raised in the discussion that follows. Some of you may have felt that a language should have a written and a spoken form. The writing issue is simple as many of the world's languages do not have written form, and yet the linguistic status of these languages is taken for granted. The speech issue is more complex as the vast majority of languages are spoken. Chomsky in his original definition of language seemed to imply that a spoken element was necessary and spoke of 'sound–meaning correspondence'. When challenged on this, however, he modified it and said, 'It is an open question whether the sound part is crucial. It could be but there is certainly no evidence to suggest it' (Chomsky, 1967).

Roger Brown defines language as 'an arbitrary system of symbols which make it possible for a creature with limited powers ... to create and understand a variety of messages' (Brown, 1965).

Roger Brown thus isolates three aspects of language: that it is an arbitrary system, that it comprises symbols and that these are organized systematically to convey meaning.

- *Arbitrariness:* One of the main areas of debate as to whether sign languages are genuine languages concerns the arbitrariness of signs (i.e. whether they are independent of their meaning or simply direct representation). It is the case that a few signs such as 'smoking' and

Table

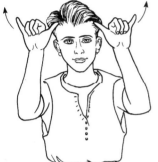

Cow

Smoking

Playing a violin

FIGURE 1 Signs from British Sign Language.

'playing a violin' can be easily guessed and are known as transparent. It is also true that some signs cannot be guessed, but once their meaning is known a connection can be made and a derivation presumed, for example, 'table', 'cow'. While this probably occurs more often than in spoken languages it is not the case for the majority of signs. Moreover such links are more often made by, and are more apparent to, those unfamiliar with the language or who are learning it, than to native users. For most native users of sign languages the links are not made and signs function for them as if they are arbitrary.

- *Symbols:*   Words are symbols in that a word represents or stands for an aspect of the world. Signs are symbols in a similar way.
- *Systematic properties:*   The way in which signs are organized can convey meaning, serving the same function as word order in English, for example, 'John helps Mary' and 'Mary helps John' both contain the same words but the meaning is different. Likewise while the sign for 'helps' is the same in conveying both messages, the movement of the sign is different in each case to convey the different meaning. In the first case it moves from a location in space already established as indicating John to one indicating Mary, while in the second the movement is in the reverse direction.

Until recently, in the UK, the approach used in the early advice to parents of deaf children and in the education of deaf children was an oral one, emphasizing the use of speech to the exclusion of any signs or gestures, which were seen as inhibiting speech development. Oralism reigned supreme from the Milan Congress of 1880. This was the second International Congress on the Education of the Deaf, the first having been held in Paris in 1878. It decreed:

> Considering the incontestable superiority of speech over signs in restoring the deaf mute [*sic*] to society and in giving him a more perfect knowledge of the language, the Congress declares that the oral method ought to be preferred to that of signs for the education and instruction of the deaf and dumb [*sic*] … and considering that the simultaneous use of speech and signs has the disadvantage of injuring speech, lip reading and precision of ideas declare that the pure oral method ought to be preferred.

Despite the lack of success of oralism, for many years it remained the recognized approach to education. It was constantly buoyed up by the promise of evolving technological advances. Hearing aids have improved over the years, but there is still a substantial number of deaf children who fail to benefit from them and thus cannot utilize speech through hearing.

Isabel and Philip grew up at a time when attitudes to sign language were changing and this is reflected in their interviews. Both families were told not to use signs or even gestures when their children were small. Isabel's parents found themselves using gestures some of the time but felt guilty about it. Both the young people would have liked sign language within their education and the parents tend to support this view, though close reading of the interview with Isabel's mother reveals some ambivalence.

5 PSYCHOLOGY AND DEAFNESS

It is not possible in a chapter such as this to present a complete picture of deaf children's development. We have thus chosen to focus on three specific topics to illustrate different aspects of development and the influence of psychology.

(a) How is language best acquired by deaf children? Should speech or sign be used in the early stages? Does sign language inhibit or facilitate the development of English or other spoken languages?

(b) Why are the attainments of deaf children so low? Is this an inevitable consequence of deafness? How do deaf children learn to read and write?

(c) What are the consequences of being deaf for the development of identity and self-esteem?

5.1 Language development

It is clear from the case histories that the acquisition of spoken language was difficult. At 4 years of age Isabel could only say three words and Philip at 2 had no spoken language. Obviously this is not simply of concern for language development but has consequences for social and cognitive development. To appreciate this, one only has to consider how many questions a 4 year old will ask, or the nature of negotiation with a 2 year old. In fact Philip's parents described his temper tantrums at that time as a consequence of frustration arising from lack of language. The findings from Isabel and Philip are typical of those from other research in this area.

ACTIVITY 4

Allow about 10 minutes

DEAFNESS AND LANGUAGE DEVELOPMENT

Most deaf children are born to hearing parents who do not sign. From your understanding of the way in which language is acquired in hearing children, how would you expect deafness to affect the development of language?

Comment

You will probably have thought of the general effects of not hearing the speech of another person. You may have wondered about not being able to monitor the sound of your own voice. You may also have speculated on the significance of the pre-linguistic period and whether hearing is necessary for interaction here.

Much research into children's language development in the 1980s focused more on the interaction between the mother and child than on language *per se*. A particular area for attention was the way in which the establishment of good communicative skills was seen as a prerequisite for later language development, though the nature of the relationship between pre-linguistic and linguistic competence remains an area of debate.

Studies of deaf children with hearing parents showed that the hearing mothers had difficulty at this pre-linguistic stage. Interactive games (peek-a-boo, round and round the garden) were more difficult to initiate (and turn-taking and joint reference were difficult to establish) (Gregory and Mogford, 1981). The question arose as to whether these difficulties were an inevitable consequence of deafness. The deaf child was, after all, having to use the visual channel both for communicating through lip-reading and watching the face, and for attending to toys or games.

A study of acquisition of the first words in deaf children of hearing parents showed, not suprisingly, significant delay.

TABLE 2 Age (in months) at 1, 10, 50, and 100 words for deaf and hearing children

	First word	10 words	50 words	100 words
Deaf children	16m	23m	29m	34m
Hearing children	11m	12m	19m	20m

(Gregory and Mogford, 1981)

The table is based on diary records for six deaf children and fourteen hearing children. Two of the deafest children originally in the study are excluded here as they did not acquire ten words by the end of the study (when the children were 48 months) so the figures present a more positive picture of the language attainments of deaf children. However, it is the pattern that is of interest. First, hearing children, once they have the first word, rapidly get to the ten-word stage. This is probably because it is very difficult to decide when a hearing child has a word, as it generally emerges from meaningful babble and once one word is attributed others quickly follow. The situation is different with deaf children where the growth in vocabulary is slow. Words are systematically encouraged rather than emerging. Both deaf and hearing children start to combine words at the ten-word stage. However, with hearing children this is at a time of rapid vocabulary growth, yet this is not the case with deaf children. This could have consequences for the development of syntax.

There are further differences in the type of words in the children's early vocabularies. In her analysis of the vocabulary development of hearing infants, Nelson (1973) used six categories of words, general nominals that name a particular class of objects, such as 'car'; specific nominals that name a specific object or event, such as 'Mummy'; action words that describe or demand an action, such as 'fall'; modifiers that describe an attribute or quality such as 'red'; personal social words that are used in personal or social relationships, or to describe affective states, such as 'please'; and function words that have a solely grammatical function such as 'in'.

While nominals formed a high proportion for both deaf and hearing children in their 50 and 100 word vocabularies, deaf children had significantly fewer of them compared to hearing children. They also had significantly more personal social words. These are words that comment on something that is or has happened such as 'thank you', 'bye, bye' or requests such as 'more' or 'look'. You may remember that the first three words of Isabel were 'hello', 'no' and 'flower'. This suggests that first words are words that are meaningful for the child. For hearing children, nominals can be salient as the caregiver can comment on the focus of attention. This is more difficult with deaf children as the same activity of commenting on the child's focus of attention is not possible. However, this can happen with personal social words, where the interaction and comment can occur in the same visual field.

The whole area of language development in deaf children was illuminated by information from another source. A growing interest in sign language in the 1970s had led to an interest in sign-language acquisition. A focus for study was deaf mothers with deaf children. Studies showed the acquisition of sign language proceeded at the same rate as the acquisition of spoken language. Some even suggested there was evidence that the development of sign language was faster than speech (Schlesinger and Meadow, 1972; Bonvillian *et al.*, 1983) though this was discounted following more systematic analysis (Volterra, 1986). However, it is certainly clear that sign language does not develop more slowly than speech and more recent studies have reinforced these findings (Volterra, 1986). It has also been suggested that babbling of the fingers with deaf children parallels the sound babbling of hearing children (Petitto and Marentette, 1991).

Because an area of concern with hearing parents and deaf children was their difficulty in establishing pre-linguistic communication routines, a number of studies looked at interaction between deaf mothers and their deaf babies. Here the difficulties apparent with hearing mothers with deaf children did not emerge. Despite the fact that the visual channel needs to be used for play and communication, the deaf children were able to develop ways of dividing their attention and interaction was smooth. There was also evidence of turn-taking and games involving joint reference.

In analysing these situations it was found that deaf mothers intervened less in the interaction than either hearing mothers with hearing children or hearing mothers with deaf children. If we look at the act of a child that immediately follows that of the mother, or alternatively that of the mother following the act of a child, we find the two acts are significantly more likely to be related for deaf infants with deaf mothers than for deaf infants with hearing mothers (Kyle and Ackerman, 1989; Gregory and Barlow, 1989).

ACTIVITY 5

Allow about 20 minutes

ADVISING HEARING PARENTS OF YOUNG DEAF CHILDREN

How would you use the information here in considering the advice that should be given to hearing parents of young deaf children on facilitating early language? If you decide that there is more information you need in order to answer this, try to formulate this response in the form of specific questions to answer.

Comment

There would appear to be a number of critical points here.

- Deaf children learn words that are salient to them.
- Deaf parents find it easier to establish pre-linguistic communication with deaf children than do hearing parents.
- Deaf children developing sign language do so at least at the same rate as hearing children learning speech.

An immediate response might be to say all deaf babies should have sign language from the start, but to justify this we would need to be sure that the greater facility of deaf parents was due to the use of sign language and not other skills of understanding deaf mothers have.

Even if you were satisfied that, in the case of deaf mothers with deaf children, sign language was an important factor, you would need to be sure that hearing parents could learn to sign adequately with their children. You might further consider how to encourage a language environment for deaf children where meanings were clear from the context.

Probably at this stage you will have more questions than answers.

- What features of the behaviour of deaf parents facilitate language development in deaf babies?
- Can hearing parents learn to sign in a way that is useful for deaf children?
- How is language made salient to the language-learning child?

As we have seen, at the time when Isabel and Philip were small, oralism was still the predominant orthodoxy. Before starting school, advice was given to most parents through weekly visits by a peripatetic teacher. The emphasis was on the parents (usually the mother) speaking to their child as much as possible. Calculations were made as to how much a hearing child heard before they started to speak and the aim was for the mother to create the equivalent input for her deaf child.

A clear link can be made between this approach and the linguistic theory of Noam Chomsky which was influential at that time. Chomsky was concerned to evolve a general grammar that applied to all languages. One of the questions arising from his work concerned how children acquire syntactic rules when the language they hear is often ungrammatical. During the 1970s this led to research which involved detailed analysis of mothers' speech in the search for an answer to this question. The research showed how mothers apparently supported and promoted the development of their children's speech in a variety of ways and encouraged the conclusion that the role of the caregiver was complex and demanding. The potential implications for mothers of deaf children were enormous and had the effect of placing an increasing burden on them. Parallel to this, teachers of the deaf became concerned about the input to deaf children, because the fact they could not hear meant they were receiving less speech.

This emphasis on speaking as much as possible to the child had two particular consequences, one specific and one more general. In general it gave parents a major responsibility for the development of language in their child. Analyses of advice to parents in general at this time have described the onus placed on parents (Riley, 1983; Urwin, 1985). However, the situation for parents of deaf children is that they are much more vulnerable to advice. Advice to parents ordinarily takes place in the context of a wide peer group of other parents in similar situations, advice (or interference) from the extended family and a general scepticism about the role of professionals. Parents of deaf children often do not know any other families in the same position; their advisor is their only access to information about deafness. As another mother of a deaf young man commented on her feeling that she had somehow failed her son:

MOTHER: When you have a handicapped child you want what is best and you take advice from professionals as to what is best. We thought we were doing the right thing.

A more specific consequence of the advice was in its focus on the mother's behaviour, which shifted the emphasis in the interaction onto what the mother did. Yet observations of mother's behaviour with hearing children of this age shows them to be child-centred and follow the lead of the child. Studies of mothers' speech to deaf children, however, showed them to be more directive and controlling than mothers speaking to hearing children.

What then are the implications of more recent research for advising mothers of deaf children? Superficially, the interpretation of the results might seem simple. If deaf mothers are establishing better communication skills and their children contribute more in interaction, then maybe it is because they sign. Unfortunately it was not as simple as this, for while some of the deaf mothers signed, some of them did not, probably because they had internalized a rejection of sign language early in their own lives. Signing was rare in any case with children under 12 months of age. What we can establish though is that deaf mothers were less controlling and directive in play and intervened less. Whether or not to encourage signing remains unclear. While good communication can develop without signs at this early stage, it is possible that it is beneficial for mothers to sign as it alerts them to the visual properties of the language.

Two important points emerge, however. First, deaf children can acquire language at the same rate as hearing children and reach linguistic milestones at equivalent ages. Secondly, the use of signs with young deaf children does not inhibit language development and there is incidental evidence that it may facilitate it.

5.2 The attainments of deaf children

One of the major concerns in the two case studies was the low educational attainment of the two young people despite their apparent general competence. Isabel has difficulty with both writing and reading and her family felt she did not reach her full potential at school. Philip's parents were disappointed with his GCSE results, because they felt he could have done so much better. He does not read or write with any confidence. The issue which seems to have upset his parents the most is the attitude of the schools which see such attainments as reasonable for deaf children. Both Isabel and Philip have been affected in their career choices by low attainments. In contrast to this, both would seem competent young adults in terms of general living skills.

While attainments were reported as low in all areas, the parents of both Isabel and Philip focused on literacy as a particular area of concern, and because of its importance it is the area we concentrate on here. It would seem that literacy might be especially important to deaf people in providing access to information and as a means of communication. In addition to information from the printed word, access to television for most deaf people is via subtitles. Also, one means of keeping in contact with others is a visual display telephone, where each participant types their message which is then displayed on a screen at the other end, but this too requires literacy skills. Writing letters can be an important way of keeping in touch with friends, particularly for those who have been to boarding school. However, despite the particular importance of literacy for deaf people, skills are not necessarily developed in this area.

The findings for Isabel and Philip are reinforced by other studies of deaf children. For example, Gaines, Mandler and Bryant (1981) demonstrated that only 1 per cent of deaf 16 year olds read at their age level. The large-scale research of Conrad (1979) had great impact in deaf education. He tested all pupils leaving schools for the deaf and partially hearing units, and reported their median reading age to be 9 years of age. While this study was published some time ago, there has been no evidence to suggest that there have been substantial improvements since that time. In fact, the findings have been confirmed by more recent studies in this country (Wood *et al.*, 1986) and elsewhere (see, for example, Kampfe and Turecheck, 1987, for the USA). Overall, studies indicate that children with more severe hearing loss experience more difficulty than those with less severe loss.

ACTIVITY 6

Allow about 10 minutes

DEAFNESS AND READING

Before reading on, consider the ways in which being deaf could affect the development of reading skills.

Comment

It is generally suggested that there is a sequence of stages that children go through in learning to read. They start with word recognition, building up a sight vocabulary. In the second stage, the child also uses sound-to-letter mappings, thus enabling decoding of some words and more informed guesses by using the initial letters of others. In the final stage the child is able to use the above skills plus more complex rules of English orthography, using higher-order spelling patterns (for a summary see Oakhill, 1995). The other skill that may be relevant is context: using semantic knowledge to guess at individual words. How this is used and at what stage is a more complex issue. While better readers are more able to use context, as evidenced by their better ability to predict a next unseen word, they seem to be less likely to use this in actual reading as other reading skills are of more use in decoding words (once again, for a summary see Oakhill, 1995).

It seems clear that deaf children could be expected to have difficulty in most of these areas. Hearing children know a great deal about how words sound before they begin to read. It has been suggested that children's understanding of sounds, that is the ability to split words down to specific sounds or blend sounds together to make words, affects their progress in learning to read (Goswami and Bryant, 1990). Training in analysing words in terms of sounds has also been shown to improve the development of reading skills. Deaf children will not have a complete knowledge of the sound of words and deafer children will rely almost entirely on lip patterns, which are ambiguous.

ACTIVITY 7

Allow about 20 minutes

HOW EASY IS LIP-READING?

Spend a few minutes in front of a mirror. Identify those sounds which look the same on the lips and those sounds that are invisible (see the end of this chapter for some suggestions).

Then watch a news broadcast on the television with the sound turned down. How easy is it to lip-read? Which words can you pick out? What facilitates lip-reading?

You will probably find that if you can determine the general content of an item it is much easier to lip-read/guess, although it remains very difficult and these are probably optimum conditions. You should note that a deaf child will not have available the same linguistic or world knowledge that you have to aid lip-reading.

In general, deaf children bring less knowledge about phonology (the sounds of words) to reading than do hearing children. They have less access to sound, and lip-reading cannot fully compensate for this. Also, because of delay in spoken language development they are less able to utilize their linguistic knowlege to the same extent. For example, Quigley and Kretschmer (1982) have demonstrated that the gap between deaf children's understanding of syntax and the syntax of reading materials which they are expected to read makes use of syntactical knowledge almost irrelevant. In fact, many deaf children, rather than using syntactical knowledge to read, are having to acquire linguistic knowledge through the process of learning to read.

A number of questions arise:

Do deaf children go through the same stages in reading development as hearing children, only with less competence, or are they approaching reading in a totally different way?

As might be imagined, the evidence on these issues is controversial. It does appear that deaf children, like hearing children, do use word recognition in the early stages of reading. However, they do not move on to using phonological coding at the same age level of reading competence as hearing children. Whereas a reading age of 7 years is achieved by hearing children using a significant degree of phonological skills, many deaf children who achieve a reading age of 7 years are still using mainly word recognition (Harris and Beech, in press).

How do competent deaf children learn to read?

Research shows that deaf children are a much more heterogeneous group than hearing children in their reading. In general the better readers are those with the lesser degrees of hearing loss and the better knowledge of English, which is not surprising. However, interestingly, a number of studies have reported that deaf children of deaf parents are among the most competent readers of all. This is usually reported as an incidental finding. In Conrad's seminal work (1979) two-fifths of those who were profoundly deaf and reading at their chronological level were deaf children of deaf parents, yet only 5–10 per cent of all deaf children have deaf parents. A similar finding is reported by Wood *et al.* (1986), and by Kampfe and Turecheck (1987). Harris and Beech note that:

> three out of four native signers (that is deaf children of signing deaf parents) were in the top seven of our 36 deaf children in terms of their reading quotient. The best reader in our entire sample of deaf children was one of our native signers with a reading quotient of 114. The fourth native signer had had a disrupted educational background but even he had a middle ranking in the sample.

> (Harris and Beech, in press)

While this may seem to indicate that signing facilitates reading, there is other evidence that makes the picture more complex. Comparisons between deaf children educated orally and those using signs together with English (not BSL) showed no difference between the development of reading skills in the two groups. Moreover, the orally educated children were no more likely to use phonological coding than those taught some signs. It may be that the best readers among deaf children are those with a good basic knowledge of a language, albeit a different language from the one that they are reading, and in fact with no written form. There may of course be other factors operating, as deaf children from deaf homes often score better on a number of linguistic and cognitive measures (for a discusion of this see Quigley and Kretschmer, 1982).

On the basis of our knowledge of the process of learning to read, what advice can be given concerning the teaching of reading to deaf children?

Clearly the complexity of the evidence means that this can only be speculative. Before reading any further, you may wish to consider for yourself which factors you would identify in discussing how reading should be taught to deaf children. There are several possibilities. While with hearing readers phonological cues may be important, perhaps deaf readers need to be encouraged through development of their general linguistic knowledge. Wood *et al*. (1986) suggest that a greater linguistic foundation prior to reading may be advantageous.

Approaches based on reading for meaning, direct access to text, have been largely rejected for hearing children and this may be appropriate as phonological based strategies are more effective for them. However, a number of writers do advocate this for deaf children (see for example, Ewoldt, 1990).

Certainly, some teachers using bilingual programmes in the education of deaf children see direct access to text as the key. The following extract from a document developed by a practising qualified teacher, who is herself deaf, demonstrates this:

> Children should be encouraged to develop silent reading skills. How, when and if 'reading aloud' is appropriate is a question that needs some discussion …

> The teacher can begin to introduce reading materials made for the children. Ideally a 'bank' of 'silent reading' materials could be kept in the school, and added to by members of staff as and when they produce new sheets. 'Silent reading' materials require a response from the children e.g. draw a line between the word and the picture, colour the picture, follow an instruction, draw a picture etc. all from following a written passage. This can be from the simple to the more complex depending on the language ability of the children.

> Books can be made by the children or about the children.

> When the child has sufficient language competence on BSL and an understanding of story they can be introduced to books outside their experience, remembering that all the time the teacher is looking for the child's understanding of what the text means. Children can be either asked to read silently and then asked questions in BSL which show how much they have understood *or* they can be asked to read 'aloud' (having read it to themselves first).

Here the teacher should look for evidence of 'conceptually correct' signing of the text. This is where the children must have an understanding of 'phrase for phrase' translation and be taught to look for units of meaning e.g. 'woke up' 'made a face'.

(Head, 1992)

5.3 The development of identity and self-esteem

The development of identity

I do not intend here to address all the issues around the development of identity but rather to highlight particular aspects which are different for the developing deaf person. Isabel and Philip were born into hearing families as are most deaf children (at least 90 per cent). Yet many of them will grow up not only as members of their own families and communities but as members of the deaf community which may well play a signficant role in their lives. While there may be some parallels with the way in which most children grow up and move away from their parents, there are significant differences. It has been argued that deaf people form a community which can be compared to ethnic minority communities. They have a common language, culture, art forms and history. Isabel and Philip are likely to identify themselves as deaf people as well as with the family in which they grow up. Part of their developing identity will be the understanding that they will grow up to be deaf adults.

It was not until Isabel was 8 years old that she realized that she would be deaf all her life. She had only ever met deaf children until then and had never met a deaf adult. This is a relatively common finding. For instance one-third (19 out of 57, 33 per cent) of deaf young people in an interview study reported that as children they had thought they would grow up to be hearing (Gregory, Bishop and Sheldon, in preparation).

PHILIP: I was 9 or 10 when I first went to deaf club. That was the first time I realized that adults could be deaf and not just children. When I was young I thought everybody was deaf, but as I grew older I realized it was not everybody, but then I thought it was only the children. Then when I saw deaf adults, I realized that they could be deaf too – and I realized I would grow up to be a deaf adult.

When I was in the second year ... I'd never met a deaf adult so I told Mum, 'When I grow up I will be hearing like all the teachers are hearing.' I was upset when she told me I would always be deaf. I was worried I would be the only one; that there would be no other deaf adults.

Philip had wanted to be hearing when he was a child. He remembers thinking about his own deafness and he describes the 'pain'. Now he accepts that he is deaf; it is an integral part of his identity. He talks of having a natural bond with deaf people.

READING

You should now look at Reading A. This looks at the issue of deaf/hearing identity but from a different perspective, that of children of deaf parents.

What this illustrates powerfully is that identity comes not only from our perceived similarity or identification with others but also from our perception of difference from others. It suggests that in that situation a deaf identity is learnt from the hearing world.

Self-esteem

It is generally suggested that self-esteem develops from a sense of being valued within the family and the outside world. How might being a deaf child within a hearing family affect this development?

First, a diagnosis of deafness can be a shock to parents, most of whom will know nothing about deafness, although it is interesting that many report relief at the initial diagnosis because a reason has been found for their children's behaviour. However, the diagnosis of deafness in a child will influence the family through their own perception of professional help; they will become recipients of that help, which may change the way they see their children and themselves. Furthermore, it would seem possible that, just as with other labels, being told a child is deaf will affect parental behaviour (see Das Gupta, 1995). Isabel's mother talked of it being good to have a period of normality before diagnosis, implying that after diagnosis things were different.

Secondly, bound up with deafness is the issue of language and communication with the family and beyond, in the outside world. The deaf child may develop speech, though more slowly, and while one-to-one conversation may be straightforward, participation in groups is likely to be more difficult. Alternatively they may develop sign language as their primary means of communication, and use English (or their family language) only in its written form. The effects of this are likely to be complex. Language is significant in socialization, in affirming aspects of identity (Lee and Das Gupta, 1995) and providing information about one's place in society. Exclusion from the usual family group conversations may restrict the information available but, probably more importantly, it may also make a person feel marginal rather than integral to the group. To give just one example, in a study of deaf young people, 80 per cent (39 out of 49) said there had been important family events of which they had not been made aware at the time, such as deaths in the family, accidents, etc. (Gregory *et al.*, in preparation).

Thirdly, there is a body of psychological literature which presents deaf people in a negative way. This informs the views of some professional groups and is likely to affect both their dealings with deaf people and their families, and their expectations of them. A recent review of the literature concluded that deaf people 'are said to exhibit a lack of sensitivity for others, overdependence, unsociability, impatience and to react to frustration with anger or overt aggression' (Rodda and Grove, 1987). It has also been suggested, by for instance Lewis (1968), that deaf people are deviant in their understanding of morality. Even as recently as 1991, a study by Markoulis and Christoforou advocated that deaf children need special teaching because of their poor moral development.

ACTIVITY 8

Allow about 20 minutes

A DEAF PERSONALITY?

The perception of deaf people as described above is extremely negative.

(a) How does this match up with your view of deaf people? You may find it useful here to review the case histories of Philip and Isabel, looking particularly at the comments that they themselves make. They were chosen to illustrate a number of points and not because they were exceptional or different in a significant way from the other young people interviewed.

(b) How does such a negative portrayal of deaf people arise?

(c) What are the consequences of this deficiency view of deafness for:

Hearing parents of deaf children?

Professionals working with deaf people?

Deaf people themselves?

See the end of this chapter for a comment on this activity.

SUMMARY OF SECTION 5

- Section 5 has looked at the contribution of psychology to the study of deaf people in three particular areas; language acquisition, educational attainments, and self-esteem and identity.

- In the area of language acquisition it is suggested that deaf children can acquire language at the same rate as hearing children and that the use of signs does not inhibit language development.

- Reading is taken as an example through which to consider educational attainment. Different approaches to the teaching of reading are considered and the implications of them for deaf children examined. Most deaf children are born to hearing parents who have no pre-experience of deaf people. The consequence of this in the development of identity and self-esteem is reviewed.

6 DEAFNESS AND PSYCHOLOGY

So far in this chapter we have looked at the ways in which psychological understandings have been applied in the field of deafness. In reading this you may have occasionally been aware of how an understanding of the impact of deafness could influence psychological thinking in a particular area.

ACTIVITY 9

Allow about 10 minutes

DEAFNESS AND PSYCHOLOGY?

From your reading of this chapter, and from your experience, consider the areas in psychology which could be illuminated by studying deaf people. You might like to consider how such studies could be carried out and any pitfalls that might occur.

6.1 Deafness as deficiency

Space constraints prevent us from discussing in detail the contribution that a study of deaf people can make to our more general understanding of psychological processes. However, deaf people have for long been seen as a natural experimental group in the area of the relationship between cognition and thought. Furth, writing in 1971, said:

> ... a number of new studies with deaf subjects has been reported. It seems that psychologists are beginning to recognise the potential offered by the presence of linguistically deficient persons to test theories about the influence of language on various cognitive activities which are here subsumed under the word *thinking*.
>
> (Furth, 1971, p. 58)

In his book *Thinking Without Language* (1966) Furth reported a series of studies he carried out in the 1960s examining Piagetian concepts to see whether they were affected by children's language. Seeing deaf people as linguistically deficient has also been the basis of studies looking at reasoning and language. However, all these studies are based on a deficiency view of deafness which focuses on the sensory impairment and assumes a linguistic deficit evidenced by poor oral language skills. Sign-language competence was seen as irrelevant.

Recently, a more positive approach has been taken specifically concerned with the relevance of studying the acquisition of sign language to the study of language development. Is there a consistency in the pattern of language development which applies to all languages, such as the onset of babbling, the first sign or word, the development of syntax, etc? What is the relationship between pre-linguistic and linguistic communication?

Sign language is particularly relevant to looking at the relationship between gesture and lexical unit (i.e. sign or word) as many gestures become signs and continuities and discontinuities in this development are significant. Other studies have established that pronouns develop at a similar time in speech and sign although the pronominal system is very different in each case. As signing involves pointing intuitively it could be considered easier to acquire (for further discussion of this issue see Petitto, 1987).

So far the view of deafness that has been presented in this section is one of deficiency, of loss, of absence of hearing. This, of course, is the generally held view. As was pointed out at the beginning of this chapter, the most usual view of deafness relates to those who become deaf and thus have lost their hearing. In education too this view is confirmed, most services for deaf children being known as services for hearing-impaired children. The approach is to normalize deaf children as far as possible using hearing aids, and to use teaching techniques based on those used with hearing children but with an explicit emphasis on the teaching of speech and language.

Psychological studies too have largely reinforced this view, seeing deaf people as a natural experimental group considered as without language. The studies of deaf people have largely been used to examine the consequences of hearing impairment on linguistic, cognitive and personality development.

6.2 Deaf people making sense of the world

The last section began to hint at something which we develop further here, that, rather than seeing deaf people as lacking hearing or lacking language, we can understand them as actively constructing and understanding their world in a different way. Three aspects of this are discussed below: deaf children processing the world differently; the strengths of sign language; and deaf children as actively making sense of their world.

By way of introduction let us look at two particular experiments with deaf children.

HEARING CHINESE CHILDREN

DEAF CHINESE CHILDREN

TARGET STRUCTURE   POINT LIGHT MOTION

FIGURE 2
Spatial analysis of dynamic displays.

RESEARCH SUMMARY 1
SPATIAL ANALYSIS OF DYNAMIC DISPLAYS

This experiment tested deaf and hearing Chinese children who were just beginning to write (Fok and Bellugi, 1986). The deaf children had deaf parents and were competent signers. They were all shown a Chinese character through the movement of a point of light on a video screen and thus the character in totality was never viewed. The hearing children found the task very difficult, while the deaf children found it easy. The latter were significantly better than the hearing children at remembering, analysing and decoding the movement in space into its discrete components.

RESEARCH SUMMARY 2
FACIAL DISCRIMINATION UNDER DIFFERENT SPATIAL ORIENTATIONS

In a study of facial recognition by Bellugi *et al.* (1990), children were given a picture of the front view of a face. For the first test they had to pick out a match for this picture from six front views. In the second part, the six are three-quarter views and in the third part they were shown six front views under different lighting conditions. The stimulus face is always a front view (the Benton, Van Allen, Hamsher and Levine test of facial recognition, 1978, cited in Bellugi *et al.*, 1990). Forty-two deaf children who had deaf parents or deaf older siblings took part. The deaf children consistently scored higher than their hearing counterparts at all age levels. For example, the norms for hearing children begin at the age of 6 years, yet deaf children of 3 years were performing at the same level as the 6-year-old hearing children.

Let us also consider the possible role of sign language for deaf people. In the past, sign language was often discussed in terms of what it could not express. Much of the early work on sign language asked how it achieved certain linguistic notions. Because the standard taken was the spoken language one, sign language was found to be either the same or deficient. However, more recently attention has focused on the potential of sign language.

READING

You should now look at Reading B. Different languages mark out the world in different ways and while sign language is often described in terms of its weaknesses, this paper gives examples of possible strengths.

Suppose we consider deaf children as actively making sense of their world in terms of the information they get rather than in terms of their misunderstanding or lack of information. We have an illustration of this in the material we have already considered. Isabel, when young, thought that she would be hearing when she grew up, a view she shared with many other young deaf children. But for a deaf child to think they will grow up to be hearing is not stupidity but a legitimate inference from the information they have received. Many of them have never encountered a deaf adult.

As further evidence, let us consider the following extracts from classroom interaction of 5- and 6-year-old deaf children individually integrated into mainstream classes.

(a) Individual session, deaf child, 5½ years.

TEACHER:	What did you do? Did you stay in bed all day?
DEAF CHILD:	*(nods yes)*
TEACHER:	In bed all day?
DEAF CHILD:	*(nods yes)*

TEACHER: You didn't stay in bed all day, did you? (*she shakes her head*)

DEAF CHILD: No.

(b) Individual session, deaf child, 5½ years.

TEACHER: Do you know what vegetables he grows?

DEAF CHILD: Pink.

TEACHER: Peas?

DEAF CHILD: (*nods*)

TEACHER: Do you keep saying pink?

DEAF CHILD: (*nods then shakes head*)

TEACHER: No, well don't keep saying 'pink'. That's a colour isn't it? Now what sort of vegetable does he grow?

DEAF CHILD: White.

TEACHER: Pardon?

DEAF CHILD: White.

(c) Group session, deaf child, 6½ years.

TEACHER: Three o'clock. Now what's that? (*points*)

HEARING CHILD: Five past three.

TEACHER: Five past three. Five past three.

DEAF CHILD: Three.

[…]

TEACHER: Twenty-five to …?

HEARING CHILD: Four

TEACHER: Twenty-five to four.

DEAF CHILD: Five to four.

TEACHER: No, twenty-five to four.

(Gregory and Bishop, 1991)

At first sight, these extracts appear to illustrate deaf children's mistakes or deficiencies based on their inability to hear what is said. Looked at more closely (and those excerpts are drawn from numerous similar ones that could have been used), they provide examples of positive strategies developed by deaf children to cope with the situation in which they find themselves. The first child nods his head but a clue from the teacher modifies the nod into a shake. The second child uses an extremely common strategy for deaf children, to name a colour in response to a question that is not understood. The extent to which this is used is an indication of how often such an answer must be appropriate or acceptable. In the third excerpt the child can clearly hear something, but cannot answer the question and so repeats the last few words every time.

All these examples contribute to a view of deafness which does not focus on hearing loss as deficiency but on deaf people as actively understanding and constructing their world. Considering deafness in this way raises a number of questions for educationists. First, should we not be basing the educational approach on what deaf children can do rather than what they cannot? Secondly, rather than seeing deaf children as deficient in English should we not be considering the implications of introducing sign language as a language for learning?

> **SUMMARY OF SECTION 6**
>
> - While Section 5 considered how psychology has been used in the study of deaf people, Section 6 has examined how deaf people have been used in the study of psychology. The section argues against the simplistic view of deafness as deficiency and suggests ways in which deaf people can be seen as actively making sense of the world.

7 CONCLUSION

There is no formal conclusion to this chapter. Rather we ask you to review for yourself the ideas by carrying out the activity below.

ACTIVITY 10

Allow about 20 minutes

ISABEL AND PHILIP REVISITED

To conclude your work on this chapter, you should re-read the case histories of Isabel and Philip and the notes you made at the first reading. Consider whether your general impression or your ideas about specific issues have changed at all. Review your list of topics for psychological investigation. How would you change or modify this?

COMMENTS ON ACTIVITIES

ACTIVITY 1

There is no right answer to this question and the following are just suggestions:

Similarities

- Not being aware of sound indications of danger, alarms, etc.
- Not being able to use a voice telephone.
- Not being able to hear television or radio.
- Not being able to be called from different parts of a house or building.
- You may have noted not being able to hear music or bird song, but this may be different for someone who has never heard these things from the way it is for someone who has. It probably should be included as a difference.

Differences

- Deafened people have a sense of loss while deaf people have never known anything different.
- Deafened people's first language is the spoken language of their community while deaf people may use sign language.
- Deafened people usually have their friends in the hearing world while deaf people have them in both deaf and hearing worlds.
- Deaf people are more likely to have deaf spouses or partners, while deafened people are more likely to have hearing spouses or partners.

ACTIVITY 7

Many sounds have identical lip patterns, e.g. 'p' and 'b', 'f' and 'v'. Others are invisible on the lips, e.g. 't' and 'k'.

ACTIVITY 8

- While Isabel and Philip underachieved educationally, in terms of their social development they seemed to be competent. There is nothing in these case histories (or in other information which is available about them) to suggest they are deviant in terms of personality.
- This is difficult to answer but parallels can be drawn with characteristics attributed to other minority groups. Lane (1988) compares the characteristics used to describe deaf people with the traits attributed to African people, and finds similarities.
- You are likely to have your own view on this. However, it is worth pointing out that while the deficiency view of deafness may not be explicitly put to the groups mentioned, it is likely to pervade practices with deaf people. Also, it can be used as a device to explain aspects of the behaviour of deaf people which focus attention on the deaf person themselves rather than the situation in which they find themselves.

REFERENCES

BELLUGI, U., O'GRADY, L., LILLO-MARTIN, D., O'GRADY-HYNES, M., VAN HOEK, K. and CORINA, D. (1990) 'Enhancement of spatial cognition in deaf children' in VOLTERRA, V. and ERTING, C. (eds) *From Gesture to Language in Hearing and Deaf Children*, London, Springer-Verlag.

BONVILLIAN, J. D., ORLANSKY, M. D. and NOVAK, L. L. (1983) 'Early sign acquisition and its relation to cognitive and motor development' in KYLE, J. G. and WOLL, B. (eds) *Language in Sign*, London, Croom Helm.

BRENNAN, M. (1976) *Can Deaf Children Acquire Language?*, supplement to *British Deaf News*, February.

BRITISH ASSOCIATION OF TEACHERS OF THE DEAF (1981, amended 1985) 'Audiological definitions and forms for recording audiometric information', *Journal of the British Association of Teachers of the Deaf*, **5**, p. 3.

BROWN, R. (1965) *Social Psychology*, New York, Free Press.

BULWER, J. (1644) *Chirologia: or the natural language of the hand*, London, Whitaker.

BULWER, J. (1648) *Philocophus: or the deaf and dumb man's friend*, London, Humphrey Moseley.

CHOMSKY, N. (1967) 'The general properties of language' in DARLY, F. (ed.) *Brain Mechanisms Underlying Speech and Behavior*, New York, Grune and Stratton.

CONRAD, R. (1979) *The Deaf Schoolchild*, London, Harper and Row.

DAS GUPTA, P. (1995) 'Growing up in families' in BARNES, P. (ed.) *Personal, Social and Emotional Development of Children*, Oxford, Blackwell/The Open University (Book 2 of ED209).

EWOLDT, C. (1990) 'The early literacy development of deaf children' in MOORES, D. F. and MEADOW-ORLANS, K. P. (eds) *Educational and Developmental Aspects of Deafness*, Washington, Gallaudet University Press.

FOK, Y. Y. and BELLUGI, V. (1986) 'The acquisition of visiospatial script' in KAO, H. (ed.) *Graphonomics: Contemporary Research in Handwriting*, Amsterdam, North Holland.

FURTH, H. G. (1966) *Thinking Without Language: psychological implications of deafness,* New York, Free Press.

FURTH, H. G. (1971) 'Linguistic deficiency and thinking: research with deaf subjects 1965–1969', *Psychological Bulletin,* **76**(1), pp. 58–72.

GAINES, R., MANDLER, J. M. and BRYANT, P. E. (1981) 'Immediate and delayed recall by hearing and deaf children', *Journal of Speech and Hearing Research,* **24**, pp. 463–9.

GOSWAMI, U. and BRYANT, P. (1990) *Phonological Skills and Learning to Read*, Hove, Erlbaum.

GREGORY, S. and BARLOW, S. (1989) 'Interaction between deaf babies and their deaf and hearing mothers' in WOLL, B. (ed.) *Language Development and Sign Language*, Monograph No. 1, International Sign Linguistics Association, Centre for Deaf Studies, Bristol, University of Bristol.

GREGORY, S. and BISHOP, J. (1991) 'The mainstreaming of primary age deaf children' in GREGORY, S. and HARTLEY, G. (eds) *Constructing Deafness*, London, Pinter Press (first published in 1989).

GREGORY, S., BISHOP, J. and SHELDON, L. (in preparation) *Deaf Young People and Their Families*, Cambridge, Cambridge University Press.

GREGORY, S. and MOGFORD, K. (1981) 'Early language development in deaf children' in KYLE, J. K., WOLL, B. and DEUCHAR, M. (eds) *Perspectives in British Sign Language and Deafness*, London, Croom Helm.

HARRIS, M. and BEECH, J. (in press) 'Reading development in prelingually deaf children' in NELSON, K. and REGER, Z. (eds) *Children's Language,* vol. 8, Hillsdale (N.J.), Lawrence Erlbaum Associates.

HEAD, S. (1992) *Language in the Curriculum*, Internal Document, Royal School for the Deaf, Derby.

KAMPFE, C. M. and TURECHECK, A. G. (1987) 'Reading achievement of prelingually deaf students and its relationship to parental methods of communication: a review of the literature', *American Annals of the Deaf,* **132**, pp. 11–15.

KYLE, J. and ACKERMAN, J. (1989) 'Early mother–infant interaction in deaf families' in WOLL, B. (ed.) *Language Development and Sign Language,* Monograph No. 1, International Sign Linguistics Association, Centre for Deaf Studies, Bristol, University of Bristol.

LANE, H. (1988) 'Is there a psychology of the deaf?', *Exceptional Children,* **55**(1), pp. 7–19.

LEE, V. J. and DAS GUPTA, P. (eds) (1995) *Children's Cognitive and Language Development*, Oxford, Blackwell/The Open University (Book 3 of ED209).

LEWIS, M. M. (1968) *Language and Personality in Deaf Children*, London, National Foundation for Educational Research in England and Wales.

MARKOULIS, D. and CHRISTOFOROU, M. (1991) 'Sociomoral reasoning in congenitally deaf children as a function of cognitive maturity', *Journal of Moral Education,* **20**(1), pp. 79–93.

NELSON, K. (1973) *Structure and Strategy in Learning to Talk,* Monograph 38, Society for Research in Child Development, 1–2, No. 149.

OAKHILL, J. (1995) 'Development in reading' in LEE, V. J. and DAS GUPTA, P. (eds) *Children's Cognitive and Language Development,* Oxford, Blackwell/The Open University (Book 3 of ED209).

Petitto, L. A. (1987) 'On the autonomy of language and gesture: evidence from the acquisition of personal pronouns in American Sign Language', *Cognition*, **27**(1), pp. 1–52.

Petitto, L. A. and Marentette, P. F. (1991) 'Babbling in the manual mode, evidence for the ontogeny of language', *Science,* **251**, pp. 1493–6.

Quigley, S. P. and Kretschmer, R. E. (1982) *The Education of Deaf Children: issues, theory and practice,* London, Edward Arnold.

Riley, D. (1983) *War in the Nursery: themes on the child and mother,* London, Virago.

Rodda, M. and Grove, C. (1987) *Language, Cognition and Deafness,* Hove, Erlbaum.

Schlesinger, H. and Meadow, K. (1972) *Sound and Sign: childhood deafness and mental health*, Berkeley (Calif.), University of California Press.

Urwin, C. (1985) 'Constructing motherhood: the persuasion of normal development' in Steedman, C., Urwin, C. and Walkerdine, V. (eds) *Language, Gender and Childhood*, London, Routledge and Kegan Paul.

Volterra, V. (1986) 'What sign language research can teach us about language acquisition' in Tervoot, B. (ed.) *Signs of Life: proceedings of the Second European Congress on Sign Language Research*, The Institute of General Linguistics of the University of Amsterdam, Publication No. 50.

Wood, D., Wood, H., Griffiths, A. and Howarth, I. (1986) *Teaching and Talking with Deaf Children*, Chichester, Wiley.

Reading A   Learning to be deaf

Carol Padden and Tom Humphries

Before beginning our journey through the imagery and patterns of meaning that constitute Deaf people's lives, we must identify the community of 'Deaf' people with which we are concerned. Following a convention proposed by James Woodward (1972), we use the lowercase *deaf* when referring to the audiological condition of not hearing, and the uppercase *Deaf* when referring to a particular group of deaf people who share a language … and a culture. The members of this group … have inherited their sign language, use it as a primary means of communication among themselves, and hold a set of beliefs about themselves and their connection to the larger society. We distinguish them from, for example, those who find themselves losing their hearing because of illness, trauma or age; although these people share the condition of not hearing, they do not have access to the knowledge, beliefs, and practices that make up the culture of Deaf people. As we will emphasize in subsequent chapters, this knowledge of Deaf people is not simply a camaraderie with others who have a similar physical condition, but is, like many other cultures in the traditional sense of the term, historically created and actively transmitted across generations.

[…] Sam Supalla once described to us his childhood friendship with a hearing girl who lived next door (this account also appears in Perlmutter, 1986). As Sam's story went, he had never lacked for playmates; he was born into a Deaf family with several Deaf older brothers. As his interests turned to the world outside his family, he noticed a girl next door who seemed to be about his age. After a few tentative encounters, they became friends. She was a satisfactory playmate, but there was the problem of her 'strangeness'. He could not talk with her as he could with his older brothers and his parents. She seemed to have extreme difficulty understanding even the simplest or crudest gestures. After a few futile attempts to converse, he gave up and instead pointed when he wanted something, or simply dragged her along with him if he wanted to go somewhere. He wondered what strange affliction his friend had, but since they had developed a way to interact with each other, he was content to accommodate to her peculiar needs.

One day, Sam remembers vividly, he finally understood that his friend was indeed odd. They were playing in her home, when suddenly her mother walked up to them and animatedly began to move her mouth. As if by magic, the girl picked up a dollhouse and moved it to another place. Sam was mystified and went home to ask his mother about exactly what kind of affliction the girl next door had. His mother explained that she was HEARING and because of this did not know how to SIGN; instead she and her mother TALK, they move their mouths to communicate with each other. Sam then asked if this girl and her family were the only ones 'like that'. His mother explained that no, in fact, nearly everyone else was like the neighbours. It was his own family that was unusual. It was a memorable moment for Sam. He remembers thinking how curious the girl next door was, and if she was HEARING, how curious HEARING people were.

When Sam discovers that the girl next door is hearing, he learns something about 'others'. Those who live around him and his family are now to be called 'hearing'. The world is larger than he previously thought, but his view of himself is intact. He has learned that there are 'others' living in his neighbourhood, but he has not yet learned that others have different ways of thinking. Perhaps others are now more prominent in his world, and his thoughts about the world now have to acknowledge that they exist in some relation to himself, but it does not occur to him that these others might define him and his family by some characteristic they lack.

In fact, in almost all the stories of childhood we have heard from Deaf children of Deaf families, hearing people were 'curious' and 'strange' but mostly were part of the background. The children's world was large enough with family and friends that the existence of 'others' was not disruptive. At the age when children begin to reflect on the world, we see an interesting positioning of the self with respect to 'others', people like Sam's playmate and her mother. Sam has not yet understood that the outside world considers him and his family to have an 'affliction'; to him, immersed in the world of his family, it is the neighbours who lack the ability to communicate.

But before long, the world of others inevitably intrudes. We can see children learning about the minds of others in stories Deaf adults tell about their childhoods. A Deaf friend of ours, Howard, a prominent member of his community, made a revealing comment to a mixed audience of hearing and Deaf people. All members of his family – his parents and brother as well as aunts and uncles – are Deaf. He told the audience that he had spent his early childhood among Deaf people but that when he was six his world changed: his parents took him to a school for Deaf children. 'Would you believe,' he said, pausing expertly for effect, 'I never knew I was deaf until I first entered school?'

Howard's comment caused the intended stir in the audience, but it was clear to us that some people thought it meant that Howard first became aware of his audiological deficiency when he was six – that he had never realized before that he could not hear sounds. But this was not his meaning at all.

Howard certainly knew what 'deaf' meant. The sign DEAF was part of his everyday vocabulary; he would refer to DEAF people whenever he needed to talk about family and friends. When Howard arrived at school, he found that teachers used the same sign he used for himself at home, DEAF. But it did not take him long to detect a subtle difference in the ways they used the sign.

The child uses DEAF to mean 'us', but he meets others for whom 'deaf' means 'them, not like us'. He thinks DEAF means 'friends who behave as expected', but to others it means 'a remarkable condition'. At home he has taken signing for granted as an activity worth noticing, but he will learn at school that it is something to be talked about and commented on. Depending on what school a child attends, he may be forbidden to use signed language in the presence of his teachers. He will then have to learn how to carry out familiar activities within new boundaries, to learn new social contexts for his language. Skills he learned at home, such as to tell stories with detail about people and events, are not likely to be rewarded by teachers who do not know the language. His language will be subordinated to other activities considered more important, notably learning how to 'use his hearing', and to 'speak' (Erting, 1985b).

The child 'discovers' deafness. Now deafness becomes a prominent fact in his life, a term around which people's behaviour changes. People around him have debates about deafness, and lines are sharply drawn between people depending on what position they take on the subject. He has never thought about himself as having a certain quality, but now it becomes something to discuss. Even his language has ceased to be just a means of interacting with others and has become an object: people are either 'against' signed language or 'for' signed language. In the stories we have collected from Deaf children of Deaf parents, the same pattern emerges over and over: 'deafness' is 'discovered' late and in the context of these layers of meaning.

As a final example to drive home this point, we turn to the story of Joe, the youngest child of a Deaf family on a farm in the heart of Indiana. Joe told us, 'I never knew I was hearing until I was six. I never suspected in any way that I was different from my parents and siblings'.

It seems ludicrous to imagine a hearing child who does not know he can hear. Is a child like this unresponsive to sounds? Are we to imagine a hearing child who discovers sound at the age of six? Of course not. Joe did know about sound. He responded to sounds, and his conception of the world included sound. But in the flow of everyday life he had no cause to think about sound in anything but an incidental way. He probably thought about it as often and as consciously as children reflect on the fact that they have feet.

The key part of his comment lies in the sentence 'I never suspected I was in any way different from my parents and siblings.' This is not a case of pretended deafness: Joe did not fail to hear, but simply understood sound in a way he could reconcile with the experiences of his family. We can imagine a range of phenomena in this child's world that have double but compatible interpretations: a spoon falls and makes a sound as it hits the floor. Someone picks it up, not simply because it made a sound but because it slipped from view. The farmer goes out to milk the cows not only because they make noises, but because it is daybreak, the time set aside for milking. A door slams, air rushes into the room, and objects on the table rattle and wobble. Many sounds coincide with non-auditory events, to which Joe would have seen his parents responding. His parents' world gave him no reason to identify sound as a primary cause of events.

One might ask how a hearing child would understand a sound that had no corresponding non-auditory event. What if the door slammed in another room and his family did not respond? Would he not see this as odd, or even as a contradiction? We might imagine a moment when the child is startled by a loud noise, looks at his family, and is puzzled by their lack of response. But the child does not yet have a basis for being 'puzzled'. He does not have an alternative explanation. The most striking observation hearing children of Deaf parents make about their early years is that it never occurs to them until they are older that there is anything unusual about their abilities. For young children immersed in the world of their families, there is not yet space for contradictions.

These stories by adults about their childhood memories reveal a rare perspective on the question of how the world comes to mean what it does. The conventional belief is that there are certain immutable events, such as sound, that do not need translation and can be known directly. But Joe's story reminds us that very little is not filtered through the larger pattern of everyday life. Sound is not an entity that is free of interpretation, but something that emerges within a system of knowledge. One does not merely 'hear' thunder, but also must assimilate its place in relation to all other activity of the world, how to react to it, how to talk about it, how to know its relationship to other sounds. For both Deaf and hearing people, sound finds its place against the larger pattern of everyday life.

References

ERTING, C. (1985a) 'Cultural conflict in a school for deaf children', *Anthropology and Education Quarterly*, **16**, pp. 225–43.

ERTING, C. (1985b) 'Sociocultural dimensions of deaf education: belief systems and communicative interaction', *Sign Language Studies*, **47**, pp. 111–25.

PERLMUTTER, D. (1986) 'No nearer to the soul', *Natural Language and Linguistic Theory,* **4**, pp. 515–23.

WOODWARD, J. (1972) 'Implications for Sociolinguistics Research Among the Deaf', *Sign Language Studies,* **1**.

SOURCE: PADDEN, C. and HUMPHRIES, T. (1988) Deaf in America: voices from a culture, *London, Harvard University Press, pp. 7–12.*

Reading B   Language in another mode

H. Lane

Let us see how adroit oral language really is, then, in this fundamental task of spatial description. How well does English convey arrangements and distances of people and things in three-dimensional space? Both literally and metaphorically, we will need to refer to left–right, in front–behind, and above–below. Suppose I am giving a lecture and I look into the audience at two adjacent people – say, Will and his wife. In English I might say, 'Will is to the left of his wife,' but in that case I can also say he is on his wife's right – that is, 'Will is to the right of his wife.' So I have been quite unclear. Which is it? Is Will to the left or the right of his wife? The answer is: both. Anna, who is seated behind them, disagrees with me; Will was never to the left of his wife. If you followed that and think that English is clear although complicated about left and right, try this one: Arrange Will, his wife, and Anna so that Will is to the left of his wife, his wife is to the left of Anna, and Will is to the right of Anna.

I have tried to illustrate that in English we must give different accounts of the same array, depending on two things: first, the speaker's point of view, and, second, whether the speaker is using verbal pointing or intrinsic reference. Verbal pointing, called deixis, requires the English listener to know where the speaker is. The intrinsic system requires an interpretation of the scene and an intrinsic orientation. It applies to people and houses, but it will not work for trees, tables, or heaps. To illustrate, let's go for a picnic. If I ask you to put the little picnic table in front of the tree, you can comply with the instruction by putting it anywhere on the planet Earth; I have been quite unclear.

There is a nearby dog track, and we take our seats at the start line. As they leave the gate, the only dog I can see is the dog closest to me, which is, of course, in front of the other dogs; but he may be behind them as well – especially if I bet on him. The rabbit that runs around the inside rail of the track is behind all the dogs up to the turn, even though it is always in front of all of them.

My dog loses, and the sky darkens. 'The sun is behind the clouds,' you say. When the sun comes out from behind the clouds, is it then in front of the clouds? Actually, the sun is only behind the clouds when there is no sun.

I have brought two balloons to the picnic and tied them to a branch so the red is above the green. You, however, are lying on your side on the grass, looking at the vault of heaven, and the red is to the left of the green – or to the right of the green, depending on which side you're lying on. Unless, of course, you can see the horizon, in which case the red is above the green. 'My friend,' I tell you, 'there's a spider dangling above your head.' You go to brush it away, but where to swing? Is it close to you or far? Is it near your cheek or near the top of your head? Who knows?

Will is to the left of his wife. The table is in front of the tree. The black dog is in front of the others. There's a spider above your head. All of these sentences are ambiguous, but they are like those we use all the time. Then we must be rather poor at communicating in English that most essential of human messages, spatial arrays. I decided to do an experiment.

I bought a dollhouse – my first – that came with a few pieces of plastic furniture and, most important, a picture on the box showing how to arrange the furniture in this two-story home. There was a sofa, a TV, a stereo, a picnic table and two chairs, and a barbecue. A graduate assistant and I asked pairs of English speakers to assist us, as follows: With the house set up and the furniture in a pile in front of it, one of the pair was to look at the box and tell the other where to place each item of furniture, in an effort to reproduce the arrangement shown in the photograph on the box. We asked the furniture mover not to talk, and we tape-recorded the speaker. Seven pieces of furniture to place in common ways: should be easy. Here is a typical transcript, influencies and all, from a native speaker of English.

> Okay, we'll start with the table and chairs on the bottom floor. In front of the house, um, there's a patch of green, like a patio, and the round table goes in the – in the – uh – top corner of the pa – of the green square. Okay. And in front of the – at – in front of the table – um – between the ladder and the table – goes one of the red chairs. Okay. And across from that red chair, on the other side of the table, goes the second red chair. Okay. Now, the barbe – the barbecue goes on the strip of patio between the green square and the house. Um, um, over to the left, almost in the left corner. Not quite. Okay, now let's go upstairs. Oh, excuse me, we have to go back downstairs; I forgot the record player. Now we're in the house, and as you face the house, it's a – the – the right – your right corner; okay, that's where the record player will go. Against the wall, well against the wall in the corner. Okay? Now let's go upstairs. Okay. Now, on the second floor – the floor's divided into a terrace and a bedroom, and just where the terrace and the bedroom are divided there's no – there's a frame but no wall there and the couch or the little red seat goes in that frame, at an angle, so it's mostly in the room but it seems to stick out onto the terrace just a little bit. Okay. And the television goes – okay, the floor in that room is separated

by – there's a little ridge that sticks out of the floor, so the couch is on one side of the ridge – the television goes in the area that's separated with the other side of the ridge – and it's facing so that the person who is sitting on the couch can't see the TV screen – in other words, the TV screen is facing into the – is facing out of the house. Okay. Sort of facing the ladder. Okay. So we're done.

Now, because ASL is a spatial language, it can communicate arrangement and relative distance of things and people in quite a different way than English, or, indeed, any oral language. This makes interpreting signed into spoken language and vice versa unique among translation tasks in that the interpreter must mediate between spatial and linear languages, utterly restructuring spatial discourse as he or she translates from the one language into the other. ASL, instead of conveying a spatial array by a linear chain of words, can map that spatial message right onto its surface form. Moreover, once ASL establishes a location for an object, it need not be reestablished in order to refer to it. When I asked pairs of signers to do my experiment, they were not only quicker at it than English speakers, they followed a different strategy: they created a verbal map of the dollhouse by naming fixed parts of the house and locating those parts in space. Then they named the movable items that had to be placed by their partner and positioned them in the verbal space they had just created. I don't really know how to translate their spatial sentences into a nonspatial language like English, but I have tried to do it using the words 'here' and 'there' to translate the locating of an object in a position relative to the others.

Okay, take the round white table and put it outside, in front of the house, in the green area. The two chairs go next to the table. So the table's here and the chairs are one here and one here in front. Now, the cooking grill, you know, with the black hood that opens – the table's here, the grill goes here. The round table goes here, the chairs go here, the grill goes here. Now, the stereo – careful, it's heavy; find the living room wall with the bookshelves and the mirror and put it there in the corner, like this. Now, the TV – go upstairs, up the steps, enter where the roof begins, see where there's a dresser, pictures, and a lamp – put the TV there. Now, the chair, which folds open like a bed, it's red and white, take that upstairs. You see where the TV, the dressers, and the lamp are? Put it there. That's it.

So is speech, in the words of the Milan resolution, 'incontestably superior to sign,' or is it the other way around? My point is that no language is superior to any other, and none is beneath you if you look up to it. Languages have evolved within communities in a way responsive to the needs of those communities. ASL is attuned to the needs of the deaf community in the United States; English is not.

Source: Lane, H. (1992) The Mask of Benevolence: disabling the deaf community, *New York, Alfred A. Knopf, pp. 122–5.*

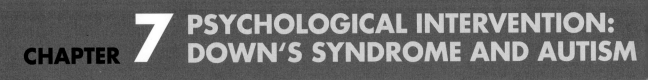

CHAPTER 7 PSYCHOLOGICAL INTERVENTION: DOWN'S SYNDROME AND AUTISM

Dorothy Faulkner and Vicky Lewis

CONTENTS

OBJECTIVES

When you have studied this chapter, you should be able to:

1 recognize that there is more than one approach to understanding intellectual impairment;

2 identify the various explanations of the causes and nature of Down's syndrome and autism;

3 explain the contribution of psychological research to our understanding of the development of children with Down's syndrome and autism and discuss how recent psychological research is changing our understanding of the nature of these impairments;

4 evaluate the implications of this with regard to concepts of intellectual impairment and psychological approaches to intervention.

1 INTRODUCTION

Intellectual impairment is a term used to describe people who have specific learning difficulties resulting from the fact that their intellectual abilities differ from those of the general population. However, as we shall see, such a definition depends upon how intellectual ability is measured and the criteria which are adopted to decide who falls into the 'disability' bracket as opposed to the so-called 'normal' bracket. The majority of these people are likely to be identified as learning-disabled as children and will receive some form of special educational provision. According to a report by Her Majesty's Inspectorate (1992), there are 168,000 children in England and Wales (or 2.1 per cent of the total school population) who need such help. This chapter will consider the identification of such children and ways in which their early development can be helped. In particular, we shall focus on children with Down's syndrome and children with autism.

We shall look at two different approaches to the identification and understanding of intellectual impairment. The first relies on using clinical diagnostic criteria and standardized measures of intelligence to identify the degree and possible causes of intellectual impairment. Broadly speaking, this way of looking at impairment could be described as a 'medical' or 'clinical' approach. The second attempts to understand whether psychological processes, such as attention, memory, perception and reasoning, develop in different ways in people with intellectual impairment, and whether specific patterns of impairment can be identified with particular causes. This approach takes a 'developmental' or 'psychological' stance towards identifying the various natures and causes of intellectual impairment.

Later in this chapter we will be looking at what psychologists have managed to discover about the nature of the perceptual and cognitive impairments associated with Down's syndrome and autism. They have discovered that while all children and adults with autism suffer from a particular form of cognitive deficit which produces a distinct pattern of social impairments, not all of them are intellectually impaired. In attempting to understand the nature of autism, therefore, psychologists must try to determine which features of autistic behaviour can be accounted for in terms of general intellectual impairment, and which features can be explained by more specific changes in the nature of particular psychological processes. Unlike autism, however, it has proved very difficult to identify any one pattern of impairment common to all children with Down's syndrome, even though Down's syndrome has a clearly identifiable genetic cause. Today, psychologists studying Down's syndrome are trying to discover exactly how the various cognitive processes develop in children with the syndrome.Their findings are beginning to indicate that psychological processes in children with and without Down's syndrome develop in very different ways. The findings also suggest some novel approaches to intervention.

In the final two sections of the chapter we shall examine the development of children with Down's syndrome and children with autism from a psychological perspective, and will move on to consider how recent research is changing our ideas about the kind of intervention and education programmes most appropriate for these children. Drawing on this research, we shall argue that a 'developmental' approach to understanding intellectual impairment is likely to be more fruitful than a 'clinical' approach, particularly when it comes to devising ways of facilitating the intellectual development of children with an impairment.

2 APPROACHES TO INTELLECTUAL IMPAIRMENT

In this section we want to contrast two approaches to the study of intellectual impairment in children which have potentially different implications for remediation and intervention. The first has traditionally been employed by the medical profession and involves quantifying the degree of intellectual impairment and identifying the precise nature of the problem. The second is more qualitative and is characteristically taken by psychologists. It involves understanding how developmental processes differ for children with and without impairments.

2.1 Intelligence and identification

According to the first approach, people are described as intellectually impaired either because their intelligence, as measured on standardized intelligence tests, falls below a certain level or because they are diagnosed as having an identifiable condition associated with a characteristically lower than average intellectual level. In the two sections which follow we shall explore features of both aspects.

Intelligence

The decision that a person has an intellectual impairment depends upon what is taken as 'normal' intelligence and where the cut-off between 'normal' and 'not normal' is set. Neither of these is fixed and both depend on a variety of factors (see Lee and Das Gupta, 1995, Chapter 5, for a discussion). However, if intelligence tests are used to identify people as having an intellectual impairment it is important to realize that:

(a) The intellectual potential of a particular population may be slightly greater or lesser than that of the population the tests were standardized on.

(b) The number of people classified as having an intellectual impairment crucially depends on where the cut-off point between 'normal' and 'impaired' is set. In the UK, the cut-off point has been set at 2 or more standard deviations below the mean. (One deviation equals 15 percentage points.) In the US, however, the American Association on Mental Deficiency has set the cut-off at 1 standard deviation. This means that the incidence of impairment in the US is apparently higher than it is in the UK.

The effects of having a standardized reference population and a fixed cut-off point on the incidence of impairment amongst children in a particular population is illustrated by Rutter's Isle of Wight study (see Research Summary 1).

Reseach Summary 1 shows that the number of children identified as having an intellectual impairment depends upon the characteristics of the population to which they belong.

Although intelligence can be described as a numerical continuum of IQ scores, children are seldom labelled with particular IQ scores. Rather, children of fairly similar intellectual levels are much more likely to be grouped together and described by a verbal label. These labels are not fixed and are subject to general views and expectations held by society at any one point in time. Reading A and Activity 1 give you an opportunity to explore how you might use certain verbal labels to characterize two children.

RESEARCH SUMMARY 1
RUTTER'S ISLE OF WIGHT STUDY

The Wechsler Intelligence Scale for Children (WISC) was administered to all children aged 10 to 11 living on the Isle of Wight in 1970. Using the WISC norms, 34 children were identified whose IQs fell two or more standard deviations below the mean. However, the WISC was administered to 302 children on the Isle of Wight and when an IQ distribution was constructed for this population it was found that the average IQ of these Isle of Wight children was greater than that of the population on whom the test had been standardized. When the distribution of Isle of Wight IQs was used to determine those whose IQs fell two or more standard deviations below the mean, 59 children were identified.

(Rutter, Tizard and Whitmore, 1970)

READING

At this point you should turn to Reading A, which gives brief case histories of two children, Pauline and Peter. The extract is taken from Barbara Furneaux's book *The Special Child* published in 1969. At this time, as Furneaux explains, it was extremely difficult to identify the cause of such children's obvious intellectual impairment.

Now try Activity 1.

<table>
<tr><td>

ACTIVITY 1

Allow about 20 to 30 minutes

</td><td>

PUTTING LABELS TO CASES

Select one of the following labels which you feel most adequately describes Pauline and one for Peter, then note down in the space provided why you have chosen this label in preference to the others.

Educationally subnormal child; mentally deficient child; child unsuitable for education in school; child with learning difficulties; mentally retarded child; child with special educational needs; mentally handicapped child.

              Pauline   *Peter*

Label

Reasons

</td></tr>
</table>

Some of you might have felt quite uncomfortable with this activity, and may have been unwilling to attach any one particular label to Peter and Pauline. Usually, with an activity of this nature, people want to know more about the children and their backgrounds before they are willing to make any judgements about how they should be labelled. Categorizing children in this way, however, was, and to some extent still is, common clinical practice.

According to Furneaux (1969), Peter's mother was told that he was 'clearly subnormal', and Pauline was declared to be 'unsuitable for education at school'. At the time these children were perceived as being profoundly 'handicapped' and were deemed to be unsuitable for education in normal schools. Furneaux argues, however, that to a significant extent even children who have severe intellectual difficulties can benefit from education. Take a few minutes to consider your choice of labels in Activity 1. Do they reflect the more recent educational emphasis?

From Table 1 you can see that there has been a shift from mental health classifications to classifications based on education. There has also been a shift in responsibility. Before 1971 children and young people with an intellectual impairment were the responsibility of the health authorities. In 1971 responsibility shifted to the education authorities, resulting in

TABLE 1 Changes in the relationship between IQ levels and labels applied to intellectual impairment over time.

IQ (MEAN=100; STANDARD DEVIATION=15)	0	20	35	50	70 75	85	100

OLD SCIENTIFIC TERMINOLOGY — INTELLECTUAL IMPAIRMENT

Idiot   Imbecile   Feeble-minded/moron

1959 MENTAL HEALTH ACT — SUBNORMALITY

Severely subnormal   Mildly subnormal

1968 WORLD HEALTH ORGANIZATION — MENTAL RETARDATION

Profound   Severe   Moderate   Mild

PRE-1971 EDUCATIONAL TERMINOLOGY

Unsuitable for education in school   Educationally subnormal

PRE-1978 WARNOCK TERMINOLOGY — EDUCATIONALLY SUBNORMAL

Severely subnormal ESN(S)   Moderately ESN(M)

1978 WARNOCK TERMINOLOGY — CHILDREN WITH LEARNING DIFFICULTIES

Severe   Moderate

POST-1981 ACT — CHILDREN WITH SPECIAL EDUCATIONAL NEEDS

much greater emphasis on educational provision in recent years. This emphasis on education arose as a result of the Warnock Committee's report, *Special Educational Needs*, published in 1978. The report recommended replacing classifications of children in terms of various physical and mental 'handicaps' with the broader definition of 'special educational needs'. It also advocated that primary schools were the most appropriate places to educate the majority of children with learning difficulties, particularly as, for many children, those difficulties were often transient. This report influenced policies set out in the 1981 Education Act (England and Wales), and encouraged local education authorities to establish policies for the integration of children with learning difficulties into mainstream schools.

These changes are reflected in Table 1, where you can see that today children with special educational needs are no longer labelled as being 'less able' than other children. Thirty years ago, however, children were given labels such as *sub*normal, mentally *deficient,* or *retarded*. These labels reflected the view that the children so labelled were at worst ineducable, and at best in need of some form of special segregated education.

Nowadays, fortunately, attitudes are more enlightened. Some children with intellectual impairments will always need specialized schooling, especially when they also have particular physical and social needs. Regardless of the severity of the impairment, however, attitudes today are that all children with learning difficulties can be given an education which will allow them to optimize their development. Unfortunately, this does not mean that all sources of stigmata have been removed from public consciousness. In the next section we shall discuss the reasons why clinical definitions of various forms of intellectual impairment result in people with very differing needs being grouped together under a common label.

Identification

Today, the label 'child with special educational needs' is used to describe any child with physical, emotional, or intellectual difficulties. Some of these children may also be labelled according to the medical diagnosis of their difficulties, although not all children with learning difficulties have a medically identifiable condition. In some cases these labels are non-specific, for example, Pervasive Developmental Disorder (PDD). This label indicates that while a child is failing to develop in the same way as other children of the same age, no single factor can be identified to explain why this should be the case. In other instances, where there is a clearly identifiable reason for a child's intellectual impairment, the label attached to that child may be highly specific, for example 'Down's syndrome'. Whatever the particular label, it is important to consider, in general terms, how children are diagnosed and the influence of diagnostic labels on people's expectations and attitudes towards intervention and education. Although labels have their uses, they are purely descriptive. A label in itself can tell us nothing about the form a particular impairment might take in an individual. Nor can they tell us much about the underlying changes to psychological processes which may be brought about as a result of the impairment. (See Chapter 1 for a more detailed discussion of the issue of labelling).

There are many conditions which are associated, or likely to be associated, with intellectual impairment. A person with an intellectual impairment may have other well-defined characteristics, genetic, physical and/or behavioural, which are a consequence of a particular condition. Usually a child is given a diagnostic label on the basis not of one single characteristic feature but of a cluster of features. When a specific cluster of features commonly occurs together in association with a particular condition, the condition is commonly known as a *syndrome*. Children displaying some or all of the characteristics of the syndrome are given the diagnostic label attached to the syndrome.

There are three things to notice about this process of identification. The first is that many of the features associated with particular syndromes are found in the general population. The second is that a child need not have all of the features within the cluster. However, the more features which are present the more likely the child is to be identified as having the syndrome. Also, in some cases, such as autism, a particular subset of features must be present before the syndrome is diagnosed.

Finally, the age at which a child can be identified as having one syndrome or another varies according to the defining features. If there is good reason to suspect an identifiable genetic disorder, perhaps due to family history, genetic tests may be carried out prenatally. Down's syndrome is an example of a genetic chromosomal disorder which can be detected prenatally. It is known that the likelihood that a child will have Down's syndrome increases with the age of the mother. The overall incidence in the general population is about 17 in 10,000 births. This incidence increases from about 10 per 10,000 births for women under 28 to 470 per 10,000 births for women over 40. As a result it is usual practice to offer pregnant women who are over 35 a prenatal test. If, as is usually the case with younger mothers, prenatal tests have not been carried out, when a newborn baby shows any of the distinctive physical characteristics associated with Down's syndrome, then behavioural and genetic tests will be carried out to see whether the syndrome is present.

People with autism, by contrast, do not have easily identifiable physical or genetic characteristics. Usually, these children come to the attention of professionals during early infancy because their parents are concerned about their behaviour and the fact that they are failing to meet developmental milestones. Initially it can be difficult to diagnose autism because the syndrome shares many features with other developmental language disorders. The original definition of the syndrome was given by Kanner in 1943. For Kanner the outstanding feature of children with autism was their inability to relate to and form relationships with other people. He also described various areas of development which were severely delayed in children with autism, including language acquisition; verbal communication skills; pretend play; and symbolic development. At the time, however, Kanner did not recognize that the majority of children with autism are also likely to have some degree of intellectual impairment.

Nowadays it is recognized that autism is associated with a variety of cognitive deficits as well as with social, emotional, and behavioural disturbances (e.g. Lockyer and Rutter, 1969). As there is great individual variation in the nature and severity of autistic features, and in the degree of intellectual impairment, many would argue that autism can be more usefully thought of as reflecting a continuum of impairment, rather than a syndrome (e.g. Waterhouse, Wing and Fein, 1989).

How early or late a syndrome can be identified in childhood has a number of implications for the way in which children are treated. Early identification and labelling as a result of physical features may be advantageous since it may allow children and their parents early access to specialist medical help and to appropriate intervention and educational programmes. On the other hand, early labelling may lead to lowered expectations of the child's developmental potential which may hinder subsequent development. Knowing that other people's lower expectations may persist throughout a child's life has led some parents to have the facial features of their child with Down's syndrome altered surgically, in the hope that this may change other people's attitudes towards their child's potential achievements. This 'solution' is of course very radical and raises all sorts of questions about why, to counteract society's prejudice, a child should have to undergo one or more painful operations so that he or she looks more like a child without Down's syndrome.

Where a problem is not identified in early childhood, however, opportunities for early intervention may be missed. Also, in cases where the identification is not clear cut, as with autism, initially an incorrect label might be attached to the child leading to inappropriate intervention.

There are other consequences of giving children diagnostic labels. One is that people may assume that children sharing a label will develop and behave in similar ways. In reality, although children with the same syndrome will share a number of characteristics, their development will differ in many ways. A diagnosis does not predict the exact course of development of any one individual. There are two main reasons for this. The first is that although they may share, for example, a genetic disorder, and will display the physical and psychological characteristics common to that disorder, they will also have inherited those genetic characteristics common to other members of their immediate family. This means that, as the genetic contribution from the family is greater than that of the disorder, family resemblances will be more evident than resemblances between unrelated children with the same disorder.
The other reason is that development is also influenced by the environment. Two children may have the same genetic disorder, but will grow up in distinctly different environments which will result in different developmental outcomes. It is therefore wrong to assume that if several children are assigned the same label their development will be identical.

Understanding how developmental processes differ for children with and without intellectual impairments is vital if we are to help children meet the challenges of their environment. A psychological approach to understanding intellectual impairment concentrates on identifying whether psychological processes operate differently in people with different kinds of impairment. This approach is discussed next.

2.2 Developmental processes

By developmental processes we mean the perceptual, cognitive, linguistic and social mechanisms which are responsible for developmental change. One of the most effective approaches to intellectual impairment is the detailed study of these mechanisms. There are three ways of conceptualizing how developmental processes may be influenced by impairment. Differences in ability can be explained in terms of either:

(a) a process being *missing* (deficit); or

(b) a *delay* in the development of a process; or

(c) a process operating in a *different* way from how it normally operates.

These three different sorts of models have been called *deficit*, *delay* and *difference* models respectively. Zigler (e.g. Zigler and Balla, 1982) has restricted the deficit explanation to people who have clear organic brain dysfunction where there is evidence of physiological abnormality or damage, and considers the difference and delay models relevant to people who have no evidence of brain dysfunction but who nevertheless have some form of intellectual impairment. Increasingly, however, all three models have been applied to the development of children with possible organic brain abnormalities, such as children with Down's syndrome and autism, even though in these cases the type and cause of the abnormality is less easily identifiable.

The problems with adopting any one model as an explanation of particular patterns of impairment lie with what the term may be taken to imply. For example, a deficit model implies that the missing process may never develop, leading to little optimism for intervention and justifying ignoring development in that area. A deficit model could also be used to justify views that affected people are different. This view could be used to support the segregation of people with the deficit from those without. If a delay model is proposed this too may suggest that nothing special needs to be done; the individual will develop the skills, albeit more slowly, without additional intervention. The third view, the difference model, implies there are different routes and mechanisms to promote development and that ways need to be found to exploit these. Such a view permits a more optimistic outlook for developmental change.

In reality it can be difficult to be certain how a developmental process is affected in a particular disorder. Down's syndrome children, for example, usually take much longer to acquire language skills compared with other children, and, while they may eventually become reasonably proficient, their language use is unlikely to be as sophisticated as that of other children. This outcome could be the result of a difference or a delay in the development of various cognitive processing mechanisms. In autism there is also disagreement about the exact nature of the underlying problem despite there being general acceptance that some form of socio-cognitive deficit is responsible.

Given the difficulties and drawbacks of explaining particular developmental disorders in terms of a single model, it is more important to consider the nature and patterns of development in such children by examining their psychological development in detail, rather than resorting to one or other model. As Wishart writes:

> … It may well turn out that the contrast between difference and delay theories of development hinges ultimately on the level of analysis used: studies in which the evidence appears to support a slow development theory may, on more detailed analysis, reveal the existence of important differences.
>
> (Wishart, 1988, p. 17)

One of the advantages of examining in detail the psychological development of children with disabilities is that such knowledge should enable us to design appropriate intervention programmes. Ideally intervention programmes should focus on the most important (or primary) impairment underlying a particular disorder. In some disorders, however, there is no consensus, as yet, on what the primary impairment is (e.g. autism). In other cases the primary impairment may not be amenable to intervention (e.g. some forms of brain damage). More often, therefore, intervention is targeted at the secondary impairments which can arise as a result of environmental factors such as lack of appropriate stimulation and encouragement. These issues are discussed in more detail in Chapter 1.

SUMMARY OF SECTION 2

- In this section we have examined how the identification and labelling of intellectual impairment changes depending upon the characteristics of the reference population and according to a society's attitudes and expectations.

- Labels may be useful in providing a summary or snapshot of a group of people, but they are extremely dangerous if they distract from the individual's own characteristics. Giving a child or group of children a label can lower society's expectations of children's potential. All children have aptitudes and skills which can flourish provided environment and expectations are of the highest order.

- Three psychological models – deficit, difference and delay – have been used to understand the nature of intellectual impairment. These models have different implications for intervention. Understanding how underlying psychological processes operate in cases of intellectual impairment offers more hope for designing effective interventions than descriptions of impairment in medical terms.

3 DOWN'S SYNDROME

We have suggested that labels, such as Down's syndrome, are associated with particular expectations and that these expectations may not be beneficial to the development of the children concerned. Such labels, because of their associations, may also cause great distress to parents when they are first told of the child's condition. In the following article a mother recalls some of her feelings:

A mother celebrates the birthday of a very special baby

My third child was born just before Christmas, a beautiful baby boy with squashy fingers and crinkly ears. I was overjoyed – and relieved. I was 37 and the triple test had given me a slightly worrying result. Carried out in pregnancy, it uses a sample of blood to estimate your chances of having a baby with Down's Syndrome. Women scoring 1/250 or less are considered high risk and offered an amniocentesis. I scored 1/260, so had no further tests.

I tried to pick the baby up but the umbilical cord was very short. He was reluctant to feed but after much persuasion took the breast. He lay in my arms, a curiously serene little bundle with a dusting of fine hair. I couldn't wait to get him home but the doctor said they would carry out some routine tests because of his initial refusal to feed.

'I'm sure there's nothing to worry about,' smiled a young nurse as she hung up mistletoe. Walking down the ward, I thought I heard whispering break out behind my back.

The paediatrician arrived just as we decided to call the baby Euan. He let the baby slip through his fingers, stroking the back of his head with a practised hand. Sitting on the bed, he glanced at John, then back to me. 'Here comes the tricky bit,' he said calmly. 'I think your baby's got Down's syndrome.' He went over the telltale signs – the short umbilical cord, stubby fingers, low-set ears, poor muscle tone. We listened numbly, unable to comprehend that the nightmare had come true: there was something wrong with the baby.

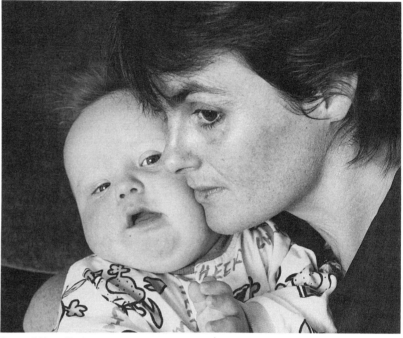

Pat and Euan Evans.

As John leant over the cot and kissed the sleeping child, I realised I was crying, great sheets of tears moving slowly down my face. Inside I felt cold, hard, cruel. The paediatrician kept on talking, as if his words were a charm to keep our suffering at bay. 'You've ordered from a catalogue and got something back you didn't expect. There's nothing *wrong* with this baby, he's just different. He's not suffering, you are. He'll be in touch with things we aren't.' He made it sound as if anyone in their right mind would have Down's syndrome.

'What about intelligence?' I asked sharply. 'Only intelligent people worry about intelligence.'

He correctly predicted the emotions we would feel: grief for the child we thought we would have, sorrow for the disastrous human being we thought he would be.

The other mothers stared as we were led into a room of our own. Some of the nurses were crying and the doctor who had examined me in pregnancy averted his eyes and scurried away. John went home to see the children and I was left alone with the baby who didn't belong to me but Mr and Mrs Down's Syndrome. He didn't bear our features but theirs, his personality rose from their union, not mine and John's.

They offered to take him to the nursery but I refused, terrified that in his absence I would reject him. I had to keep him close, make him mine once more. Waking in the dead of night, I stared into his sleeping face. He almost frightened me, this tiny, alien being wearing a mask which separated him from the rest of humanity. He was branded, set apart and now so was I. Stroking his head, I felt an agony of guilt, pity and fear. I had done this to him, I had blighted the flower before it had a chance to bloom. What terrible blackness inside me had afflicted my own child?

Later on they struggled to take blood from a vein in his head and I felt upset in a remote kind of way, as the needle made him cry out. He was given a heart scan and I watched, curious about my own reactions. Did I want him to be healthy? Would it be better if he slipped away now?

Three doctors sitting like a military tribunal pronounced judgment. The scan was normal. I took Euan home, just in time for the parties.

Twelve months later, it's nearly Christmas again. A chill mist shrouds the hills outside our house; inside Euan plays near the foot of the Christmas tree, like a present from Santa delivered express. He has slanted eyes, sticky-out ears and a tongue that pops from his mouth like the label of a collar which refuses to lie flat. He might not go to primary school, let alone university, but every time he smiles – which he does all the time – my heart turns over. Love has grown in the rubble of broken dreams. Take ego away from parental love and what flowers is more passion than I had ever thought possible. And not everyday love but a superior version because the selfish element is cut to the bone.

Euan has taught me so many things: that the ability to communicate is more important than IQ and may have nothing to do with it, and that creating love in others is so simple, a child can do it. Try as I might, I can't feel tragic about a baby who shakes with silent laughter as his sister wraps tinsel round his head. Most of all, Euan has made me realise just how we underestimate our capacity for loving.

Every woman who gives birth to a handicapped child does so in a climate of rejection and fear. Yet even as I struggled to come to terms with Euan's birth, I continued to bond with my baby. With every passing moment, the gap between us closed, changing my perceptions, banishing my fear.

In the end, loving him was as easy – and I cannot emphasise the word enough – as natural as falling off a log. Loving Euan, I find I like myself better too. I stared the bogeyman in the face and he ran away, not me.

When next you see the parents of a handicapped child, don't automatically feel sorry for them because you have absolutely no idea what they are feeling. Love, in the words of the song, changes everything.

(Evans, 1992, p. 11)

Clearly, this mother's feelings towards her son have changed dramatically over his first year. One way to conceptualize this change is that at the time when she was first told, she was responding to the label *Down's syndrome,* whereas twelve months on, she is responding to her son *Euan.* Nevertheless, even twelve months later, although she no longer views her son as 'a disastrous human being' she still has expectations which result from the label, for example, expectations concerning his education. It is certainly true that in the past most children with Down's syndrome have attended some sort of special school. However, more recently, as knowledge and understanding of their potential has increased, many more are attending mainstream schools, such as the 11-year-old girl described here:

> Every morning before her parents come downstairs, Kirsty Arrondelle lays out the breakfast things; her father's favourite yoghurt and his orange juice, cereal bowls and spoons. If it is a weekend she will play with the family's two cheerful golden retrievers or read aloud to herself from one of her favourite books before the neighbourhood wakes up and the stream of children in and out of the house begins. If it is a weekday, she will set off with her mother for the local primary school.

> Kirsty, now 11 years old, has just moved into the top juniors for her last year at primary school in Bishop's Stortford, Hertfordshire, where she will prepare for transfer to secondary school alongside all her other classmates. Kirsty's parents hope that transfer will be to the nearest mixed comprehensive – a Catholic school with 700 children on roll. They have chosen it because it offers the most appropriate learning environment for their daughter.

> (Allen, 1987, p. 1)

It is quite clear that the abilities of people with Down's syndrome have been underestimated in the past and that we still do not know their potential. In the sections that follow we shall consider what psychologists have discovered about the processes underlying their development and the implications of this understanding for intervention.

First, however, it is worth briefly considering the evidence for organic damage. A number of studies have reported structural differences in the brains of people with Down's syndrome; for example, they have smaller than average cerebella. However, more suggestive of damage is evidence indicating that neuronal development in the brain is less extensive and less developed than is found generally (for a review see Kemper, 1988). This evidence does not in itself enable us to distinguish between the three models of deficit, difference and delay. Let us take a look at the evidence concerning cognition, perception and language. We have selected these areas since they are all crucial to development and are therefore of particular significance when development fails to keep pace with chronological age. Because of their importance they are often prime targets for intervention.

3.1 Cognitive abilities of children with Down's syndrome

Much of the research into the cognitive abilities of children with Down's syndrome suggests that their development follows a similar route to that of ordinary children but that these developments are delayed (e.g. Dunst, 1990). However, a growing number of studies suggest that there may be important differences in their development which cannot just be explained in terms of delay. The study by Morss (1985) described in Research Summary 2 is an example.

RESEARCH SUMMARY 2
DOWN'S SYNDROME – DELAY OR DIFFERENCE?

Morss (1985) carried out a longitudinal study of the performance of babies with Down's syndrome on a range of Piagetian object permanence tasks. Interestingly he found that, compared with other babies, they did pass the tasks at a later age, supporting a delay model, but that, importantly, they seemed to be following a different developmental sequence. In particular, whereas when an ordinary baby succeeded on one task, she would also succeed on easier tasks and would continue to succeed on these tasks on subsequent occasions, the babies with Down's syndrome might pass a task on one occasion and then fail the same task on a later occasion. In other words the sequence with which the children with Down's syndrome passed tasks was different from that of the other children and the performance of individual children with Down's syndrome was not consistent over time.

Similar findings have been obtained by Wishart (1988, 1990), who, as already mentioned, points out that the reason for some studies reporting differences, while others report delay, may be the methodologies employed. It is important to note that choice of methodology can influence the way we understand the underlying nature of a particular disorder. Researchers reporting differences in children with Down's syndrome have tended to study their development in more detail, more frequently and over a longer period of time than researchers who concluded that their development is delayed.

You can see, therefore, that in the area of early cognitive development there is good reason to suppose that children with Down's syndrome may be developing differently from other children. Clearly, this will have implications for intervention. How about other areas of psychological development?

3.2 Perceptual abilities of children with Down's syndrome

The majority of studies comparing the visual abilities of children with and without Down's syndrome have reported few differences providing the children are of similar developmental level (i.e. where children in the comparison group are matched with those with Down's syndrome on the basis of mental age, rather than chronological age). Such findings alone would support a delay position. However, there are some suggestions that there may be differences in how the children are processing information. For example, Cohen (1981) examined habituation and dishabituation in babies with and without Down's syndrome all aged between 19 and 28 weeks of age (for descriptions of habituation and dishabituation see Oates, 1995, Chapter 3). However, Cohen found that although the number of trials to reach a criterion of 50 per cent fixation to the habituated stimulus was the same in the two groups, on each trial the babies with Down's syndrome were taking longer to process information, perhaps because their ability to process visual information was different from that of the ordinary babies.

There is also some evidence of a processing difference when the tactile modality or sense of touch is involved. A study by Lewis and Bryant (1982) found that 1- to 4-year-old children with Down's syndrome were less able than other children of similar developmental level to visually distinguish an object they had previously felt from one which they had not felt, although there was no difference when they had previously seen the object. These findings could be explained in several ways:

- Perhaps children with Down's syndrome are poor at coding and remembering information from the tactile modality. There is some support for this from studies of adults with Down's syndrome.

- Perhaps children with Down's syndrome are poor at translating tactile information into its visual equivalent.

- Perhaps children with Down's syndrome just need longer to process tactile information.

Whichever explanation turns out to be correct, it does seem clear that the way in which children with Down's syndrome process tactile information is different from the way in which other children process the same information. Given that the children were matched for developmental level in this study, a delay cannot be the explanation for observed differences in perceptual processing.

3.3 Linguistic and communicative abilities of children with Down's syndrome

When we look at the child's earliest interactions with other people, research has shown that there seem to be some differences between children with Down's syndrome and other children. For example, from about 6 months babies with Down's syndrome shift their gaze from one thing to another – whether it be from caregiver to objects in their environment, or between people – much less than children who do not have Down's syndrome. This means that young children with Down's syndrome spend much less time exploring their environment and much more time focused on one part of their environment than other children. Given the findings on perceptual abilities these findings are perhaps not surprising and could also be caused by a difference in how children with Down's syndrome process information.

Researchers have also noticed that there is less turn-taking in the proto-conversations between children with Down's syndrome and their caregivers, and that caregivers of babies with Down's syndrome seem to take greater charge of the interaction than is the case with other children. They talk for a greater proportion of the interaction and give more verbal directions to the child than is normally observed. Let us consider what might be going on here. Imagine a baby and her caregiver. The baby does something, the caregiver responds, the baby reacts to the response and so on. But if the baby has Down's syndrome and is processing what is going on differently and taking longer to make sense of her caregiver's response she may therefore not react as soon as an ordinary baby. Since nothing happens the caregiver does something else. The result of this is that the caregiver seems to take over the interaction and the rhythm which is so characteristic of the interaction between caregivers and other babies seems absent.

In support of this interpretation Berger (1990) found that when mothers of 3- to 7-month-old babies with Down's syndrome were asked to imitate what their babies were doing, some of the children became more socially responsive and played more. However, this was not the case for all of the children. Also some of the mothers found what they were asked to do very unnatural and off-putting. Nevertheless, it is encouraging that for some of the children this strategy did seem to work.

When we look at language in children with Down's syndrome the evidence seems quite clear that their language development is slower and less advanced than would be expected on the basis of their general developmental level (e.g. Fowler, 1990). This is particularly the case with the development of syntactic or grammatical structures (e.g. Chapman *et al.*, 1991). Since in most children without Down's syndrome there is a strong relationship between developmental level and language ability, this evidence again implies a difference rather than a delay. However, the reason behind the difference is not clear. For example, it could be a result of the sorts of differences we have already observed in their early interactions with caregivers. On the other hand it could be that the hypothesized difference in information processing results in particular difficulties when it comes to language. Alternatively it could be due to some combination of these or to something else.

Some evidence which supports the idea of different processes underlying language development in children with Down's syndrome comes from dichotic listening experiments. In these experiments people are required to pay attention to one of two different messages being relayed to them through a headphone set. People are asked to attend either to the message being relayed to their right ear, or to the one going into their left ear. Normally, dichotic listening experiments show a right ear advantage for linguistic material, indicating that the left hemisphere is dominant for language. Studies which have explored this with relation to Down's syndrome (e.g. Hartley, 1985), have found no evidence of this right ear advantage for linguistic material, indicating that children with Down's syndrome may process language in a different way from other children.

ACTIVITY 2

Allow about 20–30 minutes

DELAY VERSUS DIFFERENCE – SUMMARIZING THE EVIDENCE

In this section we have presented several arguments for and against both delay and difference explanations of the processing abilities of children with Down's syndrome. To get these distinctions clear in your own mind, go back and reread Sections 3.1–3.3 and then use the following headings to summarize the evidence.

Evidence for a delay explanation   *Evidence for a difference explanation*

3.4 Intervention with children with Down's syndrome

Currently most intervention techniques which are used with children with Down's syndrome are based upon our understanding of 'normal' development and therefore reflect assumed 'normal' pathways of development. In this section, after briefly describing an approach to intervention which is currently available in the UK, we shall consider the implications for intervention of our current understanding of the processes underlying psychological development of children with Down's syndrome.

One of the best known intervention programmes available in the UK is Portage. This programme, which began in Wisconsin in the US in 1969, is often used with children with Down's syndrome. It involves a keyworker visiting the parent/caregiver and child on a regular basis and, using developmental checklists, working with the carer to select areas which need further development. Together they then decide how the caregiver should work on these areas in the coming week(s). This will involve decisions about *when* to work on a particular skill as well as *how* best to teach it. At the next visit, again using the checklists, the carer and worker review progress and identify further skills to be acquired and how to go about developing these.

Although parents are often reported to find the Portage system of value, it is not clear that it has much long-term benefit for the child. One of the main difficulties is that, as with many intervention programmes, the checklists are based on the development of ordinary children and the main model of development that the keyworker is following is likely to be that of 'normal' development. In this sense the approach could be seen as one of 'normalizing' the development of the child with Down's syndrome. Such an approach may be fine with a child who is following the same pattern of development as an ordinary child, and is achieving the same landmarks by the same route. However, our argument in this chapter has been that this assumption may be unfounded for children with Down's syndrome. We therefore need to consider how intervention should proceed.

Also, although we know that children with Down's syndrome are liable to achieve a great deal more than was thought possible in the past, it is still not clear what their potential is. We have already indicated that the limited ability of people with Down's syndrome reported in the past may have reflected the limited expectations that society, professionals and families had of these people. Intervention programmes may raise parental expectations and as a result overcome hidden deprivation effects. A useful review of some different programmes involving children with Down's syndrome has been written by Hughes (1985), who points out that approaches to intervention have been affected by society's attitudes and expectations of people with Down's syndrome.

However, it is not enough just to raise expectations. It is also necessary to develop intervention strategies in line with our understanding of how children with Down's syndrome develop. In this section we have argued that the cognitive, perceptual and linguistic achievements of children with

Down's syndrome do not simply develop more slowly than in ordinary children; rather they develop in *different* ways. The implication of this and other evidence for intervention is clear: we need to develop ways of supporting and facilitating this different development. This argument is put forward by Wishart in Reading B.

READING

At this point you should turn to Reading B at the end of this chapter. Here Wishart argues that intervention programmes may have failed to produce lasting changes in the development of children with Down's syndrome because they have assumed that development is delayed rather than different.

In agreement with Wishart we would argue that it is crucial to develop intervention programmes based on our present understanding of the psychological development of children with Down's syndrome. Unless this sort of approach is adopted we shall not develop appropriate and effective programmes. Activity 3 gives you the opportunity to review the arguments in Section 3.4 and to consider their implications for intervention.

ACTIVITY 3

Allow about 15-20 minutes

IMPLICATIONS FOR INTERVENTION WITH CHILDREN WITH DOWN'S SYNDROME

Based on your reading of Wishart's article and on your reading of Sections 3.1–3.4, what implications can you identify for intervention? List below what you would try to include in any programme of intervention. Once you have drawn up your list you might like to compare it with ours.

Comment

We have identified a number of implications:

- It is important to repeat activities so that newly-acquired behaviours can be consolidated and fully incorporated into the child's repertoire.

- Checklists of current behaviour and abilities need to be used and interpreted with caution, as at any one time, children with Down's syndrome may fail to demonstrate a behaviour they have previously developed and current behaviours may drop out of the child's repertoire.

- Care must be taken not to overload the child with too much information as they do not seem as able as other children to sample a great deal of information at any one time.

- The child also needs to be given plenty of time to process information about his or her environment. Caregivers need to be encouraged to adopt a contingent style of teaching (i.e. one of waiting for the child to respond and then reacting at an appropriate level) rather than a formal, didactic style.

- It is important to be aware that there are alternative routes to development for children with Down's syndrome. For example, although ordinary children usually learn to speak and some years later learn to read, it has been reported that children with Down's syndrome benefit from being introduced to reading long before they have reached the stage of language proficiency usually considered necessary for learning to read (e.g. Buckley, 1986).

In conclusion we would argue that although intervention programmes such as Portage may be beneficial and raise expectations, they may not be as effective as intervention programmes based on a detailed understanding of the psychological processes underlying the development of children with Down's syndrome. Such programmes do not yet exist. Their development should be encouraged.

In the next section we look at autism and the various models and explanations which have been proposed to account for it. It is generally agreed that autism cannot be explained in terms of a developmental delay and that a deficit or difference model is needed.

SUMMARY OF SECTION 3

- In the area of early cognitive development there is good reason to suppose that children with Down's syndrome may be developing differently from other children.

- Babies with Down's syndrome take longer to process visual information than other babies. They also process tactile information differently, A delay model cannot explain these findings.

- Evidence suggests that different processes underlie language acquisition in children with and without Down's syndrome. The nature of the differences is not yet clear, but they are difficult to accommodate within a delay account of development. This strengthens the argument that there are real differences in the way in which children with Down's syndrome acquire language, compared to other children of equivalent developmental level.

- Wishart argues that intervention programmes may have failed to produce lasting changes in the development of children with Down's syndrome because they have assumed that development is delayed rather than different.

4 AUTISM

4.1 Introduction – characteristics of autistic behaviour

When the full spectrum of autistic disorders is taken into account, recent estimates of the incidence of autism in the general population suggest that 23 people in every 10,000 may be affected (Aarons and Gittins, 1992). We still do not have all the explanations for autism but we have come a long way in our understanding of this strange and puzzling condition since it was first described by Kanner in 1943.

ACTIVITY 4

Allow about 10 minutes

YOUR OWN VIEW OF AUTISM

What does the term 'autism' mean to you? Make a list of what you know about this condition.

Even people who have had no personal contact with a child with autism or their family have some idea of what is meant by 'autism', as the syndrome has had a fair amount of media attention over the past ten years. It would be fair to say, however, that much of this attention has been directed towards so-called 'high-functioning' people with autism, i.e. those with special talents like Stephen Wiltshire, the artist; those who have written their own personal account, like Donna Williams (1992); and people who, although they display markedly odd behaviours, are able to survive in the community, like Dustin Hoffman's character in the film *Rain Man*. These accounts may give the impression that autism is a disorder which can be largely overcome in time given the right kind of circumstances.

It is now recognized that autism is a life-long condition. Although successful specialist educational and therapeutic training programmes may improve an autistic person's behaviour and communication skills, they will continue to show features of autistic behaviour throughout their lives. We also know that autism is not restricted to any one particular subset of the population and there is no real evidence for the once popular theory that children become autistic as a result of having parents who are cold and unresponsive towards them. What then are the characteristics of autistic behaviour?

ACTIVITY 5

Allow about 15 minutes

CHARACTERISTICS OF AUTISTIC BEHAVIOUR

Read the following descriptions written by the parents and siblings of children with autism. Compile your own list of features and behaviours which these children display as compared with non-autistic children.

For years Jon never looked back at me, never would say 'goodbye', although he greeted you. Jon could not bear ... any kind of frustration as an early infant running into all the rooms of the toddler clinic; all over the park into people's picnics, to every possible boundary, over the fence, into the road; you found that your life consisted of chasing him everywhere. And if he would not walk, he would just lie down upon the pavement and had to be hoisted in a 'fireman's lift' on my husband's back for several hundred yards.

(Cheale, 1990, p. 71)

The doctor was about as brutal as it's possible to imagine. Without any preamble she stated that Katy was autistic and severely mentally handicapped ... Test after test followed, which proved that Katy was physically sound. She had brain-scans, hearing and sight tests, EEGs, etc., but after all of this, it was clear that there was something not quite right. She attended a Mothers and Toddlers Playgroup ... ; she had no imaginative play – for example, she wouldn't play with dolls or play with any object to which she had to inject an element of pretend. No, Katy preferred the sound of music boxes; she liked spinning objects; watching flashing lights, tearing paper and, when she was not doing that, she was of course rummaging through the drawers and cupboards trying to find the most dangerous article in the house to play with.

(Ford and Ford, 1986, p. 1)

Christopher had always been a lazy baby – he did not crawl until he was fifteen months old and he was well over two before he walked. He would sit for hours screaming, flapping, banging his head against the walls. His behaviour was often embarassing particularly when out shopping, at other people's houses etc ... Christopher did not relate to us in any way, shape or form; he did not feel pain and often appeared not to even recognize us. I think that this is the most painful part for the parent of an autistic child. We felt so unloved.

(Pain, 1985, p. 1)

As we saw earlier, in Section 2.1, Kanner (1943) identified difficulties in forming relationships and delayed or abnormal language development as the characteristics of autism. He also mentioned that the play of children with autism appears to be repetitive and stereotyped, and that they need a lot of routine and structure in their day-to-day lives. Children diagnosed as autistic may also show a number of specific characteristics, such as hyperactivity, obsessive behaviours, particular talents, and self-injurious behaviours. Their main problem, however, lies in relating to and communicating with other people.

Figure 1, from the British National Autistic Society's journal, *Communication*, illustrates *some* of the many ways in which autism is displayed.

Autism is...

a perplexing life-long mental handicap affecting about 80,000 people in Britain today. Isolated in a world of their own, autistic people need help to fit in. The first step towards progress is recognition of the condition.

These pin men illustrate *some* ways in which autism is displayed.

Displays indifference

Joins in only if adult insists and assists

One-sided interaction

Indicates needs by using an adult's hand

Does not play with other children

Talks incessantly about only one topic

ARE YOU GOING?   ARE YOU GOING?

Echolalic - copies words like parrot

- Difficulty with social relationships
- Difficulty with verbal communication
- Difficulty with non-verbal communication
- Difficulty in the development of play and imagination
- Resistance to change in routine

Bizarre behaviour

Handles or spins objects

Inappropriate laughing or giggling

FAMILIAR ROUTE   DIFFERENT ROUTE

No eye contact

Variety is not the spice of life

Lack of creative, pretend play

But some can do some things very well, very quickly but *not* tasks involving social understanding

FIGURE 1
The National Autistic Society's characteristics of autism.

Early diagnosis is essential if autistic people are to achieve full potential. It is only when their handicap is understood that they can be helped to maximise skills and minimise problems.

Children with autism vary a great deal in the type and severity of their symptoms. This has led to the view that autism should be conceived of as a continuum. At the end of the continuum are the so-called low-functioning autistics who display many of the behaviours shown on the outside of Figure 1. These are the people who will also have a significant degree of mental impairment (IQs below 70). At the other end are the so-called high-functioning autistics. These people may have some of the behaviours shown in Figure 1 but they are not mentally impaired to any significant extent. *All* adults and children with autism, however, will show the principal impairments listed in the box at the centre of Figure 1. While labels such as 'high-' and 'low-functioning' may be a useful form of shorthand, however, we should not let them colour our expectations as to the possible potential of individuals with autism.

4.2 Autism and intelligence

In Kanner's day it was assumed that the intellectual potential of people with autism was usually above that of the average population. There were two reasons for this assumption. One was that the parents of the children Kanner studied were themselves highly intelligent professional people, leading Kanner to suspect that their children were likely to be intelligent too. Later review studies (e.g. Bettelheim, 1967), which have examined much larger samples of children, have shown that there is no relationship between parental intelligence and the incidence of autism.

The second reason is that some children with autism show a precocious talent in one particular area. Often, as is the case with Stephen Wiltshire whose extraordinary architectural drawings are well known, this talent comes to the attention of the media (e.g. Wiltshire, 1989). The linguist Christopher Taylor (described by O'Connor and Hermelin, 1991), who can speak many different obscure and archaic languages, is

FIGURE 2
Stephen Wiltshire
at work.

another example of a young man with autism who has a very unusual talent. Unfortunately in Christopher's case he cannot use his remarkable knowledge to communicate with other people very well.

These people have what are known as *islets of ability*. The existence of these islets frequently led people to overestimate the intellectual potential of children with autism. During the 1960s and 1970s it was believed that their difficulties were not due to mental impairment, but could be accounted for in terms of disturbed or delayed emotional and social development. This belief also gave rise to the view that the communication barrier between autistic children and the rest of the world could be overcome by intensive educational and therapeutic intervention. The current view, however, is that these special aptitudes are simply islets of unusual ability; they do not reflect general cognitive potential.

Even within the subset of people who do demonstrate islets of ability, there can be large differences in their measured IQ, and this is another reason for making a distinction between 'high-functioning' and 'low-functioning' people with autism. High-functioning people may be able to lead relatively independent lives as adults, but many low-functioning people cannot cope with the demands of society and may remain with their families or in some form of institutional care for the whole of their life.

4.3 Diagnosing autism.

As we mentioned in Section 2 the diagnosis of children with autism is not easy and for many parents and children it may take a very long time for the condition to be recognized for what it is. Children with autism cannot be distinguished by their physical appearance. Even as babies, however, their behaviour is distinctly different from that of non-autistic babies. Look back at the descriptions of children in Activity 5. You can see that by the time the children were toddlers, their behaviour was sufficiently different from other children to be causing considerable concern.

As with Jon and Christopher (see Activity 5), interactions with other people, particularly parents, will be unusual. 'Christopher did not relate to us in any way, shape or form'; 'For years Jon never looked back at me'. This extreme difficulty in relating to other people is common to all people with autism and has been described as *autistic aloneness*:

> Exactly what this is cannot be identified with a specific behaviour. It can only be inferred from behaviour ... This intangible difference of autistic children, pervading all sorts of behaviour, is highly conspicuous to the experienced clinician. Theirs is not just any social abnormality. In particular it is not the same as shyness, rejection or avoidance of human contact, although autistic behaviour has sometimes been interpreted in this way. *Autistic aloneness* ... has nothing to do with being alone physically, but it does have to do with being alone mentally.

(Frith, 1989, pp. 11–12)

Frith maintains that although there are no definitive tests for autism, experienced clinicians can recognize the condition by careful observations of children's behaviour. If the following 'triad of social impairments' (Wing, 1981, 1988) are all observed to be present then it is likely that a diagnosis of autism will be made:

(a) an impairment of social recognition (e.g. indifference to other people and avoidance of social contact);

(b) an impairment of social communication (e.g. absence of desire to communicate verbally or engage in reciprocal conversation);

(c) an impairment of social imagination and understanding (e.g. lack of pretend play, little recognition of what goes on in other people's minds, and little understanding of how to find out what other people's intentions might be).

Taken singly, these characteristics are not unique to children with autism. What is unique to autism is the fact that these three impairments occur in combination. Also, as with Down's syndrome, it has recently been recognized that in autism the developmental paths of various psychological processes are very different from those in other children. Rutter and Schopler (1988) go so far as to apply the label 'deviant' to some of the developmental processes observed in cases of autism, such as those underlying language development, for example. So, as with children who have Down's syndrome, the pattern of development for children with autism may be very different from that of other children.

The fact that autism is still difficult to diagnose is borne out by numerous accounts of the parents and relatives of children with autism who have been referred to one specialist after another before a final diagnosis has been made, as the following quotation illustrates:

> … one morning, just before his third birthday [Ben] dropped onto the floor making terrible noises. It was a major epileptic fit, the first of hundreds. This marked the end of the Ben we thought we knew and the beginning of an endlessly desperate family situation. I watched helplessly as his intelligence and personality deteriorated daily … doctors were at first calm, enigmatic and non-specific. Then, unthinkable, obscene words began to filter into their vocabulary: 'brain damage'; 'mental handicap'; 'severely subnormal'. Needing, above all, to make sense of this outrage, I raised the question of autism with one eminent specialist. 'I would be very cautious about applying that label to any child,' he replied, adding that it was a matter experts disagreed on.

> … By Ben's late teens no expert, whether educational or medical, had given to his many oddities the name which might have lighted the way ahead. It was then that I took the plunge and joined the National Society for Autistic Children. I was soon reading papers by Drs Lorna Wing and Elizabeth Newson. And I found described, for the first time, a world of people like Ben.

(Marlow, 1988, pp. 1–2)

Diagnosing autism is also problematic because as many children with autism also have low IQs it is difficult to separate out effects specific to autism from those specific to intellectual impairment. Aarons and Gittins (1992) argue that an assessment of autism should not be a matter of subjective clinical judgement alone; professionals should collect a detailed medical history *and* a developmental profile of a child's perceptual, cognitive, social and linguistic abilities. As with Down's syndrome, having the label 'autism' attached to their condition could have unwanted repercussions for children and parents. A failure to identify a child with autism correctly, however, can have equally unwelcome consequences. Because Ben was not initially diagnosed as having autism he failed to receive the specialist educational help that he so desperately needed. Instead he was placed first in a school for children with epilepsy and then in a school for 'educationally subnormal' children.

4.4 Explanations for autism – past and present

Psycho-social explanations

There has always been considerable controversy surrounding explanations of autism. These centre on the question of whether it is caused by environmental factors or by factors within the child, such as some form of organic brain damage or genetic disorder. Kanner's original explanation was that autism resulted from 'an innate inability to form the usual biologically provided affective contact with people' (Kanner, 1943; cited in Bettelheim, 1967, p. 386). Nowadays this would be seen in terms of a deficit model. In his later writings, however, he also identified environmental factors, namely an impoverished emotional climate, as playing a role in the development of autism. This led to the unfortunate concept of the 'refrigerator parent'. Kanner (Eisenberg and Kanner, 1956) was careful to point out, however, that parents' lack of emotional warmth towards their child could equally well be a result of the child's innate inability to relate to them, rather than a direct cause of the autism.

The psychiatrist Bruno Bettelheim (1967) reported an extensive study of 46 children with autism who were attending a special school for emotionally disturbed children attached to the University of Chicago. He disagreed radically with explanations which suggested that autism was due to an innate deficit. Analysis of his own detailed case histories led him to suggest that autistic behaviours were symptoms of delayed personality development.

Drawing on the work of Freud and other psychoanalysts, Bettelheim claimed that if babies' and young children's needs were not catered for appropriately during various critical periods in early infancy then they would react by withdrawing into an autistic state. As a consequence of this withdrawal they would miss out on the social and emotional interactions with other people which are, according to psychoanalytic theory, responsible for the development of a mature personality.

He advocated psychotherapy as a way of promoting personality growth in children with autism. Unfortunately there is little evidence that psychotherapeutic intervention has any benefit for the majority of children with autism.

A second prominent environmental explanation was proposed by Niko and Elizabeth Tinbergen in the 1970s. They argued that autistic behaviour could be explained in terms of a 'motivational and emotional imbalance' in the child, resulting in an extreme avoidance of social contact and unfamiliar situations. Their detailed naturalistic observations compared autistic children with ordinary children of the same developmental level. Children were observed at home to see how they behaved towards their parents, siblings and other people, and also how they reacted to their non-social environment (i.e. towards their toys, possessions and physical environment).

The Tinbergens concluded that *all* children experience *'approach / avoidance conflicts'* in certain situations. When faced with a new toy, unfamiliar situation, or person, children experience conflict between their natural curiosity to approach and explore, and their natural fear of the unfamiliar. Most children are able to overcome this conflict; in children with autism, however, the strong emotions aroused are so overwhelming that they show extreme withdrawal and avoidance even in relation to familiar objects and people.

The Tinbergens proposed that *'there is in reality a continuum*, all the way from merely "shy" or "timid" or "apprehensive" children, through very mildly and less mildly autistic children, to severe autists' (Tinbergen and Tinbergen, 1983, p. 119). They also proposed that particular environmental risk factors, including adverse circumstances at the time of the child's birth, could disturb the normal processes of attachment between mother and baby, causing a breakdown of the mother–child bond and a predisposition to the development of autism. In terms of intervention and therapy, the Tinbergens advocated a technique called 'holding therapy' (Welch, 1988) which was designed to reinstate the mother–child bond. The Tinbergens' explanation would fit in with a difference model: nothing is missing or delayed, but development fails to proceed according to the usual pattern because the nature of the mother–child bond is different.

Biological and genetic explanations of autism

Advances in medical technology have begun to allow us to unravel the extremely complex set of factors underlying autism. You will have noticed from the account of Katy's experiences (see Activity 5) that in addition to observational assessment of their behaviour, children suspected of autism are often put through a battery of physiological tests such as brain scans and hearing and sight tests designed to test whether they have some form of organic brain damage.

A recent article on the origins of autism (Morton, 1989) suggests that there may be both a genetic and an organic basis for autism, and that if we suppose that some specific brain system is necessary for ordinary non-autistic development, then the greater the degree of non-specific brain damage, either at or before birth, the greater the likelihood of this specific system being damaged and the greater the likelihood of the processes controlled by this system taking a deviant or different developmental path. It is clear, from reading early environmental explanations of possible causes of autism, that many of the phenomena Kanner, Bettelheim, the Tinbergens and others observed can now be accounted for in biological and/or genetic terms. The following subsections briefly describe the evidence for an organic/biological explanation of autism.

Evidence for brain damage

Gillberg comments that while we do not yet know what causes autism a number of research findings strongly implicate abnormal brain functioning as a contributory factor. For example, there is an association between autism, infantile spasms, and epilepsy pointing to both brain-stem and temporal lobe dysfunction. Both neuroaudiological studies, which use brain scanning techniques, and neurochemical studies have confirmed that brain functioning in people with autism is different compared with other people. On the basis of evidence such as this, Gillberg states that 'There is overwhelming evidence that infantile autism has major biological roots. There is no scientific evidence that purely psychological or psychosocial stressors or circumstances can lead to autism' (Gillberg, 1989, p. 13).

Another source of evidence comes from studies of those children with autism who demonstrate an extreme oversensitivity to sensory stimuli such as sound and touch. Reviewing the available evidence Grandin (1989) suggests that abnormalities of the cerebellum, the area of the brain which modulates sensory inputs, could explain why many children and adults with autism have abnormal sensory reactions.

As yet we do not know whether abnormalities in brain functioning are caused by adverse environmental circumstances (for example, poor diet during pregnancy), or whether they are caused by some innate genetic imbalance. Research into possible environmental causes of organic brain disorder has, however, led to various drug and dietary treatments being proposed as providing a 'cure' for autism. The evidence both for brain pathology and miracle cures, however, is often based on very small samples of children, and it would be premature to jump to firm conclusions about either causes or cures until more research is undertaken.

Genetic evidence

While it is becoming clear that biological and organic factors are implicated in the aetiology of autism, it is also evident that genetic factors play a part, particularly where autism is associated with mental retardation. The relationship between autism, genetics and mental retardation is highly complex, but the following findings (reviewed in Szatmari and Jones, 1991) are all strong indicators of a genetic basis for some types of autism.

(a) Male autistics outnumber females by 4:1.

(b) The recurrence risk of autism amongst siblings is at least 50 times the general population rate.

(c) The concordance rate for autism amongst monozygotic twins is greater than amongst dizygotic twins.

As not all autistic children have learning difficulties, however, and there are no very clear-cut correlations between the IQs of autistic children and their parents and siblings, it seems likely that autism may be an example of what is known as *variable expressivity* (that is, the genes responsible may manifest themselves as autism in one child but as cognitive impairment, without autism, in a sibling or parent). While this complicated picture gives us a basis for understanding the link between autism and intellectual impairment, and why its social, cognitive and behavioural characteristics take so many forms, our state of knowledge is not yet sufficiently advanced for a reliable genetic test to be developed.

Psychological explanations

Knowing that autism is linked to various biological and genetic dysfunctions, however, does not really provide a satisfactory explanation for the social impairments and disorders of language and communication observed in people with autism. Recently psychologists have come up with an explanation which proposes that a particular cognitive deficit is responsible for the social impairments of autism.

Most people have what has come to be termed a 'theory of mind' (TOM), that is they know that other people have mental states and they are able to use this knowledge to interpret other peoples' behaviour and intentions (Woodhead *et al.*, 1995; Perner, 1991). This knowledge also enables people to communicate their own intentions and needs during the course of a social exchange, both verbally, and through gesture and facial expression. In an influential paper, Baron-Cohen, Leslie and Frith (1985) proposed that children with autism lack this appreciation that other people have 'mental states'. These children simply do not understand that other people have intentions, needs, desires and beliefs, nor do they understand that these may be different from their own beliefs and intentions.

Experimental studies have demonstrated that most young children develop TOM by about 4 years of age (e.g. Wimmer and Perner, 1983). Children with autism do not appear to have this knowledge, as experiments like the one described in Research Summary 3 demonstrate.

According to Frith (1989), for children to develop a coherent TOM they need plenty of experience of social interactions and also they must be able to 'mentalize'. Mentalizing is a complex higher-order cognitive process, or possibly a series of processes, which involves integrating considerable amounts of information from people, objects, events and behaviour in order to make sense of one's experience. Mentalizing also involves drawing on stored 'metarepresentational' knowledge (i.e. representations of other people's possible states of mind) in order to

RESEARCH SUMMARY 3
THE SMARTIES-BOX EXPERIMENT

Perner, Frith, Leslie and Leekham (1989) compared the performance of 12 children with specific language impairment (SLI) with that of 26 autistic children on a task which has come to be known as the 'Smarties-box task'. Both groups of children were matched according to mental age, which in this study ranged from 3–13 years. Figure 3 is a pictorial representation of the task, and illustrates the typical response of a child with autism.

FIGURE 3 The pencil in the Smarties box (Frith 1989, p. 162).

The children with SLI correctly predicted that the second child will think that there are Smarties in the box, as this new child has no knowledge of what is really in the box. Children with autism, however, failed to predict what the second child will think is in the box. They consistently answer 'pencil' to both the question, 'What will Billy (new child) think is in the box?' and to the question, 'What is in the box really?' They could not take into account the fact that someone else's mental state or knowledge could be different from what they themselves knew to be the case.

make new inferences and formulate theories about the behaviour and motivations of other people. People with a TOM do not necessarily assume that other people's mental states are identical to theirs. Nor do they accept literal, face-value interpretations of behaviour and events. This, however, is precisely what individuals with autism seem to do, as the experiment outlined in Research Summary 3 shows.

> Autistic children are behaviourists. They do not *expect* people to be kind or to be cruel. They take behaviour as it is. Therefore, intentions that change the *meaning* of behaviour, for instance, deception, flattery, persuasion and irony, present difficult problems of interpretation. While the autistic individual interprets behaviour in a literal fashion, the opposite is true for the compulsive mentalizer; behaviour will be interpreted not in its own right but from the point of view of the intentions behind it. Such is the effect of a theory of mind.
>
> (Frith, 1989, p. 166)

According to Leslie (1987) the ability to mentalize develops alongside children's ability to engage in pretend play, which first appears at around the age of 2 years. Leslie argues that as the impairments associated with autism (i.e. lack of pretend play and inability to mentalize) are so specific, this implies that some specific brain mechanism is absent, or non-functional in individuals with autism. He has devised a complex model (e.g. Leslie and Roth, 1993) to explain both the usual pattern of development and the specific pattern of autistic impairments. At the core of the model is a 'Theory of Mind Mechanism' (ToMM) which is needed for the development of the ability to pretend, to understand pretence in others, and to understand that other people have states of mind. Leslie proposes that ToMM is an innate mechanism which is usually fully matured by the second year of life. In children with autism, however, biological damage, before or shortly after birth, means that components of this mechanism fail to develop, leading to an impairment of the capacity to acquire a theory of mind. According to Leslie, therefore, a deficit model can explain the delayed and abnormal pattern of cognitive development observed in children with autism.

It is important to recognize that ToMM is a *hypothetical construct*. That is, no actual brain structures have been identified which correspond to the hypothetical cognitive architecture proposed by Leslie. We have presented a brief description of the model here, as it is currently one of the most influential psychological explanations for autistic behaviour. It is also worth mentioning that Leslie's model is not without its critics. Few psychologists would deny that children and adults with autism lack a ToMM, although there is much disagreement as to how this develops, and not all psychologists agree that it is the product of an innate mechanism (see Roth, 1990 for a more detailed discussion). Also as Roth (1990) points out, while the model provides a satisfactory account of theory of mind deficits in children with autism, it cannot account for the other characteristics of autistic behaviour, nor does it suggest particular strategies for intervention.

ACTIVITY 6

Allow about 40 minutes

EXPLANATIONS OF AUTISM: SUMMARIZING THE EVIDENCE

Section 4.4 presents various explanations for autism. Using the grid printed below, decide which explanations are primarily deficit models, which are delay models and which are difference models. You may like to look back to Section 2.2 to remind yourself what these models are.

Explanation	Deficit model?	Delay model?	Difference model?
Psycho-social/ innate disorder			
Psycho-social/ personality disorder			
Psycho-social motivational disorder			
Organic/biological disorder			
Genetic disorder			
Cognitive disorder			

Leslie's ToMM explanation attempts to come to grips with the primary impairment underlying autism. As we mentioned in Section 2.2, however, it is not always possible to treat the primary impairment. Intervention techniques must be directed towards the secondary impairments which arise as a consequence of the primary impairment. The next section examines some of the intervention techniques developed by psychologists to help children with autism.

4.5 Psychological approaches to intervention and education

Educational provision and management

As autism is a developmental disorder, the nature and severity of the condition changes as children grow older. Secondary impairments such as temper tantrums, repetitive and obsessive behaviours, sleep and dietary problems, if appropriately managed, become less severe, and many children with autism acquire some functional language and communication skills as they grow older. In early childhood intervention is mainly directed towards managing the behavioural, attentional and communication difficulties experienced by children. Behavioural programmes based on operant conditioning techniques are frequently used, as are various music and play therapy techniques.

All children with autism are recognized to have special educational needs, but the type of school a child will attend will depend on the severity of the condition, and on his or her degree of intellectual impairment. Once children with autism reach school age there are several different educational options open to them. Not all children with autism will necessarily need to be placed in special schools or centres: some may be able to attend mainstream schools; some may be placed in schools for children with moderate learning difficulties (MLD), or special units within mainstream schools; some may be placed in schools for children with severe learning difficulties (SLD) or schools for children with developmental language disorders. Many children are placed in schools or centres managed by the National Autistic Society, some of which are residential. Table 2 gives a rough guide to the criteria used to place children and the various types of provision available. Choice of school is also affected by what is available locally and by what parents want for their child.

As Table 2 shows, in theory there are numerous educational options available to children with autism, although in reality a family's options may be restricted by a whole host of practical and economic factors, such as a local education authority not being able to fund a child to travel to a school in an adjacent county. Where choice is available, however, the families of children with autism may choose according to the types of intervention programme offered by various schools and units. As the range of intervention programmes is as diverse as the types of educational provision on offer, we have decided to concentrate on programmes which have been designed to teach language and communication skills to children with autism, and also on programmes designed to help children's symbolic development. By examining these examples we hope to show how approaches to developing these abilities in children with autism have been informed by psychological theory and research.

TABLE 2　Educational options available for children with autism.

Severity of the disorder	Mainstream school	LEA schools for MLD children and language units in LEA mainstream schools	LEA schools for SLD and LD children and special schools and centres for children with autism
Learning difficulties	Yes	Yes	Yes
Degree of intellectual impairment	IQ and 'Reading Age' within normal limits	IQ in the 51–70 range	IQs 50 or lower
Number of autistic behaviours	Few	Some	Many and persistent
Degree of functional speech	Functional speech and comprehension	Some speech but child is not able to use it appropriately	Very limited or no functional speech and language
Nature of social interactions	Can interact with others but rarely initiates interaction	Interaction with other people is infrequent and often inappropriate	Child rarely interacts with others

Language interventions for children with autism

Attempts to teach language skills to autistic children have been influenced by psychological research concerning the nature of the difficulties children with autism face in developing language, and by research which has investigated how language normally develops during infancy and early childhood.

We now know that unless a child with autism has acquired some useful speech by the age of 5 years, he or she is unlikely to develop any expressive language at all. We also know that children with autism do not have difficulty in understanding language, as they often do quite well in standardized language assessments provided they do not have to make verbal responses. Their problem lies in using language and expressing themselves appropriately in different contexts. It is extremely important, therefore, to try to develop speech in young children with autism.

During the 1960s, speech and language therapists were encouraged to use behaviour modification and operant conditioning techniques to develop the language skills of children with autism. At that time Skinner's view, that children developed language through imitation and reinforcement, was prominent (see Lee and Das Gupta, 1995, Chapter 2, for a discussion), and it was thought that one could teach children with autism to talk by making them work through carefully designed operant conditioning programmes. These speech-training programmes would start by rewarding children when they successfully imitated first individual sounds, then whole words, then phrases, and finally sentences. A description of this approach is given in Example 1.

EXAMPLE 1
A BEHAVIOURIST APPROACH TO SPEECH TRAINING

One of the earliest detailed reports on the application of behavioural principles was the case study by Hewett (1965) on speech training with a 4-year-old mute autistic boy. In order to control the interference of disruptive behaviour, the experimenters used a specially designed experimental booth consisting of two sections separated by a shutter. The child was located on one side of the shutter and the clinician on the other. As the child engaged in off-task behaviour, such as screaming, the shutter was closed and the child was deprived of light, rewards and the presence of the clinician. Once the child had quieted down, the shutter was again raised. The initial emphasis was placed on the reduction of disruptive behaviour rather than on the teaching of speech and language skills. Actual speech training was implemented as soon as the boy had learned to stay in his seat and remain quiet. The boy reportedly developed a repertoire of 32 single-word labels by the end of a six month verbal imitation treatment program. The rationale behind speech training was that improvement in the verbal ability of the autistic child would provide him with naturally occurring social reinforcement opportunities, and thereby reduce his social isolation.

(Schuler, in Fay and Schuler, 1980, p. 140)

This way of teaching language to children with autism has been heavily criticized. Subsequent research showed that children who received this type of speech training were unable to generalize what they had been taught to new contexts and situations (e.g. Lovaas, 1977) and that they appeared to have little understanding of the rule-based nature of language. What appeared to be happening was that the children were learning an isolated set of context-dependent behaviours, rather than a set of rules for generating and using language appropriately in a variety of different contexts. Also, it is quite clearly unacceptable to subject children to this sort of inhuman regime.

READING

FIGURE 4   Zowie (age 7) at work at the National Autistic Society's Storm House School.

In Reading C, Joan Taylor (1976) describes a different approach to teaching language to children with autism. At the time that Taylor wrote this paper, information-processsing models were in full sway, and it was thought that a cognitive, information-processing deficit was the central deficit underlying autism. It was recognized that developing a child's *spoken* language skills was not necessarily the most appropriate route to take in order to develop children's appreciation of the rule-based nature of language. It was also recognized that children with autism needed to be able to appreciate sequential information and they needed to be able to process symbolic information. Mastering these abilities is particularly important for learning how to read and write. In Taylor's paper she describes a series of simple 'games' using things like building bricks, beads, stacking rings and jigsaws, designed to develop young children's perceptual discrimination; their abilities to match, sort and categorize; their memory performance; and finally the skills needed for later language development. As you work through the reading you should do two things:

(a) make a list of the skills that can be developed using the games Taylor describes;

(b) make a note of the principles she advises should be adopted when teaching young children with autism.

Now try the following activity.

ACTIVITY 7

Allow about 30 minutes

SPEECH TRAINING VERSUS SYMBOLIC UNDERSTANDING

This activity is designed to consolidate your understanding of the principles involved in the behavioural and information-processing approaches to teaching language to children with autism. First re-read Example 1. Then, using the notes you made for Reading C, complete the following grid. You should put a tick or a cross in each cell of the grid depending on whether you think a particular teaching principle is present or absent on either approach.

TEACHING PRINCIPLES	BEHAVIOURAL APPROACH		INFORMATION PROCESSING	
	present	absent	present	absent
Approach is highly structured				
Adult controls pace of session				
Child controls pace of session				
Reduction of disruptive behaviour emphasized				
Emphasis on teaching single words and phrases				
Emphasis on teaching rules and concepts				
Adult/child interaction exclusively verbal				
Adult/child interaction both verbal and non-verbal				
Emphasis on improving child's attention span				
Approach attempts to teach child to understand sequencing and rules				
Approach attempts to teach symbolic awareness				

Aspects of both behaviour modification and information-processing approaches to teaching language to young autistic children still have their place, although nowadays research into early language development in non-autistic children has suggested alternative approaches. Recent thinking on intervention is that it is more valuable to design programmes tailored to children's developmental level which build on their existing competencies. In a recent review, Prizant and Wetherby (1989) argue strongly for a 'developmental approach' to intervention and education, and a shift in focus away from 'simply listing absent behaviours that need to be developed and/or prioritizing so called "deficits" for eradication' to a focus on developing a child's 'current competence and ability' (p. 293).

Recent research studies (summarized in Prizant and Wetherby, 1989) are beginning to show that children with autism are not as totally unresponsive and aloof as had once been thought. Observational studies have shown that, like other children, children with autism do direct more social and attachment behaviours towards their caregivers than they do towards strangers. In fact the attachment behaviours shown by children with autism are very similar to those of children with other forms of developmental disorder and mental impairment. It has also been found that far from being meaningless, the echolalia or repetitive imitation of apparently meaningless words and phrases characteristic of children with autism, may actually have some communicative intent behind them (Dawson and Adams, 1984).

> ... the communication attempts of individuals with autism are often idiosyncratic and not easily readable. In a developmental approach the two general tasks are, first, to understand an individual's relative levels of functioning in communicative and social-cognitive domains; and, second, to help the individual acquire more conventional means to communicate, emphasizing the conceptual and social-cognitive 'meanings' encoded by the communicative acts.
>
> (Prizant and Wetherby, 1989, pp. 296–7)

Studies of how babies and their caregivers develop effective communication strategies under normal circumstances show that parents usually treat their baby's vocalizations and non-verbal behaviours *as if* the baby has a deliberate intent to communicate (see Oates, 1995, Chapter 7). They also imitate their baby's behaviour, play games which encourage turn-taking, and engage the baby in 'proto-conversations', all of which are highly effective means of stimulating social and communicative growth. For most children the development of these pre-verbal skills is also a necessary precursor of later language development. It is therefore important to try and give children with autism similar experiences if they are to develop language later. Dawson and Adams (1984) have found that the social responsiveness of young children with autism can be increased by using very similar techniques to those used by parents with their babies.

As you saw from Reading C, it is also important to try to develop an understanding of the *symbolic function* in children with autism. Most children begin to develop this through their interactions with other people and through pretend or *symbolic play*. For children with autism, however, the nature of the autistic disorder means that they rarely engage in spontaneous symbolic play, although they can play in this way in highly structured play situations where adults provide facilitation and support (Lewis and Boucher, 1988).

FIGURE 5
Music therapy.

A number of studies have been designed to provide autistic children with the type of pre-verbal experiences which might be expected to lead to symbolic awareness. For example, Christie and Wimpory (1986) have developed and evaluated the therapeutic technique, communication therapy with synchronized music (CTSM). In CTSM, a familiar adult deliberately contrives 'patterns of prolonged pre-verbal interaction' with the child, by imitating the child's vocalizations and non-verbal behaviours. The hallmark of CTSM, however, is the use of improvised music synchronized to the child's behaviours and the adult's attempts to use these behaviours to engage the child in an interactive sequence. Each session between therapist and child is therefore accompanied by a skilled musician. Christie and Wimpory have found that synchronized music helps develop a sense of 'social timing' in children with profound communication difficulties. This is important if reciprocal, turn-taking exchanges between the child and therapist are to develop successfully. Furthermore, there is also growing evidence that CTSM may facilitate the development of symbolic functioning and pretend play (Wimpory and Chadwick, 1992).

This subsection has discussed some of the language intervention programmes for children with autism. As with the section on intervention and Down's syndrome, you can see how current psychological research indicates that different routes to development have to be taken in order to help develop these children's symbolic awareness and linguistic skills.

SUMMARY OF SECTION 4

- Autism is a lifelong developmental disorder associated with profound social, cognitive and linguistic impairments.

- In a large proportion of children, autism is also associated with intellectual impairment. 'Low-functioning' children with autism have low IQ scores and severe learning difficulties, although they may have special 'islets of ability'. 'High-functioning' children are not intellectually impaired, but will still show the characteristic 'triad' of social impairments.

- Diagnosing autism can be very difficult as in young children it may be confused with more general mental impairment.

- There is little evidence to support psycho-social explanations of autism. Most psychologists now accept that a cognitive deficit underlies the inability to mentalize and to develop a theory of mind which characterizes people with autism. Current research suggests that some form of organic brain damage might be responsible for this deficit. Genetic factors may also be implicated, especially where autism is associated with mental impairment.

- In the main, intervention strategies focus on managing the secondary impairments of autism. Psychological models of ordinary children's language development play an important role in understanding why various interventions are more or less successful. The development of children with autism may need to proceed according to different routes from those of other children.

CONCLUSION

At the beginning of this chapter we pointed out that while psychometric testing and the clinical diagnosis of intellectual impairment might be useful in discriminating between different types of impairment, they do little to further our understanding of the causes of impairment and they do not necessarily help in deciding on appropriate intervention techniques. Furthermore, attaching a diagnostic label or IQ score to individuals often has the effect of lowering expectations about what they might be capable of achieving even when appropriate intervention and educational opportunities are available. It was argued that it was more fruitful to take a psychological or developmental approach to understanding intellectual impairment. This approach attempts to identify whether the patterns of intellectual impairment observed in children and adults are due to a general developmental delay, a specific deficit, or some difference in the way psychological processes develop throughout a person's life.

In the following sections we described some of the psychological research on the development of various psychological processes in children with Down's syndrome and autism. Recent research on Down's syndrome by psychologists such as Morss (1985), Wishart (1990) and Buckley (1986) was briefly described in Section 3. This has shown that the development of basic cognitive, perceptual and linguistic processes in children with Down's syndrome seems to follow a very different route from that of other children. This has important implications for intervention. Intervention programmes, such as Portage, have been based on the premise that the development of children with intellectual impairments such as Down's syndrome is delayed in comparison with that of other children, but that essentially it follows a very similar path. The programmes therefore use modified versions of teaching techniques found to be effective with non-impaired children. As Wishart has pointed out, however, it may be a mistake to attempt to 'normalize' the development of children with Down's syndrome in this way. Along with other psychologists who have undertaken detailed longitudinal investigations of children with Down's syndrome, Wishart argues that 'to be effective, any early intervention programme will need to be tailored to the specific needs and skills of the child with DS and will have to be firmly based in an understanding of the developmental processes operating in handicap' (Wishart, 1988, p. 251).

Section 4 described the various theories which have been put forward as explanations of autism over the past 40 years. Initially, autism was not associated with intellectual impairment and was thought to result from delayed social and emotional development. The first breakthrough in our understanding of autism came about when it was recognized that many, but not all, individuals with autism also experienced profound learning difficulties, as well as delayed social, emotional and linguistic development. Regardless of their degree of intellectual impairment, however, all people with autism show the distinct pattern of social impairments described by Wing (1981, 1988). As with Down's syndrome, it is now recognized that a developmental delay explanation cannot account for autistic behaviour. Nowadays psychologists such as Baron-Cohen, Leslie and Frith (1985) and Morton (1990) propose that a specific cognitive deficit is responsible for autism. According to Leslie (1987) an innate processing mechanism, the Theory of Mind Mechanism (ToMM), fails to develop in individuals with autism so that they are unable to appreciate that other people have mental states which differ from their own. This deficit explains the profound social and communication difficulties experienced by people with autism.

This theory is still controversial, and as yet has not suggested any particular method of intervention. As with Down's syndrome, however, it is clearly mistaken to suppose that intervention techniques based on models of 'normal' development will be successful for children with autism. Section 4 described some of the techniques that have been moderately successful in improving the linguistic and symbolic development of children with autism. Techniques such as those devised by Taylor (1976) and Christie and Wimpory (1986) rely on exploring novel ways of helping children with autism to develop their linguistic and social skills. In this chapter we hope that we have shown how research has led to a better understanding of the ways in which psychological processes develop in children with Down's syndrome and autism, and how this, in turn, will eventually lead towards more sophisticated methods of intervention. Finally, as the full capabilities of children with Down's syndrome and autism are recognized, we should begin to see an improvement in society's attitude and expectations concerning people with the type of intellectual impairments resulting from these conditions.

FURTHER READING

FRITH, U. (1989) *Autism: explaining the enigma*, Oxford, Blackwell.

LANE, D. and STRATFORD, B. (1987) *Current Approaches to Down's Syndrome*, London, Cassell.

LEWIS, V. (1987) *Development and Handicap*, Oxford, Blackwell.

ROTH, I. (1990) 'Autism' in ROTH, I. (ed.) *Introduction to Psychology, Volume 2*, London, Erlbaum/Open University (DSE202).

REFERENCES

AARONS, M. and GITTINS, T. (1992) *The Handbook of Autism*, London, Routledge.

ALLEN, L. (1987) *Like Other Children*, Surrey, Centre for Studies on Integration in Education.

BARON-COHEN, S., LESLIE, A. and FRITH, U. (1985) 'Does the autistic child have a "theory of mind"?', *Cognition, 21*, pp. 37–46.

BERGER, J. (1990) 'Interactions between parents and their infants with Down's syndrome' in CICCHETTI, D. and BEEGHLY, M. (eds) *Children with Down's Syndrome: a developmental perspective*, Cambridge, Cambridge University Press.

BETTELHEIM, B. (1967) *The Empty Fortress – Infantile Autism and the Birth of the Self*, New York, Free Press.

BUCKLEY, S. (1986) *The Development of Language and Reading Skills in Children with Down's Syndrome*, Portsmouth, Portsmouth Polytechnic Down's Syndrome Project.

CHAPMAN, R. S., SCHWARTZ, S. E. and KAY-RAINING BIRD, E. (1991) 'Language skills of children and adolescents with Down's syndrome: I. Comprehension', *Journal of Speech and Hearing Research, 34*, pp. 1106–20.

CHEALE, T. (1990) 'Jonathan's story', *Communication,* **24**(3), pp. 71–2.

CHRISTIE, P. and WIMPORY, D. (1986) 'Recent research into the development of communicative competence and its implications for the teaching of autistic children', *Communication,* **20**, pp. 4–7.

COHEN, L. B. (1981) 'Examination of habituation as a measure of aberrant infant development' in FRIEDMAN, S. L. and SIGMAN, M. (eds) *Preterm Birth and Psychological Development,* New York, Academic Press.

DAWSON, G. and ADAMS, A. (1984) 'Imitation and social responsiveness in autistic children', *Journal of Abnormal Child Psychology,* **12**, pp. 209–26.

DUNST, C. J. (1990) 'Sensorimotor development of infants with Down's syndrome' in CICCHETTI, D. and BEEGHLY, M. (eds) *Children with Down's Syndrome: a developmental perspective,* Cambridge, Cambridge University Press.

EISENBERG, L. and KANNER, L. (1956) 'Early infantile autism 1943–1953', *American Journal of Orthopsychiatry,* **26**, pp. 556–66.

EVANS, P. (1992) 'The best Christmas present of all', *The Guardian,* 22 December.

FAY, W. H. and SCHULER, A. L. (1980) *Emerging Language in Autistic Children,* London, Edward Arnold.

FORD, A. and FORD, P. (1986) 'Can cope', *Communication,* **22**(2), pp. 1–2.

FOWLER, A. E. (1990) 'Language abilities in children with Down's syndrome: evidence for a specific syntactic delay' in CICCHETTI, D. and BEEGHLY, M. (eds) *Children with Down's Syndrome: a developmental perspective,* Cambridge, Cambridge University Press.

FRITH, U. (1989) *Autism: explaining the enigma,* Oxford, Basil Blackwell.

FURNEAUX, B. (1969) *The Special Child,* Harmondsworth, Penguin Books.

GARBAT, A. (1988) 'The first three years', *Communication,* **22**(2), pp. 31–2.

GILLBERG, C. (1989) 'The neurobiology of infantile autism', *Communication,* **23**(1), pp. 10–13.

GRANDIN, T. (1989) 'An autistic person's view of holding therapy', *Communication,* **23**(3), pp. 75–7.

GRIFFITHS, D. (1988) 'I have a brother Simon who is autistic', *Communication,* **22**(3), p. 5.

HARTLEY, X. Y. (1985) 'Receptive language processing and ear advantage of Down's syndrome children', *Journal of Mental Deficiency Research,* **29**, pp. 197–205.

HEWETT, F. M. (1965) 'Teaching speech to an autistic child through operant conditioning', *American Journal of Orthopsychiatry,* **35**, pp. 927–36.

HOBSON, R. P. (1991) 'Methodological issues for experiments on autistic children's perception and understanding of emotion', *Journal of Child Psychology and Psychiatry*, **32**, pp. 1135–58.

HOWE, M. J. A. (1989) *Fragments of Genius: the strange feats of idiots savants,* London, Routledge (paperback edition, 1991).

HUGHES, J. M. (1985) 'Down's syndrome – changing attitudes and their effect on the provision of educational services', *Links,* **10**, pp. 15–22.

KANNER, L. (1943) 'Autistic disturbances of affective contact', *Nervous Child,* **2**, pp. 217–50.

KEMPER, T. L. (1988) 'Neuropathology of Down's syndrome' in NADEL, L. (ed.) *The Psychobiology of Down's Syndrome*, London, MIT Press.

LEE, V. J. and DAS GUPTA, P. (eds) (1995) *Children's Cognitive and Language Development*, Oxford, Blackwell/The Open University (Book 3 of ED209).

LESLIE, A. M. (1987) 'Pretense and representation: the origins of "theory of mind"', *Psychological Review*, **94,** pp. 412–26

LESLIE, A. and ROTH, D. (1993) 'What austism teaches us about metarepresentation' in BARON-COHEN, S. and TAGER-FLUSBERG, H. (eds) *Understanding Other Minds: perspectives from autism,* Oxford, Oxford University Press.

LEWIS, V. and BOUCHER, J. (1988) 'Spontaneous, instructed and elicited play in relatively able autistic children', *British Journal of Developmental Psychology*, **6**, pp. 325–39.

LEWIS, V. A. and BRYANT, P. E. (1982) 'Touch and vision in normal Down's syndrome babies', *Perception*, **11**, pp. 691–701.

LOCKYER, L. and RUTTER, M. (1969) 'A five to fifteen-year follow-up study of infantile psychosis: III Psychological aspects', *British Journal of Psychiatry,* **115,** p. 865.

LOVAAS, O. I. (1977) *The Autistic Child*: *language and development through behaviour modification*, New York, Irvington.

MARLOW, S. (1988) 'When is autistic not autistic?', *Communication,* **22**(1), pp. 1–2.

MORSS, J. R. (1985) 'Early cognitive development: difference or delay?' in LANE, D. and STRATFORD, B. (eds) *Current Approaches to Down's Syndrome*, London, Holt, Rinehart and Winston.

MORTON, J. (1989) 'The origins of autism', *New Scientist*, 9 December, pp. 44–7.

OATES, J. K (ed.) (1995) *The Foundations of Child Development,* Oxford, Blackwell/The Open University (Book 1 of ED209).

O'CONNOR, N. and HERMELIN, B. (1991) 'A specific linguistic ability', *American Journal of Mental Retardation,* **95**(6), pp. 673–80.

PAIN, P. (1985) 'It's not the end of the world', *Communication,* **19** (4), pp. 1–2.

PERNER, J. (1991) *Understanding the Representational Mind,* Cambridge (Mass.), MIT Press.

PERNER, J., FRITH, U., LESLIE, A. M. and LEEKHAM, S. R. (1989) 'Exploration of the child's theory of mind: knowledge, belief and communication', *Child Development,* **60**, pp. 689–700.

PRIZANT, B. M. and WETHERBY, A. M. (1989) 'Enhancing language and communication in autism: from theory to practice' in DAWSON, G. (ed.) *Autism: nature ,diagnosis and treatment,* New York, The Guildford Press.

ROTH, I. (1990) 'Autism' in ROTH, I. (ed.) *Introduction to Psychology, Volume 2,* London, Erlbaum/Open University (DSE202).

RICHER, J. and ZAPPELLA, M. (1989) 'Changing social behaviour: the place of holding', *Communication,* **22**(2), pp. 35–9.

RUTTER, M. (1978a) 'Diagnosis and definitions of autism', *Journal of Autism and Childhood Schizophrenia,* **8**, p. 39.

RUTTER, M. (1978b) 'Diagnosis and definition' in RUTTER, M. and SCHOPLER, E. (eds) *Autism: a reappraisal of concepts of treatment,* New York, Plenum Press.

RUTTER, M. and SCHOPLER, E. (1988) 'Autism and pervasive developmental disorders: concepts and diagnostic issues', in SCHOPLER, E. and MESIBOV, G. B. (eds) *Diagnosis and Assessment of Autism,* New York, Plenum Press.

RUTTER, M., TIZARD, J. and WHITMORE, K. (eds) (1970) *Education, Health and Behaviour,* London, Longman.

SCHULER, A. L. (1980) 'Guidelines for intervention' in FAY, W. H. and SCHULER, A. L. (eds) *Emerging Language in Autistic Children*, London, Edward Arnold.

STRATFORD, B. (1989) *Down's Syndrome: past, present and future,* Harmondsworth, Penguin.

SZATMARI, P. and JONES, M. (1991) 'IQ and the genetics of autism', *Journal of Child Psychology and Psychiatry,* **32**(6), pp. 897–908.

TAYLOR, J. E. (1976) 'An approach to teaching cognitive skills underlying language development' in WING, L. (ed.) *Early Childhood Autism,* second edition, Oxford, Pergamon.

TINBERGEN, N. and TINBERGEN, E. A. (1983) *Autistic Children: new hope for a cure,* London, Allen and Unwin.

WATERHOUSE, L., WING , L. and FEIN, D. (1989) 'Re-evaluating the syndrome of autism in the light of empirical research' in DAWSON, G. (ed.) *Autism: nature, diagnosis and treatment,* New York, The Guildford Press.

WELCH, M. (1988) *Holding Time,* New York, Simon and Schuster.

WILLIAMS, D. (1992) *Nobody Nowhere*, London, Doubleday/Transworld.

WILTSHIRE, S. (1989) *Cities*, London, Dent.

WIMMER, H. and PERNER, J. (1983) 'Beliefs about beliefs: representation and constraining function of wrong beliefs in young children's understanding of deception', *Cognition*, **13**, pp. 103–28.

WIMPORY, D. and CHADWICK, P. (1992) 'Communication therapy with synchronized music for children with autism: two year follow-up of an evaluative case study', paper presented to the British Psychological Society (Developmental Section) conference, Edinburgh, September 1992.

WING, L. (1981) 'Language, social and cognitive impairments in autism and severe mental retardation', *Journal of Autism and Developmental Disorders*, **11**, pp. 31–44.

WING, L. (1988) 'The continuum of autistic characteristics' in SCHOPLER, E. and MESIBOV, G. B. (eds) *Diagnosis and Assessment of Autism*, New York, Plenum Press.

WISHART, J. G. (1988) 'Early learning in infants and young children with Down's syndrome' in NADEL, L. (ed.) *The Psychobiology of Down's Syndrome*, London, MIT Press.

WISHART, J. G. (1990) 'Learning to learn: the difficulties faced by infants and young children with Down's syndrome' in FRASER, W. I. (ed.) *Key Issues in Mental Retardation Research*, London, Routledge.

WOODHEAD, M., BARNES, P., MIELL, D. and OATES, J. (1995) 'Developmental perspectives on emotion' in BARNES, P. (ed.) *Personal, Social and Emotional Development of Children*, Oxford, Blackwell/The Open University (Book 2 of ED209).

ZIGLER, E. and BALLA, D. (1982) *Mental Retardation: the developmental difference controversy*, Hillsdale (N.J.), Lawrence Erlbaum Associates.

READINGS

Reading A   The special child

Barbara Furneaux

[...] Pauline is the youngest child in a family of six and was born when both her parents were nearing forty. Both her parents and also her older brothers and sisters were completely normal and healthy and there is no history of mental illness in the family. Although the pregnancy was normal the birth was three weeks later than expected and the actual labour a long and difficult process culminating in a forceps delivery. All her early development was normal or early and she was an active adventurous baby. When she was about two and a half years old and suffering from a heavy cold with some bronchial trouble, she began at times to tremble violently, then to rush into a corner of the room where she would remain still with her eyes fixed for about five seconds. A year and a half later she developed a high temperature and was obviously feeling very unwell. This persisted for some days at the end of which she had a long and severe fit of major epilepsy and during the next few days this was followed by several more fits. She was rushed to hospital where she was seen by two specialists who put her on drugs to control her epilepsy. Since her behaviour was disturbed she was also seen by a psychiatrist who afterwards saw her once a week for lengthy periods.

She went to the local infants school but, according to her parents, 'learned nothing'. At seven she was admitted again to hospital and after a period of treatment with a different drug was taken off drugs altogether for six months. During this time she seemed to be much better, could be 'talked to' and also learned to read. She then went to a special boarding school. Some months later she became ill, her fits recommenced and she was put back on drugs. She no longer appeared to be learning anything, became very disturbed and was ultimately excluded from her boarding school. She was readmitted to the hospital and it was found that her score on intelligence tests was much lower than it had been the year before. This period of Pauline's life proved to be typical of the next few years. Her ability to learn appeared to be steadily decreasing and her behaviour became progressively more disruptive and disturbed.

[...] Peter is a second child. (As in the case of Pauline, all other members of his family are normal and healthy.) His parents were delighted when he was born; their elder child was a girl and they had hoped the second would be a boy. Until he was three Peter developed normally in every way, including starting to talk. One day he fell down the stairs, but this did not seem to affect him badly, and there has never been any evidence to show that his fall affected his subsequent behaviour. His mother, however, still wonders. The first sign that things were going wrong was when his speech began to deteriorate. He suddenly seemed unable to bring out words which he had been using fluently. This steadily became more noticeable. Then, as his mother puts it, he 'began to try to shape the words with his mouth and would put his hands up to it and manipulate them as if he was desperately trying to force his mouth to make the sounds or as if he was trying to pull the words he wanted out with his hands'. His parents, who were seriously worried by now, took him from hospital to hospital trying to get advice and help. He was investigated for deafness and was also seen by many specialists. The mother was told that he was clearly subnormal and advised to 'put him away and forget him'. When he reached school age he was seen by a school medical officer and … sent to a training centre where he quickly outstripped the other children in his ability to do puzzles, etc. However, his speech was now completely gone, although he made loud grunting and other noises. He became very restless and would sometimes frantically beat his own head or bite his hand. Eventually he became too disturbed in his behaviour for the training centre staff to cope with him so his mother was asked to keep him at home.

SOURCE: FURNEAUX, B. (1969) The Special Child, Harmondsworth, Penguin, pp. 24–6.

Reading B   Learning to learn: the difficulties faced by infants and young children with Down's syndrome

J. G. Wishart

[…] Down's Syndrome (DS) is the best known but probably the most misunderstood of all of the mentally handicapping conditions. Although recent research in genetics and the neurosciences has led to huge advances in our understanding of DS, many professionals working in the community still hold outdated conceptions of the nature of DS and of its developmental implications. More importantly, many hold unnecessarily pessimistic views on the level of ability attainable by children with DS. These views are frequently passed on to parents, often insensitively and with little consideration of the adverse effects this may have on the way parents will then respond to and interact with their DS child.

Although it is important to be realistic about the limits imposed on development by the genetic imbalance present in DS, there would nonetheless still seem to be cause to be optimistic about the prospects of improving developmental outcome in DS. Recent years have seen numerous examples of children and young adults with DS achieving skills previously thought to be outwith their limited capacities to learn. These achievements have ranged from the practical, passing a driving test, to the more 'academic', successfully learning to read at 3 years of age (Buckley, 1985). Such achievements must lead us to question our previous estimates of the ceiling imposed on development by the genetic component in DS. How far previous estimates of potential are inaccurate remains to be seen (Rynders et al., 1978), but sufficient evidence has already accumulated to suggest that with the appropriate support and input, children with DS in future generations will undoubtedly fare better than previously.

A major focus of psychological research into DS should be to define that appropriate support and input. The majority of early intervention programmes being used at present are largely based on teaching principles already known to be successful with non-handicapped children. Despite their wide-scale adoption and their undoubted popularity with parents of handicapped children, these programmes have been shown to have disappointingly little effect on subsequent levels of cognitive achievement. Any gains demonstrated have tended to be insubstantial, short-term and highly specific; 'untreated' DS children soon catch up. This is not to deny that overall levels of achievement have risen in the present generation of DS children. This, however, would seem more likely to be due to factors such as improved health, better educational provision, changing medical, social and parental attitudes to mental handicap, factors other than early intervention.

The failure of present intervention methods to produce lasting benefits should not lead to premature pessimism over the prospects of further facilitating developmental progress in children with DS. In the design of most intervention programmes, it has been implicitly assumed that cognitive development in the mentally handicapped is simply a slowed-down version of normal development – equivalent in structure and organisation, only progressing more slowly and to a lower ceiling. Increasingly, however, research studies are finding evidence that learning processes in children with mental handicap may differ in quite fundamental ways from those seen in normal development (Morss, 1983, 1985: Duffy & Wishart, 1987; Wishart, 1986).

If this *is* the case, the failure of present methods of intervention to produce lasting benefits is perhaps not surprising. To be effective, any early intervention programme will need to be tailored to the specific needs and skills of the child with DS and will have to be firmly based in an understanding of the developmental processes operating in handicap. Our present understanding is woefully inadequate for this purpose. To date, most studies of development in handicap have concentrated on the end product rather than the dynamics of learning, providing development information on 'milestone' achievement but giving little insight into cognitive processes.

References

BUCKLEY, S. (1985) 'Attaining basic educational skills: reading, writing and number' in LANE, D. and STRATFORD, B. (eds) *Current Approaches to Down's Syndrome*, London, Holt, Rinehart and Winston, pp. 315–43.

DUFFY, L. and WISHART, J. G. (1987) 'A comparison of two procedures for teaching discrimination to Down's syndrome and normal children', *British Journal of Educational Psychology*, **57**, pp. 265–78.

MORSS, J. R. (1983) 'Cognitive development in the Down's syndrome infant: slow or different?', *British Journal of Educational Psychology*, **53**, pp. 40–7.

MORSS, J. R. (1985) 'Early cognitive development: differences or delay?' in LANE, D. and STRATFORD, B. (eds) *Current Approaches to Down's Syndrome*, London, Holt, Rinehart and Winston, pp. 242–59.

RYNDERS, J. E., SPIKER, D. and HORROBIN, J. M. (1978) 'Underestimating the educability of Down's syndrome children', *American Journal of Mental Deficiency*, **82**, pp. 440–8.

WISHART, J. G. (1986) 'The effects of step-by-step training on cognitive performance in infants with Down's syndrome', *Journal of Mental Deficiency Research*, **30**, pp. 233–50.

SOURCE: FRASER, W. I. (ed.) (1990) Key Issues in Mental Retardation Research, London, Routledge, pp. 249–51.

Reading C   An approach to teaching cognitive skills underlying language development

Joan E. Taylor

[…] A child with a severe language problem cannot be expected to give concentrated attention for long periods. He needs tasks which can be performed in a short space of time but which require him to think. Their completion brings the immediate reward of a successful outcome of effort geared to the child's level of development. It is best not to present a long series of exercises all based on the same principle, but to vary the kinds of tasks so that the child has to attend and think afresh about each one.

Visual analogies of language

At this stage, the games aim to develop the flexible use of symbols by means of visual analogies of language. The simpler exercises at this level involve the use of arbitrary symbols for objects or concepts such as the colour red to symbolise 'warm' or a cross to mean 'yellow'. These symbols can be used in one game only, or they may be continued through a series of games. For example, when the child has the idea that a cross (X) is being used as a label for yellow, he can be shown an X followed by an uncoloured picture of an object such as a car. This means that he has to find a yellow car. The arbitrary symbols may be displayed for the child to refer to, or, in a more difficult version, he may have to recall them from memory.

When a child finds a yellow car in response to the X and the drawing of a car, as described above, he has in effect 'read' the information presented. The game can also be played so that the child observes the yellow car and then arranges the pictures to describe it, which is analogous to the process of writing. The correct order of the 'words' can be emphasised in these exercises.

The last game to be described here is the most complex and demonstrates most clearly the learning processes necessary for the development of useful language as distinct from a vocabulary of labels.

The language model uses four miniature toy animals; a sheep, a pig, a hen and a cow and five small, square section, coloured rods, such as those available in the Cuisinaire apparatus, one each of red, green, yellow, pink and brown.

The child is asked to associate the red rod with the sheep and green with the pig. The two animals are placed on the table handy for the child. In front of the child are arranged the red rod, placed horizontally and the brown rod standing upright to the right of it. The child is invited to do something about the red rod. He places the sheep by it. The brown rod is then 'walked' with large, slow, deliberate steps to the right. A slight gesture, pointing to the child and then to the sheep, indicates that he is do so something about it. He is not told what to do. The brown rod again begins to walk, and the child should reason that he is to do the same with the sheep. As soon as he begins to make the sheep walk, the brown rod is returned to its position, standing upright to the right of the red rod and the child is congratulated.

A new arrangement of rods is made: the green rod lying horizontally on the table and the brown rod standing to the right. The child should infer that the pig is to walk and makes it do so. If the child touches the brown rod, he is told that that belongs to the teacher: the pig is his.

The sheep and hen are now put beside the child and another arrangement of rods is made. The green rod is laid horizontally and on its right, the brown rod is also laid in the horizontal position. The child is asked to watch carefully. The tutor picks up the brown rod and clappers it quickly along to the right. making a 'running' noise, then replaces it as before to the right of the green rod. The child who has already learnt to associate the pig with the green rod should now make the pig run. Other arrangements of the rods are made and the child makes the animals walk or run as appropriate.

When the child has grasped the general idea, the yellow rod should be placed in a horizontal position, like the rods representing the sheep and the pig. He should infer that this represents the hen which can also be made to walk or run in response to the positions of the brown rod.

Next, the cow is put with the other animals and the pink rod is laid horizontally. While the child is giving close attention, the brown rod is stood to the right and made to fall over backwards. This is done again with deliberation, and left lying down, but at right angles to the horizontal position of the rods representing the animals. The child is to deduce that the pink rod represents the cow and the brown rod lying down means 'fall'.

The child now has four 'word-labels' (nouns); red for sheep, green for pig, yellow for hen, pink for cow. He also has three verbs, brown rod standing upright for walk, brown rod lying horizontally for run, and brown rod lying vertically for fall.

The child may be exercised in several ways:

1. 'Read' – the teacher makes an arrangement of rods and the child moves the animals.

2. 'Observe and write' – the teacher makes the animals move and the child places the rods appropriately.

3. 'Write something' – the child arranges the rods and the teacher reads the arrangement and moves the animals.

4. 'Do something' – the child moves the animals and the teacher writes what the animal did.

The whole exercise has required the child to associate two word-labels with animals and deduce the association of a third and fourth; associate three 'verbs' with their actions; classify 'nouns' as coloured horizontal rods and 'verbs' as indicated by the position of the brown rod; make observations about word order (word-label on the left and verb to the right of it). It has asked him to use short-term memory and to scan, internally, his memories of association of label and object, verb and action.

Aims and uses of the programme

All this does not pretend to be a method of teaching language. It attempts only to alert the attention of the children and foster the learning of skills needed for the development of language. A list may be made of matters on which the child's attention is focused, such as the attributes of things, association of perceptions in different modalities, similarities and differences, association of ideas, patterns and categories, simple analogies, but these are means to the end that the children should become generally more alert intellectually.

The programme should take its place as one part of the general plan of teaching. After working for a period of time which varies for each child, a change may be seen. The child becomes more alert, more ready to be involved, busier, more aware of the teacher as a person, making deliberate efforts to gain approval. When this happens there is often a spurt in progress in other aspects of learning and development, such as drawing and writing. Executive speech may improve together with the ability to comprehend and use symbols. The child who benefits in this way is more observant and watchful and begins to go forward on his own. The use of the series of games can be terminated at any point if it becomes obvious that the child's language development has progressed sufficiently to make their continuation unnecessary. They should also be terminated if it is clear that the child can make no further progress.

The methods of working described here are in many ways, different from those used in operant conditioning. Both approaches are structured in the sense that the teacher decides what the child should be doing, but the essence of the series of games is that the child is allowed to find the rules for himself, as the normal child seems to do when acquiring language. Most operant programmes, on the other hand, try to build up skills such as language by the direct teaching of every tiny step in performance.

Both approaches have their place, and the art of teaching handicapped children is to know when to choose one and when the other.

These games have been used with pre-school children with severe language problems, some of whom were autistic. The latter were clearly less able to create ideas spontaneously and to use associations freely. Much work remains to be done on the eventual results of using this approach for children with different syndromes of impairments. In the meantime, it is useful for assessing in detail the level any child has reached in his ability to form concepts and use symbols. It may also, if started early enough, help a little towards overcoming the severe handicaps characteristic of early childhood autism.

Source: Taylor, J. E. (1976) Early Childhood Autism, *Oxford, Pergamon, pp. 217–20.*

CHAPTER 8 CHILD THERAPIES

John Oates, Masud Hoghughi and Rudi Dallos

CONTENTS

1 LOCATING CHILDREN'S PROBLEMS

1.1 Whose problem is it?

A major difference between children's and adults' psychological problems is that children rarely seek treatment themselves, whereas the majority of adults seeking help are self-referred. Children's 'problems' are almost always defined as such by other people involved with the child: parents, teachers or social workers, for example. Typically such a person will report some aspect(s) of a child's behaviour as being in some way 'abnormal'; in other words, as deviating from some expected norm to an extent that it is seen as needing some sort of reaction that the adult feels unable to give, and hence leads them to seek professional help. Such judgements by adults are clearly subjective, since there are no firm norms of child development, nor are there agreed amounts of deviation that unambiguously define pathological behaviour. They are basically judgements against social standards, and it is quite clear that these are not absolute, but vary from person to person, between families and from cultural group to cultural group. What one person may find deviant may not be so viewed by another: for example, parents in one family may be highly tolerant of children expressing their own views and disagreeing with their parents, while the parents of a family next door may believe that such behaviour is disrespectful and impertinent. A child from the first of these two families, placed with the second, might very well evoke feelings that 'here is a child with a problem', when the child repeatedly engages in what may be perceived by these parents as 'confrontations'.

ACTIVITY 1

Allow about 10 minutes

SOCIAL STANDARDS

What do you think would be the reaction of the 'tolerant' family to the 'respectful and non-confrontational' child?

Are they likely to feel that this child 'has a problem'? In what way?

Have *you* ever been involved with a child whose behaviour you find challenging or worrying? To what extent do you feel this may have been due to the child experiencing different standards from your own in their home environment?

The vast majority of reported problems concern behaviours, thoughts and emotional responses that are common to all children. It is only when one or more of these aspects of a child are seen as being abnormally intense, frequent, inappropriate or lacking, that a 'problem' is likely to be identified. A good example of this is given by considering childhood 'phobias', which are a common presenting problem. A phobia is normally defined as a specific fear (of a particular object, event or situation) which:

1   is excessive;

2   cannot be reasoned away;

3   is beyond voluntary control;

4   leads to avoidance behaviour;

5   persists;

6   is maladaptive.

(Marks, 1987)

ACTIVITY 2

Allow about 10 minutes

WHEN IS A FEAR A PHOBIA?

This activity will help you think about the extent to which 'problems' represent deviations from rather unclearly defined norms of behaviour.

Imagine a 3-year-old boy unexpectedly encountering a small spider in the washbasin when he goes to wash his hands. Work down the following list of reactions, and decide which levels you think would count as a 'problem' that needs to be dealt with, assuming that the child shows the same reaction several times over a period of months. You might find that you get more out of this activity if you discuss it with another person, preferably a parent.

(a) child picks up spider, pulls its legs off and squashes it;

(b) child picks up spider with bare fingers and puts it on the floor;

(c) child picks up spider with a tissue and puts it out of the window;

(d) child backs away and goes to ask parent to remove spider;

(e) child screams and calls frantically for parent, calms down when comforted by the parent and the spider is removed;

(f) child screams, calls frantically for parent, takes a long time to calm down, will not wash at the basin and wakes that night from a nightmare involving spiders attacking him.

Comment

Your response to this activity will obviously depend on your own feelings about spiders in washbasins. Go back through the above list and this time pick out which reaction is closest to your own. Did you expect the imaginary 3 year old to have the same reaction as your own? Would you apply different standards in judging a 10 year old's reaction? Do you think that you would count a reaction as abnormal partly in terms of how far it is different from your reaction? For example, if you have a fairly strong fear of spiders, you might find it quite disturbing for a child to show either of the first two reactions. The point is that there is no wholly objective measure available for deciding when a particular behaviour is an indication of a problem, but rather that people appeal to personal norms, and their perceptions of developmental and social norms, in judging children's behaviour.

A phobia is basically an excessive fear. All children show fears, and it is clearly important that some things should be feared. Typically, behaviour is judged to be abnormal not only because of its unusual nature, but also because of the frequency, duration and intensity of its occurrence. For example, crying, being clingy and being withdrawn are all developmentally normal behaviours, but may be judged to be abnormal if they occur with excessive frequency or, conversely, if they rarely or never occur. Some behaviours may be considered abnormal if they are seen as developmentally or situationally inappropriate: clinginess in a 2 year old would arouse less concern than the same behaviour in a 12 year old; 'slouching' can be appropriate behaviour for an adolescent watching TV but not in class. There is also the complex issue of what may be seen as gender inappropriate behaviour. All of these judgements depend in part on the characteristics of the child (such as age or sex), in part on wider cultural standards of acceptable behaviour and also on our psychological theories of 'normality' in development and social behaviour.

As you will see in the case study in the next section, an important part of a therapist's task will be to assess the nature of a child's difficulties in relation to the sorts of judgements made by the people who have brought the child for treatment. Of course, the therapist's judgements should also be subject to the same considerations.

The question that a therapist will be trying to answer is 'to what extent is this child's behaviour a problem for the child, and to what extent is it a product of other people's perceptions or their own difficulties or biased judgements of behaviour?' The clinical judgement on this issue, which will still be a subjective one, although backed up by experience and knowledge, will be an important factor in decisions about the most appropriate form of treatment, and the extent to which it will be focused on the child and/or on the child's social environment.

SUMMARY OF SECTION 1

- Children's 'problems' are most fruitfully seen as *social constructions*, that is, located in social relationships and arising from how other people in the child's life view the child's behaviour.

2 UNDERSTANDING CHILDREN'S PROBLEMS

Working with children in a therapeutic context can be one of the most rewarding but also one of the most depressing experiences. On one hand it is possible to hold the view that the problems are being 'nipped in the bud', that by offering some early assistance the problems do not escalate and become chronic, perhaps leading the child into a 'psychiatric career'. This parallels the belief that many adults might have been 'helped' or 'saved' from a lifetime of hospitalization, misery, medication and a place on the outskirts of society if only they and their families could have been 'treated' earlier. On the other hand clinical work with children can be depressing because of the scale of the damage that may seem to have been inflicted on them often at a very early age: this might be physical and sexual abuse, emotional and psychological abuse and neglect or simply an over-involvement of the child with his or her parents' problems to the extent that their childhood fun, games and creativity are sacrificed.

Working with children can arouse strong emotions in all of us and clinical psychologists are no exception. However, an important distinction to make from the outset is between *sympathy* and *empathy*. To start with a feeling of sympathy and caring about a child's problems is a necessary prerequisite to establishing a constructive working relationship. On its own though it is not enough and may even be counter-productive. Clinical psychologists, in addition, attempt to be empathic, to try to understand from the child's point of view what their world is like. Carl Rogers (1955) emphasizes that this combination of sympathy and empathy, which he calls *non-evaluative warmth*, is a fundamental quality in any therapeutic relationship. The starting point for child therapy, therefore, is a curiosity about what it is like to be the child, and this raises the fundamental question: 'How are this child's experience, family, relationships, friendships and so on, similar to or different from the therapist's own experience as a child?' George Kelly (1955) refers to this as a 'reflexive' position; in other words the psychologist tries to take account of how their own experience may be influencing what they can construe. It is not a question of attempting to 'remove' these intrusive feelings, or thinking of them as biases. Instead, the therapist should try to use, in a conscious way, their own experiences, beliefs and understanding from their own childhood or relationships with their own children, in any therapeutic encounter with a child.

2.1 The child as passive

Much developmental psychology emphasizes that the child's social context is fundamental for emotional, cognitive and social development. A significant part of this context is inevitably the child's family. Children find themselves in many different types of family situation and also, increasingly, struggles and conflicts between separating parents are a great source of anxiety for many of them (Wallerstein and Kelly, 1980). Psychologists have tended to focus on how the family dynamic influences children. A young child who acts out of control, breaks things and will not 'do as he is told', may be seen to be acting in this way because of inappropriate modelling in the family, lack of discipline or unclear rules. Likewise, a child who is seen to be 'emotionally withdrawn' may be regarded as having been deprived of attention and affection, as witnessing a cold relationship between his or her parents and generally lacking experience of emotional trust. You can probably think of many more such examples but in general these carry two linked assumptions: that the child is shaped by what his or her parents have done and that they (the parents) have 'got it wrong' somehow. Though this is a 'sympathetic' position (towards the child but not necessarily the parents), the child is seen as passive and effectively a 'victim' of the family. This view often underlies learning theory and psychodynamic models of child development.

2.2 The child as active

In contrast, perspectives from the work of Piaget and humanistic psychology, including the work of George Kelly (1955), see children as actively trying to understand, and in Kelly's terms 'predict and . anticipate', their social worlds. Children are therefore seen as potentially autonomous and capable of making choices about how they wish to act. Consistent with an emphasis on the importance of establishing 'empathy' in work with children, a clinical psychologist will attempt to try to 'see things from the child's point of view'. Of course this is more easily said than done since often children have become distrustful, morose and uncommunicative, perhaps as a result of some of the bitter experiences they have had. It typically requires patience and the use of a variety of modes of self-expression, such as drawing, painting, sculpting, play and drama, to assist some children to communicate.

2.3 A dilemma for therapy

To see children as having their own beliefs, understandings and explanations, and as potentially free to make their own choices, presents us with a dilemma: how is it that children appear to act in their families in ways that are damaging to themselves and to others and are predictably repetitive? On the one hand we can answer this question by seeing the child as a passive 'victim' of her family life and the parents as 'villains', 'incompetent' or 'uncaring' and so on. In cases of child abuse, neglect and so on this can be an extremely seductive perspective. On the other hand, even in fairly extreme cases, we can contend that children are capable of making choices: for example, to stay loyal to parents who have been abusive to them, or to find ways of understanding and changing their situation through insights gained from reading, watching television or discussing their feelings with friends, etc.

2.4 Families and empowering children

This dilemma between the child as determined and shaped like a 'piece of clay' as opposed to autonomous has been central to theories of developmental psychology. It has also, unfortunately, led to some unproductive polarizations of positions in clinical work with children. In contrast it is possible to consider that a key aspect of family life is the extent to which children are assisted to learn to become autonomous, to think for themselves (Dallos, 1991). This should not be confused with the idea of children simply doing whatever they want but they should have the 'emotional space' in their families to be able to reflect upon their actions and to anticipate how these might influence others.

Initially many clinical psychologists and psychiatrists worked individually with children attempting to 'eradicate' their problems. Prompted by the failure to achieve significant or durable changes they started to invite parents to attend along with their children in order to gain more information about the problems at home. These consultations led to the discovery that frequently the parents were themselves experiencing severe conflicts or difficulties and in fact the child's problems often seemed to be adaptations to their parents' problems (Haley, 1976). Further observations led to a number of important insights about how children could become caught up in these conflicts:

- *Conflict detouring* – when parents are in conflict or are too emotionally drained by a variety of possible stresses, a child can become pulled in to take sides or to become a scapegoat, for example by developing a problem such as truanting from school. The child is in a sense *compelled to make a choice*, usually an unconscious one, to save her parents by becoming disturbed or ill, which serves to distract them from their own conflicts and worries.

- *Enmeshment* – families can become extremely immersed in each other's feelings and thoughts so that a child finds it difficult to have any sense of privacy, 'when someone itches, everybody scratches' (Minuchin, 1974). Even bodily experiences can become the property of the parent rather than the child, for example when they 'know' better than the child whether she is 'ill' or 'upset'. Within such a context the only way a child may be able to find some privacy and emotional space is to develop some problem that her parents, by definition, cannot understand and control.

- *Distortions of reality* – children may be placed in a position of falseness or denial in the family, for example when the truth about certain events is kept from them or they are required to collude in denials or distortions of events. Sometimes there may be a denial of something which is painful for the family, for example that a member has a serious psychological disability (Pollner and Wikler, 1985) or parents may offer conflicting versions of events. Faced with such continual falsifications it may become difficult for a child to differentiate between what is 'real' and what is not (Laing, 1969).

These are but a few examples. A grave danger here can be to 'blame' families and especially parents. In all of these examples the parents can be seen to be acting for quite benign and socially approved reasons; for example, in conflict detouring they may be worried that their conflicts are upsetting their child and therefore be continually searching her for signs of distress. Unfortunately this very concern may detour the conflict onto the child.

Such an analysis of the child's life in the family can therefore help us to see how children do, or do not, develop a sense of autonomy and ability to make decisions and solve their own problems. This is a central question for therapy with children: the task is not simply to remove problems but to try to ensure that children are able to use their intellectual and emotional resources to solve problems and make effective decisions in later life. This often requires work, not only with a child but with her family, so that new ways of relating and of being able to formulate courses of action and make decisions become possible.

> **SUMMARY OF SECTION 2**
>
> - Trying to reach an understanding of difficulties from the *child's* point of view is an essential part of therapeutic work.
> - Two contrasting models of the child can be seen as underlying therapeutic work: the *passive* and *active* models.
> - Commonly, children's difficulties are most fruitfully viewed as resulting from disrupted or dysfunctional family dynamics.

3 TYPES OF THERAPY

The previous section argued for a 'systemic' theory of children's problems, but therapeutic interventions involving children have many different theoretical orientations. There are numerous styles and types of therapies practised, with their roots in a range of psychological schools of thought. Kazdin (1988) suggests that there may be as many as 230 distinguishable styles and types. There are two main dimensions along which therapies can be differentiated:

1   Problem is located in child vs. problem in child's environment.

2   Focus on current behaviour vs. focus on earlier experiences and child's understanding.

The first of these centres on the extent to which a child's problems are seen as being located within the child, this being one end of the dimension, as opposed to these problems being seen as located in a broader social, physical and economic system, the other end of the dimension. A central issue here is to do with the extent to which a problematic environment *outside* the child impacts on the development of the child and brings about changes *inside* the child with long-term or permanent consequences. Along this dimension, therapies differ quite widely in how much they are based on a belief that treatment of the child should be focused on the child or supplemented with or even largely replaced by attention to and intervention in the child's environment. The connection between these two aspects, location of causes and direction of therapy, is by no means straightforward.

ACTIVITY 3

Allow about 30 minutes

NARROW OR BROAD? CAUSES AND INTERVENTIONS

This activity is intended to encourage you to think about possible explanations of the origins of a child's difficulties, possible approaches to their treatment and the links between these.

Read the following case study, bearing in mind the following questions:

- Is Emma's 'problem' one that lies mainly in her? In other words, is there something in *her* that is contributing to her display of these particular symptoms?

- Do you think that attempting to achieve a change in Emma, such that her symptoms are removed or alleviated, could be successful?

- Do you think that attempting to bring about changes in her family environment might potentially be a more fruitful approach?

- Do you think that a combination of approaches might be best?

- Finally, what would you consider to be a successful outcome in this situation?

Emma Harbour

Emma was referred via the family GP because she had taken an overdose of paracetamol in an apparent 'suicidal gesture'. In addition she was reported to be upset and socially withdrawn and said she was unable to attend school. The 'overdose' was not large enough to have done any damage but was sufficient to prompt her mother to seek therapy for her. The initial assessment of Emma's problem suggested that she missed her friends back at her previous school, did not like where her family had moved to and was generally sad and unhappy. It also seemed clear that a variety of family factors related to her distress.

Emma, her younger sister Jane and her mother had moved from the North of England to the South to join her father who had moved away to start a new job. They soon discovered that he was having an affair with his neighbour and he eventually left to move in with his new partner whose house backed on to theirs. This was a particularly painful situation for the girls because they could see their father when he went outside in his garden but could not speak to him, since this would upset their mother who was extremely angry at this 'betrayal'.

The initial clinical hypothesis was that Emma had found it more difficult to adjust to moving to a new town than her sister and as a result of this, coupled with the conflicts at home, had become depressed and withdrawn. She was invited to attend for family sessions with her mother and Jane. Talking with her on her own, with her sister and in the presence of her mother partly confirmed this, but it also became clear that she played a significant role as a 'mediator' in the conflict between her parents.

To explore this further her father was invited to attend a session with the two girls and Mrs Harbour. Emma chose to sit between her parents and showed clear signs of agitation when conflicts arose in their discussions. Jane appeared less concerned, being content to leave the worrying more to Emma and showing more alliance to her father. Significantly, Emma continually looked to see if her mother was upset or not and was unable to answer any questions without consulting her first. Mrs Harbour admitted that Emma was her confidant and they spent many hours talking about her father and how upset she felt. In contrast Jane was able to get on with her own life and had started to establish a network of friends at school.

Comment

The following is a summary of the interpretation of the difficulties Emma found herself in and the approach taken by the psychotherapist involved in the case. You should read this and compare the approach taken with your answers to the questions at the beginning of this activity.

The suggestion was made by the therapist, and acknowledged by all of the family members, that Emma was caught in the role of conflict mediator. Her parents were persuaded to discuss their feelings without Emma being involved, and to accentuate this point Emma was asked in the session, and subsequent ones, to move from between her parents and to sit next to her sister. Her parents were then encouraged to take turns to express their feelings to each other. This was clearly painful for all the family members but some resolution started to occur and, though they accepted that their hostility would continue, they also agreed to try to put this aside in order to co-operate as parents for the girls. In addition it emerged that Mr Harbour's new partner felt insecure about his relationship with Mrs Harbour and feared that a reconciliation might occur. Once it became openly acknowledged that these competing emotional demands were causing Mr Harbour to act in an apparently 'insensitive' and 'cold' way towards his wife and daughters the tensions between them started to ease a little.

As Emma was allowed to abandon her position as support for her mother and mediator between her parents, her sadness lifted and she willingly agreed to start at a new school when her parents agreed that they would both accompany her on her first day. They emphasized though that this did not imply a reconciliation but that they would try to co-operate in a mature way to act as parents for their girls.

The family members were seen a total of seven times over a period of five months. It seemed that an alteration in the demands made upon Emma in her family allowed her to start to make some new choices and to escape from the desperate final choice of 'opting out' of an unbearable situation through attempting suicide. Psychotherapy which includes the whole family in this way is based on the assumption that people are essentially social beings who are inevitably *connected* with others. A problem such as this is therefore seen as not simply personal but as arising out of a social, in this case family, situation. Therapy therefore involves work initially with the individual presented as having a problem, but also with the family, in an effort to 'free up' the situation to allow some new avenues of choices to emerge.

A belief that a particular problem may have arisen as a consequence primarily of environmental conditions that are in themselves disordered or problematic for the child does not necessarily sit uncomfortably with a belief that the problem solution should be directed, at least in part, at the child. Neither does a belief that a child's problem is primarily caused by some constitutional or acquired disorder necessarily preclude treatment that is directed at modifying the child's environment. To the extent that a child has over time established particular ways of responding to situations and people, particular ways of dealing with disorder in their lives, the child will often need assistance in helping to develop different, alternative ways of behaving.

3.1 The complexity of a clinical formulation

In the early stages of a practitioner's involvement with a child, the prime focus will tend to be on developing a specific clinical formulation of the nature of the problem, including its possible sources in various aspects of the child's life and its development over time. The purpose of this is to develop a set of recommendations for treatment on an informed basis. The following diagram indicates the range of factors that is likely to be considered in developing a picture of the specific problem.

Figure 1 shows a model where 'problem behaviour' is seen as potentially being caused by both personal and situational variables. The arrows between these two indicate that attention should be paid to the possible transactional nature of their impact on a child's behaviour. In other words, personal and situational variables may interact with each other and with the child's own behaviour. For example, Emma's reaction to the situation that she is living in probably affected the behaviour of her parents towards her, creating, effectively, a new environment within which her 'problems' were located.

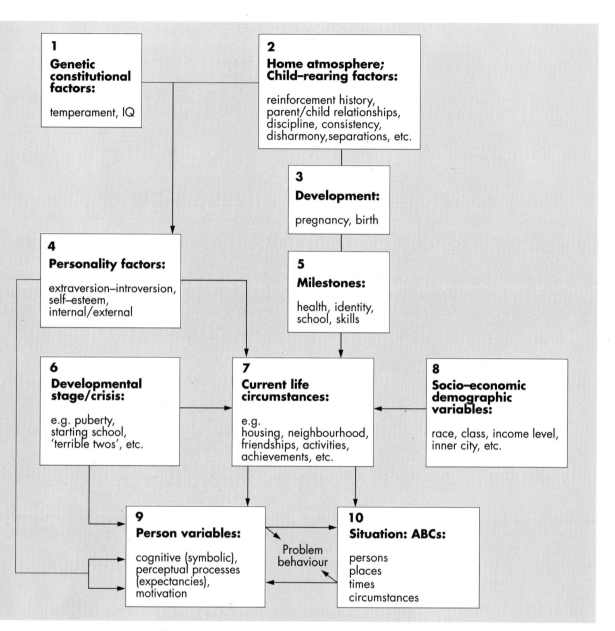

FIGURE 1   A 10-factor model of causes to be considered in developing a clinical formulation (Herbert, 1991, p. 45).

ACTIVITY 4	**A CLINICAL FORMULATION OF EMMA'S DIFFICULTIES**
Allow about 10 minutes	This activity will help you to understand the process of developing a clinical formulation.

Re-read the case study of Emma and work through each of the 'boxes' in Figure 1, making notes of possible causes within each of these areas.

3.2 Personal histories versus current behaviour

The second dimension along which therapies differ is the extent to which the therapist works with a child's *personal history* and the child's *understanding* of their difficulties, based on a 'talking' relationship between child and therapist. For the more 'environmental' therapies, this would focus on working (talking) with other people in the child's social environment: parents, siblings and other relatives or caregivers. This end of the dimension contrasts with the other, which concerns itself with the modification of the child's *behaviour,* the therapist's role being to arrange schedules of rewards, witholding of rewards and (rarely) punishment to achieve this modification, with the implementation of this schedule possibly being undertaken by one or more other people, such as the child's parents or teachers.

Given these two major dimensions along which different types of therapy vary, it can be seen that therapy with children is not a unified area, with universal approaches and frames of reference: it is one of the areas within applied psychology where the disagreements between practitioners of different theoretical persuasions are at least as great as any commonality in method.

SUMMARY OF SECTION 3

- The different types of psychotherapy that are employed with children differ in two main respects: first, whether problems are seen as *inside* or *outside* the child, and second, whether the focus is on *current behaviour* or *personal history*.

- An early stage in therapy is the development of a *clinical formulation*: an identification of the nature of the difficulty and its contributory 'causes'.

---

4 METHODS OF TREATMENT

4.1 Classification of methods

Assessment and classification of problems and difficulties encountered by the patient/client are the necessary precursors to carrying out focused, purposive treatment. There are numerous classifications of problems, ranging from the general, such as the *International Classification of Diseases* (WHO, 1988), to the specific, such as speech disorders (for example, Fundudis *et al.*, 1979). The prerequisites and difficulties of classification systems are numerous (see for example Hoghughi, 1992; Rutter and Gould, 1985).

One such classification groups treatments according to the *medium* or *modality* they use in order to alleviate problems. Seven broad categories of treatment can be distinguished by the modality they use:

* provision of goods and services;
* physical treatments;
* behavioural therapies;
* cognitive treatments;
* talking therapies;
* group therapies;
* environmental treatments.

This classification is not comprehensive: there are many other types of therapy in the treatment literature, often supported by organizations and specialist practitioners, such as 'dance therapy', 'transcendental meditation', 'yoga', 'faith healing', 'hypnosis' and many others. These approaches to treatment have not been included in the above list because of the relative infrequency of their use with children or the poor research literature on them (Schaefer, 1988).

Nor can the methods and techniques offered be neatly and exclusively compartmentalized. Giving a pair of spectacles (service provision) is accompanied by instructions for use (cognitive); surgery (physical) is usually preceded and followed by reassurance (talking therapy); and behaviour modification is invariably concerned also with environmental contingencies. Hardly any treatment is based on a single treatment method and classifications therefore cannot be pure.

Distinction should be made between 'methods' and 'techniques'. Usually the two are lumped together and treated as interchangeable. However, the distinction permits drawing out theories and elements of practice which are common to the *variants* of a method – here called 'techniques'. Method is, therefore, the superordinate or wider category, of which the technique is an example. The number of techniques can be enlarged, as has happened in the behaviour modification method, without losing the common theoretical or practice threads that bind them together.

As already indicated, all the above methods and many more, are used, more or less systematically, by a wide range of people involved in treating children's disorders. In this chapter, we will concentrate on three methods – behaviour modification, 'talking therapies' and group therapies. These are the methods most frequently used in the formal treatment of children's emotional and behavioural disorders, apart from the use of drugs and surgery for medical problems.

SUMMARY OF SECTION 4

* Seven main categories of treatment can be distinguished, although few actual therapies involve only a single method.
* Each approach is based on a different set of assumptions.

5 BEHAVIOURAL THERAPIES

Behaviour therapies consist of a set of procedures derived from experimental research into the psychology of learned behaviour. Their basic premise is that, if behaviour is learned, it can also be unlearned, using psychological principles. They are an approach to dealing with and changing behaviour that has been judged to be 'disordered' in some way, and are a collection of techniques rooted in relatively objective and measurable evidence. They aim to modify current behaviour by focusing on how that behaviour is manifested in observable responses. Although in the past behaviour therapies have tended to emphasize *current behaviour* and have, as a result, paid little attention to *antecedents, causes* or *longer-term outcomes,* there is now increasing systematic attention to these latter areas (Herbert, 1991; Johnson, Rasbury and Siegel, 1986).

EXAMPLE 1
THREE CHILDREN

At age 6, Johnny is liable to throw frequent 'temper tantrums' when denied his demands, accompanied by sufficiently serious head banging to draw blood. His alarmed parents always give in, which can be seen to *reinforce* his behaviour. After reassuring them that he is unlikely to 291 hurt himself seriously, the psychologist advises them to ignore his head banging for a week and go back and see her for debriefing. By the end of the month, parents' ignoring, combined with *anticipating* Johnny's demands and diverting him to other rewarding activities, have succeeded in eliminating Johnny's head banging.

Alison, an abused girl, is terrified of standing her ground when faced by stronger peers. The teacher pursues a programme of rewarding her for her assertiveness in the classroom towards both herself and other pupils. Over a six month period of such *positive reinforcement*, accompanied by personal tutorials and much reassurance that she will be protected, Alison is better able to stand up for herself and assert her wishes and needs.

Danny is being treated in a residential setting, because of his violent temper and persistent offending. He is on a *token economy* programme which rewards him when he is behaving appropriately and fines him for attacks. Occasionally, when he is building up to a temper outburst, he is sent to his room as a 'time out' for five minutes when he will neither receive attention nor material rewards for his behaviour. Over a six month period, the frequency of his tantrums is reduced from several times a day to about once every three weeks.

ACTIVITY 5

Allow about 5 minutes

'PURE' FORMS OF THERAPY

Reread the above examples and consider the extent to which each 'treatment' is *purely* to do with manipulating rewards for behaviour and to what extent other factors, such as the quality of the therapists' relationships with the children, are also involved.

5.1 Theoretical basis

There are two major underlying assumptions in behaviour therapies: (1) that current observable behaviour is the most appropriate and effective focus of treatment and (2) that both normal and abnormal behaviour share the same principles of learning (Herbert, 1991; Hoghughi *et al.*, 1988; Ollendick, 1986; Russo and Varri, 1982).

Every behaviour has antecedents ('causes') as well as consequences. Behaviour therapists do not deny this but they emphasize *current behaviour*, not only because this is what is deemed 'unacceptable' but also because this is the only segment of the past-present-future of the child's behaviour that is directly *available* for treatment. For example, we cannot undo the death of a child's mother or an episode of being bitten by a dog, but we may be able to do something about his present depressed state or her debilitating fear of dogs.

In the past, this led some behaviour therapists to emphasize current behaviour so heavily that they seemed to ignore the shaping of that behaviour by past events. This left them open to the charge particularly by psychiatrists and psychoanalysts, that they were concerned with *symptoms* which, even if successfully removed, would only be replaced by *other* symptoms. The early emphasis has now been corrected by a more balanced approach which looks at the background and contextual factors in the comprehensive assessment of the child's problems, though with a behavioural focus.

The second assumption of behaviour therapies is that both normal and abnormal behaviour are governed by the same laws. This assumption is both an article of faith and a hypothesis. It is an article of faith which arises from the scientific training of psychologists and their conviction that the universe (which includes human beings and their behaviour) is governed by *laws* which determine all fundamental processes – whether normal or abnormal. It is a hypothesis in that clinical psychologists use an ever more sophisticated (but not always more productive) array of concepts and methods derived from experimental research on normal processes such as learning, perception, group behaviour, memory and personality development. It is scientifically wasteful to look for new principles and explanations until those already acquired in this way have been shown to be inadequate or inappropriate. But, of its nature, the conviction cannot be logically disproved and must, therefore, always remain hypothetical.

Behaviour therapies recognize two major groupings of disorder. The first is *deficient behaviour,* when a person has failed to learn acceptable and/ or adaptive responses and therapy seeks to make up for and teach him these responses. The second category comprises *inappropriate behaviour* when a person has learned inappropriate responses to a variety of conditions, so that she cannot cope with the demands of the environment in a manner acceptable to significant persons in that environment, including herself. As noted in Section 1, behaviour, deficient or inappropriate, is deemed to be 'disordered' not exclusively because of its unusual nature (such as wrist cutting) but also because of the *frequency, duration* and *intensity* with which it occurs or does not occur. For example, crying, running around or fighting (all developmentally normal behaviours) may be judged abnormal when they occur with *excessive frequency*. On the other hand, being able to speak properly, look after basic personal needs or play with other children may show abnormality if their rate of occurrence is *too low*. Other behaviours are considered abnormal because they occur at an *inappropriate age* (such as highly sexualized behaviour in little children) or *situations,* such as an adolescent wetting himself in the classroom. Note, however, that the judgement of a child's behaviour as 'deficient' or 'inappropriate' is a *social construction,* subject to all the caveats raised in Section 1.

Whether the problem behaviour is deficient or inappropriate, treatment involves *learning, unlearning and/or relearning*. This corrective action is known as *behaviour therapy*. It assumes that behaviour can be modified (hence the synonym 'behaviour modification') by studying in detail the *current conditions* under which behaviour occurs and planning a remedial strategy on the basis of the information obtained. This will often involve working with parents, teachers, etc. by encouraging them to co-operate in the strategy and view the 'problem' in different ways. Many behaviour therapists use the experimental methods of psychology to monitor the appropriateness of their treatment by looking at treated and untreated groups; evaluating the child's response before and after treatment; varying the intensity of the treatment; and a wide range of other methods. These are essential for the long-term development of a *discipline* of treatment as well as for the evaluation of an individual treatment programme.

All behaviour results from the interaction of the psychological organism with the environment. A newborn infant has a certain innate potential for becoming a normal child but she has to *learn* all the behaviours which will achieve that normality. Thus learning is the central *process* of behaviour change and is itself also the end product. The three major forms of learning are achieved through association ('classical'), by outcome ('operant') and through observation ('social').

At its simplest, classical conditioning (and the learning which results from it) is achieved by *associating* or pairing an ordinary or neutral stimulus with another until the latter elicits the same response as the former. An important feature of this form of treatment is that the child has little control over his responses (which are involuntary and controlled by the autonomic nervous system) and can, therefore, be treated *passively*. If the taking out of a handkerchief (which is a neutral act) is sufficiently often followed by a shout (which is frightening), then eventually the handkerchief by itself will arouse fear.

This form of conditioning, which is associated with the name of Pavlov (1927) is the basis of many forms of psychological treatment where emotional responses such as fear, anger, relaxation and happiness are concerned. Perhaps the most successful and universal application of this form of behaviour therapy in the area of children's problems is the bell-and-pad technique for treating bed wetting (e.g. Herbert and Iwaniec, 1981).

In *operant conditioning*, by contrast, the child is an *active* operator of her environment, and her behaviour is instrumental in bringing about a consequence, and this consequence is the chief reason for the learning that occurs. If the consequence ('reinforcement') is positive or thought to be positive (other things being equal), the behaviour is more likely to be repeated. A positive reinforcement can take the form of either a *reward* (smile, money, late-night TV) or the cessation of something unpleasant (going to bed later, parents stopping fighting). Conversely, negative reinforcement can take the form of either active punishment (being put in own room, loss of pocket money, having to do more chores) or the withdrawal of something positive ('loss of privileges', being ignored).

What complicates the use of operant conditioning to treat problem behaviour in children is that positive and negative reinforcers vary quite markedly for different children (dependent on their history and personality). Although there are certain common physiological (for example, pain of physical punishment) and cultural patterns (for example, loss of privileges), there are so many differences among children in their responses that we cannot be at all sure that what is intended as a reinforcer (positive or negative) will be perceived and responded to as such by the child.

This form of treatment is associated with the name of Skinner (1938, 1953) and has now been developed into a variety of sophisticated techniques for reshaping many forms of behaviour.

EXAMPLE 2
VARIETIES OF BEHAVIOUR MODIFICATION

There are perhaps more numerous and varied techniques that can be described as forms of 'behaviour modification' than any other treatment method. The principal ones include: *'aversion therapy'* (use of unpleasant stimuli to eliminate a behaviour); *'chaining'* (stringing unconnected behaviours together); *'cognitive behaviour modification'* (attempts to alter maladaptive beliefs and attitudes); *'contingency contracting'* (use of a contract to guarantee particular outcomes); *'covert conditioning'* (use of visual *imagery* of outcomes or associated factors instead of real rewards and punishments); *'differential reinforcement'* (developing discriminant responses); *'extinction'* (eliminating a specific behavioural response); *'fading'* (gradual reduction of a response); *'flooding'* (swamping with an unpleasant experience to reduce its impact); *'negative practice'* (repetitive practice to decrease or eliminate a behaviour); *'negative reinforcement'* (removal of an unpleasant stimulus); *'paradoxical intention'* (expressing an unexpected view to jolt child out of current thinking); *'positive reinforcement'* (rewarding); *'shaping'* (gradual approximation to desired behaviour); *'systematic desensitization'* (gradual reduction of anxiety or fears); *'time out'* (removal of child from rewarding experiences when badly behaved); and *'token economy'* (use of coins or tokens with which to buy real rewards).

5.2 Advantages

The theory and methods of behaviour therapy are based on scientific and experimental evidence and are clearly related to observable behaviour. Thus, subjective inference and intuition, though still present, are minimized. Changes in *observable behaviour,* not interpretations, serve as the basis of monitoring behaviour and the results of treatment. Behaviour therapy is not as time-consuming and protracted as other approaches, and 'reinforcers' can be identified and implemented in treatment without segregating the child from his environment.

Children can often understand the behaviour therapy explanation of their behaviour, thus aiding insight. They are, therefore, more inclined to be motivated to change. Paradoxically, this suggests that one of the effective elements in behaviour therapy, its role in helping children to reinterpret their difficulties, is much closer to the types of therapy dealt with in the next section. Behaviour therapy demystifies the treatment of behaviour and turns it into a publicly observable and accountable form of problem solving and 'repairing'. Its techniques are efficient in terms of resources, whether one refers to personnel, time, equipment or materials. It also 'fits in' with the natural order of things – it lends itself to, and can be implemented in, any number of different settings, from the child's own home and school to specialist hospital and other settings. Behaviour therapy allows more than one problem to be tackled, either simultaneously or consecutively. Its techniques do not preclude the use of others, for example, use of medication or family therapy.

One of the attractions of behavioural techniques is that many can be implemented by a wide variety of personnel, provided that a sound technical base and therapeutic format (a behavioural prescription) have been drawn up. So parents, nurses and teachers can potentially do as well as psychologists and, indeed, many do (Herbert, 1991, Hoghughi *et al.,* 1988). Proponents of behaviour therapy emphasize its scientific and evidence-based orientation, and there is no doubt that a voluminous experimental and research literature exists claiming to support it (Garfield and Bergin, 1986, Kazdin, 1988). Its status is so well established that even the British and American Psychiatric Associations believe that behaviour therapy procedures have much to offer informed clinicians in the service of modern clinical and social psychiatry; indeed, they advocate instruction in behaviour therapy techniques for trainee psychiatrists.

From the viewpoint of a discipline, behaviour modification has the enormous advantage of a clear focus and an accountable process of treatment. The fact that there is by now a large and varied literature on its use with children also helps towards its almost universal applicability and gradual adoption as a sane and ethically defensible approach as a main (but rarely exclusive) plank of treatment.

Unlike the use of medicines, behaviour therapy has no side effects. Unlike talking therapies, it does not demand a high level of verbal ability and unlike group and environmental therapies it does not require the involvement of a range of other people.

5.3 Criticisms

Behaviour therapy procedures, nevertheless, continue to engender scepticism in many mental health practitioners, especially those inclined towards the more 'insight' and psychoanalytically oriented therapies. Certain forms of behaviour modification (such as aversive conditioning and 'time out') can be used and perceived as euphemistic substitutes for straightforward punishment or withholding of 'rights'. Indeed there are environments in which such terms are used to dress up what are plainly punitive measures. The 'Pindown' regime (Levy and Kahan, 1991) which so scandalized the UK was claimed to be a 'behaviour modification' regime.

Most seriously of all, behaviour modification in one setting may not (and often does not) transfer and generalize to another. Much effort may be expended in changing behaviour which simply reverts to its previous state upon *discharge* from the treatment setting. This is what accounts for some poor outcomes from behaviour modification, for example with delinquent children. Although there is no theoretical reason why the new learning through behaviour therapy should not be generalized and pervasive, in practice most of such learning is too shallow and context-bound to be more than a means of survival for a child in an environment bent on securing his conformity. An answer to this problem might be found in deeper and more real-life 'conditioning' and the setting up of 'continuation strategies' when the child has returned to his normal environment. After all, 'inappropriate behaviour' may be more appropriate in an abnormal environment than socially conforming behaviour. On balance, however, the advantages of behaviour therapy have to be set against its disadvantages, particularly in modern usage, which acknowledges the importance of other influences and the advisability of combining a range or 'package' of treatment methods in the interests of effectiveness (Kazdin, 1988).

SUMMARY OF SECTION 5

- Behaviour therapy (behaviour modification) is based on 'laws of learning' such as *classical conditioning* and *operant conditioning* derived from psychological research into learning in 'normal' people.
- It treats children's problems as arising from inappropriate learned behaviour which can be changed by new patterns of rewards (and sometimes punishments).
- While the methods of behaviour therapy are well theorized and relatively easily implemented, doubts are expressed about the power relationships implied between child and therapist, about the 'generalizability' of improvements and about the lack of concern with social context.

6 TALKING THERAPIES

EXAMPLE 3
TWO CHILDREN

Counsellor: 'John, I don't know very much about why you've come to see me. Dr R. mentioned it might be helpful if we met. Can you tell me if you agree?'

John: (*tentatively and barely audible*) 'Well, I was recently in some trouble with my parents.'

Counsellor: 'Do you want to tell me what sort of trouble?'

John: 'Well, they came home when I wasn't expecting them (*long pause, going red and breathing rapidly*). They found us in bed, Peter and I. They practically went berserk, calling us all sort of names. Peter got into quite a state and my father has avoided me since. Eventually my mother thought I should see Dr R., which I did. He was very nice and asked me a lot of questions about whether I was attracted more to boys or girls. Eventually he said there was nothing wrong with me and he thought perhaps I would find it helpful if I could have some counselling to help me clear up my own mind about my sexuality.'

Jessica is a girl of 12 whose mother left her when she was 8 years old. Father has just been investigated for sexually abusing her, but has been exonerated. Since her brother died six months ago it has become evident that she is increasingly withdrawing into herself, beginning to be slovenly and not looking after her personal hygiene. She is clearly very forlorn and isolated from her age mates and her schoolwork has taken a tumble. There is no formal psychiatric diagnosis but she clearly needs help. She is referred to the psychotherapist to identify what is going on inside her and how she might be helped to come to terms with the complex experience of the loss of her brother and her problematic relationship with her father.

Talking is probably the most pervasive medium of treatment. It is also most lay people's idea of what goes on between a therapist and the client.

Talking is also the most common, yet unique, human activity, particularly as a means of communicating and reducing distress. Though this activity increases in range and complexity as a person gets older, it is also reasonable to use it as a means of understanding and resolving children's difficulties. From the earliest age, parents augment their touching and hugging by cooing and talking to understand and comfort their distressed children. There is hardly any therapeutic activity with children that does not involve talking; indeed, this very fact makes it difficult and inadvisable to be definite about which exact element of any treatment programme may be the main reason for its efficacy.

However, there are therapies which use talking almost exclusively as the medium of treatment. Such talking is usually seen as a means of unblocking and reorganizing past experiences; enabling the child to identify choices and their consequences, and recognizing and reordering thinking patterns and their consequences, and many other variants (Hoghughi *et al.*, 1988; Kazdin, 1988; Johnson *et al.*, 1986).

The major influence on talking therapies comes from the ideas of Sigmund Freud (1946), who saw the root of problems as unresolved conflicts in the course of a child's development. Though he was himself less interested in children than in adults, some of his most influential followers, such as Melanie Klein, Karen Horney and Anna Freud, did their major work on children's problems. Despite the heated debates amongst practitioners regarding the finer points of their theories, their similarities are sufficient to allow them to be grouped together. Practitioners of these therapies also believe, in varying degrees, in a particular view of personality; the existence of the 'unconscious' and 'defence mechanisms' as a means of coping with anxiety (with the arguable exception of 'rational-emotive' therapists and a new breed of cognitive therapists). These defences are believed to become manifest in various maladaptive responses that can be cleared up only through certain forms of therapy – principally free association, dream analysis, analysis of defences and, more in the case of children, playing, drawing and story-telling (Reisman, 1973; Winnicott, 1971; Wolman, 1972).

Cognitive therapy, another variant, is concerned with identifying thoughts and perceptions which trigger and justify maladaptive emotions and behaviours. Cognitive therapists also try to discern patterns of distortion of thoughts about self and others (referred to as 'cognitive schema') such as 'I am always made to do things' – 'victim schema' or 'I cannot do anything without other people's help' – 'dependent schema'. If the cognitive therapist emphasizes skill-based techniques to change thinking and coping patterns or the behavioural elements, such activity could also be classified under other treatment methods such as behaviour therapy (Ellis and Bernard, 1983; Kendall and Holton, 1979; McAdam, 1987; Ollendick and Hersen, 1985).

Distilled to their essence, talking therapies are a form of *focused conversation* as a medium of helping. The client's verbal and non-verbal communications are interpreted as a means of understanding the source of difficulty. The interpretation is intended to provide insights which are meant to unravel and resolve conflicts and thereby lead to better adjusted behaviour. This is why talking therapies are also sometimes referred to as 'insight therapies'. This approach can be applied to a wide range of difficulties, from asthma and bed wetting to antisocial behaviour and phobias.

Newer forms of talking therapy began to proliferate in the 1960s and 1970s due to the growth of humanistic psychology, which emphasized the integrity and primacy of the client – even a disordered child – and asserted that talking through problems was an ethical and effective way of resolving 'psychological' problems.

6.1 Theoretical basis

The core element of all talking therapies is that, in the context of a 'therapeutic relationship', talking can be used to give the client insight into her difficulties and thereby help overcome them. The 'therapeutic relationship' possesses particular characteristics, of which the most important are:

- regard for the child;
- consistency between what the therapist says and what she does;
- genuineness towards the child; and
- empathy.

It takes time to build up such a relationship, which, though sensitive to change, must be robust enough to withstand crises in the circumstances of the child and pressures on the therapeutic relationship.

A particular difficulty, to be noted in passing, is the emphasis in the literature (particularly counselling and cognitive therapies) on the term 'client' – that is, someone who seeks help. However, as we noted at the start of this chapter, children with difficulties rarely *seek* help but rather have forms of help decided upon for them. This can potentially distort the therapeutic relationship. Of necessity, the relationship between the child and the therapist is not an equal one; the latter has, in every important sense, more power and is frequently required by other people than the child to undertake the therapy. For these reasons, although in talking therapies no less effort is made to establish a therapeutic relationship with the child, it is recognized that this relationship may not conform to the ideal in all respects.

So much emphasis has been put, both in theoretical writings and in empirical research, on therapeutic relationships that the relationship itself has been held to be at least as important as the use of talking, which is its medium. Clearly language has to be used in the process of establishing the relationship, which in turn will affect what language is used and how either party will interpret and respond to it. Though 'silence' is taken and interpreted as a significant element, it has to be bounded by speech (whether verbal or in sign language). This raises many logical problems of interpreting the special roles of language and relationship in achieving treatment. In turn, this also has implications for the practice of talking therapy.

The special characteristic of therapeutic language is that it is the medium for enabling the (child) client to gain 'insight' into the motives, beliefs, emotions and other underlying 'causes' of their actions. Inadequate understanding of these causes is believed to underlie disordered behaviour from aggressiveness and fire-setting to bed wetting and asthma. Greater insight will, therefore, increase control over the behaviour and lead to improvement in the problem condition. Unlike behaviour therapy, emphasis is less on active behaviour change (except in cognitive techniques) than on uncovering hidden causes and thereby *facilitating* change.

Focus on 'insight' is central to all talking therapies, even though it is given different names and varying emphasis in the different techniques. Furthermore, with the exception of cognitive therapies, all entail an implicit acceptance of psychodynamic views of personality which derive originally, more or less, from the work of Freud.

The differing emphases in the techniques might warn against lumping them together as 'talking therapies'. Also, sometimes these and other techniques have been promoted as 'group therapies'. This is particularly true of counselling and 'transactional analysis'. However, bringing them together in the present chapter seems legitimate on the grounds that talking is the main medium of treatment. Although their power may be enhanced by the addition of group pressure, the main emphasis is on verbal interaction rather than on group dynamics.

EXAMPLE 4
VARIETIES OF TALKING THERAPY

Talking therapies include counselling; 'gestalt therapy' (a therapy emphasizing integration of thought, feeling and action); 'psychoanalytic therapy' (with many variants); 'rational–emotive therapy' (emphasizing the importance of thinking in shaping behaviour); 'interpersonal cognitive problem solving' (emphasizing linkage between distorting 'schema' and behaviour) and 'transactional analysis' (changing entrenched behaviour patterns through verbal feedback).

6.2 Advantages

We define reality by the language we use to describe it. Talking (including 'self-talk') is the embodiment of language. It is, therefore, not surprising that it should have such a central and significant place in the understanding of children's difficulties. Talking is such an early and well-established skill that both the child and therapist can engage in it without much troublesome preparation.

Although the reality may be different, rarely do talking therapies have the same 'mechanistic' or authoritarian image as, for example, behaviour therapy. In an age of concern with empowerment, the fact that the therapist is not doing something (coercive) *to* a passive child is an important consideration. A lot of people can participate in widely available courses of one sort or other, which enable them to engage in counselling, transactional analysis and other forms of therapeutic talking.

6.3 Criticisms

There are three main criticisms of the use of talking therapies with children as the primary or sole element in treating their difficulties:

- talking therapy requires expensive and lengthy involvement with highly trained therapists;
- the theoretical justifications for the therapeutic practices and their effectiveness are poorly supported by evidence;
- children are less able than adults to make use of insights gained through verbal interpretations of their behaviour offered by therapists.

The first point highlights the difficulty in providing sufficient therapeutic help for children who are seen as needing it, given that most talking therapies involve many sessions, extending over at least months, and sometimes years. There is general agreement that it is necessary for therapists employing such methods to undergo extensive and lengthy training. These two factors together mean that many talking therapies are expensive and time-consuming, and, for them to be treatments of choice, should be capable of being shown to be more effective than other, less costly methods. Countering this criticism, there is an argument that the improvements achieved by this type of therapy are more long-lasting and that they generalize from the treatment setting more readily than is the case with behavioural methods.

The second criticism is most often levelled at the more psycho-dynamically oriented therapies, and particularly at those employing the use of interpretations derived from classical Freudian theory. Such interpretations may often aim to expose underlying, unconscious motivations that are predominantly sexual in nature (in a broad sense, to do with the seeking of erotic satisfaction). Many people are uneasy not only about the idea that such motivations (such as Oedipal wishes) exist in younger children but also about the possible harmful effects on the child of offering such interpretations where they are not justified, particularly given that it is not easy to give empirical support for them, other than the therapist's clinical judgement. Against this criticism is the experience of therapists who encourage children to express themselves through play and who find that many children quite commonly act out horrific and disturbing events involving sexual and violent acts.

The third criticism asserts that children lack a sufficient capacity to reflect on their thoughts, feelings and actions in such a way as to be able to make use of the therapist's suggestions as to useful insights. While there is a great deal of evidence that such 'metacognitive' abilities do indeed increase and elaborate during childhood, thus lending some support to this argument, it has also been argued that for many children talking therapies allow them to be 'given a voice'. To be genuinely listened to by a sympathetic and empathic adult may be a novel experience for a child whose predominant experience has been one where adults are critical and controlling.

SUMMARY OF SECTION 6

- Talking therapies originated with Freud and the development of psychoanalysis.
- There are many modern variants associated with new theoretical developments.
- They use conversation as the prime medium for bringing about change.
- Talking therapies are arguably less 'authoritarian' than behavioural approaches.

7 GROUP THERAPIES

EXAMPLE 5
THREE CASES

A psychiatric unit for adolescents has recently admitted a relatively large number of girls who suffer from anorexia. Staff of the unit believe that individual therapy is likely to take a long time to make impact and, in the meantime, individual patients may undermine each other's treatment programme. It is decided that a group therapy programme will be initiated to tackle the problem.

A substance misuse specialist brings together a group of adolescents for evening therapy sessions – to explore their reasons for misuse and teach them alternative and socially desirable means of getting a 'kick out of life'.

Rachel has just taken an overdose following suspension from school and episodes of unexplained absences from home. The psychiatrist does not detect mental illness in her but picks up evidence of considerable tension and anger about her family and life circumstances. He refers the matter to the family therapist for assessment and work with the whole family.

Most people live in groups, experience their problems in groups and have to rely on groups to accept and define them as social entities. It is, therefore, not surprising that group therapies are prominent in the treatment of children with problems. A considerable literature has grown around the topic of group therapies, and many forms of group practice have been claimed to be therapeutic (Douglas, 1986; Harris, 1977; Minuchin and Fishman, 1981; Schaefer *et al.*, 1982; Sugar, 1975; Vorrath and Brendtro, 1985).

Groups are used for a variety of purposes, even in specialist settings for children. These include gatherings for the purpose of exchanging information, providing support, joint decision-making and problem-solving, sharing normal life activities, as well as treatment. Indeed, in residential settings for disordered children this range of activities constitutes much of the therapeutic benefit of the service (e.g. Trieschman, Whittaker and Brendtro, 1969).

Group therapies, however, are different from these, because they involve the application of therapeutic techniques to groups for the purposes of ameliorating the difficulties of group members. For example, a group of anxious adolescents may be brought together for counselling as a means of helping them to manage their condition. Or a group of antisocial children may be brought together and subjected to mutual scrutiny and pressure, in the context of a *'positive peer culture'*, to modify their attitudes and behaviour. In both these instances, groups are used as both a *medium* and a *focus* of treatment, with a view to changing individual behaviour patterns.

7.1 Theoretical basis

The power of group therapies derives from two sources: the *group dimension* of some problems and group *dynamics*. Externalized difficulties (such as aggression and social insensitivity) are thus identified either in a group setting or according to group-related norms. Indeed, virtually all problems (such as sub-clinical depression) contain group-related elements. This becomes all the more important when we consider the prevalent view that certain behaviours are generated by *faulty* group functioning. This is the basis of all family therapy and much group counselling.

Whereas family-related problems such as attempted suicide or anorexia nervosa may be manifested alone or in the family, certain other problems become obvious only in groups. These include social skills problems (such as poor empathy or uncooperativeness) and aspects of personal development (such as emotional immaturity or 'indecent behaviour'). Such problems are best resolved in a group setting. Thus, theoretically, groups must be used to tap both the 'causation' of the problem and the context in which it is manifested and maintained.

Much socialization takes place through group processes, first in the family and subsequently in school and a widening social environment. Every citizen is a walking testimony to the power of groups to shape individual behaviour, from the family to the most amorphous social groupings, such as football crowds. Group power is exercised through its much greater ability to identify unacceptable behaviour; lay it out for public scrutiny, shape it through positive or negative feedback, provide a range of appropriate or alternative methods of adaptation and do so with sufficient diversity to make it withstand changes in the child's physical and social condition.

The power of the group is encompassed by the term 'group dynamics'. It includes such elements of group influence as group size, the group atmosphere, the composition of the group, communication media, task and leadership. Much less is known about the power of these elements in clinical contexts, particularly in relation to children, than in experimental and industrial settings (e.g. Douglas 1986; Rose 1972).

Family therapy is firmly based on the notion of the family as a *system* of interacting members and functions which, in disarray, can cause problems for one or more of its members as we saw in Section 2. A variety of techniques is used to create and use group pressure to enable family members to gain insight into and control over their dynamics.

Group counselling, in contrast, does not focus so much on group processes as causative in problem behaviour but uses them as a medium for highlighting and sharing problems and discovering common means of resolving them. The same is done in *group behaviour-modification* which replaces insight-giving by behaviour modification in a group setting. The propensity of group members to give *feedback* and *reinforcement* is used as a major medium for shaping behaviour.

A similar theoretical conception underlies *positive peer culture,* only here greater emphasis is laid on the peer-group origins of much antisocial behaviour. Therapeutic work, therefore, concentrates on transforming the pressure towards antisocial behaviour into a powerful dynamic for emphasizing prosocial and positive aspects of individual functioning.

Psychodrama and *role-play* have theoretical roots in Freudian psychology as well as in the group genesis and resolution of problems. The acting out of conflicts relates to group dynamics mainly in the tendency of other group members to react to each other's behaviour and this provides both feedback and a means of shaping it.

7.2 Advantages

As with talking therapies, living and working in groups is such a pervasive activity that it is difficult to be categorical about its scientific and professional status. Its very commonness and familiarity is one of its greatest strengths. There is generally no stigma attached to being in a group, though that depends on the name given it and the composition of its members. The mere fact of being with others who have difficulties is likely to lighten the personal burden of being the only one troubled, provided the group does not exacerbate an individual's problems.

The greatest appeal of group therapy is in its efficiency. The effort of one therapist can be used much more economically in ameliorating the problems of a whole group than those of one young person alone. This efficiency is further extended when we consider that, because of the greater numbers of other young people in the group, they can act as prompters and reinforcers more frequently than the therapist can alone. There are, in any case, some problems, such as those generated and sustained by the family, where treatment can only take place through reordering family interactions.

While there are undoubtedly high skill requirements for group therapists, dealing with groups is also a fairly common experience for most workers with children. Depending on the particular form of group therapy to be used, the skills can be acquired in anything from a few days to a few months, though almost everyone benefits from longer practice.

7.3 Criticisms

A generally accepted limitation is that group therapies are less useful with very young children than with teenagers because of both susceptibility to pressure and social development. There are also limits to the type of problem for which it can be used. Broadly speaking, physical and intellectual problems are not susceptible to group therapy. Thus, while there are numerous studies of group therapy with, for example, drug abusers or psychotics, therapeutic work is directed more at changing some cognitive and emotional components of the behaviour and providing support for participants than the condition itself.

People who can conduct *productive* group therapeutic sessions often need considerable training and experience, and these are not easy to come by. Also, depending on the particular form of group therapy used, a child can be subjected to intense and unaccountable group pressure to change. Children may find it difficult to leave behind the feelings of exposure and stress aroused during therapy sessions and they sometimes vent their anger and anguish on themselves and others subsequently.

The very large literature on group therapies does not provide a ready conclusion about the efficacy of this method in comparison with others. Some researchers show improvement for their clients, while others do not. Some studies claim advantages over other methods, some do not. There is little satisfactory way of accounting for these results, given the huge diversity of studies which are not readily comparable (e.g. Kaul and Bednar, 1986; Kolvin *et al.*, 1981).

There are some practitioners who see forms of group therapy as treatments of choice for everything from delinquency and absconding to attempted suicide (e.g. Fishman, 1988, for family therapy). Others limit it to more focused interventions (e.g. Michelson *et al.*, 1983, for social skills), but even allowing for their limitations, group therapies still have a wide application.

SUMMARY OF SECTION 7

- Group therapies are based on ideas from social psychology about the impact of social processes on individual behaviour.
- The most obvious advantage of group therapy is its efficiency: one therapist can simultaneously work with many young people.
- Group therapy is less appropriate for young children: it is more suited to adolescents and adults.
- There are limits on the types of problems for which it is suitable.

---

8 EVALUATING THERAPIES

Given the range of styles and types of therapies, of which we have given some examples, and referred to others, it is clearly a matter of interest both to practitioners and researchers to have answers to two important and interlinked questions:

- How effective are these therapies in alleviating or removing psychological problems?
- Are some therapies more effective than others for particular types of problems?

If clear-cut answers were available to these two questions, it would greatly aid practitioners in deciding which type of therapy might be most appropriate (likely to succeed) for each problem they find themselves having to deal with.

Unfortunately, we are a long way from having even partial answers: this is because these questions – while they appear, superficially at least, to be simple and potentially easily answerable – are in fact extremely problematic. This section will alert you to some of these difficulties and show you why they arise, help you to treat claims for the effectiveness of particular therapies with extreme caution, and give you some tools of critical analysis for evaluating such claims. More generally, it will help you to be more aware of the issues surrounding the evaluation of interventions, which is one of the themes running through this book.

ACTIVITY 6

Allow about 15 minutes

DESIGNING AN EVALUATION STUDY

This activity is intended to focus your attention on some important issues in evaluating therapies. Read the following vignette and then answer the questions below:

Two clinical psychologists, one based in a psychiatric hospital out-patient unit and another based in a clinic run by a charitable trust, have each followed up 20 children whom they treated about a year ago, by contacting the children's parents. They asked whether or not the child had needed further therapy since they had last been seen. The psychologist working in the out-patient unit, who is strongly committed to behaviour modification as a method, and treated all these children without spending much time with the parents, found that four of his sample had re-entered some sort of therapy. The other psychologist, who insisted on working with all family members and exploring family dynamics as part of his therapeutic approach, found that none of his sample had.

Could these psychologists validly conclude that the behavioural approach is less effective?

Hopefully you have answered with a resounding NO!

Note the reasons why you might have doubts about them making this interpretation, and any thoughts you have about further information they might need to collect, any flaws in their approach, and what you think they might to do gain more useful results if they were to repeat the study with groups of children with whom they have not yet started therapeutic work.

To structure your analysis, consider what factors might influence 'therapeutic effectiveness', using the following headings:

How is a problem assessed (as discussed in section 3)?

Match between therapy and problem.

What counts as a successful outcome?

> Families' social and economic circumstances.
>
> Developmental changes in children.
>
> Personal characteristics of children.
>
> What events/choices lead to children being assigned to a particular type of therapy?
>
> Life events; both positive and negative.
>
> Depth, intensity and duration of therapy.
>
> Therapist's personal qualities and their training.

The above activity will have made you more aware of the multitude of different factors that might be likely to have some impact on the outcome of a therapeutic intervention. For us to have any confidence in the results of a study that sets out to compare the effectiveness of different therapies, we need to be assured that the study has measured and taken account of the possible effects of all such variables. Otherwise, differences in measured effectiveness might have arisen because of differences in these other factors between the groups rather than being the result of any differences between the therapies themselves. This is a general problem that has to be dealt with in most areas of developmental research, particularly where the focus is on the effect of a particular treatment on some aspect of children's behaviour, thoughts or feelings. The model of experimental design that has been developed within psychology offers a well-constructed set of solutions to these problems, and many evaluations of therapeutic work with children have attempted to meet the stringent requirements of this model.

Central to this model is the importance of either:

(a) assessing the likely impact of these confounding variables on the outcome measure(s) (effectiveness of therapy);

(b) controlling these variables so that their influence on outcome is minimized.

For the first of these, the approach is to use some measure of each child's position on each variable and to analyse the data to see if there are any consistent links between this variable and outcome measures.

For the second, two ways of controlling variables are appropriate for assessing therapeutic effectiveness:

• Matching children in the two (or more) treatment groups on as many as possible of the confounding variables. This will help to ensure that differences in therapeutic effectiveness are not attributable simply to differences between the groups of children in the different treatment conditions.

• Studying a matched control group of children who undergo no form of therapy, but have the same range of difficulties as the treatment group.

DESIGNING AN EVALUATIVE STUDY: FURTHER CONSIDERATION

This will help to illustrate how the effects of various factors that might influence therapeutic effectiveness could be accounted for in a research design.

Go back to the previous activity and work through the list of possible factors and your notes on them.

For each factor, decide which of the following could/should be done and any problems that you can foresee in so doing:

- *Measure*: what could you measure to assess this factor and how would you do it?
- *Control*: what would you seek to control and how would you do it?

Do the above before you read the following comments.

Comments

In doing the above, you have been faced with the sorts of decisions that would have to be made by someone designing an evaluation study. These decisions are concerned with making judgements about what factors might influence treatment effectiveness. Judgements would have to be based on reasons for choosing which factors to take account of and which to reject as unimportant. What this really means is that there has to be a *theory* (hopefully with evidence to back it up) about what factors make a difference to a therapy's success.

In the circumstances that we are considering, that is, comparing two or more therapies, it is quite possible that such a theory could suggest that these other factors might interact differently with different therapies. For example, as far as families' social circumstances are concerned, the amount of talk about personal difficulties in a child's home might make a difference to how effective different therapies could be.

Families in which there is a lot of talk about personal matters, and in which rewards and punishment are little used to control children's behaviour, might support a talking therapy better than a behavioural therapy, whereas families where the opposite is the case might better support a behavioural approach.

When you consider that similar complications might arise for most of the variables covered by the factors in the list above, you can see that an evaluation of therapeutic effectiveness has to be based on a good theoretical understanding of how therapy is embedded in, and affected by, a very complex background.

Another issue that arises is to do with the therapies being evaluated. All therapeutic work is carried out by people, and hence all therapy involves a human relationship (or set of relationships). For talking therapies this is clearly a central, essential element, while for behavioural therapies, the human relationship element may (possibly incorrectly) be seen as less central, although it is still undoubtedly essential.

It is very difficult, then, to consider effectiveness solely in relation to the therapeutic activity itself. No therapy is wholly 'pure', and it is a mistake to consider this as being even possible: all therapies depend on people discussing, negotiating and implementing the therapeutic 'regime'. It can be argued that the *active* elements of most if not all therapies are the same: qualities such as warmth, respect, kindness, hope, understanding and the provision of explanations. Without the presence of these, the co-operation of child and family is unlikely to be encouraged.

In the practice of therapy, it is also quite common for approaches to be electic or mixed, so that 'purity' is further compromised. This is not to say that purity is something to be aimed for: that could be seen as a restricted, inflexible approach by some practitioners who would advocate a responsive choice of a variety of approaches in each case.

Therapists' levels of experience and training, and their personal qualities, will also affect what is actually done with a child and family, further diluting the 'purity' of the therapy. To summarize, the idea of a pure 'type of therapy' being susceptible to evaluation seems more difficult to sustain the more one considers the reality of therapeutic interventions in real-life situations.

There is then a wide range of difficulties facing evaluation studies. Stevenson (1986) has summarized concisely the major issues in this area which were identified by Rutter (1982):

> Firstly, the construction of an appropriate evaluation design for assessment of change produced by treatment in children is more complex than with adults. In adults change attributable to therapy is easier to identify since it occurs against a background of relative stability. The situation with children is very different. Here the effects of therapy need to be disentangled from behavioural changes induced as part of maturation or as a consequence of environmental changes. Secondly, evaluation has to recognise changes in the goals of treatment that include the recognition of symptom reduction as an appropriate goal (as opposed to restricting successful outcome to the more nebulous psychodynamic notions of the end point of treatment), the promotion of normal development, the fostering of autonomy and self-reliance, generalisation of behavioural gains and to establish the longer term consequences of treatment. Thirdly, evaluation needs to establish the relative merits of treatments compared to each other as well as compared to no treatment. As part of this exercise it will be possible to establish whether there are certain treatments that are simply ineffective and should be abandoned. Fourthly, evaluation should provide some guide as to the match between treatment and condition. It is unlikely that any one treatment is going to be the most successful with all disorders, and which therapy is most effective with which disorder needs to be established. Fifthly, a related issue is that not all children will benefit from even the treatment of choice, and therefore the

evaluation needs to answer the question of which characteristics of the child and its family are related to individual differences in the response to treatment. Sixthly, the evaluation enterprise could provide data on the process underlying the effectiveness of therapy i.e. what is it that actually produces change. This question is of obvious importance if therapy is to be made more efficient. Lastly, the question of acceptance of the treatment by the child and its family needs to be investigated. The take up of different therapies will vary and to restrict evaluation of outcome simply to those attending for treatment overlooks a considerable problem facing clinicians in the subsequent dissemination of therapeutic technique. If the clients do not accept the treatment then whatever its potential benefit, it cannot be effective in that particular case.

(Stevenson, 1986, pp. 3-4)

In conclusion, we have shown in this section how complex and problematic are the issues facing evaluative studies of therapy that follow the strict requirements of experimental design. These difficulties have led to few studies having been completed that do not fall down in one or more of the areas that have been discussed. Hence, although it would have been nice to be able so to do, we are not in a position to present you with a summary of which types of therapy work best for which types of children's difficulties. Indeed we would go so far as to say that such a summary may never be fully achievable, at least not in the near future.

This is not to say, though, that concern about how therapies work, how they interact with all the factors we have been considering, and what sorts of outcomes they produce, is unimportant. Indeed, concern with these issues is growing amongst the profession, and alternatives to the strict experimental paradigm are being actively explored. An increasing commitment to the scientific principles of the paradigm is reflected in many therapists paying more attention to the issues of establishing causal effects and clarifying their theories about the origins of need for therapy and the many factors affecting outcome.

SUMMARY OF SECTION 8

- Different ways of evaluating therapies have been looked at together with considerations that must be taken into account during the course of evaluation.
- Amongst the difficulties are: the confounding effects of social and economic circumstances, children's developmental changes, differential allocation to treatments, therapy–problem matching, outcome criteria and qualities of therapist and treatment.
- The state of current research does not allow us to present an evaluation of the various forms of therapy – the situation is under continuing review.

FURTHER READING

LANE, D. A. and MILLER, A. (1992) *Child and Adolescent Therapy*, Buckingham, Open University Press.

HERBERT, M. (1991) *Clinical Child Psychology*, Chichester, Wiley.

HOGHUGHI, M. S. (1992) *Assessing Child and Adolescent Disorders*, London, Sage.

REFERENCES

DALLOS, R. (1991) *Family Belief Systems, Therapy and Change*, Milton Keynes, Open University Press.

DOUGLAS, T. (1986) *Group Living: the application of group dynamics in residential settings,* London, Tavistock.

ELLIS, A. and BERNARD, M. E. (eds) (1983) *Rational Emotive Approaches to the Problems of Childhood,* New York, Plenum.

FISHMAN, H. C. (1988) *Treating Troubled Adolescents: a family therapy approach,* London, Hutchinson.

FREUD, A. (1946) *The Psychoanalytic Treatment of Children*, London, Imago.

FUNDUDIS, T., KOLVIN, I. and GARSIDE, R. (1979) *Speech-retarded and Deaf Children,* London, Academic Press.

GARFIELD, S. L. and BERGIN, A. E. (1986) *Handbook of Psychotherapy and Behaviour Change,* New York, Wiley.

HALEY, J. (1976) *Problem Solving Therapy*, New York, Harper & Row.

HARRIS, G. (ed.) (1977) *The Group Treatment of Human Problems: a social learning approach,* New York, Grune and Stratton.

HERBERT, M. (1991) *Clinical Child Psychology*, Chichester, Wiley.

HERBERT, M. and IWANIEC, D. (1981) 'Behavioural psychotherapy in natural home-settings: an empirical study applied to conduct disordered and incontinent children', *Behavioural Psychotherapy,* **9**, pp. 55–76.

HOGHUGHI, M. S. (1992) *Assessing Child and Adolescent Disorders*, London, Sage.

HOGHUGHI, M. S., LYONS, J., MUCKLEY, A. and SWAINSTON, M. (1988) *Treating Problem Children,* London, Sage.

JOHNSON, J., RASBURY, W. C. and SIEGEL, L. J. (1986) *Approaches to Child Treatment – Introduction to Theory, Research and Practice,* New York, Pergamon Press.

KAUL, T. J. and BEDNAR, R. L. (1986) *Research on Group and Related Therapies* in GARFIELD, S. L. and BERGIN, A. E., *Handbook of Psychotherapy and Behaviour Change,* New York, Wiley.

KAZDIN, A. (1988) *Child Psychotherapy – Developing and Identifying Effective Treatment,* New York, Pergamon Press.

KELLY, G. (1955) *The Psychology of Personal Constructs*, Chicago, University of Chicago Press.

KENDALL, P. C. and HOLTON, S. D. (1979) *Cognitive Behavioural Intervention: theory, research and procedures,* New York, Academic Press.

KOLVIN, I., GARSIDE, R. F., NICOL, A. R. and MACMILLAN, A. (1981) *Help Starts Here: the maladjusted child in ordinary school,* London, Tavistock.

LAING, R. D. (1969) *The Politics of the Family and Other Essays*, London, Tavistock.

LEVY, A. and KAHAN, B. (1991) *The Pindown Experience and the Protection of Children: the report of the Staffordshire Child Care Inquiry,* Staffordshire County Council.

MARKS, I. M. (1987) *Fears, Phobias and Rituals*, New York, Oxford University Press.

McADAM, E.(1987) 'Cognitive behaviour therapy: a therapy for the troubled adolescent' in COLEMAN, J. C. (ed.) *Working with Troubled Adolescents,* London, Academic Press.

MICHELSON, A. W., SUGAI, P., WOOD, R. P. and KAZDIN, A. E. (1983) *Social Skills Assessment and Training with Children,* New York, Plenum Press.

MINUCHIN, S. (1974) *Families and Family Therapy*, London, Tavistock.

MINUCHIN, S. and FISHMAN, H. C. (1981) *Family Therapy Techniques,* Cambridge (Mass.), Harvard University Press.

OLLENDICK, T. H. (1986) 'Behaviour therapy with children and adolescents' in GARFIELD, S. L. and BERGIN, A. E., *Handbook of Psychotherapy and Behaviour Change,* New York, Wiley.

OLLENDICK, T. H. and HERSEN, M. (eds) (1985) *Handbook of Child Psychotherapy,* New York, Plenum.

PAVLOV, I. P. (1927) *Conditioned Reflexes: an investigation of the physiological aspects of the cerebral cortex,* London, Oxford University Press.

POLLNER, M. and WIKLER, L. (1985) 'The social construction of unreality', *Family Process*, **24**, pp. 241–59.

REISMAN, J. M. (1973) *Principles of Psychotherapy with Children,* New York, Wiley.

ROGERS, C. (1955) *Client Centred Therapy*, New York, Houghton Mifflin.

ROSE, S. D. (1972) *Training Children in Groups: a behavioural approach*, San Francisco, Jossey Bass.

RUSSO, D. C. and VARRI, J. W. (eds) (1982) *Behavioural Pediatrics: research and practice*, New York, Plenum.

RUTTER, M. (1982) 'Psychological therapies in child psychiatry: issues and prospects', *Psychological Medicine*, **12**, pp. 723–40.

RUTTER, M. and GOULD, M. (1985) 'Classification' in RUTTER, M. and HERSOV, L. (eds) *Child and Adolescent Psychiatry*, Oxford, Blackwell.

SCHAEFER, C. E. (ed.) (1988) *Innovative Interventions in Child and Adolescent Therapy*, New York, Wiley.

SCHAEFER, C. E., JOHNSON, L. and WHERRY, J. N. (1982) *Group Therapies for Children and Youth: principles and practices and group treatment*, San Francisco, Jossey Bass.

SKINNER, B. F. (1938) *The Behaviour of Organisms: an experimental analysis*, New York, Appleton-Century-Crofts.

SKINNER, B. F. (1953) *Science and Human Behaviour*, New York, Macmillan.

STEVENSON, J. (1986) 'Evaluation studies of psychological treatment of children and practical constraints on their design', *Association for Child Psychology and Psychiatry Newsletter*, **8**(2), pp. 2_11.

SUGAR, M. (ed.) (1975) *The Adolescent in Group and Family Therapy*, New York, Brunner/Mazel.

TREISCHMAN, A. E., WHITTAKER, J. K. and BRENDTRO, L. K. (1969) *The Other 23 Hours*, Chicago, Aldine.

VORRATH, H. H. and BRENDTRO, L. K. (1985) *Positive Peer Culture*, New York, Aldine.

WALLERSTEIN, J. S. and KELLY, J. B. (1980) *Surviving the Break-Up*, London, Grant MacIntyre.

WINNICOTT, D. W. (1971) *Therapeutic Consultations in Child Psychiatry*, London, Hogarth Press.

WOLMAN, B. B. (ed.) (1972) *Handbook of Child Psychoanalysis*, New York, Van Nostrand Rheinhold.

WORLD HEALTH ORGANISATION (WHO) (1988) *International Classification of Diseases*, tenth edition (ICD.10), Geneva, WHO.

ACKNOWLEDGEMENTS

Grateful acknowledgement is made to the following for permission to reproduce material in this book:

Chapter 1

Table 1: Fielding, D. 'Working with children and young people' in Marzillier, J. S. and Hall, J. (eds) *What is Clinical Psychology?*, by permission of Oxford University Press.

Chapter 2

Text

Reading A: Robert F. Biehler and Jack Snowman (1993, 7th edn) *Psychology Applied to Teaching*, copyright © 1993 by Houghton Mifflin Company, used with permission; *Reading B*: Pinder, R. (1987) *Why Don't Teachers Teach Like They Used To?*, Hilary Shipman Limited, © Rachel Pinder 1987.

Figure

Figure 1: Pinder, R. (1987) *Why Don't Teachers Teach Like They Used To?*, Hilary Shipman Limited, © Rachel Pinder 1987.

Photograph

Page 57: C. Turner, W. Kent and the Norfolk Living History Group.

Cartoons

Page 34: cartoon by Dish reproduced by kind permission of the Editor, *Education*, published by Pitman Publishing, *Education*, 26 February 1993, p. 146; *page 49*: Ray Mutimer; *page 64*: Derek Eastoe.

Chapter 3

Text

Bates, S. (1992) 'Pupils lead way on computers', *Guardian*, 24 December 1992.

Figures

Figure 1: Blaye, A., Light, P., Joiner, R. and Sheldon, S. (1991) 'Collaboration as a facilitator of planning and problem solving on a computer-based task', *British Journal of Developmental Psychology*, **9**, pp. 471–483, British Psychological Society, © 1991 British Psychological Society; *Figure 2*: Light, P., Foot, T. and Colbourn, C. (1987) 'Collaborative interactions at the microcomputer keyboard', *Educational Psychology*, **7**(1), Carfax Publishing Company, PO Box 25, Abingdon, Oxfordshire, OX14 3UE.

Cartoon

Page 104: from *The Fanatic's Guide to Computers*, cartoons by Roland Fiddy, reprinted by permission of Exley Publications Ltd, Watford.

Chapter 4

Photograph

Page 123: the Board of Trustees of the National Museums and Galleries on Merseyside (Walker Art Gallery).

Chapter 5

Table

Table 1: Bishop, D. V. M. and Adams, C. (1990) 'A prospective study of the relationship between specific language impairment, phonological disorders and reading retardation', *Journal of Child Psychology and Psychiatry*, **31**(7), pp. 1027–50, (c) 1990 Association for Child Psychology and Psychiatry.

Cartoons

Page 162: Nick Newman; *page 176*: Nigel Paige.

Chapter 6

Text

Reading A: reprinted by permission of the publishers from *Deaf in America: voices from a culture*, by Carol Padden and Tom Humphries, Cambridge (Mass.), Harvard University Press, copyright © 1988 by the President and Fellows of Harvard College; *Reading B*: from *The Mask of Benevolence* by Harlan Lane, copyright © 1992 by Harlan Lane, reprinted by permission of Alfred A. Knopf, Inc.

Figure

Figure 2: Bellugi, V. *et al*. (1994) 'Enhancement of spatial cognition in deaf children' in Volterra, V. and Erting, C. (eds) *Gesture to Language in Hearing and Deaf Children*, Gallaudet University Press.

Table

Table 2: Gregory, S. and Mogford, K. (1981) 'Early language development in deaf children' in Kyle, J. K., Woll, B. and Deuchar, M. (eds) *Perspectives in British Sign Language and Deafness*, Croom Helm.

Chapter 7

Text

Evans, P. (1992) 'A mother celebrates the birthday of a very special baby', *Guardian*, 22 December 1992; *Reading A*: Furneaux, B. (1970) *The Special Child*, Penguin Education Special, copyright © 1969 Barbara Furneaux; *Reading B*: Wishart, J. G. (1990) *Key Issues in Mental Retardation Research*, Routledge, copyright © 1990 Jennifer Wishart; *Reading C*: Taylor, J. E. (1976) 'An approach to teaching cognitive skills underlying language development' in Wing, K. (ed.) *Early Childhood Autism*, Pergamon Press Ltd, copyright © 1976 Lorna Wing.

Figures

Figure 1: back cover from *Communication*, **25**(2), June 1991, National Autistic Society; *Figure 2*: concept and photography by the Clockwork Marketing Company Ltd, commissioned for charity by Redland Bricks Ltd; *Figure 3*: Frith, U. (1989) *Autism: explaining the enigma*, Basil Blackwell Ltd, copyright © Basil Blackwell Ltd; illustration on page 162 by Axel Scheffler; *Figure 4*: National Autistic Society; *Figure 5*: National Autistic Society, photo by Ed Barber.

Photograph

Page 236: Sue Adlen.

Chapter 8

Figure 1: Herbert, M. (1991) *Clinical Child Psychology*, John Wiley and Sons Ltd, reprinted by permission of John Wiley and Sons Ltd.

NAME INDEX

Adams, John 3–4, 5

Bettelheim, B. 251–2
Beverton, S. 59–60
Bishop, D. 156–60, 171
Bradley, L. 171–4
British Psychological Society 11, 20, 21, 26
Brown, A. 60
Bruner, J. S. 42–3, 47, 56
Bryant, P. 171–4

Childs, A. 57
Classroom Action Research Network 37
Claxton, G. 12–13

Davis, A. 9–10

Frith, U. 166–7

Gardner, H. 58
Goldstein, D. 174

Hardman, F. 59–60
Hinshelwood, J. 167
Howe, C. 95

Jacobson, L. 66–7
Kanner, L. 245, 247, 248, 251

Miller, G. 10–11

Orton, S. 167, 174

Palinscar, A. 60
Papert, S. 82–7, 96
Piaget, J. 7–10, 16, 41, 52–3, 85, 96, 97
Pinder, R. 53–4
Pond, M. 57

Rogoff, B. 47, 58
Rosenthal, R. 66–7
Rutter, M. 228

Scottish Council for Research in Education 37
Skinner, B. F. 48–50, 62, 72–3

Thorndike, E. 48
Tinbergen, E. 252
Tinbergen, N. 252
Topping, K. 59

Vygotsky, L. S. 41, 42–3, 47, 56, 96, 97

Yule, W. 167

SUBJECT INDEX

ability, relationship with age 3
accuracy, of reported accounts 116, 118, 119, 137
accused, facing, in court 122, 123, 124
achievement:
    and questioning styles 15, 29–31
    and teacher expectations 66–7
active model, in child therapy 282, 284
alliteration 173, 174
American Sign Language 195, 196, 224
anticipation, in behavioural therapy 291
anxiety, 'defence mechanisms' and 298
approach/avoidance conflicts 252
arbitrariness, in language 196–7
assessment:
    and labelling 23
    and statementing 24
assumptions, and children's comprehension 128
attachment behaviours 262
attainments, low, in deaf children 189, 191–2, 193, 198, 203–7

attractive children, and teacher expectations 67
audiograms 194–5
autism 26, 226–7, 232–3, 245–64, 265–6
autistic behaviour, characteristics 246–8
autonomy, sense of, in children with problems 283, 284
aversion therapy 294, 296

babbling of the fingers, in deaf children 200
backward readers 167
basic skills 81–2, 87
behaviour:
    current 284, 289, 292
    deficient 278–80, 292–3
    inappropriate 280, 292–3, 296
    learning/unlearning/relearning 293
    modification 259, 261, 293–4
behavioural therapies 290, 291–6
behaviourism 40–1, 43, 48–52, 62, 68
biological basis, for autism 252–3, 264

boys see gender
brain:
    damage, and autism 252–3, 264
    development, in Down's syndrome 238
British Sign Language 189, 195–6, 206–7
Bullock Report 36–8, 39

career, choice 192, 203
category formation 55, 74–5, 260, 275
Catherine, case study of 155
causes:
    of children's problems 285–8, 289
    of intellectual impairment 264
centration 94–5
change in routine, resistance by children with autism 247, 252
child development see development
child psychologists:
    roles 16–17, 20
    and valid evidence from children 135
Child Study Movement 4
child therapy, 'reflexive' position 281, 284